Haunted Liverpool 27

Tom Slemen

The Tom Slemen Press

Copyright © 2017 Tom Slemen

All rights reserved.

ISBN-10: 1544696361
ISBN-13: **978-1544696362**

IN MEMORIAM

Dedicated to the memory of
Marjorie Elizabeth Entwistle

CONTENTS

A Couple of Unexplained Ghosts	1
Two Shadows on a Stage	13
The Gloater	19
The Coffin in the Classroom	38
Two Evil Spirits	41
Tales of Tealeaves and Cards	55
Phantom Legs in Fazakerley	75
Lydia	81
A Haunted Bus Stop	91
Women Only	99
The Ghostly Mime Artist	105
The Strange Tail of Cat Morrison	113
Sawney	141

Strange Fare	146
The Scotch Uncles	150
Nameless Horrors in Sefton Park	157
The Sad Tale of James	178
Mr Impossible	181
The Boots	185
Marianne	190
Trix	208
Radio Moolah	215
Jeremy	223
Knowsley's Evil Ghostly Nun	238
Strange Liverpool Cults	245
Merseyside's Haunted Crossroads	259
As Young as You Think	285
Auras of Truth	296
Strange Goings-on in Lydiate	304

Mrs Broome	313
The Everton Witch	323
A Bike named Geoff	328
Never Over	342
Huyton's Phantom Houses	347
Something in Disguise	352
The Life-swappers	370
The Purple Girl Mystery	381
More Liverpool Vampires	387
Letters to the Lost	424
Spring-Heeled Jack – Vigilante and Caped Santa Claus	430
Timewarps and Spaceslips	435
Love Across Time	458

A COUPLE OF
UNEXPLAINED GHOSTS

There are some unexplained ghosts knocking around in Liverpool; ghosts that appear, scare the witness, and elude the ghost hunter who tries to unearth their history. One such ghost that comes to mind is one I've never personally seen, but I've spoken to dozens of people who have, and this is a bizarre and disturbing apparition that appears in the vicinity of Camp Hill, a place I have written about before. Camp Hill in Woolton was once an Iron Age fort about 150 years before the birth of Christ, and it has quite a supernatural history. Many people – myself included – have seen the appearance of a long white tent at the foot of the hill, on the Hillfoot Road side, and this flimsy structure, when seen at night, often features rows of silhouettes of people on its translucent fabric, but no one knows its history. But that is not the terrifying apparition I am referring to. The ghost I'm talking about is one of a huge diamond-shaped kite – some have estimated that it is 30 feet in length and about 25 feet in width – and hanging from this kite by some thin rope is a schoolboy of about twelve years of age. He is not hanging onto the kite by his hands; he is hanging from it by his neck; in other words, the end of the thin rope looks like a noose pulled tight about the schoolboy's neck. The rope runs from the centre of the kite frame and is about twenty feet in length. The lad's hanged corpse wears an old black school cap, a grey overcoat, shorts, and his thin legs have on grey socks and shiny black shoes. The boy's head is leaning left at an angle of about forty-five degrees – his neck obviously broken - and some reports say his tongue is protruding and very dark. The boy's arms are hanging by his sides – but why on earth is he hanging from a kite? The kite, which is of a pale green fabric, always seems to come from the direction of Woolton Manor – from the north – and just above treetop height, so the shoes of the boy are almost touching the upper reaches of the sturdy old trees of Woolton Woods as he dangles from the heavier-than-air diamond-shaped craft. The kite does not hover in a stationary manner, but almost behaves like a hang-glider, coasting steadily through the air at some 20 mph at around 200 feet above sea level, heading south, sometimes visible for about half a mile, before it vanishes before the eyes of observers somewhere over Allerton Cemetery. John Marshall, a 45-year-old man, saw the grisly airborne apparition whilst walking his dog up Camp Hill in the 1970s on two occasions. The first time was around 9.40 am one windy morning in March 1974. Curiously, John had an inexplicable urge to look up as he reached the top of the hill, and he saw the giant kite, and the body of the schoolboy suspended from it shoot out from behind the trees. The kite must have cleared the crowns of the trees by about forty feet, and as it moved silently south, John initially thought the boy hanging from the frame of the soaring rhombus was alive, and only when the kite had passed overhead and made a slight descent of Camp Hill did the dog-walker notice that the schoolboy was suspended by a rope which terminated in that noose around his neck. The boy's body was inert, but seemed to turn slightly, probably because of the motion of the kite and maybe from the updraft of air from the hill. The second time John saw the hanged schoolboy suspended from the gargantuan kite was in the September of the following year, and like the previous occasion, the kite and its suspended boy appeared over Camp Hill at about twenty minutes to ten in the morning, and on this occasion, as John Walked his dog, the animal barked at the kite and a couple in their twenties who had taken to running of a morning, also saw the surreal but sad spectacle as the kite passed over Hillfoot Road. What is being re-enacted when this strange spectacle glides over Camp Hill? Was the boy deliberately hanged from the kite long ago for some sadistic reason, or was it an accident? I've scoured the local newspapers, hoping to find some reference to a murder or mishap relating to an oversized kite but can find nothing, and this absence of any information merely deepens the mystery.

Another unexplained apparition is the old woman in black with huge feet who has been seen in the living room of a certain terraced house on Wavertree's Grosvenor Road. I have received five reports of this strange ghost over the years and am still at a loss to explain her. As far as I know, the weird entity was first seen in 1969 when a couple in their twenties – Terry and Margaret – moved into the two-bedroom house.

While Margaret was at her mother's house in nearby Methuen Street, Terry and a friend named Fred painted the walls of the living room with rollers, and at around 5.40pm, Fred left to go home for his tea. Terry also left the house to get pie and chips from the local chippie. It was a bright summer's late afternoon, and Terry's thoughts were focused on getting the new house decorated; he was not thinking of ghosts or the supernatural when he returned with his tea from the fish and chips shop and a bottle of cream soda. He passed the living room window of the new house - which had no curtains on because the walls around the window were wet with paint – and he could see the front room quite clearly. He also saw a woman sitting on the sofa, and she had white hair, a prominent aquiline nose, large protruding eyes, hollow cheeks and a very small mouth. She was dressed in some black tightly clad outfit, and her feet, encased in long black slippers, looked freakishly long. Terry froze, and then he gingerly tapped on the window, but the strange old woman did not look at him. She simply sat there on the sofa, but she did smile, revealing she had no teeth. Terry tapped on the window again, this time using his wedding band to make a sharper sound. The next door neighbour, Phil, came out at this point and Terry called him to the window. 'Seen this?' he said, and nodded at the window.

'What?' Phil looked in and smiled. 'What's she got on her feet? Is that your Nan?'

'I haven't got a bleedin' clue who she is,' Terry told him, 'she's let herself in, whoever she is. I've just come back from the chippie and noticed her there!'

'She must have lived there – she must have the key

or something,' Phil suggested.

'Come in with us mate,' Terry put the Yale key in the door and went inside. As he reached the doorway of the living room he started to say: 'Alright love, who let you – '

But there was no one in the living room.

Phil looked in and seeing she was gone, he swore, then told Terry: 'That's a ghost that, mate.'

'Where's she gone?' Terry went into the kitchen, and saw it was empty. He checked the rooms upstairs and still there was no sign of the woman in black with the big feet. When Terry came back downstairs he found Phil standing outside in the street. Phil said he had a feeling he was being watched as he stood in the hallway.

'Nah, she's not a ghost, mate,' Terry told his neighbour, 'there's a rational explanation – '

'Yeah, there is – she's a ghost,' Phil told him, then looked at his watch, 'I've got to get going Terry mate. I'd get a priest in if I was you – get the place blessed.'

And he walked off.

Terry went back into the house, but left the front door ajar, and he put on the radio, and then he sat at the table in the kitchen and ate his pie and chips. He actually felt the hairs rise up on the nape of his neck and he also saw goosepimples rise up on his forearms, and he recalled how his old grandmother used to tell him that such goosepimples mean a ghost is about.
Terry tried to drive these superstitious thoughts from his mind.

There was a bang at the front door, and Terry jumped up from the table, startled. It was just a football hitting the front door, kicked by a boy playing outside. Terry's wife Margaret wasn't due back till around 7pm, and his friend Fred said he'd call round at about nine. He and Terry planned to have a few pints at the Grosvenor pub just down the street. Terry naturally wondered about the ghostly woman, and he went back outside, where it was still sunny, and he stood on the spot where he'd seen the figure earlier on. He could see the sofa clearly. He could see that the ghost had not been the product of some reflection, and he obviously hadn't been seeing things, because Phil from next door had seen her too.

'Excuse me!' the boy down the road shouted – it was the one who had kicked the football at Terry's door before by accident. That boy's plastic-skinned football was rolling towards Terry, so he picked it up, and then he booted it to the boy and his friend.

He turned, and looked into the front room again – and his pie and chips nearly came back up from his stomach.

She was sitting on the sofa again – the old lady with the huge long feet. This time she opened her mouth, and her tongue came out and seemed to lick the tip of her nose before withdrawing into her toothless mouth again.

Terry didn't tap on the window this time. He wondered if he should go in and confront this thing, but he lost his nerve and walked off to the shop with his heart pounding. He didn't enter the shop; he stood at the entrance of the place for a few seconds, then turned and walked back, his mind clouded with confusion. He hesitated to look through his window, but mustered up enough courage to finally do so – but now the woman was gone again. He put his hands in his pockets, felt his house keys, then took them out and locked the front door. He then walked to Methuen Street to call on his wife at his mother-in-law's house. When he got there, Margaret was surprised to see him, as Terry never really got on with her mother. She asked him if everything was okay. In reply, without even setting foot inside the house, he said: 'The house is haunted.'

'What?' Margaret didn't laugh, for she knew Terry was telling the truth from the fear in his eyes, and she also knew the supernatural was a subject he had always been scared to even talk about, as he had been brought up to believe that talking about the spirit world would attract ghosts and such.

'Come in,' Margaret told him.

He reluctantly went into the house and his mother-in-law Jill, who was sitting in the kitchen eating strawberries and ice cream, remarked: 'Bloody hell – Terry – and to what do we owe this pleasure, eh lad?'

'The house is haunted,' Terry replied, flatly, and stood by the sink, gazing out the window into the backyard. He jumped when Jill's Alsatian, Juno bounded up to the window and barked at him.

'What?' Jill asked with a bemused mock attempt at shock.

Margaret ignored her mum and went to Terry. She softly asked him: 'Did you see something?'

Terry nodded. 'I think we should try somewhere else – I've heard you never get shut of them.'

'I've heard everything now,' said Jill, and she pulled the spoon of ice cream from her mouth and asked Terry: 'have you been on the bounce to the new neighbours?'

'This is why I don't want her round at ours!' he told Margaret, pointing his thumb at Jill. 'She's always making out I'm causing trouble.'

'Oh shut up, Terry I was joking,' Jill told him, and when he swiftly turned his back on her she gave him the two fingers gesture.

'What did you see?' Margaret asked her husband and put her arm around him as the dog barked incessantly.

'Shut up Juno!' Jill said, getting up from the table. She took her plate to the sink and as she passed Terry, she said: 'I'm sorry son, I thought you was having us on.'

Terry rolled his eyes and hugged Margaret, then went with her to the table.

'I'll make you a cup of tea, Terry, now tell us what happened and I swear I won't laugh,' Jill told her son-in-law. She filled the kettle at the sink.

Terry told them what he had seen, and Jill said it had been a reflection.

Terry sighed. 'It was no reflection, and Phil next door saw her, so I know I'm not going round the bend.'

'Could someone have got into the house with a set of keys?' Margaret asked, and then she made a suggestion which annoyed her husband: 'Maybe they want to scare us off because they want the house. Did you look round to see if anyone was hiding?'

'I checked the kitchen, the bathroom, the two bedrooms – not a soul anywhere,' Terry told Margaret.

'How could she get up the stairs if she had those big feet anyway?' Jill joked – but no one was laughing.

'Come and have a look and see for yourself, Jill,' Terry challenged his mother-in-law, 'you won't be laughing when you see her yourself.'

'It's not ghosts *I'm* afraid of – ' Jill begun, and Terry ended it.

'I know, I know – it's the living! Well come and have a look at this ghost!' he said.

'Alright,' Jill got up and went to the hallway, 'just getting me coat and we can all get to the bottom of this rubbish.'

'Great!' Terry said, with mock enthusiasm in his voice, and he pretended to smile. Margaret looked a bit scared, and she told her mother that perhaps Phil was right – a priest should be brought in to bless the house.

All three of them set off within minutes for Grosvenor Road, just a hundred yards away. When they reached the house, Terry showed them where he'd been standing on the last two occasions when he had seen the woman in black, and Jill looked through the window but Margaret was so afraid she wouldn't even look, and averted her gaze. They all went in the house and Margaret stuck to her husband everywhere he went, but Jill went upstairs on her own and had a good look about. She came back down and said: 'There's an old woman in your bed upstairs and her big feet are sticking out from under the blankets.'

'What?' Margaret felt faint.

Her mother smiled and said to her: 'Go way you stupid thing, I'm joking.'

'You alright love?' Terry held his wife close, then told his mother-in-law: 'Don't joke like that Jill, she's scared stiff of anything like this.'

'There's eff all here, kids,' Jill announced, and looked at the clock on the mantelpiece. 'I'll get a move on in a minute. There's a horror film on tonight that I want to watch: Mrs Big Feet.'

'Mum, will you shut up?' Margaret protested, her nerves frayed by the stupid non-jokes.

Jill gently slapped her daughter's upper arm and said: 'Oh calm down will you? No, there's a film with Cary Grant and Ingrid Bergman on at ten to eleven. *Notorious*. Love Cary Grant.'

As they stood there, the distant sounds of someone on Grosvenor Road having a heated argument could be heard.

'Ooh, who's that? Someone's having a barney,' Jill went to into the hallway to go and have a nose.

'Mum, don't be so nosey – mum!' Margaret went after her.

Jill stood at the front of the house, and looked up the street where a couple were having a blazing row as a gang of children watched them. 'Do you know them?' she asked her daughter.

'Mum, will you get in you nosy cow? They'll be turning on us in a minute!' Margaret tried to pull her mother into the house but she said: 'I'm coming in now. Ooh, hear what he just called her?'

Margaret went back into the house in a huff and she and Terry hugged, and then they sat on the sofa.

'What are we going to do?' Margaret asked him, and Terry could feel her hand shaking slightly.

'Hopefully we won't see it again. Maybe it came out because new people were moving in, love.' Terry squeezed her hand.

'You should have asked Phil next door if this place has had them in the past,' Margaret said, avoiding the word 'ghosts' in her sentence.

'Phil told me this morning he's only lived on this road for six months himself, so he probably wouldn't know,' said Terry, adding: 'We'll be okay. Your mum's right, it is the living you should be scared of, not *them*.'

'Wonder who's on the other side?' Margaret pondered.

'You mean beyond the grave?' Terry asked, not clear what she was referring to.

'No, soft arse, the house next door, on the other side from Phil's.'

They both chuckled at the misunderstanding.

'I don't know,' Terry admitted, trying to recall if he'd seen the neighbour to his left. 'I'm almost certain it's an old man.'

They both looked over to the window – and standing there, with an expression of face-contorting fear, was Jill. She was looking in horror at Terry and her daughter. They saw her back away from the window, and then dash off.

'Mum!' Margaret was up like a shot from the sofa, and Terry ran after her. They caught Jill three doors down the street.

'You alright Jill?' Terry asked, gently seizing her elbow. Margaret poked her face close to her mum's face and asked: 'Mum, what's wrong?'

'I saw her!' She said, and she looked down the street towards the door of her daughter's new home with terror in her eyes.

'What?' Terry muttered. 'You mean *her*? The ghost?'

'She was horrible,' Jill stammered, 'she was sitting next to Margaret on the sofa, and I don't think you two could see her!'

An icy chill coursed through Margaret's abdomen at

the thought of sitting right next to the ghost. 'What?' she asked weakly. 'What, mum?'

'She was all in black, and I saw her feet – they were huge. She looked at me and pulled tongues,' Jill closed her eyes, and grimaced, and then she pulled away from her daughter and son-in-law to try and get as far away from the house as possible. She swore and told Margaret: 'You and Terry will have to stay in mine tonight till you can move somewhere else.'

And this the couple did, and they found a house to rent on Martensen Street, off Wavertree Road, about a mile away. Believe it or not, the new house was also haunted, but the ghost was very low key, merely switching off lights now and then and occasionally tapping on the cellar door, but it was nothing like the woman in black with the huge feet at that house on Grosvenor Road. I have had four other reports of a ghost which matches the description of the unknown ghost of the weird old lady at that Grosvenor Road address, and the most recent one is 2012. I have gone through censuses, put out appeals to the public via my newspaper columns and asked listeners if they know who she is whenever I'm on a radio programme – but I remain in the dark – that woman in black with the white hair, crooked nose and those big feet remains anonymous. She must be connected to someone, somewhere, and I would dearly like to know her backstory.

TWO SHADOWS
ON A STAGE

One rainy night many years ago at the Liverpool Playhouse down in Williamson Square, long after a play had ended and all of the theatregoers had left the building, the director of the play (we'll call him Roger) and his assistant Mal, stayed behind and discussed a particular scene in the production which – in Roger's eyes – was not working. Long after midnight, Roger and Mal walked around the stage, trying the lines of the actors at various spots and noting down ideas for lighting effects. By one in the morning, Mal was yawning, but Roger was an unflagging perfectionist and so he took Mal and himself off to the seats in the second row, and over a late supper of cold steak and kidney pies and a few bottles of stout, Roger jotted down more ideas and extra lines of dialogue for the actors – until the theatre was suddenly engulfed by blackness. All of the lights had gone, and for some reason, only the green exit signs burned in the void of blackness. A small bright spark appeared briefly, high above the stage, and from it shone a spotlight which threw its wide disc of greenish light upon the stage.

Two startling figures dressed in period costume, were revealed by this inexplicable spotlight. The stagehands had long gone home, so Roger and Mal knew no one could even be operating the spotlight at this ungodly hour.

Mal swore and said, 'Who are they?'

'Quiet!' whispered Roger, surprised but fascinated. He somehow sensed straight away that these players were ghosts.

The taller one looked aristocratic and was dressed in some sort of black costume with a white ruff collar, snugly-fitting doublet, codpiece, long cloak, breeches and square-toed shoes. He sported long hair and a van dyke. The smaller figure looked plebeian, and wore a linen collar, a leather jerkin, scuffed calf-length boots and coarse trousers. His hair was cropped short and he was brandishing a sword as he looked at the other actor. Twelve feet to the left of the eerie thespians there was a large antique, polished wooden globe of the world set in a four-legged stand.

'The world is a net!' cried the man with the sword, 'And the more we stir in it, the more we are entangled! Your merciless ambitions have taken you to these heights, but high places have their precipices!'

'Oh my God,' whispered Roger, gripping Mal's forearm, 'I recognise that voice; it's Burton.'

The taller refined-looking actor spoke in a velvet voice abounding with energy: 'In the hour of your greatest triumph you sowed the seeds of your own destruction! Your wife was diamond pure, but you drove her into my arms, and her loose tongue has brought down your house!'

'I know that voice,' Mal muttered, and Roger turned

to him and nodded, saying: 'It's Michael Redgrave.'

Richard Burton and Sir Michael Redgrave had passed away over ten years before, yet this was clearly those two great actors in the spotlight. Both of these giants of the British theatre had been regulars at the Playhouse decades before world fame came their way.

Mal started to tremble and mumbled the word: 'Ghosts.'

'Shush!' Roger put his index finger to his lips, and in a hushed tone he declared: 'This is fascinating!'

Burton turned his back on the other player and began to walk slowly in the direction of the globe as he went into a soliloquy – and the character played by Redgrave sneaked up on him and tried to wrestle the sword from his hand, but after an impressive struggle he was run through by the blade, and fell upon the globe.

'The world!' Redgrave gasped, rested his face on the globe, then kissed it before sliding off it to the floor – and the spotlight died at this point.

Roger had the urge to stand up and clap loudly, but he knew that what he had just seen was a performance by two phantoms, and he was afraid to make any noise in case the apparitions vanished.

The lights went up, and the stage was bare. Not a soul was there, and the globe prop had also gone. Roger ran to the stage and looked around. Yes, they had definitely gone, and this was no prank – this had really happened. Mal came slowly up onto the stage, and he asked, 'Why?'

'Why what?' was the producer's reply.

Mal was puzzled. 'Why did they come back and do that scene? And what play was that from?'

'I've never heard those lines anywhere before,' Roger confessed.

Mal started to scribble down the lines of the unidentified play, and Roger, who had a photographic memory, corrected some of the parts his assistant had copied down. They both researched the text and found it nowhere. It wasn't by Shakespeare, as Roger knew every play by the Bard word for word, and numerous playwrights and actors and professors of literature were consulted, but no one ever identified the play. A scene from an unknown play had been performed by two long-dead actors at the Liverpool Playhouse in the dead of night – but for what reason? In the many years I have spent investigating the world of the supernatural, I have come across reports of theatre ghosts on innumerable occasions. A lot of the older theatres in Liverpool and beyond are haunted, and I've written about the apparitions to be found in the theatres of this city in previous *Haunted Liverpool* books. A little embellishment often creeps in when some of the people conducting ghost tours tell the sad story of the widow Mary Edmondson, a cleaner who was tragically killed at the Playhouse Theatre (back when it was called The Star Theatre of Varieties) in December 1896, when the end of the "iron curtain" accidentally fell onto her as she was sweeping the stage. She was not "guillotined" as the uninformed man conducting the ghost tour claimed; Mary died from a fractured skull. Nor is Mary Edmondson the ghostly girl who is occasionally been seen at the Playhouse – Mary was in her fifties, and by no stretch of the imagination is the spectral girl roaming the theatre the ghost of the middle-aged cleaner. The latter ghost seems to be that of a girl of about thirteen. An apparition of a 'see-through soldier' was once reported to me by six people who had seen the figure in the Playhouse foyer area in the early 1990s. I mentioned this apparition on a radio programme about the paranormal and was inundated with further reports of the soldier. The ghost may be that of William Jones of the 7th Dragoon Guards, who fell down a flight of stairs at the theatre on 1 November 1883. Jones was so badly injured, he later died after being admitted to the Northern Hospital, and around Christmas 1883, his ghost, dressed in his full uniform, was seen by many witnesses at the theatre. Three witnesses noticed that, just before the soldier vanished, he touched the medal on his chest. The witnesses, all military men, recognised the medals as being the clasp for the Battle of Tel-el-Kabir, the Khedive's bronze star, and the Egyptian medal. Mary Edmondson and William Jones are just a few of the fatalities that have occurred in consequence of some tragedy at the Playhouse Theatre; there have been many others, and these deaths may well be the cause of the 'company' of ghosts at the theatre. Most theatres have a very unsettling atmosphere when the audience has gone and the players have vacated the stage. I've delivered talks on the supernatural in a lot of Merseyside theatres and I have sensed presences and cold spots backstage, sometimes even before a show. I have a feeling that there are 'night plays' acted out beneath the proscenium arches of our vintage theatres in the wee small hours. Most actors love their work; it's in their blood, and for many thespians, the applause of the audience is a drug they will remain addicted to until the curtain of life comes down. Why then, should it come as any surprise to us to realise that some departed actors want to return from 'resting' in the next world to tread the boards once again as they did in the happy hours of their lives? I think that it's highly likely that Sir Michael Redgrave and Richard Burton really did return from the grave to strut and fret another hour upon the stage. And the mystery still remains: who penned the lines of the two deceased actors? Perhaps the great playwrights and dramatists of bygone days are as restless as the players in the afterlife...

THE GLOATER

Mick hadn't seen his old friend Liam in years, but he recognised his square head and sloping shoulders even from the back, and there, standing next to Liam was another mate of Mick's nicknamed Parko. Mick was standing about twelve feet behind his old hoppos as they all stood in the queue outside one of the best chippy's in England – Byrnes, on Stuart Road, Walton. Liam, like Mick, was now fifty years of age, and yet it seemed like only yesterday when they were both depressed at the approach of their 30th birthday. It was a cold Good Friday night, and Mick had been queuing for about twenty minutes now, but the fish, chips and mushy peas meal from the family-run chippie was always worth the wait and held so much promise for his rumbling tum. 'Liam you quilt!' Mick shouted his archaic slang, and Parko's head swivelled swiftly around to face him. He was pudgy-faced now, and he obviously didn't recognise Mick at first, now that Mick's once thick black hair had taken leave of his head, and the thin grey remains had been shaved to the wood in a futile act of age-denial. Mick just gazed at him with a slight grin, waiting for Parko to recognise him, but when the penny dropped it was a bit of an anticlimax, because all Parko muttered in response was, 'Oh, 'right Mick lad.'

Mick nodded at the back of Liam's cubic head. 'Has he got no missus to cook for him then, eh? He's not *still* single is he?'

Liam looked back and he scowled with furrowed brow and mouthed the word "No" as he shook his head, obviously disproving of Mick's comments, which were made in jest of course.

'Eh?' Mick as puzzled by Liam's reaction. 'What's up?'

Liam turned – and at first, Mick thought he was pulling a face. Half of his mouth was turned down – the left half – and his left eye was almost closed. He began to speak, but Mick couldn't understand him. He realised that his old mate had had some stroke. In shock, all Mick could say, 'I'll see you in there in a minute, mate,' as he nodded at the bright windows of Byrnes' chippie. When Mick finally got into the busy eatery, he hugged his old mate Liam, and saw at close quarters how awful the stroke had left him. Liam tried to talk to Mick but it was difficult to make out his words, although Parko seemed to get the gist of the utterances very quickly and served as some translator, which seemed to anger Liam. Parko explained that Liam had suffered a stroke during an altercation in Anfield Cemetery six months back. Liam had been paying a visit to his mum's grave and had bumped into a weirdo who seemed to know a bit about Liam's late mother. This oddball made shocking jokes about Liam's mum rotting away in her grave and had cruelly remarked of her: 'She'll know by now there's no heaven, and that she's stuck in her box till the worms eat her to the bone.'

'What?' Mick recoiled, and he turned to Liam, who had tears in his eyes and asked: 'and you gave him a hiding for that, surely?'

Liam grunted something and thumped his operative right fist against the wall of the chippy. His left fist – and arm – hung motionless at his side.

'Don't get him all worked up, Mick,' Parko protested, and he stopped and looked Liam in the face, held his clenched, shaking fist and said, 'It's alright mate, calm down.'

When Mick got home he told his girlfriend Krissy about his old mate Liam having a stroke after he'd had a blazing row with some 'plantpot' in Anfield Cemetery, and his girlfriend – who had been putting her rollers in, suddenly froze, and her big green eyes swung left to Mick's face. 'That sounds like that same fellah our Dean met in the cemetery the other week, Mick,' she said.

'What?' Mick asked as he went into the kitchen to put the fish and chips onto two plates.

Krissy recalled the incident as she began winding her gold locks around the curler. 'Our Dean went to put flowers on me Nan's grave - the Saturday before last it was - and he said there was this fellah kneeling by a new headstone. Dean thought he was crying at first because the fellah was holding a hanky to his eyes, but he was crying with laughter.'

'That might be him, but there are that many dickheads knocking around nowadays – ' Mick was saying, reaching into the cupboard for the ketchup. But Krissy cut in on him.

'Yeah, anyway, listen: Dean asked him if he was alright and he looked at the name on the new grave and said "She was quite busty and attractive, and she turned heads, but she found a lump," and then he started laughing his head off and Dean was going to give him a smack.'

'What a horrible thing to laugh at, the warped bastard,' Mick came in holding the two plates of fish and chips and the knife fell off one plate.

'A sharp surprise they say,' Krissy smiled at the fallen knife. She picked it up and went to replace it in the kitchen. She got two cans of Coke from the fridge and when she came back into the living room, she saw that her boyfriend was gazing morosely into the gas jets of the fire. She knew only too well how thin-skinned and caring Mick was about other people, and she tried to take his mind off the ghoul in the graveyard. 'I'm taking these curlers out, they're crap. I was just trying them out but – '

'I think someone should give that weirdo a hiding,' Mick suddenly said in a low, far away voice.

'No, someone should have him sectioned,' Krissy reasoned, 'he shouldn't be walking the streets. He's obviously got mental problems Mick. Someone'll give him a belt if he keeps skitting at people who have died.'

That night at 9pm, as Krissy had a drink and a natter with her next-door neighbour Joanne, Mick left the house on Bedford Road, and went to the Stuart Hotel pub, where he met an old associate named Jim Asquith – or Asky as he called him. He and Mick had worked together in a soul-destroying job at a factory in Fazakerley six years before. Over a few pints, Mick mentioned the nutter going round Anfield Cemetery who was making jokes about the dead people buried there, and Asky gave a knowing nod and said, 'Yeah, I've heard about him.'

'I think someone should teach him a lesson,' Mick said, and he sipped his bitter and gritted his teeth.

'What? Do you mean like do him over?' Asky said out the side of his mouth. His eyes had been glazed from alcohol before Mick's bellicose suggestion, but now they were sharp and clear. Violence had always been Asky's amphetamine, and the thought of giving someone a good kicking energised him.

Mick nodded, produced a packet of Lambert & Butler from his inside coat pocket, then on his way to the door he replied: 'I was thinking along the lines of baseball-batting seven shades out of him, mate.'

Asky didn't smoke but he went outside the pub with Mick to continue the conversation. Outside, on Stuart Road, a chill April wind knifed Mick, who was only wearing a thin cotton tee shirt under his denim jacket. 'Mick, I never knew you had a violent bone in your body, lad,' Asky told him bluntly with a smile full of gammy teeth. 'Has this fellah offended you or something?'

Mick inhaled the cigarette and directed the smoke out of his nose. 'When someone hangs around a cemetery, skitting at people who have died of cancer and that, I find that highly offensive. He upset someone who's virtually my brother-in-law as well; that's family to me.'

'Shall we go up there now and knock his teeth down his throat?' Asky queried, thrusting his chest out and angling his head back like Mussolini.

'Not on Good Friday lad,' Mick replied. 'You can't shed blood on this day unless you're a heathen.'

'I don't believe in anything Mick, only *that*.' He held his huge fist up and almost seemed aroused.

'After the holiday, after Easter Monday.' Mick ghost inhaled; he let a thick cloud of smoke out a few inches then sucked it back in.

Tuesday evening at 7.10pm at Anfield Cemetery; the sun was now sinking below rooftop level and there was less than an hour of daylight left. Low cloud was moving in to darken what was left. Mick waited at the entrance to the cemetery and was a little impatient. Asky said he'd be here just before seven, and Mick wondered if he'd made a detour into an alehouse on his way from Carisbrooke Road. Mick had his back turned to the traffic at the junction of Walton Lane and Priory Road in case some passing acquaintance in a car spotted him standing there. He thought it might be even better if he went into the cemetery, and as he headed for the gate he heard Asky shout him. Mick turned and saw him on the other side of the road, coming from Diana Street. He was carrying a baseball bat. Mick couldn't believe the stupidity of his friend and shook his head. 'What an arsehole,' he mouthed, seething as Asky lifted the bat up with one hand as he crossed the road. Mick darted into the cemetery, suspecting the worst. Asky had either been smoking the other stuff or he'd had a few 'swift halves' in a boozer. As soon as he entered the place of the dead, Mick swore at him.

'Aye aye, what's up with you?' Asky was startled by his foul-mouthed outburst.

'You have definitely got a gene missing, mate,' Mick told him, glancing at the baseball bat, then looking down the long avenue of the cemetery. There were two old people about fifty yards away.

'Your bottle's gone,' Asky prodded Mick's beer belly with the tip of the bat.

Mick took his denim jacket off. 'Giz that here!' he said, taking the bat off his cavalier companion. He wrapped the club in the jacket and walked up the path.

'Did you bring a knuckleduster?' Asky earnestly enquired.

Mick wasn't sure if he was joking or being serious, and in reply he asked: 'Have you had a few bevies?'

Asky slowly shook his head. 'I had *one* hot toddy Mick, if that's alright. I've got a sore throat.'

'I hope you didn't go in an alehouse with that bat, Asky,' Mick gazed down at the tarmac of the path and sighed.

'Shut up Mick, you're being mad,' Asky looked away sulkily.

A few yards on the two men smiled and nodded politely at the passing elderly couple and continued their patrol.

Asky suddenly lightened up and chuckled to himself. 'There's a grave in here Mick, and the fellah's name on it is Dolphin Fish, honest.'

'Keep your eyes peeled,' said a sombre Mick, holding the wrapped baseball bat under his arm. 'Krissy's brother Dean said this freak had on a dark green jacket and black kecks and er, he looked about twenty-five. God, I'm freezing without me jacket. I'm putting it back on -'

'Mick,' Asky knocked his knuckles against his friend's forearm and slowed. 'There he is.'

They both halted and looked across rows of headstones to see a figure in a green jacket strolling along between two trees.

'Mightn't be him,' Mick felt the handle of the bat under the denim cloth. 'Let's follow him. Don't start rabbitin' – and walk light.'

They hesitated, gave the man – who looked indeed as if he was in his mid-twenties – about thirty seconds' start, and then they followed him. He walked in a peculiar way, with his right leg kicking out a bit as he moved along, and he seemed to shake a little as he halted by a black marble headstone. He startled the duo a bit by turning on the spot to face them in quite a dramatic fashion. Now they could see his pale triangular face with the pointed chin, and a prominent pair of eyes that seemed ringed with mascara. He had on a grass-green windcheater, zipped up to just below the neck, and seemed to have on a black tee shirt beneath it. His hair was quite short and jet black, and he wore black pleated trousers and what looked like winklepickers on his feet.

'I could easily take him out, no problem,' Asky muttered as he and Mick approached the man.

'Just see if it is him, first,' Mick suggested, his eyes fixed firmly on the stranger. He was about thirty yards away and already Mick could make out that the man was grinning.

'Just give me the word Mick and he'll be at home in here.' Asky clenched his fists and narrowed his eyes.

The man got down on one knee and put his right pallid hand on the top of the black marble gravestone as he read the golden lettering.

When Mick and Asky reached the man, they halted, and Mick said to the stranger: 'Paying your respects lad?'

The man didn't respond.

Asky took a deep breath, about to say something, but Mick tapped his arm and shook his head.

The man in the green jacket shook – with laughter. He sniggered and he turned to look at the older men over his right shoulder. He had a lazy eye, and those eyes were very unnerving because they had a bluish shadow around them, almost coloured like a bruise, and the mouth had unusually red lips, as if the man had on lipstick.

'He thought he had wind,' the unknown man told the budding vigilantes. 'His friends told him to get his ticker checked out. He said he would after Christmas. After Christmas never came. He had a heart attack on the toilet. Crapped he did, and he was in the right place.'

'It's him,' Mick said, and he walked over to the gloater and began to unwrap the baseball bat.

'What's funny about a man having a heart attack, lad?' Asky wanted to know.

The sinister scoffer took out a handkerchief and dabbed his eyes as he let out the strangest guffaw. 'After Christmas! He'll know now it wasn't wind!' he cried.

'Are you the bastard who laughed at the woman who died from cancer?' Mick handed the baseball bat to Asky as he put his denim jacket back on.

'Which one?' the mocker asked, sniffling as he put his handkerchief away. 'There are so many in here!'

'Is there something wrong with you mate? Something mental?' Mick asked.

'What are you going to do with that?' the weirdo asked Asky, eyeing the baseball bat.

'Gonna play baseball with your skull you shit!' Asky informed him and swung the bat back, but it glanced against Mick's left ear.

'Arrgh!' Mick fell backwards.

'Bastard!' Asky swung that baseball bat with such rage at the disrespectful ghoul, the impact sent him across the grass and he hit a gravestone.

Mick got to his feet, and mindful of the way the bat had almost smashed his face in, he walked around his friend and urged him to stop the onslaught.

Thump! The baseball bat thudded into the man's spine now as he lay face-down. Thump! Asky screamed profanities like a man possessed as he raised the bat high above his head and brought it down hard on the head of that pale-faced ridiculer of the dearly departed.

'Asky! Stop! You've killed him!' Mick shouted, and out the corner of his eye he saw two men around his age, about a hundred yards off, and their faces were looking towards him.

'That's funny isn't it!' Asky screamed, and the bat smashed down on the white triangular face and the nose was flattened as if made of putty. The man tried to shield that face with long-fingered lily-white hands but the bat ploughed into them, breaking the fingers and smashing knuckles and the force of the blow seemed to impact the hands into the face.

'Asky stop it!' Mick felt a terrible pain in his throat as he yelled at the top of his voice, and a salty taste of blood at the back of his tongue. He felt as if he'd burst a blood vessel.

There were three more strikes from that bat upon the head of the unstable skitter. Each blow accompanied the three words uttered in perfect time by Asky: 'Isn't-that-funny!'

The man seemed dead. He was motionless, and hands of broken fingers with disjointed wrists covered his face.

Asky turned to Mick, his eyes bulging. He was foaming at the mouth. 'I think that – that – taught him a lesson, Mick.'

'You've killed him,' Mick said, and he hurried away, pulling Asky by the wrist.

The two observers in the distance were now coming slowly along the path as Mick and Asky trotted off to the gates of the cemetery. Dusk was falling fast now. Asky kept asking, 'Was he dead?'

Mick kept saying, 'You've had it,' over and over. As they neared the gate, Mick looked at the bat and shouted: 'Get shut of it!'

'No, I'll burn it!' Asky told him, but Mick seized it and yanked it from the grip of his dazed friend and he hurled it into bushes.

They went to Mick's home, where Krissy was now watching a movie with Joanne, and they went to the bathroom, and in a confused state, Asky washed his hands and face and Mick washed his trainers in the shower. They didn't know what they were doing. They were panicking. They went into the spare room and Asky sat on the bed with his head in his hands. He blamed Mick. Mick said he wasn't to blame, and accused his friend of being a psychopath. They almost came to blows, but Krissy came in and asked what all the arguing was about. They assured her they were just arguing about footy.

Asky finally went home at midnight, and that night

in bed, Krissy asked Mick what he had really been arguing about and he wanted to tell her, but he maintained that he had been arguing over football. Mick was a red-hot LFC fan and Asky was a born-blue Everton supporter. That's all there was to it.

In the morning, Mick awoke about seven-thirty. He thought someone had knocked at the door. He thought it was the police, as he was expecting them. Krissy was still asleep as he got out the bed and went to the window. He looked down and saw it was Asky. He was looking up at him with a smile. He beckoned him.

Mick went down and let him in, and Asky immediately told him something he couldn't take in.

'Mick, I went to the cemetery to get the bat – '

'You didn't – ' Mick groaned.

'Hang on! Listen, I found the bat, and he was there – he's still alive. Not a bleedin' scratch on him!'

'What?' Mick didn't comprehend what he was being told.

'*Him* - the fellah we thought we'd killed. Not a scratch on him, and he said something to me, but I couldn't make it out.'

'You sure?' It crossed Mick's mind that Asky had hallucinated the young man because he was in denial at being a murderer.

'Mick, on your life!'

'Swear on your *own* life!' Mick told him. 'What time was this when you went there?'

'Five o'clock,' Asky told him, 'and Mick I was not seeing things!'

'It wouldn't even be light then, Asky – you *have* been seeing things, or you've seen some meff hanging out in the cemetery.'

'Mick, it was him! Same green jacket, that pale face, and the moon was out – a full moon lad! I saw him clearer than I'm seeing you now!'

'I'm not having it, Asky,' Mick was frank about his suspicions. 'Look mate, there is no way anyone would have survived that hiding.'

'What hiding?' came a soft voice from the stairs. It was Krissy. She stood there in the darkness.

Asky looked at her in horror.

Mick pressed his palm over his perspiring face. 'Jesus,' was all he could manage. They all went into the kitchen and he told Krissy the truth. She cried, and told her boyfriend to go to the police. She told Mick he wasn't the one who had killed the man and that Asky would 'carry the can'.

'I'm not a grass, and never will be,' Mick told her with tears in his eyes.

'Krissy he's alright, he's in better shape than me!' Asky insisted.

'Take me there – to the cemetery – and show me where it happened,' Krissy told Asky, not thinking things through.

'Alright! Alright!' Asky replied in a manic yelping voice. 'Get your coat on!'

'No, we should just sit tight, and see if anyone reports a body in the cemetery,' Mick suggested, and he reached out to the radio but didn't have the guts to switch it on. He didn't want to hear the news.

Krissy went and washed her face, fixed her hair, and she marched to the door. Mick begged her not to go, but she was adamant about it, and she left with Asky. Mick hurried after them.

Asky was right. There was no body anywhere near the scene of the brutal attack.

'You haven't buried him or something have you?' Krissy asked Asky.

Asky rolled his eyes. 'Krissy, I swear on my life, on Mick's life – on *your* life, I haven't killed anyone or got shut of any body! I saw him this morning over there! He's alive and well.'

The days dragged by, and Mick and Krissy expected a visit from Merseyside Police or to hear of the discovery of a man's body in the vicinity of Anfield, but no one ever called from the police, and no one reported finding any body or body parts in or around the cemetery. Then, about a fortnight after the strange and traumatic incident, Krissy's brother Dean remarked that he had seen 'that nutcase' again – the one he'd seen kneeling at the cancer victim's grave weeks back. Krissy asked Dean if the man looked as if he'd been beaten up. She said she'd heard that someone had attacked him for saying wicked things about loved ones. Dean had said that the loony looked had looked okay. Krissy was determined to see this repulsive but nevertheless intriguing person herself now, and she talked Mick into taking her to the cemetery. They went on the late afternoon of a Saturday, and this time there was a constant drizzle. The couple walked the cemetery holding hands for about twenty minutes without seeing the crowing creep, and then, just when Mick suggested they should leave the place, Krissy gripped his hand hard and gasped: 'Is that him down there?'

'Where?' Mick brushed the tiny droplets of mizzle from his eyelashes. He could just about see the figure in the distance; he must have been about 200 yards away, and was partially obscured by a monument. Krissy said he had on a green jacket, and seemed to be peeping around the monument at them.

'He must have good eyesight,' quipped Mick. The drizzle turned into standard rain, and suddenly they were subjected to a downpour.

Krissy pulled her hood up. 'Yes, he's watching us, Mick, honest. It's got to be him, I can see the pale face you described.'

'He's got to be superhuman Kriss,' Mick said pensively. 'Asky laid into him with that bat. It turned me off violence for good it did.'

'Maybe he's not superhuman,' Krissy pondered, 'maybe he's supernatural – did you ever think of that?'

'Don't start talking about that subject in here, love,' Mick told his partner, and he squinted through the wall of slanting rain and saw the distant figure withdraw behind the cover of the monument with amazing rapidity.

'See that?' Krissy asked, a slight grin on her face as she saw the figure take cover behind the monument.

'Yeah,' Mick nodded, 'so let's go back.'

Krissy tugged at his hand, pulling him in the direction of that monument. 'Don't you want to just see him and then you can be one-hundred per cent certain that Asky didn't kill him?'

'Er – no. Now let's go home, come on,' Mick retorted and he tugged Krissy hard and she walked back towards the gates with her boyfriend. Then, out the corner of her right eye, she saw something moving, and she turned to face it out of reflex action. It was a man with short black hair with an unusually pale face and he wore a green jacket, black trousers and black pointed shoes. Krissy knew it was him from the chalk-white face and green jacket, and also by the weird grin on his face as he looked at her. He was walking along in the same direction about thirty feet away, and now Mick noticed him too.

'Kathleen's in here, isn't she?' the gloater shouted, and Krissy went ice cold inside because she just knew he was referring to her schoolfriend Kathleen, who had died of leukaemia when she was fourteen.

'Do you want another hiding, arsehole?' Mick shouted, and he gripped Krissy's hand hard.

The deranged and morbid entity suddenly shouted: 'Poor Kathleen, laying here in the dark! Always dark! And she knows she's never going to see daylight again!'

'Asky didn't hit him hard enough!' Mick snarled to Krissy, 'I'm going to have to finish this bastard off!'

'Mick, no! Just ignore him and get out of here, come on!' Krissy marched ahead of her boyfriend, pulling him along by his hand.

'But – ' Mick was protesting.

'No buts about it, just leave him behind!' Krissy now grabbed Mick's fist with two hands and yanked at him, and he walked with her to the gates as the morbid crank shouted: 'Kathleen was always very clean wasn't she? You should see her now though! All mud and bones! Ha ha!'

'Ignore him, Mick!' said Krissy in a broken voice, close to tears at the thought of Kathleen's body lying in her grave.

The couple went home, and although they were soaked to the skin as they came into the hall of their house, they were hardly aware of it. Krissy was now convinced that the man who had taunted her about her long-dead friend was some devil – something inhuman – whereas Mick was completely baffled by the situation. He was not at all sure what that man was in Anfield Cemetery. Krissy made a secret visit to her priest, and she told him about the gloater in the graveyard and she was stunned when the priest said he had heard of the man before from other parishioners.

'Father, what – what is he?' Krissy asked the holy man.

'I'm not really sure,' the priest confessed, 'but I'm tempted to consider the possession angle.'

'Possession?' the word really unnerved Krissy.

'Yes, he may be someone who has been possessed by something evil, although from what you have told me about the beating this individual received from your boyfriend's associate, I'm not so sure. Even someone possessed would not be able to sustain such an assault with a baseball bat.'

'He really scared me, Father, the way he knew about my best friend Kathleen dying from leukaemia all those years ago.'

The priest nodded with a faraway look, then told Krissy: 'There is a ritual – not an exorcism as such – but more of a powerful curse – and it's usually carried out by Rabbis rather than men of the cloth in the Christian churches – but there are exceptions.'

Krissy didn't understand what the priest was getting at. He explained the ritual after asking Krissy not to tell anyone what she was about to hear.

'The Rod of Light curse ritual involves the reading of certain texts pertaining to kabbalistic writings. Black candles are lit and a specific instrument – a ram's horn – is sounded. This is absolutely the last resort when exorcism has failed and the Church is under threat from something evil. There's something similar in the Christian Book of Common Prayer called the Commination Service – it's a way of putting a contract out on someone in a spiritual way.'

'You mean the Church can put curses on people?' Krissy was quite taken aback by the concept. She had always imagined that the priests and reverends steered well clear of any such occult practices.

'Yes, and I recall the Commination Service being used a few years ago on two thieves who were breaking into churches across Liverpool and ransacking the poor boxes. The thieves were cursed by the service and both died in a car crash not long after.'

'So you're going to try and do something similar to this unbalanced idiot going round the cemetery?' Krissy asked.

The priest nodded. 'Not the Commination Service though; the Rod of Light ceremony, which is much more powerful – but we will have to consult a rabbi first.'

It is said that three churches on each side of Anfield Cemetery held special private masses in the evening and the Rod of Light ritual was then carried out. Terrible screams were heard in Anfield Cemetery that evening. Residents as far away as Breeze Hill and West Derby Road heard these screams that night. Since then, the gloater has not been seen in Anfield Cemetery, and hopefully the curse has rid the resting place of the sacrilegious scoundrel. I have heard of similar entities mocking the dead in graveyards and crypts, and their agenda is a strange one – perhaps the mission of these ghouls is simply to erode the belief of those visiting the graves of loved ones. When a person dies, the body that is buried is just a shell and nothing more. The essence of that person – the soul – goes on to another place after death, although some souls that are earthbound because of unfinished business in this world will hang around the sphere of the living and they'll be perceived as ghosts. I hope we have seen the last of the gloater of Anfield Cemetery, whatever it is.

THE COFFIN IN
THE CLASSROOM

At a certain Everton school in the 1960s, a 12-year-old pupil named Arthur was standing in the schoolyard one playtime on a foggy October afternoon, when his friend John dared him to retrieve a confiscated bag of lemon sherberts from the desk of the maths teacher. From where the boys were standing they could see that the teacher in question through the window of the school staffroom, having a smoke with his back turned towards them, and as there was ten minutes' worth of playtime left, this was now the ideal time for Arthur to reclaim what was rightfully his. 'Go on, Arthur,' John told him, 'I'll keep dixie for you. He'll never know you took them!'

'They mightn't even still be in the drawer of his desk, though,' Arthur wondered out loud, but John and another boy swore they had seen the bag of sweets in the teacher's desk when he had opened it during a lesson this morning. And so, Arthur went into the school toilets, but then he sneaked out of them moments later and began the careful ascent of the stairs. He could hear the headmaster telling a joke to the teachers in the staffroom and he knew he'd get the cane if he was caught snooping in the drawer of the maths teacher. He ducked as he walked along the corridor in case he was seen passing the windows by the teacher on duty in the playground, and then he reached the door of the maths classroom and slowly pushed that door open. Arthur crept into the classroom, and as he did he heard footsteps at the end of the corridor. It was the caretaker, Mr Bates. As the boy hurried to the back of the class to hide behind a desk, he noticed something very strange and alarming; there was a coffin leaning against the wall near the teacher's desk. The caretaker entered, and saw Arthur crouching behind the desk, but then he also noticed the six-foot-tall coffin, and he remarked, 'What the blazes is this?' as he walked over to it. He read the brass plate on the coffin – it was the name of the maths teacher. The caretaker seemed spooked, and he backed away and quickly left the room to inform the headmaster of the macabre find. Arthur was also unnerved by the coffin, and he froze as he headed for the door, because he thought he saw someone peeping at him from the other side of the long box. He quickly left the classroom, ran down the corridor, and almost collided with the caretaker, headmaster and two teachers coming up the stairs to see the coffin. That coffin was nowhere to be seen when Bates and the school staff entered the classroom, and the headmaster told the caretaker he'd either been seeing things or someone was playing some very distasteful prank. Mr Bates told the headmaster and teachers he was prepared to swear on a Bible about the coffin he had seen minutes ago, and he said no prankster would have been able to cart around such a huge and heavy-looking coffin without being seen by someone in the school. 'And who on earth would go to that much trouble to perpetrate such a hoax? And for what purposes?' Mr Bates asked the headmaster.

'Oh, you'd be surprised Mr Bates,' the headmaster replied.

'I'll ask the local undertaker sir,' one of the teachers told the headmaster, 'and see if any of his coffins are missing.'

'And how did this hoaxer get a brass plate with the maths teacher's name inscribed?' the caretaker asked. 'This joker would have to go to an awful lot of trouble, and where on earth has he got to with his coffin, eh?'

'Unless it was some trick of your mind, Mr Bates,' the headmaster suggested as he looked at the caretaker out the corner of his eye in a condescending manner.

Bates was furious at the audacious intimation. 'I'm not in the habit of imagining things like coffins in classrooms, sir, and I have not been drinking, just in case you are hinting at that!'

'Sir, I saw the coffin too!' Arthur told the headmaster, but his testimony was not taken seriously.

That week, a very strange thing took place: the math teacher died of a heart attack, and Mr Bates and Arthur realised that the coffin had been some omen of the man's approaching death. For years after this weird incident, Arthur had recurring nightmares about the coffin, and of the creepy person who seemed to be hiding behind it...

TWO EVIL SPIRITS

The first disturbing call was received at Mrs Rita Higginson's Garston home on the evening of Thursday 12 March 1970 at ten to nine – just as the police drama *Softly, Softly* was ending on BBC1. Mr Higginson was in the bath, so his 47-year-old wife Rita answered the telephone, and a distressed young woman's voice asked: 'Hello; is that you mum?'

Rita didn't recognise the caller's voice and she asked: 'Who is this?'

'It's Liz,' was the caller's answer. 'Is that you mum?' She sounded sniffly and emotional, as if she was close to tears.

'I don't have a daughter,' Rita told the voice, 'you must have the wrong number.'

'This number I've called is my home number,' said Liz, 'and you're in my house on Whitehedge Road, so you must be my mother.'

Rita's home was indeed on Whitehedge Road in Garston, but she told "Liz" she'd still got the wrong number.

'I've been in the dark for so long,' Liz rambled on, 'and I'm starting to realise what happened to me.' There was a pause, and then a terrible scream, and Liz cried: 'I'm dead, aren't I? I'm coming home mum!'

'If you call me again I'll have the police on you!' Rita yelled back, and slammed down the phone, feeling more scared than annoyed, but Liz called back a minute later, and again asked to speak to her mother. Rita hung up again, and on the following night, again at 8.50pm, Liz called again. This time she said she was in a telephone box 'just round the corner on St Mary's Road' and that she was on her way home. At precisely 9pm there was a knock at the door, and Mr Higginson answered to find no one there – but he felt something brush past him and he and his wife heard soft footsteps in the hallway which seemed to be headed for the kitchen. They both heard a young woman's voice ask: 'Where is everyone? Where's my mother?'

The couple clung on to one another, terrified.

The unseen woman screamed: 'I'm dead! Oh my God I'm dead! Help me!'

'Get out of this house!' yelled Mr Higginson, but the invisible ghost sobbed loudly and cried: 'I'm dead, I'm dead...'

Mr Higginson felt his door keys in his pocket before ushering his wife out of the house and locking the door behind him. The Higginsons sought sanctuary next door. Their neighbour, an old lady named Meg, said: 'Years ago, in the 1950s, a young lady who lived in your house with her mother was knocked down and killed on St Mary's Road. I'm almost sure her name was Liz.'

Meg and her neighbours could hear the ghost screaming next door, and Mr Higginson told his wife to stay with Meg while he paid a visit to his cousin – a Catholic priest named Edward. Mr Higginson explained the weird and scary predicament to his cousin that evening and begged him to help. Edward visited his cousin's home that evening at 11pm and found the ghost very evasive when he asked it if it recognised Jesus Christ. Poltergeist activity broke out, and Father Edward was pelted with pots and pans. He opened the door and went next door to see his cousin and Rita Higginson to tell them that he was going to attempt an exorcism – even though he had not recently been to confession (which is something of a prerequisite to the Rite of Exorcism). Armed with a Bible and a silver crucifix, Father Edward went into the house but the spirit had gone into hiding. Mr and Mrs Higginson stayed with their neighbour all night and slept in a spare room. Father Edward returned the next morning after confession and began to perform the Rite of Exorcism. He did not get too far into the rite when the entity, suspected of being a demon, left the house in the form of a dark vapour. It materialised at one point as a grinning woman before it faded away. Why this demon had mimicked a long-dead woman is unknown. It never called again at the house on Whitehedge Road, but I have many reports of evil spirits at large in Liverpool, and could easily fill a book with them. The two accounts featured in this chapter are just a miniscule selection of a disturbing phenomenon I have researched over the years, and what strikes me as sinister is the way in which these entities go about impersonating the living. In the 1990s, a landlord bought an old Victorian house on Wavertree's Sandown Road. The large house was in a bad state, but after some £15,000 was spent on renovation, the end result was a complex of student flats with all the mod cons. By the summer of 1995 all six flats in the house were occupied by students, and the landlord began to search for other properties around the city in the hope of repeating his success. However, one dismal Sunday evening in July 1995, a 22-year-old student named Lily was in the communal kitchen at the house when the doors of a cupboard burst open, giving her quite a start, and a rather effeminate voice came from inside the cupboard which announced: 'Ha ha! My name is Tony and I lived here before you! What are you doing in my house?'

The voice said this in a jokey manner, not as a genuine protest against the student being there, but all the same the utterance of the ghost and the way it had thrown the cupboard doors open sent poor Lily running out into the street. She went to find her boyfriend Jake, and eventually found him drinking in a local pub called the Cock and Bottle on Wavertree's High Street. When Lily told him what had happened, Jake's face twitched. It turned out that he had seen a tap turn on by itself in the kitchen sink that morning, but had said nothing because he had been brought up to believe that he'd have bad luck if he talked about the supernatural. What's more, Jake's friend Olly, a very level-headed law student, had been playing Scrabble with Jake at the flat one week before when Lily was out with her friends, and something kept arranging the Scrabble tiles on his rack so they would spell very offensive swear-words. In the end, Olly gave up on the game and went home, leaving Jake spooked. Jake left the pub with his girlfriend and went to their flat at the house on Sandown Lane. Jake saw that the doors of the cupboard in the kitchen were still open, and as he closed them, Lily let out a scream, then fled from the kitchen into the hallway, where Jake caught up with her. 'It touched me!' she said, with her hands on her crotch. She had on jeans, yet she had distinctly felt a cold hand in her knickers.

Three medical students, Oscar, George and Sophia, came out of their flat upon hearing Lily's scream and asked what the matter was.

'Our flats haunted,' Jake told them, and became annoyed when the three students all smiled. They obviously thought it was a joke.

'Haunted?' Sophia asked, the most bemused of the three.

'Yes, I wouldn't say so otherwise!' snapped Jake and he asked Lily if she was alright.

She shook her head. 'I think we should go,' she said, and her huge eyes bulged with fear as she gazed at the open door of their flat. That door was slowly closing.

'Did you see it?' the medical student Oscar asked, all tongue in cheek, playing up to his two friends.

Jake felt like punching him because of the smarmy faint grin on his face. 'No, but she saw it open the cupboard and heard it talk,' Jake replied, and he held his girlfriend's hand and suggested: 'We could stay with Olly till we find a place if you want.'

The door to the haunted flat slammed shut, Lily yelped and Jake jumped, but the student Sophia said a draught had closed the door, that's all.

'We'll go in there with you if you want,' George said, stepping forward from his two friends, and he seemed sympathetic to the couple.

'Come and have a look,' Jake opened the flat door and beckoned for his three neighbours to come in. 'See for yourself.'

'No, don't,' Lily said nervously, but the three medical students followed her boyfriend into the flat. "Tony" failed to appear, and the atmosphere now seemed back to normal in the place. The students brought over a few bottles of wine and they and Lily and Jake all watched MTV and The Box on the telly for the rest of the evening. About a week after this, Lily was due to go out to a pub with Sophia, as she had now become friends with her, when something bizarre happened. The arm came off Sophia's new leather jacket as she grabbed the handle of the front door. Lily gave a nervous laugh at first, as it was such a surreal sight, but then Sophia examined the top of the sleeve and saw that all of the thread which would have attached it to the coat had vanished. The thread was not on the seam at the shoulder, and as Sophia was ascertaining this, the brass stud-fasteners on the other cuff and the waist suddenly fell onto the floor. Lily just knew this was the work of Tony, but she was too scared to even mention the spirit as she stood in the hallway. 'Talk about bad workmanship!' Sophia said as she stooped to pick up the studs and the detached sleeve.

'I did that!' said that campy voice Lily had heard coming from the cupboard on that memorable Sunday evening.

Sophia turned quickly and looked down the empty hallway, expecting someone to be there, but saw no one. 'Did you hear that?' she asked Lily, who nodded as her eyes darted about.

'It was me! Tony!' said the effeminate speaker, and this time Sophia could plainly discern that the voice had originate from an empty space about six feet to her left, and this really unnerved the student. Sophia's two student friend's had gone to the cinema with Lily's boyfriend Jake, and the only people in the house were two students upstairs.

'Let's go, Sophia!' Lily opened the front door and looked at the sheets of rain on this typical English summer evening.

'I can't go without a coat in this weather,' Sophia was saying when there was a noise which sounded to Lily's hears like a slap – or something elastic snapping. Sophia let out a scream and lifted her skirt. Her knickers were gone.

At this point Tony started laughing and said something which neither girl could understand; it sounded garbled, and the voiced seemed much nearer now. Both girls ran out of the house and had to walk to Old Swan, where Sophia's friend Lauren loaned her a pair of knickers. When Lauren heard about the strange goings-on at the house, she advised the girls to get in touch with a local medium she knew named Mary, who never charged for her services. Sophia and Lily took Lauren's advice and telephoned Mary, and she arrived at the house on Sandown Road on the following Monday evening at 7pm. Mary was in her late fifties, dressed in a sky-blue suit and white shirt, and with her voluminous head of elaborately styled (and brightly rinsed) hair, she bore a strong resemblance to the actress Molly Sugden, who played Mrs Slocombe in the popular television sitcom *Are You Being Served?*

Mary went into the living room of Lily and Jake's flat, and said she sensed a presence. Mary had asked Lily to ensure that no one was in the flat during her inspection, and only Lily was allowed to accompany the medium as she walked about the place.

'His name's not Tony for a start,' Mary announced,

smiling as she glanced towards the kitchen.

'Oh,' was all that Lily could muster.

'Yeah, his surname is Hengler, but he's withholding his first name for some reason,' Mary informed the young student.

'You're going to have visitors in a minute?' said the ghost, out of mid-air, somewhere in the kitchen.

Lily jumped, startled at the sudden eerie outburst but Mary only smiled and casually asked: 'Really, visitors from where? The next world?'

'No, the police!' "Tony" – or Mr Hengler as Mary began to call him – told the two women.

There was a loud banging at the door, and one of the tenants from the flats upstairs buzzed the visitors in. There was a ran-tan at the door of Lily's flat, and when she answered it the student was startled to see two policemen standing there.

'You reported an incident – ' one of the policemen said.

'No, sorry,' Lily stammered, 'I didn't call you.'

'We had a call from a woman - or possibly a man - saying a girl was being raped.' The policeman narrowed his eyes and looked past a shocked Lily at Mary, who was standing further down the hallway.

'Officer, you have been hoodwinked by a spirit!' Mary bellowed down the hallway, and made her way to the front door.

'Can I come in?' the world-weary policeman asked, and Lily nodded and stood aside.

The two policemen came in and one looked in the bedroom and bathroom and the other went to the communal kitchen and then he took a look in the small toilet.

'So you didn't call us?' the policeman who had accompanied the first one into the flat sighed to Lily.

'No, no, I swear, I didn't – ' Lily was replying as her heart palpitated. She had always been scared of authority figures.

'It's alright Miss,' said the other policeman as he finished looking in the toilet. 'Probably someone playing silly buggers.'

'It was a ghost, officer,' Mary confidently told him, all matter-of-fact, but received only an annoyed glance from the copper.

The police left and the doors of the cupboard in the kitchen opened and something pushed all of the cans of food and a bag of sugar from the shelves onto the floor.

'Stop! Stop this!' Mary cried at the cupboard.

'Shut up you stinking old hag!' said the unobservable pest.

'Mary, let's go,' Lily hurried out of the living room, 'I'll find somewhere else to live!'

'No, stand your ground Lily!' the medium tried to seize Lily by the arm to stop her from leaving but the young student was too fast. She opened the front door and the two policemen who had just left were coming up the path. The one in front said: 'Sorry about this love, but we've just had another call saying there's been a stabbing at your place.'

'It's a ghost officer,' Lily told him in a trembling voice, and she wanted to run out into the street but the officers of the law were in her way.

The police entered and heard what sounded like a slanging match between two people coming from the kitchen. Mary was yelling: 'I command thee to leave here unclean spirit!' and someone with a high-pitched voice was screaming four-letter words at her and threatening to rape her.

The police stormed the kitchen and were naturally baffled to see only Mary standing there; her hair and face were covered in flour and loose tealeaves and coffee granules. The policemen heard the quasi feminine voice coming from the cupboard and one of the officers who shone his torch into the cupboard was spat upon by something he could not see.

'The laws of your world do not apply to the laws of this thing, officer,' Mary told one of the stunned policemen, and just after she said this, the cupboard wrenched itself from the wall and smashed into her head, but she just laughed and exclaimed: 'Just because you can't have your own way!'

There was roaring sound outside and the floor shook. Two fire engines had pulled up outside on Sandown Road. Someone had alerted the emergency services to a blaze at the flats. The policemen escorted Mary into the hallway as they explained to the firemen that some hoaxer was behind the calls to the emergency services. Then an ambulance turned up. Someone had called 999 and reported a lady with head injuries at the flats. The ambulance personnel treated the cut to Mary's forehead from the flying cupboard and they took her into hospital in case she was suffering from concussion.

Lily and Jake left the troubled dwelling that evening and went to stay in Olly's house. They didn't return to the house on Sandown Road, but the spirit – Mr Hengler – then turned on the other occupiers in the flats, and one by one, they all left. The landlord called in medium after medium, and also a priest, but the spirit — which now called itself Angus — refused to leave. Mary returned to the house one evening and saw the landlord sitting in his car outside the empty flats. She explained who she was and warned him that the thing was some sort of demon and that he should treat the flats as a write-off. Mary then told the landlord she had returned to warn him because she had had several dreams where the landlord had been killed by the malevolent spirit.

That evening, the landlord was found in a semi-conscious state, slumped over the wheel of his car outside the house on Sandown Road. He told a paramedic who was the first to arrive on the scene: 'I saw it; it was horrible — gave me a bad turn —' and then he started fighting with the paramedic as he suffered from what seemed to be an anxiety attack. Another witness was present while the paramedic was there, and this was the manager to a local public house who had been taking his dog for a walk that night. He and the paramedic saw the landlord point at the window of the haunted house, and then he fell down — dead. The paramedic could not resuscitate the landlord, who had died from a cardiac condition. The pub manager said he passed the empty house on Sandown Road on the following night as he walked his pit bull terrier, when he heard someone in the communal hallway of the flats singing *Blue Moon of Kentucky*. The pit bull reacted by whimpering and tugged hard on its leash as it tried to run off. Other people around this time spoke of hearing someone singing the same song at the vacant flats all hours in the morning, but just what the significance of the song (which was written in the

United States in 1946) might be in relation to the haunting, is still not known. One woman told me that she had seen the silhouette of a very tall man with a long bullet-shaped head on the blinds of one of the empty flats at the house in 1996, and whoever – or whatever – it was, the figure seemed to be doing some dance.

One evening around 7.30pm in August 1997, Lily and Jake were at the Sloop Inn in St Ives, Cornwall, where they'd been holidaying for a few days when a member of the hotel staff told Lily she was wanted on the telephone. Lily thought this was odd because no one knew she was at this hotel with Jake, as they had originally only planned on going as far as Gloucester but had decided to visit Cornwall. Lily got up from the table where she had just been served scampi. As she reached the hotel reception area she asked the man at the desk who was calling her and he shrugged and said, 'I think he said his name's *Tony*.'

Lily picked up the handset and said, 'Hello?' She immediately recognised the voice.

'Hello – it's me. Drive carefully when you come back won't you?' said the caller, and he sounded even more effeminate on the telephone line.

The line went completely dead; no clicks, breathing sounds, purring tones or crackling noises - just complete silence.

Lily slowly replaced the handset and looked over to Jake with such an expression of shock, her boyfriend and the hotel staff member thought she had just received some really bad news. Jake came over to his girlfriend and asked: 'Who was it?'

'Tony,' Lily told him, her voice barely audible

because the back of her throat had dried up with fear.

'Tony who?' Jake was puzzled at the reply, and he thought of his uncle Tony and of Tony the kind local shopkeeper who sometimes gave him and Lily food on tick when money was in short supply.

'That thing – the ghost – that Tony,' Lily said, and she almost missed her seat as she tried to sit down at the table.

Jake recalled the weird goings-on at the house back in Liverpool. 'Oh come on Lil, someone's been messing about! It'll have been George!'

'It wasn't George – it was *him*.' Her trembling hand lifted the glass of white wine to her twitching lips.

'Ghosts can't phone people up, love,' Jake said with a forced, soulless chuckle.

'He said drive carefully when we're on the way back – does he know something?' Lily shuddered, and the rim of the wineglass hit her front tooth.

'I'll kill George when I get back – ' Jake was saying as he seated himself back at the table.

'It wasn't George – I know George's voice, Jake – it was that thing,' said Lily, 'it was an omen.'

'Oh God, Lily, will you just eat your scampi and stop all this nonsense, please?' Jake pointed his fork at the untouched food on his girlfriend's plate. Jake attempted to smile and told his girlfriend: 'Don't let a crank call ruin our little break, love.'

On the following morning the couple made their way back to Liverpool in Jake's old Ford Fiesta. Lily was convinced the car would be involved in some accident. Liverpool was over 360 miles away and it would take over six hours to complete the journey. Jake kept reassuring Lily that the Fiesta was in great shape. He'd had the engine and brakes checked by a friend who knew everything about cars and he had given the vehicle a glowing bill of health – but as the car was travelling along the M5 motorway on the outskirts of Bristol, its front right tyre burst. This incident was probably cause by Jake, as he often sheared the walls of his tyres against the kerb whenever he parked and he rarely checked the pressure of his tyres. He was lucky when the front tyre blowout occurred. He recalled his father's advice about leaving the footbrake alone if there is enough space on the road ahead. The vehicle was veering to one side and Jake constantly corrected the deviation by skilfully turning the wheel to counteract the path of the car. The car lost speed naturally and came to a halt on the hard shoulder.

'I told you, I told you!' Lily screamed, and she got out the vehicle and fell down onto her knees on the grass verge in tears.

'I don't know how that happened!' Jake kept saying, and eventually he calmed down, put the Fiesta's hazard lights on and walked to the nearest emergency phone to call the AA.

Back in Liverpool, Jake had it out with George, for he believed he had made that call to the hotel in St Ives, but George maintained that he had not made any call to frighten Lily and he had not even known where she was at the time. This was true, because the couple had decided to go to St Ives on a mere whim after visiting Gloucester. Lily never heard from that spirit again, but whenever the nearest telephone would ring, the girl would always imagine the worst and wonder if *he* was calling...

TALES OF TEALEAVES
AND CARDS

There's more to cards – ordinary playing cards – than meets the eye. They are mostly used for games, but they can also be used to foretell the future, and this use is termed 'cartomancy'. My mother taught me how to read cards when I was young, and it was soon discovered that I was a spookily accurate reader. I stopped the readings because a high proportion of the cards foretold death and illness, and 'clients' (if you could call morbidly curious non-paying friends and neighbours that) did indeed die or develop serious illnesses – even though I rarely told them about the bad news in the cards. This scared me a little; I felt as if I was getting involved in some forbidden practice best left to the adult occultists. I was told that the cards are based on the old calendar of the witches. The mathematics of this claim has a lot going for it too; a pack of cards has twelve picture cards – three in each suit – symbolizing the twelve months of the year and the twelve signs of the Zodiac. There are two colours in each pack – red hearts and diamonds – and black spades and clubs – and these two colours represent the summer solstice (red) and the winter solstice (black) as well as night and day. The four suits represent the four seasons of the year in this archaic model, and if the value of each card is added together, with the aces counting as 1, and kings, queens and jacks equating to 13, 12 and 11, the sum total of this addition is 364 – and the joker makes that number 365 – the number of days in a year. The 52 cards in a pack also represent the number of weeks in a year. Some Christians have branded the pack of playing cards the Devil's Picture Book, as no good can come of gambling, although anyone who has heard the old song *The Deck of Cards* in which a soldier is caught red-handed with a pack of playing cards while he's at church, will know that religious meaning has even been drawn from a card-deck. The quick-thinking soldier claims that the humble pack is his Prayer Book and Bible; that the Ace reminds him there is only *one* God, and when he sees the number two card – the Deuce – he is mindful that the Good Book is divided into the Old and New Testaments; the three card symbolizes the Holy Trinity, whereas the number four card reminds him of the four evangelists: Matthew, Mark, Luke and John. And the soldier roams along the cards, pointing out such things as the Nine Lepers who were cured but all ungrateful enough not to thank God, and the Ten Commandments and so on. Without a doubt, there is some occult meaning in the cards which goes even deeper than hidden calendars and cryptic religious references – and you may delve at your own peril into the *real meaning* of those poe-faced knaves, queens and cards – and that sinister grinning Joker.

There was a case, many years ago in the 1930s, where a very level-headed high-ranking court official – Justice T. B. Horwood, Judge of a native High Court in Estcourt, Natal (a province of South Africa from

1910 to 1994) tried a Liverpool man named John Bailey with obtaining money by deception by taking cash off clients for reading their cards. Bailey was fined the equivalent (in English money) of £20 plus court costs and Justice Horwood gloated at the card reader by asking him: 'Why didn't you foresee yourself in court with your cards?'

'I do not read my own life in the cards, that is why, your honour,' Bailey replied.

'No one can read anyone's future in cards – ' the judge declared, but Bailey irritated him by mouthing the words: 'I can,' as he slowly nodded. The judge asked the defendant if he had a pack of cards upon his person as perhaps he could give a demonstration of his 'art'. Bailey surprised the judge by producing a pack of cards, and he told Horwood: 'I could read *your* fortune your honour.'

The judge seemed nervous as people giggled at the audacity of the Liverpool fortune teller, who smiled, then announced: 'Here is your future, your honour!'

Mr Bailey dealt the Ace of Spades, followed by the King of Spades – and suddenly stopped with a very morose expression on his face. The cards rested on the thin 'shelf' on top of the enclosure, and Bailey looked at them and said: 'The death card, and it is something to do with an important dark gentleman, represented by the King of Spades. I get the strange impression that this man is cursing you – '

'Quiet!' Justice Horwood's voice boomed and reverberated through the wood-panelled courtroom. 'Get this charlatan out of here!' Horwood instructed the two policemen flanking the defendant. Mr Bailey could not have possibly known that the judge before him was indeed on the receiving end of a curse inflicted upon him by a Zulu witch doctor. No one knew just why the judge had been cursed but it was said by some that he had called one of the Zulu witch doctor's a charlatan because he had killed an Indian man and made concoctions from the murder victim's blood and body parts. The judge believed that if he travelled home to England on a short vacation, he would be outside the range of the Zulu magic, but a few days later, just after Horwood had arrived at Heyford, Oxfordshire, intending to stay with his relatives, he dropped dead of heart failure. Relatives of Horwood said they had heard strange distant drumbeats on the night the judge had suddenly fallen down dead.

In Liverpool in the late 1970s a fortune teller calling herself Lady Haruspex opened a room above a shop on West Derby Road. She charged fifty pence for a reading, and she divined by reading standard playing cards. A 22-year-old woman named Claire, who only lived around the corner from the soothsayer on the cul de sac of Somerset Place, had recently had her palm read by an alleged Romany woman in a Chester arcade, and she had been told to expect bad news. She had asked the palm reader just what type of bad news was in the offing but the palmist had said it was hard to see exactly what it was, but she had the strong impression of it being very serious and felt that it was due to take place around a weekend in the middle of March. This naturally scared Claire, so she went to see a Tarot reader in the Globe pub on Cases Street in the city centre – and this cartomancist, who knew nothing about the palm-reader's dire warning – said very much the same thing as her – that Claire's life would be in danger around the 18th or 19th of March, the dates of the coming weekend. The Tarot reader said she could not see what the threat was, only its shadow cast over the end of the coming week. So you can imagine the state of Claire when she visited Lady Haruspex on West Derby Road; she could hardly get her words out with nerves. The seer of the cards shuffled the simple pack and told Claire to briefly touch them once with her pointing finger. She then began to deal the cards into a grid. 'The four of clubs – a doomed car,' the lady announced, and something very weird took place as she continued to deal. The face of the Queen of Hearts looked exactly like Claire – even to the mole on her left cheek, and her short light brown hair. And the Jack of Diamonds looked like Claire's boyfriend, Chris – the same Roman nose, the eyebrows that met in the middle, and the piercing dark-green eyes. Lady Haruspex said: 'That's you – the Queen of Hearts, full of love, so trusting my dear, and this one - the Jack of Diamonds is your boyfriend, an individual who is always scheming for money.'

'That's him alright, he's money mad,' said Claire, gazing at the faces of the cards in awe.

'Well he does loves you but is very lustful, and can't help himself where women are concerned, and I am afraid that a woman you know is carrying his baby.'

Claire was stunned by this claim, but then another card was dealt – the Queen of Clubs – and its face was clearly that of Claire's best friend, Sandra; the same pointed, elfin chin, upturned 'piggy nose' and huge brown eyes.

'If you get into a car with the Jack of Diamonds

you'll be dead on Sunday. Leave him my dear! Leave him to your deceitful friend!'

Sensing something very eerie about the fortune teller and those weird cards which had faces that actually resembled Claire and the people she knew, the frightened young lady left the 50p on the table and backed out of the room.

'Stay out Jack's car!' the strange lady cried after Claire as she hurried down the stairs. Claire lumbered along West Derby Road against a sudden fierce wind, and all of the words of the fortune teller and the images of the cards were tumbling round in her head. Was Sandra really pregnant with Chris's baby? When had he been seeing her? Why had her friend betrayed her like this? Claire had only recently loaned Sandra a tenner because she'd been laid off work. So many questions and issues flooded the girl's mind. She was on the doorstep of her home on Somerset Place within a minute, and she went into the kitchen where her mother was handwashing some tea towels in the sink.

'Why aren't you in work?' she asked Claire.

'I told you last night I have three days off, Mam,' Claire replied, and grabbed the kettle. Her mother stepped aside as the girl filled it at the sink. 'Mam, I'm worried – really worried.'

Her mum rolled her eyes and wrung out a tea towel. 'You're always worried, Claire, what is it this time?'

Claire told her about all of the predictions of approaching doom from the three fortune tellers and seemed close to tears.

'Claire, I have no sympathy for you, love, you're always reading horoscopes and listening to stupid ghost stories from your Nan. I think you look for things to worry about.'

'Mam, that's not all, the card reader told me more bad news – '

'You want to try paying the rent and working in a canteen in a school every day to get food on the table with a lazy husband who lives in the bookies – '

'Mam, please shut up a mo! The woman who just read my cards said Chris has been carrying on with Sandra behind my back and that Sandra is having his baby!'

'I've never heard of anything as ridiculous in all my life,' Claire's mother laughed. 'Chris and you are joined at the hip; when would he find the time to be carrying on with Sandra? And she's put that much weight on she could go on the wrestling on *World of Sport*.'

'Mam, maybe she's put weight on because she's in the club,' Claire tried to strike a match to light the gas ring for the kettle but the stalk broke.

'Ooh, that's a bad sign that,' Claire's mother pointed to the broken match.

'What? Is it?' Claire seemed horrified.

'No, you daft cow, but see what I mean? You're so gullible.'

Claire was offended by her mother's attitude and she slammed the kettle down on the unlit gas ring and went upstairs to sulk. The predictions of bad news played on her mind and she was so certain Chris's car would crash, she sneaked out of her house that night and walked to her boyfriend's house with a knife. She slashed all four of the tyres on Chris's car then hurried off home, putting the knife down a grid on the way. She wondered if she was losing her mind doing such a thing, and asked herself why she should save Chris's life when he might be seeing another girl.

Chris had made arrangements to go to a friend's house that Sunday but couldn't go because he couldn't afford to buy new tyres, and he got into a fight after he accused a local young vandal of puncturing the tyres.

Later that day, a car stolen by a youth ploughed into a vehicle of the exact same model as Chris's car – and the robbed car even had a registration very similar to Chris's vehicle. A woman from Chris's street died in the smash along with her son. The victims had the same unusual surname as Chris too. Soon after this, Sandra admitted she was pregnant to Chris, and Claire burst into tears. Chris told Claire that Sandra had practically seduced him while he was drunk one evening when she had met him in town, but Claire swore at him and said it was over. Chris told Sandra to get rid of the baby but she slapped him and later gave birth to a baby girl. Sandra also begged her friend for forgiveness but Claire never talked to her or Chris again, and she never visited fortune tellers again. I have never traced Lady Haruspex. A Haruspex was a person who practiced divination by examining the entrails of sacrificed animals to look for omens and answers to various problems.

Another traditional way of foretelling a person's future is tasseomancy – the reading of tealeaves, and again, as with the cards, I have dabbled in this form of divination (which probably dates back to ancient China) with some startling results, but found some of the readings so chillingly accurate I decided to put the soothsaying on hold for a while. Unlike cartomancy, in which the learner has to memorise what each of the 52 cards of a pack signify, the tealeaf reader merely has to look into the patterns of leaves in the bottom of a cup after the beverage has been carefully drained to see the patterns directly. Not everyone can see people and objects in the leaves, and while some occultists have stated that readers of leaves are born and cannot be trained in tasseomancy, I beg to disagree, as I know a few people over the years who have taught themselves the art with a little patience and dogged perseverance. Incidentally, grounds in the silt at the bottom of a coffee cup can also be read. Some modern readers of the leaves divide the bottom of the cup into sectors and time zones and claim that images nearer to the rim at the top of the cup are nearer to you in time. Sometimes this is so, but in my experience, you should simply empty your mind and look at the patterns and shapes and if you relax a little you *will* see recognisable images and symbols; the skill is in connecting them, and this shouldn't be forced; just leave it to your subconscious mind and you'll realise the order the symbols come in. You can use loose tea or simply open a few teabags and put them in a cup or mug and add boiled water from a kettle. Let the leaves infuse for a few minutes, and then, if the client cannot bear to sip the newly-brewed tea, add a little milk and sugar (or sweetener) if required. The client needs only to take a few sips if desired. Either you or the client can then swill the tea around (clockwise if possible) and carefully drain it into the sink so the leaves remain. Some tealeaf readers let the leaves 'fix' a little by putting the cup aside for a few minutes. The old readers often had a saucer at hand to drain the cup but the sink will suffice nowadays. I have been asked by readers if it is possible to read the fortune of a person in the leaves who is not present, and the answer is, according to the occultists of old – yes. You have to write the name of the person on a piece of paper and after folding the paper, keep it in your hand as you prepare the reading. If possible, the tealeaf-reader should keep the person in their mind as they themselves sip the tea and drain the cup.

My grandmother Rose Slemen was very good at reading the leaves, but never charged for reading fortunes. In February 1963, she visited the house of a certain lady she had worked with at a tobacconists a few years before. The house was a terraced redbrick one on Hollybank Road, which runs parallel to Penny Lane, which lies between Wavertree and Mossley Hill. Rose looked into the teacup and not only did she see a wedding between her friend and a man carrying a sack (a postman, and not the handsome coalman, because the figure wore a hat) – she also saw something much more disturbing. When I heard the story of what my Gran saw many years later I was surprised I had not heard about the tragic incident during my delving into local history. In the leaves, Rose saw a man with some sort of firearm, and he was blasting a girl. She felt that this girl was known to her friend, and that was why this terrible presentiment was so clear. Rose said she could see the letters MOC, and she felt that these were the initials relating to the girl being shot. There was a coffin next to the girl, and Rose told her friend that the man with the strange gun was possibly a soldier or related to someone with a military background. At the end of the reading, Rose's friend said, 'I'm excited in a way because of what you've seen about me and the postman, but I'm also dreading hearing about a girl being shot.'

The prediction was made on the Sunday afternoon of 10 February 1963, and just under a week after this, on the chilly but sunny afternoon of Saturday 16 February, 15-year-old Maureen Olive Cope was walking past Ferndale Road – just off Smithdown Road – possibly on her way to her friend's house, when she was blasted to death by a man she had never seen in her life before. The man was 20-year-old John Perrin, who lived on Ferndale Road with his mother and father – an Army Lance Corporal. John had no history of violence and no criminal record, yet he had casually walked out of his home with a sawn-off shotgun, and he had fired each barrel at Maureen at almost point-blank range. Maureen, of Heathfield Road, had been a model pupil at Morrison County Secondary School and was an only child. No one ever found out why John Perrin shot the girl, because seconds after he had ended the life of Maureen Cope, he shot himself dead. Like Maureen, John had been a very quiet and inoffensive person who liked to read books and watch television. He didn't have a girlfriend and had not worked in two years, his last job being in a local bakery. All of the facts of this shooting were read by my grandmother's friend in the newspapers and she felt faint when she realised that the tealeaves had foretold this double tragedy. The MOC seen in the leaves had been the initials of Maureen Olive Cope, the girl who had been shot. A fortnight after the killing of the schoolgirl and the suicide of the person who had shot her twice, my Gran's friend received a funny home-made card from the postman entitled "A Belated Valentine" – in which he declared his feelings for her in a verse. Within a year, the postman had married her.

We now come forward a little in time from 1963 to 1977, to another sinister tale of the tealeaves, and this one concerns Roger Hampton, a 40-year-old Kirkby market stall trader. Roger visited his Aunt Sylvia at her home in Maghull on her birthday on the Wednesday evening of 1 June 1977 with his wife Jane, and after the couple gave their presents to Sylvia, Jane asked her to read her tealeaves, as Sylvia was renowned for her gift of reading the leaves. Sylvia told Jane that she would have two babies in the winter of the following year, as she could see them clearly in the leaves, and she even pointed them out to Jane. 'Oh my God, yes,' Jane was amazed at the two tiny figures with big heads, and she called Roger over and pointed them out to him. 'See, love? They look like the symbol of the Gemini twins in the horoscopes don't they?'

'Pie in the sky, you lot,' Roger replied with a twinkle of amusement in his eyes. 'Women are always dabbling in black magic and hocus pocus.'

'This is not pie in the sky, Roger,' his annoyed aunt told her nephew.

'Read Roger's leaves, Sylvia,' Jane suggested, 'see what's in store for him.'

'Oh behave yourselves,' Roger grimaced and looked at his watch. 'We'd better be going.'

'No, hang on Roger, Sylvia will convert you – unless you're scared, like.' Jane seized his wrist and covered the watch with the sleeve of his pullover.

Sylvia was already making her way to the kettle.

'We've got to get back soon!' Roger complained to his whimsical wife in a forced whisper of a voice.

'She could make a living out of this you know love, she's very accurate,' Jane whispered back.

'Oh don't encourage her, please,' Roger screwed his face up again and looked at the clock on the mantelpiece.

A new cup of tea was brewed with the two teaspoonfuls of leaves in the china cup, and after Roger took a few sips, Sylvia emptied the contents into the sink and brought the cup back in. She sat with her reading glasses on, studying the cup and rotating it as Jane tried to see any patterns in the leaves. Roger sat facing in a big comfy tartan-patterned armchair, puffing and blowing with swelling impatience.

'I don't like the look of this,' Sylvia murmured, and that ominous remark instantly grabbed Roger's attention. The last time Aunt Sylvia had said that to the person who was having the leaves read, the person had died; she had foreseen a blaze on that occasion, and within a week the invitee had been burnt to a crisp in a terrible house fire.

'You don't like the look of what?' Roger stood up and came round the coffee table. He stooped to look at the cup but Sylvia pushed his curious face away.

'I don't like the look of that, either,' she suddenly added.

'I can't breathe,' Jane clutched her throat. This always happened when she had a mini anxiety attack.

'You okay love?' Roger asked. He had palpitations.

'Get her some water, she'll be okay,' Sylvia told her nephew without averting her gaze at the cup.

'I said I didn't want my tealeaves read,' Roger complained as he hurried to the kitchen, 'but no, you two witches had to start dabbling!'

'Love! I'm okay now, I'm okay!' Jane shouted.

Roger brought her a glass of water anyway, and Jane saw his trembling hand as he handed her the glass.

'Is it bad news?' Jane asked Sylvia.

There was a sharp intake of breath from Sylvia, and then she looked up at Roger's face, which looked as if it had been drained of blood. 'Be careful on the road on the way back,' Sylvia was saying when Roger started coughing. He snatched the glass back off Jane and drank all the water.

'Why, what have you seen? A car crash?' Roger asked, and his left eyebrow began to flicker.

Sylvia looked back into the cup and replied: 'I can see what looks like either a black car or a Hackney cab, and I can see the letters HLC and 3 numbers before it – and I think two of them are sixes. Keep your eyes peeled for that vehicle, as he looks like he's hit your car.'

'Never again are you to read my tealeaves auntie,' Roger said through gritted teeth, 'I don't approve of this mumbo jumbo, no good can come of it.'

'You said there was something else you didn't like, Sylvia,' Jane reminded her, and Roger threw his head back and gave a loud hollow laugh.

'Yes,' Sylvia replied, slamming the cup down in a haughty manner on the coffee table, 'but I'm sorry I opened my mouth now, the way he's over-reacting.'

'Over-reacting?' Roger pointed at his own chest, and tried to grin, 'I've just been told that I might be involved in a fatal car crash - *after* you told me and Jane we are going to be the parents of twins! What did you want me to do? Laugh?'

'Calm down Roger,' Jane playfully slapped her

husband's leg. 'It's better for you to know these things in advance instead of them just happening to you. That's why a lot of witches live long – they avoid accidents by looking into the future.'

'I'm no witch!' Sylvia swiped off her glasses.

Jane back-pedalled. 'No, I know you're not Syl; I was just explaining to Roger how it pays to be able to see the future.'

'Well be careful how you choose your words Jane,' Sylvia told her, putting her specs back on, 'there are lots of judgemental Jacks and Joanna's around here who are still in the dark ages and if they heard you call me a witch they'd put my windows in or worse.'

'God, talk about nineways to Sunday!' Roger groaned. 'Can you tell me what the other thing was that you saw? I mean, if I survive the first thing – what's the second life-threatening thing?'

Sylvia took a real close look at the cup, so her nose touched the rim at one point. 'Well, it's not life-threatening as far as I can see, but er, she's very strange – '

'She? So it's a woman?' Jane was very curious at the mention of a woman, and immediately wondered if it was her new neighbour – a young single blonde who had recently offered Roger a fiver to mow her lawn. Roger was always talking about this woman.

'An *old* woman,' Sylvia destroyed Jane's conjecture. 'An old woman who strikes me as, well – sinister – and here's the weird part: there's an eye above her, and I just have this impression of it being the Evil Eye. I can see Roger, and she is standing behind him, a bit of a distance away, but she's looking at him, and I feel it's a sort of obsession.'

'Wonder who she is?' said Jane, and she looked up at Roger.

'I'm more worried about the crash,' he said, and once again he went on about the whole thing being Jane's fault for asking for the tealeaves reading in the first place.

The couple left Aunt Sylvia's home and headed back towards Kirkby, but Roger, exceedingly mindful of the predicted crash, took a long-winded route back home. 'Where are we going?' Jane asked, gazing through the passenger side window of the Jag.

'We are going on a roundabout route to avoid the main roads,' Roger replied, constantly checking his mirrors. He took the car down dirt tracks and even took a short cut over the corner of a farmer's field.

'That's Maghull Hospital over there,' Jane observed, 'we've gone way off the beaten track.'

'I've just told you that,' Roger replied in an annoyed tone, 'it will hopefully be safer if we avoid the main roads.'

'It'll be getting dark soon,' said Jane, pessimistically, 'and she noticed that the full moon had already risen in the clear sky.

'It's only nine o'clock,' Roger retorted, and he asked Jane if she now knew where they were.

'Haven't the foggiest,' she admitted.

'That's Simonswood up there – ' Roger was saying when there was a flash of light in the road ahead. Jane screamed, and Roger quickly spun the steering wheel left in a reflexive reaction. A hackney cab came flying past the car and skidded to a halt about twenty feet away with its front stuck in a hedge.

Roger swore and was about to get out the car but his

wife dragged him back. She had turned in the seat and had seen a man with a bar or a stick leaving the cab. He was coming towards the couple's car.

'Drive off - quick!' Jane's voice was almost a squeal, and her husband fell back into the seat and restarted the car before tearing off.

'That cheeky get almost killed us and he's on the bounce with that bar!' Roger whined, watching the bellicose figure shrinking in the rear view mirror.

'Did you see the registration?' Jane asked.

'No!' Roger bawled. 'It's not worth reporting; he shouldn't have been using these dirt tracks and neither should I but – '

'Roger, the registration ended in HLC, and I'm sure the first part had a six in it!' Jane informed him.

'So? What about – ' and Roger suddenly recalled the registration his Aunt Sylvia had seen in the leaves. 'Oh, well at least that one's out the way.'

In August of that year, Roger was returning from Chester, where he had a stall selling bric-a-brac and gifts for visiting tourists. Instead of heading straight for the Queensway Tunnel to get home, he made a detour on a nostalgic whim to the Stork Hotel pub on Birkenhead's Price Street, where he had lived for a while in his younger days. He went into the pub, expecting to see a few old friends, but only saw one – Terry, his old neighbour from Brassey Street. Terry had been done for drink-driving a few months back so he insisted on buying Roger a bitter shandy so he could drive his Jag home safely. The two men talked of old times and Roger said, 'I wonder how old Billy the Brickie is going on? Haven't seen him in years.'

'He's just died,' said an old woman standing behind

the two men. She wore a green headscarf and a black calf-length coat. Her face was very pale and her eyes were deep set. She explained that Billy had been suffering from a long illness and had passed away literally an hour ago.

The two men were shocked and saddened by the news, and Roger asked the old woman if she had known Terry. She just nodded and smiled. She didn't have a drink, so Roger asked her what she was having.

Terry pulled Roger aside and whispered: 'They call her Mrs Badnews. Every time you see her she has got some news of someone dying or tragic tidings of some sort.'

The woman refused to have a drink and left the pub.

A few days later, Roger and his wife Jane flew down to Spain for a week, and on the first evening of the holiday as the couple walked into a bar – they were met by that same old woman from the Stork pub. She still had that green headscarf and black coat on. 'Go abroad and you'll hear news of home,' she told Roger with a crooked smile, 'that's an old saying.'

'Oh, hello, fancy meeting you here,' Roger told the old lady, and as he went to introduce his wife, the elderly woman said: 'I've just been talking to a man named Bob over there who knows you and he said your grandmother Peggy is seriously ill.'

This turned out to be true; Bob was a neighbour of Roger's Nan and had just arrived in Marbella with the bad news. He had told the old woman not to tell Roger in case it spoiled his holiday. Roger made a long-distance call to his brother and was told his Nan had just passed away. The holiday was ruined. Roger told Jane how Terry had called the old woman Mrs

Badnews, and how he thought she was some weird jinx but his wife said it was all coincidence and superstition – but on seven more occasions over the next twelve months, each time Roger bumped into the old lady, in places ranging from Liverpool to Lancaster, she would tell him bad news to do with family or friends. Jane eventually realised that this creepy old woman was the person Roger's Aunt had seen in the tealeaves, and she told her husband. 'She mentioned the Evil Eye above her head or something didn't she?' Roger recalled the uncanny prediction. Jane nodded. When she and her husband saw the woman in the following week, at a supermarket in Aintree, Jane asked the woman where she was from and what her name was. The old lady never answered her questions; instead, she turned to Jane's husband and asked: 'Roger, have you got an uncle in Prescot named Len?'

Roger went cold, and Jane, who really liked his Uncle Len, threw her hands to her face in grim anticipation.

'Yeah, why?' Roger asked.

'The woman who lives next door but one to me is a nurse in Whiston Hospital and she said he was admitted this afternoon saying he had pains in his chest. He died from a heart attack in the hospital bed.'

'No!' Jane cried out, and burst into tears, and Roger became both upset and yet he was also angry at the old harbinger of doom.

'Piss off you unlucky old cow!' Roger growled at the woman.

'Don't you talk to me like that, I'm just the messenger! Be thankful I'm not telling people about you dying,' was her reply, and she gave the two finger gesture towards the upset couple before turning and walking down the aisle of the supermarket.

Roger and Jane were so fearful of meeting the bringer of bad news again, they both went to St Chad's Church and got down on their knees. They earnestly prayed for God to keep this Jonah of a woman at bay. They left the church that grey afternoon, and never set eyes on "Mrs Badnews" again. I've made many enquiries about the old woman over the years, and no one seems to know just who she was. Someone said she was a Mrs Costello, but that lady died early in 1977, whereas Mrs Badnews seems to have been active till around 1980 in other parts of Knowsley and Liverpool. A man named Joe Hayes told me that in 1975, a relative of his was told that her neighbour – a young fire brigade recruit – had tragically died after becoming trapped in a mock-up of a blaze at a derelict house. The woman who broke the news was dressed in a green headscarf and also wore a long black coat, and she was known for being the first to break bad news to people, sometimes literally within a minute of a tragedy taking place, yet no one knew this woman.

Incidentally, Jane later did have twins – in February 1978, just as Aunt Sylvia predicted.

PHANTOM LEGS IN FAZAKERLEY

In the living room of a mid-terrace house on Fazakerley's Drake Road in 1972, a 39-year-old woman named Eileen got the shock of her life when she bent down to pick up her 6-year-old son David's Dinky model car. The time was 10.40pm and David was fast asleep in bed upstairs. Eileen's husband Harry was in the local pub with his brother. Eileen was about to get up from under the table after picking up the car when she happened to glance towards the door to the hall. She saw the legs of a stranger standing there in the doorway. He wore grey trousers with turn-ups and a pair of highly-polished black brogues. Eileen froze there on her hands and knees, naturally assuming that someone had broken into the house. She couldn't see the trespasser from the waist upwards, just his shoes and trousered legs, and her mind raced as she wondered what to do. Should she run to the door leading to the backyard? No, she'd have to get the keys from the hook on the kitchen wall first. Should she start screaming? Maybe that would spur the intruder to silence her – perhaps with a knife. She remained there under the table, trembling, when suddenly, she heard a knock at the front door. At that moment, the legs of the menacing stranger vanished, but Eileen thought he had simply dashed off to hide. She got up, looked about, and saw no one. Eileen ran to the front door and opened it. It was Harry's older brother, Peter, slightly intoxicated as usual. Harry had always warned his wife about letting Harry in because he had stolen money in the past to finance his drink habit, but Eileen was that afraid of the sprightly uninvited guest, she almost dragged Peter into the house, and he was pleasantly surprised to get into the house.

'Eileen I'm sorry about calling like this unannounced but my landlady has thrown me out my home – ' Peter was saying in a slurred voice as Eileen pulled him indoors. She closed the front door and walked him into the living room and looked around. 'Where the hell has he gone?' she asked, looking around. She even looked behind the curtains and behind the sofa.

'Eileen, who are you looking for?' Peter asked, 'Harry?'

'No, I *know* where Harry is; he's in the Farmer's Arms,' Eileen quipped, and then she told Peter what she had seen, and he seemed a bit scared.

'Are you sure it wasn't one of Harry's mates, Eileen?' he asked. 'Maybe Harry sent one of them back for something – money or something.'

Eileen shook her head. 'No, this fellah looked a bit old-fashioned. He was wearing grey kecks and I think they were straight and wide; they weren't flared, and he had old brogues on like my dad used to wear, and that makes me think it might have been a ghost. He seems to have vanished into thin air.'

Peter looked at the spot in the doorway where the ghost had appeared, according to Eileen, and he suddenly made an excuse to leave. 'I think I'll get out your hair before Harry comes back, Eileen; he'll only have a cob on when he sees me.'

'No, don't get off because of that, Peter,' Eileen told him with a worried look, 'I'll make you some cheese on toast and get you something to drink. I've had a bottle of sherry from last Christmas in the cupboard getting hairs on it – '

Peter walked into the hallway, and despite Eileen's calls for him to return because she was obviously scared by the ghostly incident, Peter left the house.

When Harry came home around half-past eleven he was so intoxicated he just dismissed his wife's account of the man in the kitchen doorway with an irritating wave of the hand in her face before he went to bed, but on the following Sunday, while Eileen was paying a visit to her mother in the Warbreck Moor area, it was Harry's turn to see the ghost. It was around noon, and he had just returned from the newsagents with his Sunday paper, a packet of Golden Virginia tobacco and a tube of lighter petrol. Harry closed the door behind him as he entered the hall – and immediately he saw something surreal but startling. Two legs stood in the doorway between the living room and the kitchen. They looked like the bottom half of a manikin with trousers and shoes on. The waist looked straight as if the thing was artificial – plastic perhaps. The toes of the shoes were pointing towards the kitchen, so Harry was seeing the legs from behind. There was no movement of this apparition, so Harry wondered if someone had put the legs of a shop window dummy in the doorway as some sort of prank. Then the legs moved, and they turned around, and Harry felt his stomach go into freefall with sheer fright. Those legs walked with a natural gait towards him, and he was so scared he threw down the newspaper, turned to run to the door, and in a heartbeat he was out on the street. A few people walking up Drake Road looked at him as if he was deranged as they passed by. Harry was behind a parked car as he kept watch on the open door of his house. He went to his neighbour Geoff and told him what he had seen and Geoff went into the house to see absolutely no one and nothing knocking about. He called in Harry to show him that there was no one there, but Harry remained on edge and refused to go back in the house on his own. He walked all the way to Warbreck Moor to his mother-in-law's house to tell Eileen what he had seen, and she told him: 'You've seen the thing I saw last week, but when I told you about it you didn't even listen.'

'What is it? Why's it in our house?' Harry seemed really shaken by the experience, and Eileen had never seen him like this before in all their years of marriage.

A month went by, and the strange 'half-ghost' seemed to have gone into retirement, but one windy night at around 11pm, just after Eileen had gone to bed, Harry was watching a film called *Journey into Fear* on the Granada channel, when he suddenly heard faint footsteps in the hallway. He thought Eileen had come back down from the bedroom, and when the door to the living room opened, he saw the legs in the wide trousers walk in. In the brief moment before Harry leaped clean over the sofa to get away from the ghost, he saw the waist clearly – and it seemed to be all glistening with blood. The legs walked across the living room to the kitchen but never entered the kitchen – they stopped at the doorway.

Harry bounded up the stairs and barged into the bedroom, waking Eileen. He closed the door and switched on the light and for a while he seemed out of breath and unable to tell his wife what had happened, but she knew what Harry had seen, and calmed him down.

'It's alright love, it's alright,' she said, holding his hand as he looked at the door. 'Was it the ghost?'

'Yeah, walked right past me, and I saw its waist, all full of blood, as if its body had been cut in half,' gasped Harry.

'It's alright Harry, we'll move,' Eileen told him, and she saw the look of terror in his eyes as he continued to look at the door. 'We can't put up with this, the council will rehouse us, love.'

'We've lived here for seven years,' Harry said, and he took a deep breath. 'Why has this thing started haunting us now?'

'I don't know love – ' Eileen was saying, when she was interrupted by a loud thud downstairs; it sounded like a door closing. Then she and Harry heard the sounds of footsteps coming up the stairs.

'It's coming up,' Harry gasped, and he ran to the double bed and threw the mattress and blankets from it. He then pulled the mattress to the door and lifted it so that it was pressed lengthwise along the door. The couple heard the footsteps stop outside the door. The thing never tried to enter the room, and about five minutes later, Harry and Eileen heard the footsteps going back down the stairs. They both remained in that bedroom until nearly six in the morning. Understandably, the couple decided they simply couldn't live under the same roof as this strange ghost, and they moved in with Eileen's mum in Warbreck Moor until they could get a council house elsewhere. I mentioned this ghost on a radio programme about the paranormal, and a woman who had lived at the very same haunted house on Drake Road telephoned the radio station and told how she and various members of her family had seen the ghostly legs on several occasions in the 1980s. They too had seen it loitering in the kitchen doorway. In the end the woman, who was a single parent, decided to move. A man named George also got in touch with me to say that he had lived at the house - and he correctly gave me the house number of the haunted dwelling. George said he had come home with his wife one evening, just a few nights after moving into the house, and they both witnessed the solid-looking legs of the ghost kick a can of paint across the living room. The can opened when it was kicked and the paint went all over the carpet and walls. The place was being decorated at the time because the couple had just moved in, and they had a feeling that the ghost resented the changes they were making to the dreary old decor. George told an old neighbour about the weird apparition, and this neighbour claimed that the ghost was that of a man who had worked on the docks until he lost his life in a very gruesome accident. Apparently, some cable on a quayside winch snapped and cut the man in half.

Today, the house that was the scene of these bizarre hauntings is occupied by a family, and I do not know if the ghost still makes an appearance.

LYDIA

In late January 1974, a 22-year-old Knotty Ash man named Louis Watt took a train down to London to attend his sister Rose's engagement party, and about twenty minutes before he arrived at Euston, he noticed a girl of about eighteen sitting at the window seat in the carriage. She had a head of rather thick, short hair that was a dark shade of red – a sort of carmine colour, and even from three seats back, Louis could see that the girl had pale blue eyes. Redheads with blue eyes are a genetic rarity, as red hair and blue eyes are both caused by recessive traits, and only 1% of the world's population are blue-eyed gingers. Louis didn't know that; to him, the girl simply looked very pretty. He kept looking over at her and she caught him looking a few times and coyly smiled before looking away, and at every stop along the route he wondered if she'd be disembarking, but she was still there when the train pulled into Euston. In the crush of passengers getting off the train, Louis lost sight of the girl. He hailed a hackney at the train station's taxi rank, and told the cabby to take him to Lancaster Gate, just north of Hyde Park, about three miles away. Louis had a few simple presents for his sister Rose and her fiancé Larry. An atomizer of Madame Rochas perfume, a deluxe box of Milk Tray chocolates and some expensive orchid for Rose, and for Larry he'd bought a dress box of Bolivar Bonitas cigars and a ludicrously large bottle of Long John Scotch whisky. All of this had taken a lion's bite out of the savings but Louis had always been close to his sister and was so glad she'd found someone as loving and loyal as Larry. Larry's apartment was very spacious, and the engagement party started at 7pm. Louis felt a little out of his depth among the guests. They all seemed to be bankers, university lecturers, graphic designers, antiques dealers and hoteliers. There was one young lady of about 25 named Tanya who worked in advertising, and she was very sociable. Louis had just started work in a butcher's shop in Liverpool city centre, and when he mentioned this, Tanya took hold of his free hand (the other was holding a Martini) and inspecting the fingers close she quipped: 'Ah, you haven't lost any fingers to the cleaver yet?'

Louis didn't think the remark was at all funny or witty but gave a phoney laugh – and then he looked at the far end of the room – about 25 feet away, and through the pale blue murk of tobacco smoke, he saw a familiar red bob of hair and his immediate thoughts were, *No, surely she can't be here?*

'Everything alright, Louis?' Tanya noticed the trainee butcher's distraction and followed the line of his sight across all of the heads of the room.

'Yes, sorry; just thought I recognised someone,' said Louis, turning to the brown eyes of Tanya.

'Oh, ' Tanya blinked and smiled, 'if you'd like to go and say hello to them, don't let me stop you.'

'I won't be a sec,' Louis walked away and threaded

his way to the redhead through about thirty people. When he got there he saw a tall black smartly-dressed man with an impressive Afro hairstyle, spouting what sounded like a poem to a thin blonde woman who had her hands clasped together as if she was praying. They were both about thirty. Standing to the left of the black man was that very same girl Louis had seen on the train, and she was taking alternate glances between the faces of the couple standing next to her as she smiled and gave little chuckles. She noticed Louis, raised her thin arched eyebrows, gave a tight-lipped smile, then looked back towards the couple. She wore a black polo neck sweater, a short navy blue skirt, black stockings and a pair of maroon Mary Janes.

Louis addressed the girl awkwardly; his throat seemed to have dried up. 'Sorry to bother you, but I think I remember you being on the train today.'

The girl put her hand to her ear, then beckoned Louis with her other hand, saying, 'Come over here, I can't hear you.'

Louis went to a quiet corner with the girl and she asked: 'Did you say you saw me on the train?' As Louis was about to answer the girl added: 'I'm Lydia by the way.' She had no accent but was quite well-spoken.

'I'm Louis. Yes, I thought it was a coincidence you being here.'

'I know the hosts,' Lydia's large blue eyes scanned the room as she spoke. 'I mean I don't know them well, but they asked me to come here.'

Despite the acrid aroma of tobacco hanging in the air, Louis detected the violet-like perfume Lydia was wearing. 'Oh really?' he replied. 'Do you know Rose? She's my sister. She's the one getting engaged – to

Larry.'

'Yes,' said Lydia, so what do you do with yourself?'

'I'm training to be a butcher!' Louis chuckled, attempting self deprecation. 'Can I get you a drink?'

'No, I've had enough already,' Lydia replied, looking at the Martini in his hand.

'Louis?' someone tapped Louis on the shoulder, and he turned so fast he spilt some of the Martini. It was Tanya, one eyebrow raised with a quizzical expression. 'You okay?'

'Yes, I was just talking to, er,' Louis turned back to Lydia, wondering if Tanya already knew her.

Lydia was nowhere to be seen. Louis scanned the room, and his eyes could not pick out even one person who was remotely like Lydia. 'Where's she gone?'

'A girl just went to the toilet,' Tanya nodded to the closing door on the other side of the room.

'Did she have short hair — sort of dark red?' Louis asked with a small smile of relief.

'I think she had short hair — don't know what colour it is,' Tanya said, and shrugged and pulled down the corners of her mouth in a couldn't-care-less type of frown. 'Is she your girlfriend?'

Louis shook his head of long hair and replied: 'No, I don't even know her. Her name's Lydia; only just found that out. She was on the train earlier and I just thought it was a coincidence, her being here.'

'Do you fancy her?' Tanya asked, and she smiled, but the honest language of her eyes hinted that she was a little injured by his interest in this readhead.

'Oh no, no, it's nothing like that,' claimed Louis, 'just as I said; I thought it was a bit of a fluke: her being here at the same party.'

Well, Louis and Tanya stood there, sipping drinks and talking and all the time he kept looking at the door, and when the girl with short hair came in he saw that it was certainly not Lydia. 'Is that the girl you saw going to the toilet?' he asked Tanya.

'Yeah. She isn't a redhead,' Tanya observed.

'I know, that isn't Lydia,' Louis seemed a bit mystified now. Tanya jokingly told him he'd imagined the girl and she tried to get him off the subject of the mysterious redhead, but the matter niggled him and he ended up asking the black man and the blonde woman who were still chatting near the corner, if they knew who Lydia was, as she had been laughing at the poem being spouted. The couple looked at one another baffled; neither of them had any recollection of a young redhead standing with them.

'Told you – you've imagined her,' Tanya said to Louis, and he left the room with Tanya in tow and looked around, just in case Lydia had gone into the kitchen or one of the bedrooms. Lydia was nowhere to be seen.

'Don't go in that toilet, Louis,' Tanya warned the young Liverpudlian as he placed his hand on the handle of the toilet door. 'This is becoming an obsession. Lydia probably just gatecrashed, and then once she realised that you knew the people hosting this party, she probably left.'

'No, I'm bursting,' said Louis, 'I'm not looking for her now, I admit defeat!'

'Yeah yeah,' Tanya took his drink from him as he went into the toilet.

There was no one in there. Louis waited for a bit, looked at himself in the mirror over the wash basin, and thought about his sanity. He left the toilet and saw Tanya talking to a man with an American accent. Tanya took hold of Louis's arm and said, 'This is Mike; he saw Lydia.'

'Oh,' was all Louis could utter in surprise.

'Yes, you didn't imagine her,' Mike reassured Louis, 'I saw her too. She came in here about 7.15pm and she didn't drink or eat anything, just sort of mingled, and then I lost sight of her.'

'Can you recall what she was wearing, Mike?' Louis asked. He just wanted to be sure the lady the American was talking about was the same person he'd spoken to earlier.

Mike nodded slowly and his eyes swivelled up and to the right as he recalled what Lydia wore. 'A black turtleneck sweater – sorry, polo neck as you say over here,' and a sort of mini skirt.'

'Yes, that's her,' said Louis.

'Dark red shoes too I think,' Mike added.

Lydia was not seen again at the party, and Rose and Larry did not know anyone of the girl's description. It would appear that only Mike – and Louis – saw her at the apartment at Lancaster Gate that evening. That was not the last Louis saw of the elusive redhead though. Just under a fortnight after the engagement party, Louis left a friend's house in St Helens one morning and boarded the Number 320 double-decker bus to Liverpool city centre. Louis was working half day at the butcher's shop. As Lime Street approached, he went downstairs from the top deck and rang the bell. The bus pulled up at the stop and Louis and about a dozen other passengers got off. As Louis walked alongside the bus as it started to pull away, he happened to glance at one of the people still seated on the vehicle – and saw it was *that* girl again – Lydia. Louis definitely saw her looking at him, but then she looked away in a strange shy manner. The bus continued on its way and Louis stood there in the middle of the busy street, thinking how strange it was to see that girl yet again, and an unsettling thought crossed his mind: was she following him? If so, why – and how? He went to his workplace and was so distracted by the constant thoughts of Lydia, and how she seemed to be following him, he narrowly missed slicing off the tip of his index finger with the meat cleaver. His boss loudly reprimanded him and told him to concentrate on what he was doing 'instead of going off into a dream world!'

By 6.15pm, Louis was walking down Chedworth Road in Knotty Ash to his house. He was really hungry and looking forward to his tea: Findus crispy pancakes, chips and peas, followed by rhubarb crumble and custard. After tea he told his mum about the ubiquitous Lydia and she said he had probably just seen someone who looks like her. His mum thought most girls of that day and age looked like clones of one another in their hairstyles and fashions, but Louis knew it *had* been Lydia on that bus from St Helens and no one else, but he couldn't make any sense of the sighting. Had the long arm of coincidence reached out to him yet again?

Louis watched a bit of telly, but finding *Granada Reports* rather boring, he went upstairs to his room, stretched out on his bed and closed his eyes. He thought about the new copy of *Gramophone* magazine which featured the French composer Pierre Boulez on the cover. He yawned. The room was cold, so Louis decided he'd get up and switch on the two-bar electric fire – but as he rose to a sitting position and put his right leg on the floor, he froze, and the shock to his heart was like a puck hitting the bell after the mallet had crashed down on a high striker at the fairground.

Lydia was standing there in the dark corner just to the right of the window, her arms hanging straight at her sides. She was dressed the same as last time; the black polo neck sweater, the short navy blue skirt, black stockings and maroon-coloured Mary Janes on her feet.

'You - you're a ghost,' Louis sputtered, and in a flash he had flown from the bed and was descending the stairs at a dangerous rate of descent. He fell down the last two steps and his mother and father ran to his aid. Louis got to his feet and looked to the top of the stairs, saying 'She's up in my room!'

'What are you talking about?' the young man's father asked.

Louis looked past him at his mother. 'She's a ghost Mam! She's up in my room!'

'Who, love?' Mrs Watt asked, baffled by her excited son's statement.

Louis backed away into his father as he looked up the stairs. He could hardly get his words out to answer his mother. 'That – that girl I saw on the train! The one I was telling you about at our Rose's engagement party! She's a ghost – and she's up there in my room!'

All three of them heard footsteps upstairs, and Mr Watt looked at his wife with an expression of surprise that soon changed to one of nervous caution.

'See?' Louis pointed his index finger at the hall's

ceiling. 'You can hear her.'

'I think that might be the sounds of the neighbours next door,' his father said, but his explanation was not convincing his wife and son – and he knew himself that someone really was in the room above.

About a minute later, Mr Watt went up the stairs, followed by his wife and Louis, and upon reaching the door of his son's bedroom, which was ajar, he hesitated and listened. Silence. He went in and saw no one in the bedroom. His wife and son came in seconds later, and Louis and his mum noticed what could only be described as a citrusy smell. Mrs Watt said it was a perfume her sister had worn back in the 1960s, and then she named it: Irisia – by Creed.

The scent soon faded, and Louis was overcome with a strange melancholy as he wondered if Lydia was some ghost who had fallen for him for some reason. He wondered where she was and what type of existence she had, if she had any such thing at all. And how had she lost her life? If she had been a ghost was she only seen by Mike, the American guest at the engagement party because he was possibly psychic? Louis recalled the way she had laughed with the couple at the party, but of course, they had not even known she was there and Lydia had only pretended to laugh so that it would seem to Louis that she was a real flesh and blood person interacting with the living. The more he reflected on Lydia, the more Louis felt a sadness welling up in him. He never saw her again but every now and then he would detect that scent she had worn in the years when she had been a warm-blooded living young lady.

I've researched a lot of person-centred hauntings

such as this one over the years, and while some departed spirits may be attracted to members of the living who resemble the former partner of the dead person, some ghosts have also been known to stalk people for more sinister reasons, and you will find such a story later on in this book. I've tried to discover the identity of Lydia but as of yet I cannot find anyone with that name who died locally in Liverpool with that name in the 1960s. She might not even be from the North West, and after all, Louis did first set eyes on her in the capital on the Euston-bound train, so she might be from London or any of the counties the train was passing through. I'll keep looking for the story behind Lydia though, and if I unravel it, I'll put it in a future book.

A HAUNTED BUS STOP

It was just after midnight, so technically the weird event happened in the early hours of Christmas Day 2010 – the year a white Christmas became a reality. The temperature on Belle Vale Road was minus 4 degrees Fahrenheit and 20-year-old Jessica had on a North Face Arctic Parka but the cold was invading her leggings and chilling her feet inside a pair of Doc Martens. She arrived with chattering teeth on the thoroughfare hoping to flag down a hackney cab. Two of them went past but their yellow 'For Hire' lights were off and in the second cab, two young male passengers shouted rude words at the freezing girl through the vehicle's open windows. Feeling queasy after just a few vodka shots, Jessica had just left a party early at her friend's house on Lee Park Avenue and was desperate to get home to Garston to catch up on some much-needed sleep. She'd been suffering from chronic insomnia for the past few days and now she could feel her lids trying to close all by themselves. She could also hear a faint ringing in her ears which she always noted when she was overtired. Jessica took shelter from the glacial cold at an enclosed bus stop about 25 yards away from St Stephen's Church, and here she waited for a cab as she stamped her Doc Martens in the slushy snow in the doorway of the shelter. She put up her fur-lined hood and screwed her eyes up to the bitter knifing cold breeze as she looked up the road – and there was another hackney cab coming her way, but it did not have the much-wished-for yellow lamp on its roof, so Jessica let out a yawn, closed her eyes, and wondered if she could somehow make it back to Garston on foot without dying from hypothermia. Not one of the lads at the party had been gallant enough to escort the girl to this road to get a taxi. One of them *had* tried to call for a cab earlier, but with it being Christmas Eve, it had been a dead loss; every cab was on call already.

The passing hackney cab beeped three times, startling the girl. Her eyes flew open and her mind returned abruptly from some dreamlike state as she saw the shiny white hackney decelerate and come to a halt about fifteen feet to her left. Jessica was naturally wary about the strange behaviour of the taxi driver; why had he stopped, and why had he beeped his horn at her? There had been cases in the past where rapists had gained the trust of victims by impersonating taxi drivers, and this was at the forefront of Jessica's mind. However, the cabby turned out to be female, and she emerged from the hackney and beckoned Jessica with urgent waves of her hand. She was blonde and her hair was done up in a tight bun. She looked about ten years older than Jessica and seemed genuine.

Walking towards the cab, Jessica shouted: 'You've already got a passenger haven't you?'

'Yeah,' said the cabby, 'never mind that – get in!' And she got back into the taxi, unlocked the doors, and the passenger, who also happened to be female, threw open the kerbside door and in a quietly-spoken voice she said, 'Come on.'

'This is very nice of you,' Jessica pulled down her hood, stooped, and got in the back of the taxi, almost tripping over the passenger's wedges. Before she could say where she was going, she was thrown back onto the seat by the inertia as the cab shot off up Belle Vale Road.

'Didn't you see him?' the driver said to the rear view mirror.

'See who?' Jessica asked with a puzzled look, noting the large blue eyes of the driver.

'There was a man with a knife on the other side of that bus shelter, and he was watching you!' said the passenger, and the cabby nodded to underline this alarming statement and added: 'He was peeping at you, real weird-looking he was.'

'Shurrup!' a disbelieving Jessica said, thinking they were joking, but the driver looked in her wing mirror and said, 'Look back now; that's him!'

At this point the taxi was passing the junction of Jones Farm Road. Jessica and the other passenger turned and had to wipe the slight condensation off the rear window to see the tall silhouette standing on the pavement next to the bus shelter.

'We should report him to the police,' the passenger told Jessica and the driver, but the cabby seemed very reticent about something – almost as if she knew something about the creep with the knife, and well, Jessica was plain too tired to report anything.

'It's really nice of you to pick me up like this,' Jessica told the driver. 'You saved my life.'

The driver smiled and half turned to Jessica before looking back at the slippery iced road ahead. 'Ah, it's the least I could do. Where do you live?'

'Duncombe Road North,' replied Jessica, 'Garston.' She looked at the meter. Its glowing red display read £8.50.

'You're in luck, ' said the driver, 'I'm dropping this lady off at Bathurst Road.'

Jessica turned to the other passenger and said, 'You're just around the corner from me.' And then she insisted on paying the fare, but the passenger said she'd pay, considering what Jessica had been through tonight. Jessica was dropped off first but told the cabby to hang on, and the young lady brought her a bottle of vodka (an unwanted gift), and she also threw a five-pound note at the passenger. She then went straight to bed as her mother and grandmother asked her why she was back relatively early from the party. Jessica literally fell fast asleep as soon as her head touched the pillow and she did not awake until 8.10am. Over breakfast she told her mother and Nan about the man with the knife laying in wait at the bus stop on Belle Vale Road, and the two women looked at one another with expressions that could only be described as ones of suppressed shock. Then Jessica's Nan asked, 'Was he all in black?'

Jessica shrugged and admitted she hadn't seen him close up, only as a silhouette in the distance, viewed from the cab as it moved off. He had looked tall – that was all she could recall.

'That'll be him,' the girl's mother said in a cryptic fashion.

'He's a ghost,' said Jessica's Nan. A declaration like

that, coming from a woman who never even told white lies, unnerved Jessica somewhat.

'How do you mean, a ghost?' asked Jessica, checking text messages from her phone.

'I've seen him, your dad's seen him,' Jessica's mother said, matter-of-fact.

'I saw him years ago,' Nan said.

'Nah! He looked real to me,' Jessica tried to reassure herself she had not been in the vicinity of a ghost. They were one thing that scared her; not spiders or earwigs or mice – but spirits.

'No one knows who he is,' said Jessica's mum, 'or was, when he was alive.'

'The fellah who committed suicide,' said Nan, but then she became quiet as if she was afraid to say more.

'You don't *know* that, mother,' Jessica's mum told Nan. 'No one knows who he is.'

'There was a fellah who slashed his own throat in that area years ago,' Nan told Jessica, putting her off any possibility of yoghurt and granola. 'I think it's him, I do.'

'He chased your Auntie Pam,' Jessica's mother suddenly recalled. 'That was on New Year's Eve 1988.'

'Mum, can you kindly shut up now? You know I hate this subject,' Jessica told her, and she sipped her morning coffee, then exchanged presents. The whole eerie mood left over from last night's incident threw a shadow over the festive present ritual.

Jessica's best friend Emily called that morning and she was told about the ghost by Jessica's Nan. Emily was fascinated by the supernatural and seemed hypnotised by the story of the ghost. She pulled off a mean trick that day. Emily said she was going to drive to a friend's Christmas party at 7pm, and told Jessica she was invited too. Jessica spent over an hour trying out the Mac make-up she'd got off her mother as a gift, and she painstakingly straightened her normally curly hair. The transformation left her stunning.

Just after 6.30pm, Jessica got in the car with her friend, but Emily drove to that bus stop on Belle Vale Road and admitted with a fake chuckle that there was no party. Jessica was both angry and scared, and she begged her friend to drive away, and in a supreme act of bad taste, Emily pretended she'd seen the ghost. Jessica became hysterical, and Emily apologised and drove her home – but all the way back, there was an iciness in the car, and it was not down to the rift between the two friends because of the non-existent party. Both girls felt as if there was a freezing presence in that vehicle. Emily turned the heater up but something icy brushed against the back of her neck and also touched the right ear of Jessica several times. Over the next few days, Emily kept getting little wounds similar to 'paper cuts' on her hands and breasts. One of these sinister cuts appeared on the tip of Emily's nose as she watched TV, and then her mother said she also felt as if something like a cold blade had stroked her bottom in the kitchen. The cuts really hurt, because, like paper cuts, the incision was very shallow, exposing the skin's nerve receptors to the air, so the pain was intense. Emily also started seeing a shadowy indefinable thing out the corner of her eye. A few weeks after Christmas, the girls decided to go running in an effort to lose weight (even though both of them were not overweight), and they went on a Sunday morning run with a friend named Amelia, who lived in Netherley. Amelia jokingly ran off as they all jogged along a rather secluded stretch of Naylorsfield Drive. 'She's left us standing! The show off!' panted Emily, and she slowed and stopped. Jessica stopped and turned around – and there, running up the lonely lane, was a tall figure in pure silhouette. It didn't look real, and it was moving at a phenomenal speed. As it got nearer, the terrified girls could see it had what looked like a knife in its left hand.

The girls ran off screaming, and in a blind panic they both slipped and fell in fields where snow was undisturbed and crusty with the freezing temperatures. The fleeing females had to jump over fences and force their way through prickly bushes and hedges as the shadow entity pursued them. They both felt it was the ghost with the knife from Belle Vale Road chasing them in broad daylight. The girls headed south into Childwall, and at one point they thought they'd lost the apparition, but with horror they realised where they were when Emily had to stop because of the sharp stitch in her side: it was Belle Vale Road. There was that bus stop in the distance where the ghost had been creeping up on Jessica that night. The girls flagged down a passing police car in a hysterical condition but the two policemen in the vehicle could see no 'shadow man' chasing the panic-stricken duo. About a week after this, the paper cuts started again. Emily was on the toilet when she felt something scratch her eyelid and as she screamed she saw a shadowy outline of a tall man fly away from her into the far wall. She took to wearing an old rosary she found in a charity shop, and the paranormal persecutions stopped. Jessica had no visitations from the mysterious menacing ghost, but she and Emily still refuse to go anywhere near that bus stop on Belle Vale Road. I have researched this case for years and no one seems to know the identity of the ghost with the knife. There was a theory that the ghost might be some earthbound spirit of a man who committed suicide at a house close to the Belle Vale Road bus stop in the 1980s but that person was only 5ft 2 and quite stocky, whereas the shadow entity is always described as being at least six feet in height and slim. In 2012 an investigator of the paranormal spent a few hours at the 'haunted bus stop' in the wee small hours and managed to record some strange EVP – unexplained sounds and voices captured by sensitive electronic recorders. The words 'Wilcox' and what sounds like 'Mister Rix' can be heard with some clarity, but so far, no one has linked these apparent names with any of the ghostly goings-on.

WOMEN ONLY

One dreary grey November afternoon in 2007, two friends, Andy and Parth — both in their late twenties — were walking across Williamson Square, coming from St John's Precinct, where they'd been browsing the shops for clothes. They were headed towards Whitechapel via Richmond Street, when Andy said he'd just got déjà vu. Parth said he'd just had the same sensation after seeing a woman come out the nearby Queen's pub; he felt as if he knew the woman and that everything he was perceiving was like some TV repeat.

'You're not winding me up, are you?' Andy asked with a suspicious look.

'No, for real man,' Parth reassured him, 'I feel as if I've done all this before.'

'Mike,' Andy said, pointed to a young man coming out of Sayers, 'he'll say "Mike" I just know it.'

'Yeah! I know he's going to say that too!' Parth halted and looked at the teenager in a tracksuit holding a sausage roll in a bag as he nibbled at its end. This youth suddenly stopped eating and waved to someone over by the fountain and said, 'Mike.'

And then the sense of déjà vu abruptly ceased in the minds of Andy and Parth.

This was not the end of the strangeness, because things for the duo then became even weirder. Andy and Parth got lost on Whitechapel; buildings that should have been there were missing, and shops they had never seen before were all over the place. The Gyratory in Queen's Square was nowhere to be seen and Sir Thomas Street could not be found (it seemed to have been renamed Agnes Jones Street), yet the two disoriented men could see St John's Beacon in the distance, although the logo on it was not that of Radio City, but some unfamiliar black and purple logo and a word that neither man could make sense of.

Andy and Parth found themselves on what vaguely seemed to be Crosshall Street, and as they walked along they realised they had walked in a circle, back to Whitechapel.

'I wouldn't be surprised if someone spiked our coffee with LSD in that café earlier on,' said Andy, looking at the unfamiliar street signs.

Parth suddenly asked his friend, 'Have you noticed something else that's a tad strange?'

'What?' Andy stopped to look up at a shop called Eve's Children; a clothes store with tinted red, white and blue plate glass that he had never set eyes on before, even though he was a regular visitor to downtown Liverpool.

Parth told him about his alarming observation as he pushed his friend along. 'Andy, every person on this street is female,' he muttered through his thick beard. Andy looked about and saw that his friend was right; females of all ages were everywhere – and some of the nearer women had stopped and they were looking at him and Parth. Some of them wore expressions of awe and some were smiling condescendingly. There wasn't a single male in sight. A bus came down a road that resembled Dale Street, and everyone on board – the driver included – seemed to be a female. A car slowed down and the blonde lady driving it leaned over to the kerbside window and looked at the two men as if they were from Mars. She let out a profanity, apparently more out of shock than a wish to offend as she looked at Andy and Parth. Straight after this, a little girl passing by her with her mother pointed at Parth and exclaimed 'Mummy! Look! What's that?'

'This is mad,' said Andy, feeling very paranoid, and he and Parth did a 180-degree turn and walked back up the street and onto the broad thoroughfare which *seemed* to be Dale Street, but Andy noticed that he could not see the Liver Buildings at the end of the street of milling females. Then Parth noticed that the Liverpool City Council's Municipal Buildings now bore a gleaming brass plaque that read: Kitty Wilkinson House. Andy's mind could not get to grips with the strange altered environment and he wondered if some film company had temporarily put the plaque up and changed the street signs while some movie was being shot. Film companies had done things like that when they wanted to turn parts of the town into London, New York and even Moscow – yet Andy knew deep down that this was not the case, and he could feel panic welling in the pit of his stomach.

An old woman grabbed Andy by the arm and asked him: 'Are you in drag?' which faintly amused Parth, even in the unsettling midst of all of the unrealness. The woman was evidently under the impression that Andy was a lady dressed as a man.

'No, I'm not!' Andy barked at the old lady and pulled his arm from her grasp and muttered, 'What *is* going on here?'

A tall female police officer approached from the other side of the road, and after looking Andy and Parth up and down, she told them: 'Stay where you are,' before talking into a small two-way radio. Andy and Parth simultaneously panicked and ran off down a thoroughfare named Bessie Braddock Street with the constable hot on their heels.

'Halt! Stop!' the female officer of the law yelled as she belted after them. Parth thought she was carrying a gun and had drawn the weapon but Andy didn't see any firearm.

The confused duo found themselves on a familiar Stanley Street, and to their utter relief they saw a male beggar sitting in a doorway. The policewoman had vanished and the Liverpool Andy and Parth were accustomed to had returned, but for about ten minutes the two young men experienced light-headedness and feelings of being 'unreal' – and then the normal states of consciousness returned.

Andy and Parth assured me they had not made this story up and had not hallucinated the strange events of that November day in 2007. Neither of them had ever seen a ghost or had any paranormal experiences before. They were naturally baffled by their experience and cannot explain just what happened – so they got in contact with me to see if I could possibly throw some light on the incident.

Most quantum physicists know that alternate worlds are a reality, and perhaps Andy and Parth had passed through such a world – a world where events have taken a different turn than the ones in this strand of reality - but how would a female-only society come about? Well, it's a scientific fact that the human Y chromosome is shrinking and may one day die out, which would mean the end of males, perhaps leaving women to produce female-only offspring through some biological process akin to drug-aided parthenogenesis. Mankind could also one day succumb to a deadly virus which plugs itself into the DNA sequence which governs male gender. A chilling scenario indeed.The names of the streets and buildings in the alternative reality Andy and Parth walked into were all of prominent women of local history - Kitty Wilkinson, Agnes Jones, Bessie Braddock etc.

The idea of a world run by the female may seem a far-fetched fantasy to some, but there is mounting archaeological evidence which seems to indicate that there was a great matriarchal society in the distant past that has been largely overlooked. It would seem that the peoples of that vague remote period popularly termed the Stone Age were not savage dumb brutes at all, but a peace-loving race not all that unlike the hippies of the Flower Power movement of the 1960s, and, what's more, this ancient society worshipped a deity which has come down to us via the occultists as the Great Mother – identical to Gaia, the Greek primordial goddess who symbolizes the female personification of the Earth. The Victorian anthropologist Johann Jakob Bachofen was one of the first intellectuals to stick his neck out and advance the theory of a golden prehistoric age when women ruled the planet, but as a result of his beliefs he was vehemently attacked by the male-dominated establishment of his day. All the same, Bachofen went to his grave in 1887, convinced that motherhood was the origin of all early human societies. They say that all history is a perpetually turning wheel, and what has gone before will come again, so perhaps one day, women will once again run the world. I have a sneaking feeling that they'll be a lot more successful than warmongering, planet-destroying men...

THE GHOSTLY MIME ARTIST

The following strange story took place in the December of 1970, and it's one of those rare cases where a ghost was not only seen by more than one person when it appeared (and disappeared) – it also appeared on one of Liverpool's busiest shopping thoroughfares.

Saturday night was drifting into Sunday morning as he lay awake thinking of his next victim. The dead light of a cold uncaring December moon shone through the grimy windows into his bedroom as John Saxifred pictured James Perlander, the chief clerk at a well-known bank – victim number ten. Saxifred, a deliveryman for a big retail store in the city centre, always drank at Rigby's after work, and in recent weeks he'd ingratiated himself with Perlander, who had started to call into the pub for a few drinks before going home to his mother. Whiskey had loosened the tongue of the thirty-something bank employee, and Saxifred had learned that bachelor Perlander had saved thousands, had started dating the daughter of a bank manager in Birkenhead, and loved the occasional game of poker. It was the week before Christmas, and the plan Saxifred had hatched was simplicity itself; he would get James Perlander drunk with copious amounts of Bells – nothing suspicious about that in the festive season – and then he would talk him into visiting a few friends at a flat over a shop on Hanover Street for a game of poker. But instead, the chief bank clerk would meet Saxifred's girlfriend Linda and she'd lower his resistance with more drink and exercise her talent for enticement when Saxifred was out of the room. Then Saxifred would take a few incriminating photographs of the momentary hank-panky and threaten to show them to Perlander's fiancée unless a few thousand nicker changed hands. Linda lay next to the blackmailer in bed, lost in the unconscious oblivion from a five-hour drinking binge that had started at 7pm in the pubs of Ranelagh Street.

The last blackmail victim of Saxifred, a theatre actor named Peter, had had his life ruined by John Saxifred because he was unable to pay up, and although the threats made by the blackmailer were not carried out, the actor hanged himself because he feared he would be exposed. Peter had been hiding his homosexuality from his family, friends and fiancée of two months, but John Saxifred had overheard him whispering sweet nothings into the ears of a man in the Lisbon pub – and had quickly moved in for the kill. Peter, the only son of a wealthy factory-owner, had already been plagued with depression because his agent had told him to give up the acting profession because he simply lacked talent. Peter had even resorted to street mime to collect money for a living rather than live in his rich father's pocket. It was a big shock to Saxifred when he called at his victim's bedsit and found him hanging from a banister in the communal hallway. 'You can't win them all,' he had said upon seeing the suspended legs slowly turning in that darkened hall. But back to the present.

On a snowy early evening, a few days before Christmas, Saxifred found himself guiding a swaying, intoxicated Mr Perlander up ice-glazed Church Street, bound for the make-believe poker game. 'I hope you're not setting me up, John,' Perlander said, and hiccupped.

For a moment, Saxifred thought the bank clerk had sussed him out. 'How do you mean?'

'These friends of yours aren't card sharps are they?' the naive Perlander asked, and slid sideways. His palm struck the plate glass front of a store with a thud. He leaned against the glass as a female member of staff within the store shot him a look of disgust.

'Careful!' Saxifred gently pulled him from the window and answered his question. 'No, they are pretty terrible players actually, James, and I think we might be able to make a killing tonight.'

'Jolly good,' Perlander smiled and confessed: 'I must say, I do prefer a good old manly game of poker rather than Rubber Bridge with *her* father.'

'Ah, well, I agree that poker – ' Saxifred was telling his victim when a weird clown-like man suddenly hopped out from the doorway of the Dolcis shoe store. He wore a beret and one half of his face was heavily painted in white and the other half was purple, and one of his heavily-drawn eyebrows was an arched snake. His eyes had a look of madness about them and he wore a broad inane grin. He had on a dark magenta three-piece suit, royal blue tie, white gloves (just like the ones magicians wear) and cherry red shoes. The street performer stood in the way of the blackmailer and his victim, then started walking backwards, refusing to get out of the way. He wiggled the ten fingers of his gloved hands and then, with his pointed finger he counted each of his fingers, then pointed to a perplexed and bemused Perlander, as if to associate him with the number ten – was he referring to victim ten? A confused Saxifred wondered about this.

The mime artist gripped his own tie and his tongue protruded as he lifted that tie. He was mimicking someone *who had been hanged*. This instantly reminded Saxifred about the last blackmail victim's fate. The bank clerk laughed, hiccupped, and asked, 'What's he trying to say?' And Saxifred swore at the mime artist and told him to beat it, but then the street mummer suddenly spoke.

'Remember me?' he said, and he swiftly undid his tie, unbuttoned his collar, and pointed with his gloved index finger to the appalling reddish scar around his neck. 'Rope burn, when I hanged myself!' the mimic said.

Saxifred suddenly saw through the thick make-up; it was *him* - Peter the actor - the last victim – but how? The mime artist was no longer grinning, and in a low gruff voice seething with anger he told the bank clerk that Saxifred was going to try and blackmail him, and the deliveryman reacted by taking a swing at the painted face – but his fist went straight through it, and an off-balance Saxifred slipped on the iced pavement. He crashed to the floor, breaking a front tooth in half upon impact. Perlander was so spooked by the weird-looking ghost he turned and ran. John Saxifred hauled himself up off the floor and shouted for the bank clerk to come back. Perlander fell twice on the treacherous ice of Church Street but got up each time and continued to run without even looking back. John Saxifred's tongue dared to feel the broken tooth and its tip probingly touched the exposed nerve. People gathered around the blackmailer and two Samaritans tried to help him up but he slapped their hands away and got to his feet. He pushed the stunned helpers out the way and looked for the mime artist – but he was nowhere to be seen.

Saxifred went to his flat on Hanover Street, where Linda was walking around in a negligee, waiting for Perlander. When she saw the blood on her boyfriend's bottom lip she realised something hadn't gone to plan, and he told her about the mime artist, and how he had warned the bank clerk.

'But how, Johnny?' Linda was baffled at her boyfriend's brief account of the creepy altercation. 'How would some mime artist know what we were up to?'

'I'm going to have to go to hospital, Linda,' said Saxifred, his eyes watering with the pain of the broken incisor. 'I'm in agony!'

'Do you think he might have gone to the police?' Linda asked, full of concern for herself. 'I mean, the mime artist. Maybe Perlander will contact them as well.'

Saxifred exploded. 'For God's sake will you put a sock in it – hey? I'm in agony here and you're worrying about getting nicked!'

Linda took off the negligee and put on a thick woollen jumper. 'I'm not getting involved with any more of your schemes John Saxifred! I'm going back to my mother!' she yelled. She put on a miniskirt and platforms then went to the small round teak-famed mirror on the wall to check her make-up before she left – and she screamed. Linda was so afraid at what was staring at her in that mirror, she backed up and fell over the end of the sofa. She got to her feet, screamed again and ran out of the room. John Saxifred looked at the mirror and saw the face of Peter in his mime artist make up, and he was smiling, and the grin looked twisted. The face of the ghost was lit up by a pale blue radiance.

More out of anger than fear, Saxifred stooped down and picked up a heavy brown glass ashtray with the word 'Martini' emblazoned upon it, and he hurled it hard it at the face. The mirror smashed into glittering shards and splinters and then the frame fell from the wall. He ran out of the flat and went downstairs into the street, where he saw Linda close the door behind her as she got into a hackney cab. Saxifred ran after the taxi as it pulled away and waved furiously but it didn't stop. John eventually flagged down a cab which took him to the Royal Infirmary on Pembroke Place, and after a long wait, an emergency dentist decided to pull the broken tooth. Gas was used for this, and while the blackmailer was under the anaesthetic he had vivid and surreal nightmares of being chased by the mime artist Peter. The actor's face and body would morph into strange shapes as if John was viewing him through the warped looking-glasses in some hall of mirrors, and all the time he could hear the waltz of some fairground music. Just before John Saxifred regained consciousness, Peter's painted face had come close up to his and the actor had told him: 'Tonight, the curtain is coming down on your life, and then you're off to Hell!'

John attacked the dentist, and had to be restrained by two young trainee doctors who finally convinced him that he had merely had an abreaction to the general anaesthetic gas. 'He said I'm going to die, tonight! He said I'm going to Hell!' Saxifred told the two medical rookies, and one of the young men assured him it had all been down to hallucinations from the halothane gas.

Saxifred shook his head. He felt nauseous. He told the doctors: 'No, he was real, you see I drove him to -'

'Drove him to what?' the dentist asked.

'Nothing,' said the patient, 'it was — as you say — all some nightmare dream from the gas.'

John Saxifred went home, and that night he put the lights on in every room and he kept the television set on for company and tried his best to take his mind off the spinechilling events of the evening. He watched the Spinners performing at the Philharmonic Hall on BBC1, and then, when BBC1 closed down at midnight, John switched over to Granada, but found that channel had also closed for the night a bit earlier than usual. BBC2 had gone off the air, and so he switched on the radio and listened to *Night Ride* - a BBC Radio One music programme that started at midnight and ended at two in the morning. When that show ended, John Saxifred was so convinced the ghost Peter was going to turn up to somehow kill him, he went out and went to the first prostitute he saw and paid her to sit with him for a few hours. This prostitute listened to the rambling story of the ghostly actor and how it had appeared in John's nightmare as he was under the dentist's gas, and then something terrifying took place. Saxifred was sitting on the sofa when his hands flew up to his throat, and his face went red as he made terrible choking sounds. He was then lifted into the air by something the lady of the night could not see, and the lights went out. A strange amber light then lit up the room, and this illumination from nowhere flickered on the walls as if it was being cast by flames. Saxifred hung in mid air, his kicking feet about twelve inches above the floor. The prostitute ran out of the flat and she heard weird hysterical laughter behind her – even though she knew no one else was in the room she had vacated – only the choking, suspended Mr Saxifred. Later that morning, the ruthless blackmailer was found dead from heart failure in his flat with a look of terror on his twisted face. The coroner noted that purple marks on the dead man's neck, and opined that they had been caused by blood vessels bursting during the coronary.

For many years, I have received letters and emails about the ghostly mime artist who is often seen on Church Street. He always seems to appear around December, and he was even seen peering into the windows of a well-known electrical goods store which stands close to the site of the old Dolcis shoe store, where the mime artist from beyond first jumped out on the merciless blackmailer John Saxifred on that wintry evening in 1970.

THE STRANGE TAIL
OF CAT MORRISON

The following story happened just a few years ago, and I've had to change a few little details because I promised some of the people mentioned in this narrative that I'd protect their identity – but the rest, however inexplicable, allegedly happened.

One autumn day on the campus of one of the Liverpool universities, a 25-year-old man named Ed, who was studying Psychology and Humanities and the Arts, entered the canteen at lunchtime and told his close friend and confidant Anton, who was queuing at the counter: 'I have just found the kugelblitz. She is – '

'You found what?' Anton didn't hear him right.

'Kugelblitz,' Ed replied with a dreamy smile, 'the hottest thing in the universe. You see, a kugelblitz is so hot it's even hotter than the Big Bang that - '

'Alright, don't go into all that bumph, just get the message out,' Anton interposed tetchily. 'Hate the way you go all round the houses.'

In a voice that seemed to go down continually with every slowly uttered word like a Shepard tone, Ed told him: 'I have seen a girl and I think she is the real thing and I don't even know why I'm even telling you because you always put the mockers on. End of message.'

'Why do they always have one person working at the counter at lunchtime?' Anton watched the solitary lady – Debbie (a friend of his mother) - serving the students five people away. 'So you've met *the one*?' he suddenly turned and looked at Ed as if he had a tarantula on his face.

'Yes, ' Ed replied with slow nods, 'you've probably seen her. Her name's Cat Morrison.'

'You actually blushed when you said her name,' Anton's thick eyebrows lifted, and he fumbled in his pocket, 'where's my phone? I have to capture this.'

'No, don't, stop it,' Ed cupped his hand around his eyes and nose. 'I can't have a serious conversation with you nowadays – something has dumbed you down – probably all the crap on the telly.'

Anton left the phone in his pocket. 'I don't watch the TV anymore, I only watch YouTube and Netflix, and that's when I'm not putting in long hours studying.'

'Anyway, forget it,' Ed told him and the queue moved down one.

There was a pause as both young men looked in different directions.

Anton yawned, then turned back to his sulky friend. 'Okay, tell me about this Kath wazzername – '

'Cat – Cat Morrison,' Ed corrected him immediately. ' Well what attracted me to her at first was her eyes – they're like agate, a sort of orangey gold brown – very unusual.'

Anton rolled his eyes. 'Oh come off it, Ed, no one is attracted to eyes, only tiny mayflies – you always go for legs; I've seen your search history.'

'Anyway, her eyes are incredible, and also, she sort of hardly speaks; she whispers in this really funny voice, it's *cute*.'

Anton looked behind in case someone was eavesdropping, and then he told Ed never to use that four-lettered word again.

'Anton, she looked at me and I looked at her, and we just locked on to one another like a tractor beam. It's amazing – something just pulled the two of us together.'

'Yeah, mutual insanity,' lamented Anton. 'Just shut up please, Ed, I don't want to lose this appetite.'

By the time the two men had reached the counter an argument was brewing between them.

'Look, I am not in the least interested in this Cat, or whatever her name is,' Anton's face was screwed up as he spoke, as if he was about to burst into tears, 'all I am interested in is food and drink at the moment. You've been acting weird for some time now, Ed – '

Someone butted Anton in the back, and he twisted a half circle reflexively to see who was pushing in the queue with such brute force.

It was an unusual girl of about five feet three in height with a globular bob of black hair with purplish-red highlights, and a pair of beautiful but angry-looking *orangey-brown eyes speckled with gold*. And when he saw these eyes, Anton knew it was the Morrison girl Ed had been droning on about. He recalled the saccharin description by the lovelorn lad.

'Hey!' Anton bawled, 'What was that for? Butting people!'

Cat Morrison said nothing. She lifted her hand,

closed her minute fingers tipped with dark blue nails into a small fist, and licked the knuckles. She then angled her head and rubbed her eyes and eyebrows with this fist.

'Hiya,' Ed almost gasped to the girl, and she leaned forward and began to rub her head on his upper arm, which surprised him, and caused his face to go up a shade to a sort of ham pink, and paradoxically the aberrant head-massage gave him a shudder of sensual pleasure from regions of his body he had never heard from before.

The look on Anton's face was one of shock mingled with slight bemusement. He watched this bizarre girl turn her head through some double-jointed angles as she rubbed her shiny hair and her cheeks on the part of Ed's bare left forearm protruding from his tee-shirt.

Ed, who was now an incandescent pink in the face, self-consciously looked at Anton and said, 'Well, I have this way with the babes you see,' and he reached out with right hand and stroked her hair – and she suddenly snapped at his hand with her mouth.

'Hey!' Anton shouted at her, 'Are you on drugs or something?'

Cat Morrison smiled and resumed rubbing her head on Ed's arm. People started to notice this. People queuing behind noticed and narrowed their eyes as they forced faint scornful smiles, and people in front started to rubber neck and take quick glances back at the strange behaviour of Ms Morrison.

Anton kept shaking his head and silently mouthing to his friend: 'Tell her to get lost.'

Each time, Ed shook his head at his friend's repetitive suggestion and whispered back permutations of, 'It's okay, I'm cool with it.' His Thulian-pink face was glossy with perspiration by now.

When the two young men reached the counter, Anton asked Debbie for the last two slices of chicken parmesan pizza and salad, and he also took a blueberry fancy cupcake from a basket and placed it on the corner of the glass-topped counter. Cat Morrison reached out and started pushing the cupcake by centimetres towards the edge.

'Er, don't do that,' Ed told her meekly, and she took no notice.

Anton was fishing the change out of his wallet to tip Debbie (even though she always told him not to) when he saw the oddball girl trying to knock his cupcake off the counter and he snatched it just before Morrison could push it off. 'You have *serious* behavioural problems,' Anton told her, and she hit his hand as he went to give the tip money to the lady behind the counter. Two fifty pence pieces and a twenty pence coin flew into the air. Debbie let out a howl of surprise and shielded her face from the flying currency.

'Cat! What are you doing?' Ed asked her, gravely anticipating the reaction from Anton and Debbie.

'Hey! You fruit loop!' Anton yelled at her, 'Just stay away from me, okay?'

'What did you do that for?' Debbie asked Cat with bulging blue eyes, and she bent down to pick up the coins.

Ed suddenly decided he'd have to get Cat – and himself - away from the canteen as soon as possible, and he quickly asked her what she was having but she just giggled and then she whispered something incomprehensible with her fists to her mouth as she peered through the glass at the pies, pasties and sandwiches, so Ed only ordered a yoghurt pistachio smoothie, and as he was paying for it with his uni ID card, Cat once again started nudging at the tall plastic smoothie container – and this time she managed to knock it off the counter – but the reflexes of Ed were so honed by the state of his stressed-out nervous system, he caught the smoothie as it fell. He asked Cat what she was having and she giggled and again murmured something unintelligible which only served to irritate Debbie behind the counter, who bluntly told her: 'Come on, make your mind up – there are people waiting to be served behind you! Acting childish at your age, for God's sake!'

Ed and Cat moved away from the counter, away from the sniggering and sneers and dagger-looks of the queue, and they approached the table where Anton was seated, but he presented his palm to them and shook his head. 'No, find another table – please – find some other place – not here.'

'We're supposed to be friends,' Ed told him, as Cat started to scratch at the little 10p-sized tattoo of the yin and yang symbol on Ed's elbow – almost as if she thought she could remove it.

'Our friendship is – what's the word?' A bitter-looking Anton asked with so much rage in his voice. 'Kaputski! Yes that's the word – kaputski.' And so Cat and Ed sat in a corner of the canteen overlooking a well-kept garden, and a little robin flew onto an evergreen shrub close to the window – and Cat climbed slowly onto the table, apparently fixated with the twitchy robin redbreast. Ed gave a sham chuckle as his eyes scanned all of the curious faces in the canteen watching the girl's barmy behaviour. 'Lovely isn't he?' Ed asked Cat and looked at the robin. 'Means winter's not far now.'

The girl did not respond, and instead she began to twerk and swing her backside in her jeans left and right – and then after a short period of rhythmic derriere swaying, she jumped from a position in which she was on all fours on the tabletop – and the palms of her two hands slapped the plate glass with some force. The robin was as astonished as everyone else, and flew off in fright.

Ed looked over at Anton, who had his mouth wide open in pure astonishment with the point of the pizza slice almost in it, but he didn't eat it. He put it back on the plate and without taking his eyes off Cat, he closed his mouth and looked speechless. The English language had failed him; the crazy antics of that Morrison girl were beyond a coherent phraseological response.

'Aye aye! Stop this larking about you stupid git, or you're out!' shouted Debbie, meaning business because she had walked from behind the aluminium counter. Cat ignored the warning and lay across the seats so her forehead was on Ed's lap. She somehow turned that head and he experienced palpitations as she rubbed the back of her head on his loins. 'Don't do that in here!' Ed tried to lift Cat Morrison's head and she leapt off him about four feet into the air, then sort of twisted – still in mid-air – before sprinting out of the canteen at a phenomenal speed. Ed got to his feet and walked in a daze after her, but Anton shouted something from his table, and then he came over to Ed and said: 'Don't go after her, she's got a screw loose.'

'I love her though, loose screw and all,' Ed told his friend, and looked utterly lost.

'Ed, snap out of it; you'd think you'd been married to her for years,' Anton reached for Ed's lower arm and gently pulled him in the direction of his table. 'Come on, calm down; she'll be back.'

'Did I say something wrong?' Ed asked himself, and tried to recall his words before Cat had fled from him in such a melodramatic fashion.

'Come on, sit here mate,' Anton guided him to the table and Ed sat down. 'And no, Ed, you didn't say anything wrong; she just took off – maybe she remembered she'd left the oven on or something. Wait there while I get your smoothie.' Anton went to the corner table where his friend had been sitting with cranky Cat and grabbed his smoothie. He took it over to Ed and asked him where he had first seen this Cat.

'She was on campus with some girl,' Ed recalled, gazing morosely at the tabletop, 'some girl she always hangs with, and then when I was in town, in John Lewis, I saw them there, and I dunno, I just felt like – well – I know you'll laugh – but it was like love at first sight.'

'Uh huh,' Anton responded with a cold look of disappointment in his eyes as if he thought Ed should know better. 'And when was this?'

'About, let me see,' Ed made an irritating clicking sound with his tongue. 'About a week ago I'd say.'

'A full week, eh?' Anton took a bite of pizza and then he asked: 'And you've fallen for her? And you'd never talked to her before today?'

Ed shook his head. 'No, just sort of communicated with certain looks. She knew – '

'Ed, how do you know her name?'

'I asked around and that caretaker guy Martin told me her name, and he said she acted eccentric but I didn't care. I should have gone after her now. What did I say or do?'

'Ed, unfortunately she will be back, believe me, but do you really want to get involved with someone who acts bizarre like that?'

'I wanted to tell her that I loved her earlier before she ran off, and I have never told anyone that before, not even my Nan.' Ed seemed near to tears and began rapid blinking and sniffling.

'No one says *those three words* any more Ed, it isn't cool and girls will think you're really screwy if you do.'

'I'm not ashamed to be in love – ' Ed was saying when he noticed that Anton seemed distracted. He had a puzzled look on his face.

'What *is* that?' Anton asked, and after looking under the table he recoiled as if he'd seen a snake down there.

'You okay Anton?' Ed asked, wondering what had spooked him.

'It's *her!*' Anton cried, standing up and looking at Cat, who was crouched under the table. She'd been touching Anton's knee ever so lightly, and now she was smirking with her hands covering her mouth as she knelt there. As Anton ripped the air with a barrage of swear words aimed at Cat Morrison, she came out from under the table and ran at an incredible speed out of the canteen. This time Ed ran after her.

Ed never showed for a major lecture that afternoon, and only Anton noticed his absence. Ed reappeared the following morning at 7.30 at the Halls of residence near Aigburth where Anton had accommodation. Anton had received a text message from his absent friend around 6am which had simply read: 'r u up?' and he had thrown the phone to the bottom of his bed and drifted back into the realms of sumptuous sleep grumbling. This time he heard the faint long buzz on the intercom and so he had to drag himself out of the cosy warm cocoon of the 13-tog duvet to get to it. He buzzed Ed in and intended to kill him as he heard him coming along the carpeted corridor outside. When Anton opened the door he saw that Ed had reddened eyes and a look of utter misery on his face, the likes of which he had never seen before.

'You are not going to believe this,' said Ed, not even looking at his friend. He was looking at some point behind Anton, just below ceiling level. 'You will think I've gone out of my mind.'

'You went out of it years ago,' said Anton, and he yawned and closed the door behind his melancholic mate. 'I wouldn't believe you if you said you'd found your way back *into* your mind though,' Anton said, in a dismal attempt to cheer him up.

Ed saw an English paperback dictionary on a table and said, 'Let me see if this works – I'll open it at random and see if the word at the top of the page is a sign...' And he opened the thick dictionary, looked at the word, and closed his eyes. He gave a sardonic smile. 'Saturnine! Ha! That's my whole life – '

Anton pressed his hand on his forehead and sighed. 'Ed, I am bleedin' knackered, so – whatever it is – can you just spit it out or I might start throwing things at you.'

'She's not human – there, I've said it,' Ed pounded

his fist on the dictionary and gritted his teeth.

'What?'

'Cat Morrison, who do you think?'

'What do you mean – "not human"?'

Ed turned to look at his friend and his undulating mouth and twitching face seemed to be a dam, holding back a vast reservoir of unshed tears. 'She – she's got a tail for a start!' he managed to get these words out then fell face down on the bed, biting the duvet and pounding the mattress as he made agonised howls and choking yelp-like noises.

'Ed, have you been taking drugs?' Anton tentatively asked in a low calm voice. He had to ask this question again because Ed didn't hear him the first time with all the noise he was making.

Ed reacted to the question by thrusting his legs out three times and yelping again as he remained face down. He got up and shouted: 'No! I haven't been doing drugs!'

'Alright, alright – keep your voice down Ed! You're going to wake everyone in this place!'

'Have you got any whiskey? Anything to drink, just to numb this heart of mine!' Ed slapped his closed first against the lapel of his jacket and scrunched his face up.

Anton smiled and gently took his friend by the arm and led him across the room. 'Look, let's sit in the kitchen and I'll make you a strong coffee and if you feel like eating I'll make you a full English brecky, okay?'

Ed nodded, unable to speak, and he wiped tears from his eyes with his fingers as he accompanied his friend to the kitchen.

'Here, sit down, Ed, and when you feel you're ready, just tell me what happened,' Anton pulled a chair from the small dining table. 'Just relax now mate, you'll be okay,' he said in a very reassuring voice, and then he went to the cafetière and began putting heaped scoops of ground Starbucks House Blend into it as he smiled at Ed. Ed tried to smile back but his mouth resembled a wavy line now. Anton wondered what on earth had happened to him to get him in this state; he seemed mentally unhinged. He had to make small-talk with Ed, just to keep the rapport up. 'Got this coffee at Waitrose. Used to go to er,' Anton was about to say he went to Morrisons but remembered that was Cat's surname and he certainly didn't want to mention her at a time like this. 'Er, is it just me or is it a bit nippy this morning?' Anton asked.

Ed gave two small nods and looked at the tabletop.

'When I move out of this tiny place – after I've graduated – I'm going to buy the biggest house I can afford,' said Anton, pouring the kettle into the cafetière.

'I like this place,' Ed suddenly said in a broken voice. 'It'd be easy to heat; economical.'

'Nah, it's too small for me,' Anton replied, so glad Ed was starting to talk. 'You couldn't swing a ca – ' he stopped himself and changed the subject in a flash. 'Hey, you're an Everton supporter aren't you? Did you see how much they're going to to pay for that striker? Er what's his name?'

'I support Tranmere Rovers,' Ed said in a low monotone voice. 'She's not human...' he rambled and his voice trailed off again.

About ten minutes later, Ed seemed to be a lot more

stable as he gripped the mug of coffee with both hands. He had a very strange story to tell Anton, who was now fully awake.

'When she ran out of the canteen yesterday, I went looking for her, but I couldn't find her anywhere, so I went home.'

'To your mum's in Childwall or your dad's house in Huyton?' Anton asked, 'Only you call both those places home.'

'My mum's place,' Ed answered, annoyed at the interruption. 'Anyway, I was having my tea and my mum said there was a girl looking through the window behind me, and it was Cat.'

'She'd followed you?' Anton asked. 'That's a few miles from the uni.'

'Yeah, so I went out and told her to come in and meet my mum and she did. She was wearing a black tee shirt and a short skirt. Anyway, my mum's dog, Alf – he's like a big old Labrador – he started barking his head off at her, and she let out this scream, and then started making this hissing sound, and she ran out the house. Me mum and me went out like seconds after she'd legged it out the house, and we couldn't see her on the road outside, but Alf started barking at the tree in the garden, and there she was, half way up it.'

'Cat was up a tree?' Anton paused, and wondered for a moment if he was still in bed, as this sounded like something out of a crazy dream.

Ed continued the surreal narrative. 'So I got the dog in and closed the door, and I told her it was alright to come down, and she eventually came down. Me mum was watching all this through the window.'

'And?'

'She climbed down dead fast, and kept looking at the front door of the house as if she was scared. Me mum opened the window and said that Alf had been put in the yard, and she told me to bring Cat in. So I did. Anton, here's where things get a bit trippy. She sat at the table and me mum put a bowl of scouse in front of Cat, and she sniffed the bowl, then bleedin' started clawing the tablecloth on each side of the scouse, and she had this look on her face as if she had a stink bomb under her nose. Mum went mad.'

Anton was tongue-tied for a moment, and then he stammered: 'That's what a cat does; makes a sort of clawing gesture round its food to show it doesn't like it.'

'Oh that's nothing.' Ed told him, and Anton could see he was reliving the strange incident as he watched his sad eyes. 'Me mother then said to her "Are you eating it or not?" and Cat lifted her leg – I think it was her left one – vertically – like straight up, and she had no - you know – underwear on. And you know what she did?'

'No! Don't tell me Ed,' Anton closed his eyes with a look of disgust on his face, 'I think I've heard enough.'

'And that's when I saw her tail – a grey furry tail, hanging down and writhing like a snake. I saw it first, and then my mum did, and screamed. She told me to get her out the house.'

'And because of this, you think she's not human – ' Anton said calmly.

'Well she can't be can she? What the hell is she?' Ed asked his friend, and his eyes seemed to be searching for an answer. Ed had always turned to Anton in times of need, and Anton always had an answer or some good advice – but this morning he looked baffled.

'Ed, look, she is not some half-cat half-woman! She's got some psychiatric condition, and that tail will be some trick. It'll be something she's bought online or out of a joke shop; remember that big inflatable penis Kevin got out in the toilets when we were in that club last New Year?'

'It's not a trick – it's attached to her arse!' Ed told him through gritted teeth.

'Well, Ed, let's look at this logically shall we? No one can be half human and half animal, only in some stupid horror film. Anyone with a modicum of knowledge of basic biology would know that a human cannot breed with anything outside of its own species – even an ape – it's just not possible. And don't even mention those ridiculous stories about randy farmers and sheep. She's having you on, this Cat Morrison – and I've only just realised that she's even chosen to call herself *Cat* to reinforce the idea she's some cat-human hybrid. I can't believe we are even talking about this crap at this time in the morning. Why can't I have sane friends?'

'She got up – and down – that tree really fast – ' Ed recalled.

'Ed, listen to me – just listen to the voice of reason, alright? Now, you've got to give your studies one hundred per cent. You failed last time, so let's make a success of it this time. I want you to forget this psychotic, attention-seeking screwball, and I want you to come back into the real, sane world, because you're a mate – okay?'

'But I love her,' Ed told him, and from the way he sounded, he obviously had a lump in his throat.

That lunchtime, Anton convinced Ed to give the canteen a miss, just in case Cat Morrison turned up playing her pathetic charade again, and Anton told his friend that Debbie, the lady behind the counter, would only go on and on about the nutty behaviour of Morrison. The two lads therefore went to a small quiet cafe about half a mile from the university campus, and Anton was paying. It was a surprisingly sunny day and Anton and Ed sat at a table in the window. Anton had a vegan toasted cheese and chorizo sandwich, and Ed had a jumbo hot dog. Anton saw that his old friend was apparently getting back to normal; his ravenous appetite had returned and he was smiling again – and that awful hollow sad look had gone from his eyes.

And then James York walked in. He was the last person Anton wanted to see today, because York was obsessed with the occult, and Anton had heard that his old friend was now making something of a living from reading tealeaves, palms, as well as being a self-proclaimed 'esoteric life coach' and even occasionally being called upon to exorcise spirits at troubled houses. Anton had last seen York five years ago when they were both attending a city centre college. York had been expelled from the college after he had accused three senior lecturers of being in some sort of cult, and had even challenged one teacher to a duel in Sefton Park. York did seem to have an in-depth knowledge of the esoteric, but Anton thought he was also a bit *non compos mentis*. York was dressed in a wide-brimmed black hat of plush felt which resembled a sombrero, only it was flat on top, and the most striking item he wore was a long black cape which almost went down to his ankles. This latest incarnation of York reminded Anton of the silhouetted man on the label of a Sandeman's port bottle. Anton quickly looked out the window to avoid being spotted, but York saw his old college friend's distinctive face – now lit up by the sun – reflected in the café window. York had a very theatrical way of speaking, and everyone jumped in the café when he bellowed out:

'Ah, Anton! You old reprobate!'

Anton turned to him, feigning astonishment. 'Yorkie, what a surprise.'

There was an awkward pause as Ed looked at York and his strange attire, then turned to face Anton as if to ask, 'Who is this?'

Rolling every 'r' he spoke, York said: 'Well, Anton? Are you going to introduce me your acquaintance here?'

Anton seemed to wake up at the question and seemed startled by it. 'Oh, yes, yes, er, Ed, this is James York; York – this is my friend Ed, he's studying at the same university as me.'

York held out his hand, Ed tried to give him a weak handshake, but the eccentric squeezed his hand hard and then slapped his other hand against the back of Ed's hand and shook it violently as he said: 'Pleased to meet you – Ed!'

'Yeah, same here,' said Ed, grimacing as he withdrew his crushed hand.

'I'd ask you to join us but I can't see any empty chairs knocking about,' Anton told his old college mate with a suppressed smirk.

An old man who had been eating alone overheard the remark and stood up. He smiled at Anton and said: 'Here, have my chair, I'm going now!'

'Oh thankyou good sir, you're a first-class gent!' said York, and with a flash of theatrical flourish he took the chair and spun it on one of its legs as he manoeuvred it to the table. He then swept his cloak aside, detached it from some clasp about his neck, and looked at it as he rolled it up. 'My cloak is not merely for show - it is for concealing me in the hours of darkness and has even served as a trip-mat.' Then he sat down. His elbows rested on the tabletop and his hands were pressed together, as if in prayer, with the finger tips under his chin. He looked at Anton from beneath his heavy-lidded eyes and said: 'Pray! Tell me what is troubling you! Furnish me with the details post-haste!'

'Eh?' Anton answered, puzzled.

York pursed his lips, then in a rapid-fire way of speaking he said: 'I sense that you and your friend are being troubled by a metaphysical matter.'

'No, were not actually,' said Anton, but simultaneously Ed replied: 'Yes, we are.'

'Ha!' exclaimed York, loudly, making Ed jump. 'I could see it in the auras – troubled auras. My gift scares me sometimes; what am I? *Incertae sedis* in this human species - ' York began to ramble, till Ed interrupted him.

'You're wanted over there, mate,' Ed told York, pointing to the counter, where a young lady with a barely audible voice was calling him.

'Mr York,' she was saying, and she was beckoning him with a curl of her waving palm. 'You left this – '

'Speak up child!' York boomed to her, and he got to his feet and went to see what she wanted.

'Right, let's get the hell out of here now!' Anton told Ed, speaking through a mouth that was almost closed.

'How did he know we were troubled by a metaphysical matter?' Ed asked, reluctant to get up.

The woman behind the counter was handing York some walking cane which he'd left behind after his last visit. York turned and saw Anton standing up and asked him not to leave. Anton said he and Ed *had* to be going because they needed to attend a lecture, but York could see their half-eaten meals and he knew they were just trying to get away from him.

'Please stay a moment!' he annunciated the words as if he was onstage at the Old Vic. 'Your lives may depend on this!'

'Sit down, hear him out,' urged Ed, halting at the doorway, barring a frustrated Anton, who shook his head despondently, then slowly headed back to the chair he'd vacated.

York returned to the table twirling the cane – which turned out to be a vintage (and illegal) swordstick. He sat between the students, took off his huge hat and placed it in the middle of the table, and he resumed his questioning. 'So, tell me; what is weighing heavy on your minds?'

Despite kicks to his ankle from Anton, Ed told York about Cat Morrison – her tail – and her feline behaviour. York nodded, thinned his eyes, looked at the ceiling, then turned and waved frantically at the young lady behind the counter of the café. Once she had noticed him, York roared: 'One cup of green tea! With loose leaves! No milk! No sugar! Just unadulterated green tea!'

Anton plugged his ears at the bawling from his flaky friend. When the green tea was brought over, York asked Ed to take a sip from the cup, and explained that he was going to read his tealeaves. Again, Anton said he and Ed had to attend a lecture soon, but the self-styled occultist just nodded and carefully drained the cup of tea into the saucer as Ed watched, spellbound.

'Can you really read tealeaves?' Ed asked.

'Coming events cast their dread shadows before them green knave,' intoned York in a low grave-sounding voice as he peered into the cup and studied the patterns of the leaves. 'And as you read a book, I will read the unwritten chapters of your future before they are indelibly penned by the fingers of fate!'

'Huh?' Ed returned a puzzled look as Anton made repeated symbolic glances at his watch.

'Let this mind's eye see what is in the offing. I see minions of the Moon, walkers by night, witchery, and those things which go by Diana's lunar livery! And I see the cat you speak of!'

'Cat Morrison?' Ed was very intrigued by the tealeaf scryer, and leaned forward, trying to see what York could see, to no avail.

James York shook his head of long raven black hair. 'She is not a maiden, Ed! She is an attendant spirit to a sorceress – a familiar!'

'Oh Yorkie, come on now...' Anton said in a condescending tone and he sported an uneasy smile as he shook his head - but neither Ed nor York paid an iota of heed to him.

'A sorceress? I don't understand Mr York,' Ed was naturally worried by the diviner's uncanny take on this strange situation.

'A witch, callow friend,' York told him without averting his eyes from the interior of that leaf-speckled cup. 'A playful but dangerous girl who meddles in the lives of unworldly folk.'

Ed was wrought by mounting worry now. 'What do you mean – dangerous?'

York gave a cryptic reply. 'We three are now in unknown waters and there will be no safe wading from this moment on, for she knows at this very moment that we are on to her.'

The cup in York's hand suddenly shattered, startling Ed and Anton and causing everyone in the café to look at the loud source of the breaking sound.

'You pressed on that cup, Yorkie!' Anton claimed, 'I saw your fingernails turn white!' he asserted, and yet deep down he knew that this wasn't really so; he just wanted to walk away from this scary mumbo-jumbo.

'No he didn't,' Ed told his friend, 'he didn't break it - he was holding it lightly.' And to York he asked: 'Is the witch the blonde girl? The one Cat Morrison hangs around with?'

'Who broke the cup?' the petite lady from behind the counter appeared at the table, and York gathered the fragments of the cup and placed them on a saucer. 'Not I, fair maiden, but dark forces exerted by a witch!'

Anton had clearly had enough, and he got to his feet and with a leftward tilt of his head he beckoned Ed to leave the café with him.

'You'll have to pay for that cup – and the tea – Mr York,' said the café employee with an anxious look at the cup fragments.

'Put it on the slate, my dear,' York picked up his hat, flipped it into the air, and it landed neatly on his head. He put his cape back on and swished it aside, then followed the others out the door, leaving the girl speechless.

Some twenty-five yards from the café, Anton turned and confronted York. 'Look, we're going to the uni now; we are not going on some – some – witch hunt! Now, it was nice seeing you Yorkie but buzz off!'

York halted on the pavement as an irate Anton walked on with Ed reluctantly following him. 'Charming! On your own head be it then!' York tilted his hat in some sort of salute. 'By the sun above me, without my expertise you two are marching to the edge of a cliff!' He then turned and strode away, taking swipes at falling leaves with his swordstick.

'His mental condition has gotten worse since our college days!' Anton fumed, and he and Ed turned a corner.

'Do you think Cat Morrison really is a witch's familiar?' Ed asked. In Ed's mind, York's claim did seem to have a lot going for it.

'Oh please, Ed, I can't even believe you're asking a silly question like that!'

'Yorkie does seem to possess something – ' Ed said, struggling to define just what that something was.

'Yes, I believe it's called insanity,' Anton chuckled, 'dressing like Zorro, and that foghorn voice of his; he makes Brian Blessed seem like Bob Harris. I was really enjoying that sandwich too.'

Back at the university, when Ed and Anton split up to attend different classes, he approached a know-all named Kenneth and asked him if he knew the name of the young blonde woman Cat Morrison knocked around with, and Kenneth said her name was very unusual – something that sounded like Jamara Oswith (possibly even Oswyth, an ancient Welsh name). Prying Kenneth knew nothing else about her, beyond the fact that she was studying the biological sciences and sociology. The busybody knew nothing at all about Cat Morrison though.

Unknown to Anton, Ed decided to confront Jamara that day when he spotted her in the university library, and without even introducing himself, he asked her: 'Is Cat Morrison your familiar?'

She seemed very stunned at the question, and in a well-spoken voice – and in an accent Ed could not place – she replied: 'What on earth are you talking about?'

'I said...' Ed started – but he found himself suffering from a spell of mild amnesia; he could not recall what he had intended to ask Jamara. 'I, er, I'm sorry, er – just give me a moment – ' he muttered, and the girl glared at him and swung around, twirling her long blonde hair around with her. She walked away, and left the library – and then slowly, Ed's short-term memory recovered, and he realised that she had somehow made him forget the question he had wanted to ask. Right then he realised that James York was right – this girl had to be some sort of witch. Ed waited in the corridor outside of the class Anton was attending, and approached him excitedly when he came out. He told him about the strange memory-loss episode in the library which had occurred when he had tried to question Jamara.

'Not all that again,' Anton groaned.

Ed nodded vigorously. 'Yes, and I haven't seen Cat Morrison anywhere – I was thinking of making enquiries with the Chancellor of the uni about this Jamara and Cat. There's something very fishy and sinister about them Anton, and you know it.'

'If you go to the Chancellor, he'll have you sectioned!' Anton hissed, raising the ring binder to his face to shield his words from the people filing out of the classroom. 'Just drop it, Ed, and get on with your studies. If you see Cat Morrison or her friend, just blank them. This is turning into an obsession!'

Ed decided Anton was of no use in this strange matter – he just didn't want to get involved. He wondered how to get in touch with James York. That evening he found him on Facebook. He sent a message to him via the social network, asking York if he could meet him at that café they'd all met up in earlier, sometime around 2pm. York later replied - via Facebook - that he would be there at 2pm sharp to 'render any assistance needed free of charge'. On the following day, Ed came into the café at five minutes to two and found York already sitting there in the corner. York gave his usual loud cordial welcome and then the two men sat and discussed what had to be done over coffee. York told Ed he'd have to point out Jamara to him to make sure he was pursuing the right woman, and once he had identified her, he would tackle her alone. Ed was instructed to keep well away for his own safety. Ed was very reluctant to do this but York eventually convinced him it was an absolute necessity. And so, that day, York accompanied Ed to the university, where the two men bumped into Anton, and the latter was furious with Ed for persisting with this 'bunkum' and called James York a 'dangerous charlatan'. Unabashed by Anton's outburst, York continued to hang around the campus with Ed until Jamara was seen going into the library. 'That's her!' Ed told the self-appointed witchfinder general with a sly nod to the blonde. Once again, Cat Morrison was not in her presence.

York gazed intently at the blonde disappearing into the library. 'Right, Ed, I will go and grapple with this one, but you must get as far away from here as possible!'

'Please try and find out what Cat Morrison is,' Ed asked, and as York strode off he added, 'and be careful.'

'Fear not for my safety,' York assured Ed without turning around, 'for I am well-versed in the *Malleus Maleficarum* my friend! Now begone! Get out of harm's way!'

Ed walked away, and kept expecting to see bolts of lightning dancing around the skies over the library – but he saw nothing when he looked back and never heard a rumble of thunder or so much as a single scream. He walked for about a mile, strolled through a park of trees of burnt orange, gold and bronze (like the colour of Cat's strange eyes), checking his phone almost every minute. The dull pumpkin-coloured sun hung in the barren branches of an oak, headed for dusky oblivion at chimney pot level, and Ed's eyes watered in the ice-sharp breeze that was stirring. A murder of cawing crows passing high overhead startled Ed, and he turned up the collar of his coat and left the lonely park. About forty minutes elapsed until his phone vibrated once in his pocket. York had texted him with a message to meet up at the canteen at the university. When Ed reached the canteen he found York in a pensive state, sitting in the very same corner he had sat with Cat Morrison when she had slammed into the plate glass window to scare that robin. When

Ed sat down, York told him that Jamara was now gone.

'Gone?' Ed was puzzled at the statement. 'And what about Cat?'

'Well, I was wrong about Jamara being a witch,' York told him in an uncharacteristically low voice. 'She is – er, it's hard to explain, but I'll try. She's not from this reality. This reality – the one you're used to living in – is not the only one; there are countless other ones, and Jamara was from one of them. They come to our one now and then and we interpret these visitors as angels, and aliens and all sorts of things - even the Loch Ness Monster - but well, they are just outsiders. She wanted to live as a woman – a human woman in the prime of her life, and her pet did too; that's what Cat Morrison is; she's a sort of elemental, and it's sad because she had seen you from way off in her reality, and she had fallen for you.'

'You're not making much sense, Yorkie,' Ed told the occultist bluntly. 'This is very, very trippy.'

'I knew you'd be like this, and I can't blame you,' York told him with a very sad pair of eyes. 'It's a bit like explaining colours to a blind man, or imaginary numbers to a kid at infant school.'

'Where has she gone? Cat I mean.' Ed asked, and he glanced at the windowpane where Cat had tried to seize the robin.

'Back to the place where she lives, in another reality,' said York, matter of fact. 'Look, their world and all the other realities are like the thousands of conversations on phones passing through us right now. We can't detect them with our five senses but they are there, and if you know how to tune in with the electronic circuits you can listen to the conversations. The other realities overlap ours and as we sit here in this canteen we are sitting in many worlds.'

'It doesn't make sense,' Ed talked as if someone was slowly strangling him. He was becoming so choked up. 'Why was Cat Morrison behaving like a cat?'

'That's her real nature in her reality – she's a creature almost identical to *Felis catus* - the animal we know as the domestic cat, only her nervous system is more complex. Jamara gave her a human form, and she was attracted to you for some reason – perhaps it was love.'

Tears rolled from Ed's eyes. 'I – I can't believe what you're saying, it sounds ridiculous. It doesn't make sense.'

York shrugged. 'The deep truth rarely makes sense – ask anyone who has even a rudimentary knowledge of quantum physics. I couldn't accept the deep truth at first, but I eventually realised that the blockage was my own faulty perception.'

'Can't they come back to our reality if what you say is true?' Ed had desperation in his eyes now.

York slowly nodded. 'Jamara could but I seem to have scared her off; she's not supposed to do this you see. She could choose any of the other myriad realities to sample, but she may return – I don't know – and she may not even come back as the same person.'

'I loved Cat,' Ed told York, and tried to smile but it was a disaster, 'which is crazy isn't it?'

'No, there's no such thing as crazy, and love is another prime example of something inexplicable I suppose.'

'What now then?' Ed took a paper napkin from the

table and dabbed his eyes.

'I don't know the answer to that, Ed,' was York's honest reply. 'I feel bad in a way because I confronted her and scared her off. She was a nice person. Outsiders from the other realities usually just up and go without a trace, but she explained a little, and then she vanished. She walked around a bookshelf in that library, and then she was gone.'

Ed had a sudden longing. 'Yorkie, can I study this subject that you know so much about? It's fascinating, and I'd love to be a sort of apprentice – I've had enough of the uni.'

'I don't know, Ed, it's taken me a few years, and a few nervous breakdowns along the way, and you'll be shunned by most people you know – '

'Damn people,' Ed blew his nose into the napkin, 'let them shun me, I really don't care.'

'Can you keep secrets or do you blab?' James York asked, matter of fact, with an intense gaze from under his hat.

'Oh I'm deep as the ocean, me,' Ed replied.

'I'll give you a trial period – just teach you the basics, and we'll see what happens from there then,' York told him.

SAWNEY

John Peters, a retired engine driver, was possibly one of the first to notice something strange about the pillar box which stands to this day on the corner of Childwall Valley Road and Score Lane. The pavement was white and slippery and the pillar box wore a cap of frozen snow that evening in the December of 1962, with a biting arctic wind howling down Score Lane as Mr Peters made his way to his local pub. Over the crying wind he distinctly heard a high-pitched voice shout: 'Don't get tanked up Mr Peters!'

There was not another single soul around, and 75-year-old Mr Peters thought the jokey remark came from the direction of the pillar box. He walked on stoically through the subzero weather to the Rocket Hotel pub, almost a mile distant, where he told his friend, Billy McDonough, about the brassy exclamation, and Billy said it was probably some kid messing about. 'I don't know, Billy,' John Peters told him, and relished a glass of scotch on such an inclement night.

'Well what do you think it was? A ghostie?' Billy asked with a lopsided smirk.

'There wasn't another person about,' John replied, 'and who in their right mind would be hiding somewhere in this freezing weather to play a silly prank like that?'

'A kid, that's what,' Billy answered, and he started filling his pipe. 'Kids don't feel the cold the way we do at our age John.'

'I don't know,' John raised his eyebrows, and looked at the windows to see falling flakes sticking to them now. 'Might have been someone behind the fences of one of those gardens on Score Lane,' John told himself out loud, 'and they do say sound travels further at night and that.'

'Fear is a great inventor, John,' said Billy, pocketing his tobacco pouch. 'It magnifies things and makes you think all kinds, fear does.'

Some twenty minutes later, a man named Rory, a coalman known to John and Billy, came into the pub and Billy bought him a pint of his favourite tipple. Rory mentioned something that induced an icy shudder in John Peters. He rubbed his hands, remarked upon the bitterness of the night, and as he reached for his pint, he said: 'Came up from Craighurst [Road] tonight 'cos I had to go and lend me sister a few bob, so instead of coming here down the Drive [meaning Queen's Drive], I had to come up Score Lane. Anyway, there's a post office pillar box on the corner there, and someone must have been standing behind it, and they shouted: " 'Effin Bible smoker!" '

Billy nodded to John and told Rory, 'Same thing happened to John about half an hour ago.'

'He shouted "Don't get tanked up" to me, and it sounded like someone with a high-pitched voice, like a kid,' said John.

Rory smiled and said: 'I went over to the pillar box like, and whoever it was had gone, but they must have been fast, and I couldn't see any foot prints in the snow either.'

'What's a "Bible smoker" any road?' Billy asked, and Rory shrugged. However, when Rory went the toilet later that evening, John explained the strange remark. 'Rory did time a few years ago for fiddling the coal, and he told me that someone smuggled tobacco into the prison, but he ran out of cigarette papers, so he asked the chaplain in the nick for a Bible, and made out he'd seen the light, and he used the thin pages of the Holy Book as ciggy paper.'

'Ah, that's barley that, Billy,' said John shaking his head with a look of repugnance, 'Heathens do that. I'd rather do without than burn the Bible.'

On the following day, a 10-year-old girl from Score Lane was sent to post four Christmas cards at the pillar box on the corner, but came running home in tears. The child said something inside the pillar box had snatched the envelopes as she posted them and it had sworn at her too (using the c word). The girl's father, Mr Hoyle-Jones, knew the child had been upset by something, and he visited the pillar box, and saw a pair of 'dark mad-looking eyes' glaring at him through the letters slot. 'Rob a chop!' said someone, apparently inside the pillar box, and Mr Hoyle-Jones, a butcher by trade, recoiled in shock which turned to anger, because he had been wrongly accused of stealing a leg of lamb at the butcher's shop five months ago. The butcher therefore believed that the mischief-maker in the box had to be someone who knew him; perhaps he was the child of a gossiping neighbour. A well-dressed lady coughed behind the butcher, and she held several envelopes she wanted to post, but Hoyle-Jones warned her: 'Don't put them in there, love – there's some young joker in there!'

The bemused lady asked the butcher if he'd been drinking, and he told her he was serious. To prove he wasn't crazy, the butcher leaned forward and into the letter slot he said, 'Go on you idiot, say something.' But no voices emanated from the pillar box and no penetrating eyes were visible at the slot, so the butcher tried the door handle of the box – to find it was locked. 'He's deliberately saying nothing to make me look like a crank,' said Mr Hoyle-Jones, kicking the base of the pillar box in anger.

The lady backed off, slipped and almost came to grief on the icy pavement as she hurried away. Once she was out of earshot of the pillar box, the butcher was again greeted by that falsetto voice: 'Rob a chop!'

Hoyle-Jones and a gaggle of other locals heard the voice in the pillar box, and some even searched behind a wall, thinking a prankster was throwing his voice – but no practical joker could be found. When the postman called to collect the mail later that day, he saw the crowd gathered around the pillar box, and he was told about the voice in the box and the eyes peering out the slot. The box was opened and contained nothing but letters. A gang of boys heard the pillar box 'spirit' next, and he allegedly said his name was Sawney, and stated that he read all the letters in the box and knew everyone's secrets. The boys said a pair of crossed eyes would sometimes appear at the slot, and sometimes a greenish finger. It was also noted that people walking their dogs would have to drag their cowering animals past the pillar box. One of the biggest snowstorms then hit Britain and the "Big Freeze" went on till March of 1963, and then, with the thaw and widespread flooding, Sawney was eventually forgotten. After the Spring of 1963, there were no more reports of Sawney. Ghosts have haunted some strange places, but why on earth would a ghost haunt a pillar box? Could the alleged ghost really read the mail contained in the box, or was the whole thing the work of some exceedingly gifted ventriloquist? Unless Sawney haunts that pillar box again – or some other one – we'll probably never know the truth of the matter.

STRANGE FARE

It was the evening of 6 January 2010 – Twelfth Night – and most of the country was buried under snow- Liverpool being no exception. A weary hackney cab driver named Tommy dropped three students off at the supermarket on Smithdown Road, and continued on his way. A man almost walked out in front of the cab and because of the slush and ice on the road, the cab took longer to stop. Tommy wound down his window and yelled at the jaywalker, but the man shouted: 'Sorry!' and beckoned the driver to pull over. He climbed in and said: 'Sorry about that! Maryland Street, please.'

'Minus twenty tonight they reckon,' Tommy told his passenger, glancing at him in the rear view mirror. He noticed he had no coat on, just a white shirt with the sleeves rolled up. 'And,' Tommy continued, 'they reckon we'll have 16 inches of snow in the morning. Fifteen schools are closed because of this weather and yet again they've run out of grit. Pathetic. Years ago my arl fellah used to put chains on his tyres when it snowed like this; he never got stuck. They were better prepared those days than in this so-called hi-tech age.'

The man barely nodded and bore a worried expression as he looked out the side windows. He said nothing throughout the journey. Upon reaching Maryland Street, just off Hope Street, the fare said:

'Just here. I haven't got my wallet on me; I left it in the flat, so can you hang on a sec?'

He got out of the cab, walked to a badly-lit stretch of pavement and pressed the intercom button as the taxi waited, juddering with its diesel running. A woman came to the door with a man; they both looked as if they were in their early twenties. The fare came back to the taxi less than a minute later and told Tommy. 'You know what? I think I'm going insane. That couple said they live in my flat, which is impossible. I mean how on earth - '

'Well, you owe me eleven quid mate,' sighed Tommy, waiting for the punchline. The fare got back in and said, 'She must have gone back to her mothers. Er, can you take me to her mum's? Morecambe Street, off Rocky Lane, please? Sorry about this mate.'

'Nah, don't apologise, you're paying for this mate.' Tommy replied, and drove off along treacherously slippery roads for nearly three miles. Halfway down Morecambe Street, the hackney stopped and the fare got out. He knocked on the door and a man, aged about thirty, answered. Tommy saw him shake his head and lip-read him saying 'no' to his passenger, who returned with a perplexed look. 'He has just told me he has lived there for two years!'

Tommy's temper flared. 'Look mate, I haven't got time for this rigmarole! What are you playing at?'

The fare opened the cab door and got in. 'I swear I am not a nut! I am genuinely puzzled by this. Please, take me to my sister's house on Earle Road – I should have gone there first.'

Throughout the journey, Tommy put on Radio City and to every single record that was played, he complained that it was crap, and talked about the dire state of popular music – but his passenger never said a word of reply. He had the expressions he'd had on the other fruitless trips – they alternated between worried and confused.

When the cab reached the destination, the house was not even there – it had been demolished, obviously some time ago, given the height of the weeds that were coated with snowflakes.

'I don't know what to say,' said the man, confused, and he began to cry as the snow fell. Tommy asked him where he had come from when he first hailed the cab, and suggested going back there to get some money.

'The cemetery,' said the man, 'I remember now. I'm dead aren't I? Yes, I remember now. I died. My wife moved on. I am so sorry I wasted your time. Oh I miss my wife. Oh I miss that girl so much.'

Tommy naturally thought the strange fare was mentally unbalanced, and groaned, 'Oh no; why did I even stop to pick you up?'

And then the sobbing stranger held his face in his hands – and vanished. The crying ceased instantly as he disappeared in an instant like an image of a person on a TV screen when the channel is changed.

Only then did the penny drop. Tommy reversed the cab, and jumped, startled by the horn of the approaching car he was backing into. Tommy drove away up Earle Road, and felt the hairs rising on the back of his neck. He had heard about ghosts over the years, but had never really given the subject of the supernatural much thought. When he reached home, he left the cab with his takings, and before he locked the vehicle he glanced into the hackney at the back seat, where that apparently solid man had been seated. He went into the house, and as his cat came down the stairs to greet him, Tommy went into the kitchen, put the takings down and he hugged his wife Sarah hard.

'What's got into you?' she asked, 'Your nose is freezing. Tommy? Is everything alright? Are you crying or have you got cold in your eye?'

Tommy was too choked up to answer. He thought about that nameless ghost missing his wife, and he softly told Sarah that he loved her.

THE SCOTCH UNCLES

Most pubs on Merseyside have their ghosts, from the Derby Arms in Prescot and the New Johnny Todd in Kirkby, to the Magnet bar on Hardman Street and the Bridge Inn pub in Port Sunlight - but there is one pub in particular up in Knowsley that has a pair of very solid-looking ghosts, and I will not name this pub because its phantoms are of a very rare kind – they can inflict serious physical – as well as mental – harm. The case of the Scotch Uncles begins in the 1980s. Two Scottish brothers, Roy and Alan, were born in Glasgow but had a Liverpool mum who had divorced when the lads were in their twenties and returned to Liverpool, before settling in Knowsley. The lads were wanted the length and breadth of the country for bank robberies and several violent crimes, but much later in their lives, when they visited their mother at her Merseyside home in the 1980s, they always tried their utmost to behave and stay out of trouble because their mum was in her eighties by then and never believed all the worrying stories about her sons. Both brothers were absolutely fearless, and both had taken up boxing and martial arts in their younger days and knew how to look after themselves, but Alan, the younger of the two, was said to have been nothing short of a psychopath. Paradoxically, Alan seemed to be the calmer of the two and with his receding hair and friendly eyes, he could easily pass as a bank manager or a clerk when he was suited up – but when he felt threatened - or if someone annoyed him - he would lock onto them with those eyes and in a heartbeat they'd change from friendly to a sinister laserlike stare – and then he'd move in for the kill. Roy was the bearded one with a good head of hair who was forever suspicious of everyone and was always staring people out. He seemed to have a chip on his shoulder all the time, but he was much slower to anger than his berserk brother. At the pub in question one snowy December evening in the 1980s, a beautiful girl of eighteen named Jacqueline came into the place and ordered half a lager and lime. She'd arranged to meet a college friend at the pub before going to town, but two local lads in their twenties accosted Jacqueline from either side and started asking her very 'personal' questions regarding the colour of her underwear, sexual positions she preferred, and other unsavoury matters I could never put into print. The barman told the lads to beat it but they took no notice. In the corner, Roy and Alan watched the two young men bothering the girl, and Roy shouted over: 'Hey, Laurel and Hardy, leave her alone.'

The taller of the two pests told Roy: 'Why, what's it got to do with you, you old bastard? Get back to Scotland!'

Alan, who was proudly wearing his tartan scarf, rose from the table, and he picked up what looked like a short roll of Christmas gift-wrapping paper. And he walked straight to the disrespectful lad who had addressed his brother and said. 'What makes you think a lovely lassie like this would have something to do with one ugly mug like you?'

Everyone stopped talking – and you could hear a pin drop.

'Me, ugly?' said the offended youth, who was now turning red, 'So you don't like my face eh? And his friend smirked, adding: 'The scotch egg doesn't fancy you, Davy!'

Alan moved in that close, his nose was almost touching Davy's nose. He said: 'No, I don't like your face at all. I'm going to have to alter your features.'

'Alan!' Roy shouted from the corner, 'let them go, you'll be done for murder!'

Alan lifted the iron bar swathed in Christmas wrapping paper, and pressed it into Davy's navel. 'Got a lovely present for you here, sonny.'

'That's not fair, he's got a weapon!' the other scally said to the barman, who looked anxiously at the telephone, but his wife shook her head, reading his eyes; she knew if he tried to call the police those two Scotsmen would destroy the premises.

'Alright, pack it in, mate,' said the pub landlord, 'I don't want any trouble in my pub!'

'I can't pack it in, mate,' said Alan, not moving an inch as his eyes drilled into young Davy's eyes, 'you see this young man has left me no room to manoeuvre. But I'll just let the young lady get out of harm's way first. Alright love?'

Jacqueline tottered away in her high heels to the other end of the pub. Davy tried to get a punch in, but Alan simply lifted the bar up with both hands as if he was lifting weights in the gym and 'accidentally' caught

Davy's pointed and fragile-looking jaw, and before Roy could get to his feet to help his brother there was a lightning punch thrown by Alan and it was all over. Both youths lay unconscious on the floor. Davy lay there, having some sort of fit as blood poured from his smashed teeth.

A seasoned boxer standing six feet away shook his head and admitted: 'I've never seen anyone scrap like that before.'

Before the Scots left the pub, Alan winked at a horrified Jacqueline and said, 'If the cops ask ya who sparked those two, tell them it was your Scotch Uncles.'

A few weeks later, the landlord was reading a tabloid when he saw a picture of the two Scotsmen in an article about a fatal car smash down south. He was somehow relieved the trouble-causers had died in the multiple pile-up and told his wife so, and she said 'You shouldn't say things like that, God rest them.'

And then, in the following December, a young lady from Huyton named Kelly, who was causing a scene at the pub because she was a bit tipsy from a friend's 21st birthday party, found herself being mocked by a local hard knock nicknamed Gazza. Gazza and his mates took it in turn skitting at Kelly's drunken behaviour – until someone in a corner of the pub in a Scottish accent familiar to the barman and his wife shouted to Gazza (who had blond hair): 'Hey, goldilocks – you're very brave picking on a lassie aren't you?'

The landlord and his wife froze. The Scotsmen who had died a year ago – Alan and Roy – were sitting at that same corner table they'd sat at last time – and they looked alive and kicking.

'The newspapers must have made a mistake,' the landlord gasped. Alan suddenly locked eyes with the landlord, and getting up from the table, he said: 'We're back.' He then casually picked up a stool near a radiator shelf and appeared to be taking it to the bar, perhaps to sit there – but then he halted and looked at Gazza with a smile.

Gazza and his fawning cronies smirked and giggled uneasily.

To Kelly, Roy said: 'Get over there, lassie, out of harm's way, and watch my brother spill some yellow Sassenach blood.'

Kelly instinctively knew something bad was going to happen and she hurried away and hid behind an elderly man at the end of the bar.

'Eh?' Gazza asked, thinning his eyes as he smiled at Roy. 'Can you say that in English Jimmy McJimmy?'

The bar stool was of six kilograms of padded leather and hard acacia wood, made to support the weight of a 160 kg drinker. Alan had done this so many times before, it was like swinging a golf club to him. He lifted the stool, high over his head, and it knocked against two festive balloons on the ceiling before it came down like the wrath of God on Gazza's head and right shoulder. The boy seemed to go into the floor like a tent peg under a mallet, and something flew out of his mouth. It was a false front tooth the lad wore to replace the one he had lost in a scooter accident a few years back. Screams filled the pub as Alan lifted the stool again and gazed with insane bulging eyes at Gazza's gang as they backed away towards the pub door. The stream of profanities from Alan's mouth were like the vile utterances of a man possessed, and when Roy touched his brother's shoulder and said, 'Come on, we better split,' he turned in one sharp reflexive movement and raised the stool, ready to strike.

And then, in an instant, Alan beamed a loving smile at Kelly, who was clinging on to the pensioner next to her, ready to faint at witnessing the nightmarish attack on Gazza.

Alan tried to reassure Kelly his actions were noble ones. 'Don't ya worry, my bonnie girl, your Scotch uncles were just protectin' you!'

Then, as three members of Gazza's gang were all trying to get through the doorway at the same time, Alan hurled the stool at them. One was knocked out on impact. Gazza was taken to hospital with bleeding on the brain and a shattered collar-bone.

When the police arrived at the pub, they wanted statements and were quickly briefed by the landlord and several shook-up drinkers, but the Scotch uncles were not found, despite an immediate search of the area. They had seemingly vanished – 'like Scotch mist,' quipped one detective. Another detective returned to the pub later in the evening and said that the two Scottish men they were looking for had died the year before in a car crash, so new lines of inquiry had to be initiated - all to no avail. A few years later, Alan and Roy were seen at the pub again, only this time there were no fights or confrontations, and when a medium was brought to the pub, she said that the ghosts were coming to the pub for some symbolic purpose which she could not fathom – but she detected that one of the 'Scotch uncles' had dabbled in serious hard-core Satanism during his life, and that had some bearing on the hauntings.

Every now and then, always in December – and sometimes on Burns Night - the ghosts turn up at the pub, and so many landlords have come and gone at the place because of the occasional violent antics of the unearthly tartan terrors from beyond.

NAMELESS HORRORS
IN SEFTON PARK

In the 1970s in Liverpool, a 27-year-old man named Jon Harcourt worked as a quantity surveyor by day, but in the evenings and on weekends he indulged in his long-standing hobby of investigating the sphere of the paranormal, probing such things as encounters with ghosts and poltergeists, as well as cataloguing reports of UFOs. In early 1972, a very strange and horrendous case came his way when a 30-year-old woman named Gayle took a short cut through Sefton Park one morning on her way to work. Gayle had taken this route before when she was late for her secretarial job at a hotel, and usually saw other people on the path in the park at that time in the morning, especially people walking their dogs, but on this occasion she saw no one as she passed a wooded area. She heard what sounded like a click – perhaps it was the sound of someone stepping on a twig, she wondered, and she turned right to see a tall and very muscular looking man wearing glasses with black square plastic rims. He had a head of curly brown hair, and wore jeans and a white shirt with the sleeves rolled up. This man, who looked to be about forty – perhaps a little more – wore quite a sinister smile on his face as he looked at Gayle. He came out of the wood about twenty five feet away and started to trot towards her.

He wore what looked like workmen's boots (Gayle, who was Scottish, called them "tackety boots" – meaning hobnailed boots). Gayle naturally panicked, expecting this stranger to assault her – and her expectations were correct. The man's large hands seized Gayle's shoulders, and he turned her round, then pushed her down onto her back. Gayle lashed out, and swung her clenched fist at his face, but it was like hitting wood, and the attacker laughed at the girl's attempt to defend herself. An uncapped biro fell out of the secretary's handbag and when her hand felt it, she grabbed it and thrust its ballpoint into his face. Intending to claw at his eyes, she tried to pull off his glasses as his hands grabbed her throat but the spectacles seemed to be held in place, perhaps by a rubber band that went round the assailant's head. Fearing imminent death by strangulation, Gayle spat in the park predator's face, and the spittle obscured the left lens of his spectacles, which enraged him, and he released a hand from Gayle's neck and slapped her face hard, leaving her stunned. While this attack was going on, Gayle could detect a sweet smell which she identified as church incense, and after the assaulter - and possible mugger - had left the girl stunned, she expected to be raped and murdered. Then Gayle heard a panting and growling noise, and a huge black Alsatian dog suddenly pounced onto the spectacled stranger, and he let go of Gayle's throat to fend the animal off. The attacker got to his feet, and tried to kick at the dog, but it tore into his jeans and bit his arms and legs. The owner of the dog was now advancing, and Gayle lifted herself up off the grass and saw this man was about fifty, and he was coiling the chained dog leash around his fist, ready to use it as a makeshift knuckleduster. The cowardly aggressor ran towards the woods he had first emerged from before the attack with the dog-walker and his Alsatian in hot pursuit, and yet the fleeing attacker seemed to literally disappear, seconds after he entered the wooded area. The Alsatian seemed as baffled by the apparent vanishing act as its owner, and it whined and ran back out of the wood. The dog owner went to see if Gayle was harmed and urged her to go and report the matter to the police. Gayle said the man had slapped her, and her jaw felt a bit sore, but otherwise she was okay. She promised the Good Samaritan that she would tell the police about the attack, but she went straight to work, where she made herself a strong coffee, and subsequently decided not to involve the law. She did decide, however, to never take a shortcut through Sefton Park again. About a month after this incident, Hattie, a 19-year-old female kitchen assistant at the hotel where Gayle worked came into work one morning in a shaken state, carrying a single shoe. She said she had missed her bus and had decided to take a short cut to work via the park – Sefton Park, that is. This was around 7.50am. Two young men were jogging along ahead of Hattie, so she felt quite safe, even though the sun had not yet fully risen and the low thick clouds were blotting out what little predawn light there was. Hattie *heard a clicking sound* as she passed a wooded area of the park. Then she saw a man with glasses on, peeping out from behind a tree. Alarmed by the sinister watcher, Hattie ran off down the path, and she heard heavy footfalls behind her as the spectacled man gave chase. Hattie left the path as she tried to run away, when suddenly her pursuer dived forward and landed on the floor, where he grabbed her ankles. Hattie screamed and kicked at the man, and her shoe came off. The joggers who had been running along further down the path heard the screams and stopped, and then they quickly came to Hattie's aid, but by then the attacker had fled back towards the wood – apparently with Hattie's shoe. Hattie told her employer about the attack and he advised her to make a report to the police, but the young kitchen worker didn't do that – she told her boyfriend Terry about the incident, and as he lived on Linnet Lane, which is very close to Sefton Park, he decided to go and look for the assailant with a few friends in the hope of giving the man a beating. Terry and his three mates, all in their early twenties, put on their steel toe-capped "bovver boots" and Terry armed himself with a cricket bat. The gang met up at terry's flat on a Saturday afternoon and went to the part of the park where, according to Hattie, the man had come out from the cover of the trees, and they entered the wood there. In a clearing in this wood, Terry noticed something curious. There was a circle with a five-pointed star in it, carved into the grass and mossy soil. The symbol looked as if it had been made fairly recently. One of Terry's friends said he had seen this star in a circle in a book belonging to his uncle and that the symbol had something to do with witchcraft, with the points of the star representing the five wounds of Christ when he was on the cross. Terry believed – wrongly – that the symbol was the Star of David (which actually has six points). As the four young men stood there debating the meaning of the star inscribed into the ground, they all heard a loud bang. Someone had thrown a short-handled hatchet which had flown between the heads of Terry and a friend, and the blade of the tool had caused the loud bang as it had embedded itself in a tree trunk. Terry and the gang then noticed three figures standing nearby – all with long hair, and two of them held what looked like daggers. The gang fled from the wood and were chased by the three men for about four hundred yards down Mossley Hill Drive as far as Ibbotson's Lane. Terry felt like a coward, running from the long-haired 'hippies' (as he called them), and keen to maintain his tough-guy image as the gang leader, he told his friends he was going to enlist the help of a few 'John Bulls', 'Jays' and skins tomorrow. 'They weren't playing fair, using knives,' Terry told his cronies, after he'd regained his breath from the chase, 'but if they want aggro, they're gonna get it.'

But no one wanted to know. Terry told Harry Wheeler - a vicious skinhead he'd gone to school with - about the hippies with the knives and hatchet, but when the shaven-headed aggro-lover heard about the five-pointed star and circle inscribed in the soil in that wood, he said the hippies must be part of some cult, and talked about the Manson killings. Wheeler then made it clear that the supernatural was the one thing he *was* scared of, and he advised Terry to leave the 'Satanists' well alone. Later that day, Terry called at the house of a hard-knock associate named Billy in Huyton, and Billy's mum came to the door and said her son was at work – he now stacked shelves in Lennon's supermarket in the Wavertree area. Terry went to the supermarket and spotted Billy in one of the aisles and asked him if he'd help him to 'give a few hippies a good hiding' for the attack on his girlfriend Hattie. He mentioned the weird star symbol and told Billy that Harry Wheeler, supposedly the hardest skin in Huyton, was terrified of the hippies. 'He might have a point though, Terry,' Billy suggested, 'there are some weird people knocking round nowadays. Someone's been killing loads of pigeons and impaling them on railings up in Huyton, always when there's a full moon, like.'

'Look, Billy, are you going to help me out or not?' Terry asked, putting him on the spot.

'My fighting days are way behind me now, mate,' Billy turned away and started to stack cans of Ambrosia cream rice on a shelf. 'I've got a girl in the club and I'm working to provide for her and the baby, y'know, be a responsible parent and that.'

'Bleedin' hell, what's happened to all of the hard-knocks?' Terry asked, shaking his head with a painful smile. 'You're all shit-scared of your own – '

'Er, I'm sorry to intrude into this conversation,' interposed a man who looked as if he was in his late twenties. He was dressed like a teacher in the eyes of Terry – corduroy suit with leather patches at the elbows, Jason King moustache and collar-length hair sporting the 'feather-cut' style.

Billy turned to see who the stranger was, and hoped he wasn't some associate of the supermarket manager who had been eavesdropping on him and Terry.

The interposer, who was carrying a shopping basket, smiled meekly and explained: 'My name's Jon Harcourt, I'm a quantity surveyor but my hobby is investigating the occult and the supernatural. I couldn't help overhearing you – but did you say you saw a pentagram – a five-pointed star – carved into the ground in Sefton Park?'

'I might have done, why?' Terry replied, with great suspicion in his thinned eyes. He had it in his mind that this Harcourt might be one of *them* - one of the hippie cultists. Before Harcourt could reply, Terry added: 'It's bad manners to earwig you know?'

Jon closed his eyes and nodded. 'I can assure you I am not in the habit of listening in on people's private conversations, so I apologise if that's – '

'Anyway, what about it?' Terry asked, looking the quantity surveyor up and down.

'Nothing, it's just that I'd like to see this pentagram you speak about – purely because of my interests in the occult,' Jon answered, 'that's all.'

'How do I know you're not one of them?' Terry asked, craning back his head, because Harcourt was about six feet in height, considerably taller than him.

'One of who?' Jon Harcourt returned a puzzled look.

'The hippies, that's who,' Terry replied. 'Because, if you were, I'd have to put you down, mate.'

'Billy!' shouted the assistant manager of the supermarket as he came marching down the aisle. 'What's all this here?' he gesticulated with his hands to indicate Jon and Terry. 'Are they friends of yours?'

'Anyway, it's okay,' Jon said to Terry, 'sorry for butting in.' And he walked off down the aisle as the assistant manager took Billy to task for chatting to people when he was supposed to be working.

Terry followed Jon Harcourt around the supermarket, curious as to why he was interested in the long-haired loonies in Sefton Park. He asked the well-spoken snoop what that pentagram symbol meant.

'Well, it sounds to me as if some ritual has been taking place in the park,' Jon told him. 'Occultists have probably been conjuring something up – perhaps an evil spirit.'

'Did you hear what I said about my girlfriend like?' Terry asked. 'The man who attacked her came from the woods where we found that star.'

'No, I only heard the bit about you finding the symbol,' said Jon. 'Tell me the rest if you like.'

So Terry told him the rest, and Jon Harcourt visited Sefton Park and took several photographs of the star in the circle with his SLR camera. He also took a picture of the word "SENAR" carved into one of the trees near to the pentagram. Jon then paid a visit to the hotel near the park and, via the manager, he made arrangements to interview the secretary Gayle and the kitchen assistant Hattie. The young women were interviewed separately and afterwards Jon told them that he thought there was some occult element to the attacks – especially the way the attacker had gone to ground within seconds – as if he had vanished into thin air, and furthermore, the mention by Gayle of the smell of incense seemed to tie in with this theory. Another girl at the hotel mentioned seeing a suspicious looking man in spectacles that week, but the manager told Jon he couldn't interview this possible witness and he also stated, in a rather irate manner, that he could not help him any further as he had a hotel to run.

There was no public internet in 1972, and to discover if anyone else had encountered anything strange in Sefton Park, Jon could not go asking around on social media or online forums; instead he pinned brightly coloured cards on notice boards in supermarkets and even stuck them in the window of several post offices. The typewritten text on these cards read: 'Researcher Seeking information about Sefton Park. Have you ever had a strange experience in Sefton Park which you cannot explain? Have you ever been confronted by anyone strange in Sefton Park who tried to attack you? Have you ever seen or heard of anyone dabbling in witchcraft or Devil-worship in Sefton Park? Please call me on the number below (and feel free to reverse the charges), or write to me via the PO Box detailed below. All information will be treated in complete confidence.'

Jon had resorted to this method before to obtain possible eyewitness testimony to hauntings and UFO sightings, and sometimes he'd get juvenile jokers and attention-seeking timewasters calling him late at night, but on this occasion, he received no such nuisance calls. A librarian named Alison who lived in the Allerton area called him one evening and supplied Jon with a very intriguing piece of information. In the summer of 1967, Alison had been crossing Sefton Park on her own one warm night around ten minutes to midnight. It was a Saturday night going into Sunday morning, and Alison was returning from a party at a friend's house on Penny Lane, and she was taking a short-cut through the park to get to her home near Lark Lane. Normally, Alison would not walk through the park alone, but she was filled with Dutch courage from all the Martinis she'd imbibed at the party, and the moon was full, so the park looked almost as bright as it would be during the day. However, as Alison was walking along through the 235 acres of verdant moonlit splendour, she thought she heard a strange sound. She slowed her pace and listened, and realised the sound she was hearing was a group of people chanting, but just what was being chanted she could not tell. Instead of going straight home upon hearing the eerie incantations, Alison nonchalantly went to see where the chanters where. It *was* 1967 and people of all walks of life were dabbling with witchcraft and getting involved in all sorts of cults, Alison explained, and she imagined that the chanting was just a group of harmless late-night revellers messing about in the park. But when she drew nearer to the source of the cantillations she thought that the chanters were all singing in very strange but consistent harmonies and that the intonation reminded her of a hymn. Alison reached the edge of the wood – the very same one where that pentagram would later be found – and she saw a circle of men and women, all naked, gathered around a coffin. The coffin was open and inside of it lay a figure in white. The coffin was resting on a stand (a bier), and the coffin and stand were in the centre of a large five-pointed star with two circles enclosing it. Alison thought she saw strange letters – possibly Greek or Hebrew – dotted around the annulus formed by the circles. Alison just knew somehow that the body in that coffin was going to move – was going to return to life – but she was so gripped with terror she turned and ran off. She wanted to scream but she knew the chanters would hear her and come after her – and most probably silence her. She was so scared, she halted at one point, took off her heeled shoes, and ran pell-mell all the way to the far side of the park. She was within about fifty feet of the exit, when she thought she heard noises behind her. She turned and saw two tall naked men – one of them carrying what looked like a sword – racing towards her. Alison recalls the penises of the men flapping up and down as they ran towards her, and she screamed and ran out of the park, where she saw a parked police car on Lark Lane. She ran to the car and told the policemen what she had seen and one of the officers sniffed the air and said, 'What have you been drinking, eh love?'

Alison admitted she'd had a few drinks at a party but was not drunk, and she looked nervously back towards the park, expecting to see the naked pursuers turn up, but they never did. Alison begged the policemen to go and investigate the strange ritual involving the coffin in the park, but one of the officers warned her: 'Beat it or I'll nick you for being drunk and disorderly. Off you pop!'

Alison said she wanted to go to the woods on the following day to see if there were any traces of that weird ritual but she was too scared to, and after that terrifying experience she walked around the park rather than take a short-cut through it, even in broad daylight. Alison also mentioned a number of silent telephone calls she received not long after the Sefton Park incident, and these calls were always made around midnight with the caller hanging up after a menacing minute of silence, but whether they were connected to the cultists she'd seen around that coffin was never determined.

Jon Harcourt dug deeper into the Sefton Park mystery. He visited the Central Library and scoured paper and microfilmed copies of *The Daily Post* as well as the *Liverpool Echo* and he discovered that there had been a suicide at the very site of the pentagram in Sefton Park in the 1960s. A man had hanged himself from a tree there, and his mother had claimed that he had been associating with Satanists before he had undergone a drastic personality change and taken his own life. Had this act of self-destruction some bearing on the location of that pentagram? Jon Harcourt wondered. On the Thursday evening of 24 August, 1972, at 11pm, Harcourt set up his strange square tent in a wood in Sefton Park. The tent, supported by lazy tongs and a light tubular frame, resembled a Punch and Judy booth in dimensions and shape, being about 7 feet in height, five feet in width, and five feet in depth. It was made of a dark green fabric and had plastic leaves and netting covering most of it as a form of camouflage. With binoculars and the naked eye, Jon Harcourt looked out of a rectangular opening, three feet wide and seven inches in height in the front of the tent, about five feet from the ground, and inside the dwelling he had all of the necessary equipment – SLR camera with telephoto lens, tape recorder, binoculars, a flashlight and also an electric lantern made from the red tail light of a bike – as such red (subdued) light does not blind eyes that have adapted to the dark. At hand was a flask of hot coffee with milk and sugar already mixed in, a foil-wrapped ham sandwich, and an empty plastic bottle to urinate in should the need arise. Although it was against the law, Jon also had a powerful air-pistol loaded with .22 ammunition – just in case the cultists attacked with swords. Straight ahead, at a distance of about 300 yards, was the wood where the spectacled figure was reported to have come and gone during his nocturnal attacks. On the first night, the surveillance lasted for about four hours, ending at 3am. During this time, Jon saw nothing except the odd fox and cat wandering about. On the third night, at around midnight, Jon saw movement in the wood. Something pale was definitely moving about. John slowly grasped the binoculars, uncapped the lens covers and looked back at the movement in the wood. He looked through the binoculars, focused them – and what came into view astounded him. The whiteness he had detected was the light of the moon reflecting off some shiny colourless head – a head which was clearly not human, for it had a long tubular nose, similar to that of an elephant's trunk but only about two feet in length, and the eyes were very large and black. The ears of the thing were similar to that of the large ears of the elephant, only they fanned out downwards from each side of the head and hung like the striped Egyptian headdress of the sort worn by Tutankhamen and Nemes. The rest of the entity's body seemed to be draped in a long black robe which went all the way to the floor, but it was hard to see the attire because the figure was still partially obscured by tree trunks and bushes. Jon estimated its height to be a little over six feet. The head of the unearthly being turned towards Harcourt's observation tent – as if it knew it was being watched. Already, Jon was pulling the cap from the lens of the SLR camera, and then he wound on the film with the lever as the flash attachment charged up, emitting a high-pitched noise. Would the flash scare off the weird being? Wouldn't it be wiser to observe the entity first, rather than attempt to take a picture at this distance? These were some of the questions swarming in the hive of Harcourt's mind as the uncanny life-form drifted out into the open. By the light of a waning gibbous moon, Jon could see that the thing was hovering along in the grass now with a faint green mist around it – then suddenly, in an instant, the entity vanished and was replaced by the human figure of a man, and he wore a white shirt with rolled-up sleeves, and he had a head of curly dark hair and spectacles on his face. This had to be the attacker of those women – it was that thing in another guise. Then Jon heard the sounds of someone crying in the distance; it sounded like female sobs. He looked to his left, and there, silhouetted by the moon's light, he saw what looked like a girl – perhaps she was in her teens – maybe she was even younger – and she seemed to be holding her face in her hands as she walked along the path crying hysterically. In the distance, came the voice of a young man who Jon could not see. 'I don't ever want to see you again! Got that?' he yelled, and the words echoed back and forth across the park.

In a flash, Jon realised what was going on; that entity somehow knew the defenceless girl was going to pass its lair, and it was going to attack and perhaps rape her! Jon felt for the air pistol and left the tent with the SLR camera hanging from him by the trap around his neck. Already the thing which had metamorphosed into a humanoid figure was hurrying towards the unsuspecting girl who was blinded by tears, perhaps because of some fall-out with her boyfriend.

'Hey!' Jon shouted to the thing masquerading as a man, and it turned to face him with a look of surprise upon its face. Jon lifted the camera and took a shot. The flash lit up the park and the girl stopped crying and looked over at the source of the light-burst.

The figure turned and started to run back towards the woods, and Jon fired off two shots with the repeater air pistol. He saw a black spot appear in the left side of the man's neck upon the second shot and thought he heard him cry out.

'Run! Get out of here! Go on!' Jon bawled at the girl, and he saw her turn and run off. She fell at one point but got to her feet and ran back the way she had come. Jon walked slowly to the wood and saw no one – just that five-pointed star in the concentric circles – but he did detect that same aroma of incense which Gayle had noticed around her attacker. Jon had the strong sensation of being watched as he headed back to the observation tent and packed it up. Having a darkroom of his own, he developed the Ilford black and white film roll within hours of getting home, and he saw that there was no man in that photograph that he had taken – just a large out of focus orb of light. What's more, the rest of the film was fogged, even though most of the frames had not been exposed. Then came the silent telephone calls in the middle of the night, and about a week after this, Jon was awakened at his flat one morning at 4am by a loud bang that came from the front door. When he went into the hallway, he saw something sticking through the middle of his door. He opened that door and saw it was the blade of a short-handled axe. For over a month he was followed by a white car all over town, and when he had to pay a visit to a relative in Preston, the car even followed him there. Then one evening, Jon had been working late and arrived home just before 9pm, and when he came into his living room, he was startled by the presence of a smartly-dressed debonair man in his fifties. His black hair was slicked back, and he had grey sideburns and a grey van dyke beard. Jon reflexively lifted an ashtray stand, ready to strike the intruder, who remained calmly seated in Jon's favourite armchair. The stranger raised his hand and in a cultivated voice he said: 'No need for that Mr Harcourt, please relax. I've come here to warn you, not to harm you.'

'Who are you?' Jon asked, his heart pounding.

'That is irrelevant,' the man replied. 'Your life is in grave danger because of your stupid antics in Sefton Park. You don't know what you've got yourself into.'

'Are they Satanists? Did *they* send you?' Jon slowly put the ashtray stand down and looked to the doorway of the kitchen, wondering if the man had an accomplice in there.

'No, Mr Harcourt, they are not Satanists at all; they are much more dangerous and real than all these bogeymen and scare-stories in the Press.'

'What are they then?' Jon asked, and he felt a little safer now, so he reached behind himself and closed the door. With a little caution he advanced a few steps towards the well-spoken stranger.

'I've been looking at the books you read here,' the man swept his left hand in a semi circle at the entire wall of bookshelves, 'and I am sure you will have heard of the Hindu deity Ganesha; I prefer to call him Ganapati, but that's beside the point. Anyway, you will recall that Ganesha is always depicted with the head of an elephant?'

There was a pause, and the stranger had a peculiar, perceptive knowing twinkle in his eye as Jon recalled the elephantine entity with the trunk-like nose and large ears. 'Are you trying to tell me that the thing in the park was – Ganesha?'

'Certainly not!' answered the seated stranger. 'But just as you and I are distant relatives of the ape and dolphin, the thing you saw in the park is a distant cousin to the entities the people on this plane refer to as Ganesha. The thing you saw was one of the Morgra. They have been intruding into our dimension since the days of the dinosaurs, and they have a very peculiar sexual fetish for human females.'

'How would you know all this?' Jon asked, filled with suspicion. 'What are you even telling me all this for?'

'Because the Morgra have servants who worship them, and these people are literally slaves who have been brainwashed into doing anything for them, because they believe that when they die they will be reborn in paradise. If the Morgra will these slaves to kill you, they'll simply do it without questioning it.'

Jon could hardly take all of this in. 'Okay, if this is true, how can I avoid being killed by them? I take it that's why you're here?' he asked the stranger.

'It's laughable really, but there are certain places on this earth where they have great difficulty exercising their power, and one such place is Avebury – you must have heard about this place?'

'Yes, it's a village in Wiltshire surrounded by a circle of ancient standing stones,' Jon recalled.

'Three circles of standing stones,' the stranger corrected him, 'and there's a good reason for this, lost in the mists of antiquity. Some of the ancients knew of the Morgra and their sorcerers and wizards discovered that the Morgra could be kept at bay if a dwelling was encircled by certain stones. I strongly advise you to move to Avebury, or you'll soon be dead. And even after death they can still use you. They sometimes instruct their followers to exhume the dead and they resurrect them to be used as slaves.'

Jon recalled the testimony of Allison the librarian, who said she had seen some arcane ritual in the woods in Sefton Park involving what seemed to be an open coffin.

'Why won't you tell me who you are?' Jon asked the night visitor. He was obviously a man who had a great knowledge of the occult.

'Just think of me as a guardian, Jon. I try to keep things in balance – try to even the odds a little. So, will you do as I say? Or will you become just another unsolved murder victim?'

'I don't know – I don't like running away – it's not my style – I'm not a coward.'

'Better to be a coward for a moment than dead for the rest of your life,' was the man's swift reply.

'I don't run away,' Jon insisted, 'never have done.'

'He that fights and runs away, lives to fight another day,' the stranger retorted with glaring eyes, then his harsh gaze softened and he smiled: 'I know you're not a coward; just think of this as a strategic withdrawal – and – you may be able to help me at some time in the future.'

'I don't know,' Jon told him, confused. 'I'd dearly love to know who you are though. Are you – ' And as he was still talking, Jon saw the man literally vanish before his eyes. He walked slowly to the empty armchair and felt the seat with his palm – it was still warm; he had not imagined it, and yet he almost doubted his senses. On the following morning as Jon drove to work, he discovered that his brakes were not working and so he tried to stop the vehicle by applying the handbrake – but it transpired that it had been interfered with too – and the only way Jon could bring the vehicle to a halt was by dropping to the lowest gear and driving into a park where he was stopped by a row of bushes. That night, Jon suffered terrible nightmares of weird entities with black and grey leathery skin and trunks for noses, and they were egging various people on to commit gruesome murders, and Jon felt as if he was going through time in the dream, because he could see some soldier in chainmail raping and afterwards mutilating a woman with a sword, and then the scene changed and he saw a crazed knifeman carving the breasts off a woman who lay dead on a bed in a room that looked Victorian. When he awoke, gasping for his breath with his heart pounding like a drum, he had the unfamiliar word "Senar" echoing in his mind. Jon recalled it was the very same mysterious word he had seen carved in that tree near the pentagram in the park, and he researched the word, even consulting ancient Saxon dictionaries, but never discovered what the word meant. Jon took his holidays a little earlier than normal and went to stay at a simple bed and breakfast down in Avebury, and sure enough, while he was down there, no further harm came to him and he enjoyed a restful nightmare-free sleep. With great inconvenience he resigned from his job as a quantity surveyor and after being unemployed for several months, he landed a job as an administration assistant to a small electronics firm. He felt much safer from the malevolent powers of the Morgra as long as he lived within Europe's largest Neolithic stone circles. What became of Jon Harcourt after his drastic relocation to Avebury is unknown, but I suspect that 'guardian' who appeared in his flat that night may have kept his word and enlisted Jon's help in fighting a menace few people in this reality are aware of. Sefton Park *continues* to be the scene of some very strange goings-on. In my book, *Tales of the Weird 3* I mentioned the curious case of the Sefton Park Centaur – a weird man-horse hybrid creature seen by many witnesses in the Summer of 1963. I have also collected many reports over the years of what seems to be the same frightening entity which I call the Nameless Horror because I simply can't classify it, and it fills people with intense fear whenever it confronts them. The Horror is always described as a cloud of dark smoke or something resembling a swarm of flies, and it buzzes and crackles with what sounds like static electricity as it floats along a few feet off the ground. Some witnesses reported seeing two large disc-shaped eyes in the gaseous mass and others have seen what looks like long thin arms or tentacles reaching out from the insubstantial body. A woman walking her dog in Sefton Park one wintry evening in February 1982 saw what looked like a rolling ball of smoke, about five feet in height, coming towards her. Before the globular ball of greyish vapour reached the woman, her dog yelped and ran off with such force, it yanked its leash out its owner's hand. The woman then experienced what she could only describe as a very severe panic attack, and as the cloud enveloped her she found her face and hair tingling with static electricity. She turned and tried to run but was unable to breathe, and suddenly her legs felt weak. Somehow she stumbled away, and then the cloud left her and went back the way it had arrived. I later mentioned this incident on a local late-night radio phone-in show where I'd been invited as a guest to discuss the paranormal, and dozens of calls were made to the radio station from people who had also encountered the rolling ball of electrified gas. One man said he had encountered the entity in the Palm House back in the 1960s, and had found himself suffering an asthma attack as a result of the encounter, and a woman named Helen said an object which resembled a cloud of dark smoke had chased her from the other side of the boating lake in Sefton Park one summer evening in 2012, actually crossing the surface of the lake as it closed in on her. The woman ran out of the park filled with terror, and when she got home her mother noticed that Helen's hair was literally standing on end with the amount of static electricity in her body. Helen's new quartz-regulated watch also began to lose time after this incident – perhaps because of the electrical surge from that 'cloud'. These are just a few of the many reports I've collected of the Nameless Horror, which some have dismissed as nothing more than a meteorological anomaly – perhaps a form of the much-misunderstood ball lightning phenomenon. I'm currently looking into a similar gasiform being which has been seen in nearby Greenbank Park by witnesses as varied as a landscape gardener, a birdwatcher and a postman. This entity gives off quite a stench and has even flown out of the park and chased cars and even a fox, but the miasmic menace is about only half the size of its aeriform cousin in Sefton Park, and no one has mentioned the same feeling of absolute fear which the Sefton Park entity seems to evoke in those it attacks.

THE SAD TALE OF JAMES

In 2009, two mysteries began to unfold in Liverpool's Georgian Quarter which had a supernatural connection. Tayleur, a 20-year-old student studying art at Liverpool John Moores University, received a rambling letter, purportedly from a man named James, telling her how much he loved her, ever since he had first set eyes upon her as she had passed him on Hope Street. James said he had written the letter via a medium – because he was a ghost. Tayleur thought the two-page letter – written in erratic block-letter handwriting - was just some practical joke – but more letters arrived, and they seemed to get progressively more emotional. Meanwhile, over on Huskisson Street, a 45-year-old medical receptionist named Libby had discovered that she was not only sleepwalking, but 'sleepwriting' as well. She had been seen visiting the pillar box at the corner of her street and Catharine Street, less than forty yards from her flat, dressed in her pyjamas, at 3 in the morning on two occasions by friends and neighbours. Her suspicions about her unconscious night-time trips had been alerted before she had been seen sleepwalking, because she had found four postage stamps missing from her bureau and had recalled vague dreams of a man in a top hat and black turned-up moustache dictating letters to her. Libby paid a visit to her doctor and told him about the sleepwalking and sleep-scribbling, and he called this latter sleep disorder 'somniscription' in which a person writes and even types whilst unconscious. Stress was usually to blame, said the GP, and he advised Libby to take a hot relaxing bath each night before bedtime. Libby turned detective and examined her writing pad. She could see the faint impressions of the text she'd penned on what had been the underlying page of the pad she'd written the letter on – and by rubbing a pencil lightly across the paper she saw it was addressed: 'Dear Tayleur'. She mentioned this titbit of information to her workmate Izzy, and she said her daughter had a female friend with that very name and its unique spelling – and this girl happened to be an art student. Through her daughter, Izzy discovered that Tayleur had indeed been receiving weird 'love' letters, and eventually Libby and Tayleur met up at a café on Falkner Street. Libby swore that she was not some nut, and that she really had been sending the letters in her sleep, apparently dictated by man in old-fashioned clothes named James. Tayleur was very opened-minded and said she believed Libby, and suggested contacting a medium. Libby was open to this idea, and Tayleur eventually asked a medium named Saffron in Mossley Hill to help. To test the medium, Libby and Tayleur did not mention "James" yet the psychic said the ghost of a Victorian man named James was present when she came out to Libby's house. Saffron told Tayleur: 'He saw you on Hope Street one day, and was fascinated by your coloured hair. He watched you taking pictures of flowers and things with your phone in St James's Cemetery.'

Tayleur often *did* take snaps of flowers with her phone for inspiration. The medium continued: 'He knows it's silly and very forward of him but he wants to marry you, Tayleur. He used Libby to write his messages while she was asleep. That was the only way he could tell you he loved you.'

'How can I marry a ghost?' Tayleur asked, and she grinned yet seemed tearful as she posed this question.

The medium shrugged and said: 'He's crying now. He's just walked away through the wall.'

'Tell him to come back,' Tayleur said, choked up.

'James, did you hear that?' the medium asked, her eyes looking towards the wall.

All three of them then detected a sweet smell reminiscent of violets.

After that day, Libby had no further dreams about the ghost and her sleepwalking and the somniscription ceased. Tayleur later fell in love with a living person, a boy the same age as her named David, and James was heard from no more. It may be a coincidence, but there is a ghost of a man in a top hat who is sometimes seen lingering around the part of Falkner Street where Tayleur once had her flat. It could be anyone's ghost, given the history of that quarter and the number of hauntings in that area, yet I can't help but feel that this lonely shade is that of James. In my long experience with the supernatural, I have learned that many ghosts are very sentimental beings and they seem to cling on to the memories of old loves and visit the places they walked when they were alive – and in love...

MR IMPOSSIBLE

There have been so many famous visitors to the Philharmonic pub over the years. Bing Crosby enjoyed a drink there after a charitable clandestine visit to the Convent of Notre Dame on Hope Street in the 1950s, and even Superman – the late Christopher Reeve – drank at the pub around the time of his visit to the Everyman Theatre in the early 1970s. There's also a largely forgotten claim that JRR Tolkien sometimes downed a few pints of beer at the Phil in the 1950s during his visits to Lancashire (where his sons were being schooled). Shining bright among the glittering pantheon of eminent visitors to the pub are the Beatles, who occasionally supped there in their student days, but there have also been other phenomenal performers who have graced the premises of the Phil – and one of these was "Mister Impossible" – a sort of cross between Tommy Cooper and Derren Brown - who pulled off many baffling wizardly tricks at the pub during his self-appointed tenure in the late 1960s. Impossible wore an immaculate black suit, satin green tie and a bowler hat (which he made his collection with), and this barroom Merlin usually carried a rather creepy doll named Razzmatazz that could speak, sing and tap-dance – even at some distance from its 'operator' – but just how this was achieved remains an unfathomable mystery. Impossible told very surreal jokes, did all the usual magician's card tricks, and apparently read minds too. He would also roll up a broadsheet copy of a newspaper, make cuts to it, place it in a plant pot and play snake-charmer music on a pungi as the newspaper stalk grew and sprouted leaves until it reached the ceiling. The sceptics said the newspaper plant trick was all down to hypnotism, and the cynics also maintained that hypnotic influence was responsible for Mr Impossible's levitation routine as well as his eerie ability to exhale cigar smoke that would coalesce into the faces of deceased people, but harder to explain was the magician's generation of extra limbs – known as 'pseudopods' in the psychic world. Mr Impossible would reach out from under his coat with an extra arm and shakes hands with people. Two Liverpool University students, Pru and Judy, became obsessed with discovering Mr Impossible's secrets, but could never catch him out. Judy eventually came to the conclusion that the pub entertainer was no mere illusionist but a man with genuine miraculous abilities – perhaps even someone working in league with the Devil. Pru thought her friend's notion was ridiculous – and Pru certainly didn't believe in the supernatural and the concept of a Devil. Then, one Saturday evening there was a knock at Pru's flat on Percy Street. She got out her bath, wrapped herself in a towel and went to the door. 'Who is it?' the student asked, unwilling to open the door because she only had a towel wrapped around her naked body. She was supposed to meet her boyfriend John at the Ye Cracke pub at 8.30pm and she wondered if he'd decided to call for her instead. Pru thought she heard what sounded like a child's voice shouting 'Help me!'

'Hello? Who is that?' she asked, her ear to the door.

No reply came, and worried that some child might be lost or in some danger, the student opened the door – and she got quite a start when she saw who – or what – had called at her flat.

It was Mr Impossible's puppet Razzmatazz. He stood there, twelve inches tall, wringing his hands as he looked up at Judy with a sad expression. The doll cried: 'Help me, please! I've run away from him Pru! I'm not a real puppet! He trapped my soul in this doll! Please hide me!'

Pru gathered the towel around her thighs. She knew it was just a doll, and yet she reflexively thought of it looking under the towel, and stepped back. Unsure what trick was being played by Mr Impossible, Pru stood there, gazing down at the little figure, a little annoyed at leaving a hot bath for this nonsense.

'I escaped but he'll be looking for me,' the doll said in a quivering voice. Pru believed it was all a ventriloquism act and that Mr Impossible was hiding somewhere on the landing. She hissed a swear-word under her breath and shook her head. She was about to slam the door on the doll – which, she reasoned, must be remotely controlled by the eccentric trickster, when Razzmatazz moved forward, with his tiny left foot inside the door of Pru's flat. The little man said: 'Do you *know* what Mr Impossible is? This might scare you but - '

Razzmatazz never got to tell Pru. A hammer swung from somewhere just to the right of the doorway in the hall and it smashed down repeatedly on the puppet, and as Pru screamed, a hand in a white glove grabbed the shattered doll and the student heard someone run off. All that remained of Razzmatazz was a little doll's eyeball. Mr Impossible was never seen again by anyone after that night, and for many years, Pru had recurring nightmares about that hammer smashing in the head and body of Razzmatazz. The student could not even bring herself to visit the Philharmonic public house after the weird incident, just in case she met Mr Impossible...

THE BOOTS

I've had to change a few names and some minor details in this strange account, which was reported to me many years ago. A Mr George Henry Wickham - a former Major with a distinguished military career who had served his country throughout World War Two but had reluctantly opted for retirement after the fiasco of the Suez Crisis - had become very bitter after being turned down for a post in the Diplomatic Service, apparently because he had quite a reputation for being cantankerous. Instead, Wickham landed a job as a clerk of works, and he channelled the bitterness from his disappointment with the army into being a professional overseer who would think only of the best interests of his client. One dark February morning in 1960, Wickham – now "happily divorced" from his long-suffering wife – left his flat on Knight Street and set off for a building site in Liverpool city centre. He swung his brolly as if it was a military swagger stick as he marched along in his bowler and pinstriped suit – when he suddenly realised he was being followed. The long narrow street had been empty when he had stepped into it but now Wickham could distinctly hear the metronomic thudding of someone behind him. He walked in the middle of the cobbled road and gripped his umbrella with both hands as if it was a rifle. He was ready to thrust the point of the brolly into the eyeball of this thug if he tried to rob him. He took a quick look over his left shoulder and saw no one there – and yet he still heard the heavy tread following him. Wickham was one of those rare people who somehow knew when eyes were upon him, and this uncanny sense had saved his life on many occasions when he was in enemy territory during the war and the many years of service with the army in other conflicts across the globe. He could definitely feel someone's gaze upon him, and yet he couldn't see another living soul about, and this really unnerved him. He hurried to Berry Street, where he saw a few other early risers on their way to work, and the 'invisible' robber's footfalls could no longer be heard. On the following morning when Wickham made his way to work, he again heard the heavy plodding sound of what seemed to be boots, and yet he saw no one about, although there was a fog present on this occasion. Again, as the clerk of works reached Berry Street, the out-of-sight stalker's footsteps immediately halted. As they did, the ex-military man thought he heard a voice in the fog behind him utter a profanity; it had sounded like the c-word, and had been spoken in quite a gruff way.

Wickham wondered if he was losing his sanity, and that afternoon when he was on his lunch break, he rode a hackney cab to a former military doctor named Sterling who had a surgery on Rodney Street. Wickham had known Sterling for over fifteen years, and he told the medical man about the sound of footsteps and the feelings of being followed from his flat. Sterling asked his old friend if he was still fond of the whiskey, and Wickham smiled as he proudly announced that he hardly drank at all nowadays, only on Saturday evenings at his club. 'Are you taking any medication at the moment?' Sterling inquired, and Wickham shook his head. Sterling began to light a pipe as he asked: 'You used to smoke opium with that Gaines fellow; you don't still do that in civvy life do you?'

'Certainly not!' Wickham seemed outraged by the suggestion and vigorously shook his head. 'That was a long time ago in Burma; I don't even smoke tobacco nowadays.'

'Well, George, I'm just a physician; I deal with the body, and this matter – thinking you're being followed and hearing footsteps, lies squarely in the domain of the psychiatrist.'

'I'm not hearing things or imagining this,' Wickham assured Sterling.

'Someone once said that a ghost is the outward and visible sign of an inward fear,' Sterling reflected, leaning back into his comfy leather chair as he eyed the wreaths of blue pipe smoke rising to the high ceiling. He had a slight grin on his face which vexed Wickham.

'I don't follow you Sterling; what are you trying to say?'

'Well, let me put it this way: have you got some skeleton in your cupboard old chap? Some unresolved matter from your past perhaps?'

'I came here for medical advice,' Wickham replied, already rising from his chair, ready to leave. 'I didn't expect to hear some sermon – '

Sterling coughed a cloud of smoke and interrupted his old associate. 'I'm just trying to help, but as I advised, George, you'd be better seeing a shrink.'

Wickham left in a huff and returned to the building site in a flaming mood.

The next day, as the former major went to work at 6am. Again he heard the familiar tread of intangible walker. This time, an enraged Wickham halted on Knight Street and turned to face the as-yet unseen prowler. There was no fog about on this bitterly cold morning, but Knight Street was then badly lit and the clerk of works had to narrow his watering eyes in the cold to make something of the two black objects that were approaching him along the ground; they were a pair of army boots – Wickham could see them distinctly. Whoever was in them could not be seen. Wickham shuddered at the sight, and he lifted his brolly, ready to take a swipe at the ghost. Then, from the back of Wickham's mind came the sneaking suspicion of this unearthly apparition's identity; *that* soldier they said he'd driven to suicide back in the days of extreme square-bashing because his boots were never highly polished enough. Major Wickham had made a laughing stock of the lad, telling the unit he was the scruffiest tramp of a soldier and comparing his boots to the worn-out clodhoppers of Chaplin's hobo. That lad had hanged himself with his bootlaces in the barracks. Yes! He had come from round here; he had lived in this neighbourhood. The boots ran forward and before Wickham could run they began to kick at him with a demonic power. He ended up on all fours with a fractured rib, damaged spleen, and a jaw that clicked when he opened and closed it. A policeman found the clerk of works on his knees in a shop doorway on Berry Street, and after helping him up, he asked Wickham who had attacked him.

'It's quite alright, officer, I deserved it,' Wickham admitted.

'Why sir? What did you do?' the policeman was bound to ask. Sometimes the policeman came across well-to-do homosexuals who had been beaten up after making advances to men. Homosexuality was not officially decriminalised until 1967 – and this was 1960. Wickham read the policeman's suspicious mind and assured him he had not been up to anything 'untoward' – but had simply got his come-uppance from a man whose life he had destroyed many years ago. 'It's strange, officer,' gasped Wickham, 'but I feel better – cleaner - for the hiding I received this morning. Could you do me a favour though? Could you call an ambulance for me? I'm finding it hard to breathe with these injuries.'

People talk about laying ghosts to rest, but sometimes the ghost may lay to rest an unsettled score with a member of the living. After that morning George Wickham never heard those boots again.

MARIANNE

A few years ago a 51-year-old Liverpool man named Nathan decided to apply for the position of a security officer at a warehouse in the city centre. Life was getting Nathan down of late. He'd found himself unemployed when the factory he had worked at (as a fork-lift operator) had gone bust. His wife Tracy nagged him constantly about getting another job, and his two lads, aged eleven and thirteen, had started to hang around with a violent gang. The pressures of life had become so intense, Nathan would sometimes take off in his minivan in the evenings and drive aimlessly around the city, chain-smoking and sipping diet Coke, just to escape from his awful life for a while. His wife hated it when he drove off like that and was always threatening to leave him because of the periodic desertion. Then he landed the job as a security guard. The pay was not as good as the fork-lift number but it was better than trying to live on the disgracefully low amount of benefit 'awarded' to him by the Government. The warehouse was only guarded by Nathan and a man in his early forties named Paddy, and on the third night at the job, he complained of feeling unwell and asked Nathan if he could sneak home for a few hours as he really felt light-headed.

Nathan was very sympathetic to Paddy and said he'd be okay doing the shift alone, but about fifteen minutes after Paddy left the place, Nathan was unscrewing his thermos flask, intending to pour himself a banana-mango smoothie, when he heard music somewhere. It was hard to say exactly where this music was coming from and it was just as difficult to identify the song. After about two minutes, the distant music stopped abruptly, and the cavernous cathedral silence of the vast warehouse returned to engulf the guard. Most of that warehouse was in darkness that time in the morning, and Nathan was sitting in a small area lit by a soft disk of light from a solitary energy-saving bulb. Nathan decided that the music had been from the radio of some car which had been waiting at the lights outside. The time was now approaching 3am. Nathan had a little DAB radio tuned to Radio 2, and was half-listening to the music and banter, just for company. Around this time, the sensation of being watched by someone began to unaccountably grow on the guard. He thought he heard a sound somewhere amongst the labyrinth of towering shelves stacked with dodgy clothes bound for the bargain stores of the streets. Yes, someone was definitely in the warehouse, because he could plainly hear the swish of fabric – a kind of rustle – but when he swept his high-powered torch about, he saw no one. He knew he had not imagined it, and under his breath he hissed, 'Come on you robbing bastard, I'll kill you.' He wasn't supposed to bring any offensive weapons into work but he had hidden a baseball bat in his locker. He'd use it rather than sustain life-changing injuries from some desperate smackhead or audacious young robber – and deep down, he knew the truth behind his violent stance – his life at home was really getting him down and he'd had enough. He felt that even a prison term would be better than the life he was enduring. He turned the radio off and listened. The place was as dead as the grave again. All he could hear now was the mournful drone of a plane coming in to land at the airport. He unlocked his phone and called Paddy. The guard took ages to answer and his voice was echoing because he was in the toilet. He said he'd just thrown up and was obviously coming down with something. Paddy believed it was the norovirus vomiting bug, and decided he wouldn't be coming in, and would have to stay off till he got better, he informed Nathan.

A guard aged twenty-six was Paddy's temporary replacement. His name was Curtis and he'd only been a guard for a fortnight. He was a quiet lad and always had his head in a Penguin Classics paperback when he wasn't doing the rounds. On the second night on the job, at around 1.40 am, Nathan was on the toilet, when Curtis came knocking on the door.

'Is that you, Curtis?' Nathan asked.

'Yeah, come and have a listen to this, mate!' the young man had urgency in his voice.

Nathan sighed, annoyed, and got up off the seat. He came out less than a minute later and saw that the face of his colleague looked pale.

'It's stopped now,' he said, his head tilted to the left, and his eyes swivelled to the right. 'There was a song blasting out in here!'

'What?' Nathan immediately thought of the faint music he had heard three nights ago.

'She was singing something like "you're not alone",

and something about "open your mind" – or your eyes!' Curtis told Nathan, and he seemed rather unnerved by what he'd experienced.

'Sound travels further at night, mate,' said Nathan, and he smiled, trying to reassure his nervy workmate he had not heard something supernatural. 'It's the bare brick walls in this place; it's like an echo-chamber in here at night.'

'This was deffo in *here,* mate and it was coming from over there,' Curtis pointed to the far corner on the left, towards a dark archway about thirty feet in height. 'It was a woman singing, and it sounded like the songs me mum plays – the old dance stuff from years ago.'

With a smug smile, Nathan nodded and said: 'I heard music myself a few nights ago – it was just a car radio but because it's of a night the sound carries – you think it's in here but it isn't.'

'I know what I heard mate, honest,' Curtis insisted, watching the shadowy maze of shelves. 'It wasn't outside, it was *in here*; I'm amazed you never heard it when you were on the bog.'

'Curtis, listen up a sec, mate – bit of basic advice: don't start letting your imagination get the better of you when you're on duty, because you'll freak yourself out, yeah?' Nathan's eyebrows lifted and vanished behind his short fringe.

'Wasn't imagination though, mate – ' Curtis retorted, chafed by his colleague's unshakable scepticism.

'Come on, lad,' Nathan walked back to the little table under the dreary energy-saving lamp.' Let's have a coffee and you can have one of my sarnies if you want; prawn mayonnaise they are.'

On the way to the island of light with the table and

chairs upon it, Curtis never once took his eyes off that corner near the archway.

When the guards sat at the table, Nathan began to pour out the coffees from his thermos flask as Curtis wrote short sentences in longhand with a tiny betting shop biro in a notepad.

'What are you writing?' Nathan enquired.

'Jotting down bits of the lyrics of that song I heard,' Curtis replied. 'I'll Google them and see if there was such a song.'

Nathan rolled his eyes. 'You know what, all your generation are like this – wanting things to be mysterious and spooky. Everything's a conspiracy – '

Curtis opened the Safari browser on his phone and went to the Google homepage. Deftly using quotation marks and the plus symbol he inputted the lyrics he'd heard into the search engine. Then he saw a YouTube video of a song appear in the search results: *You're Not Alone* by a 'trip hop' group called Olive. Curtis played the YouTube video – and he felt an icy shudder go down his spine – it was the very same song he'd heard in the corner of the dark warehouse earlier.

'Talk about a blast from the past,' remarked Nathan, pushing a plastic cup of coffee to Curtis. 'I used to dance to that a long time ago and – Jesus!'

'What?' a jumpy Curtis thought Nathan had seen something behind him when he made that exclamation.

Nathan began to survey the dark interior of the premises as the realisation dawned on him. 'This warehouse was the club where I used to go with Marianne. It's all been altered and changed a bit since then, but this is the place; how strange.'

'This was a club?' Curtis asked, and tiny droplets of sweat formed on his forehead. He was scared and perspiring.

Nathan slowly nodded, his mind back in 1996. 'Yeah, we used to go here – and sometimes the Buzz and a few other places, but this place had a very strange atmosphere; everyone mentioned the atmosphere.'

'Is Marianne your missus now?' Curtis asked, and sipped the sugarless coffee.

'No, she died,' Nathan replied, and his voice faltered into a pause.

'Oh, I'm sorry,' Curtis tore the little pink bag containing sweeteners and dropped two in the bitter coffee.

Nathan looked at the corner of the table as he recalled those events of so long ago. 'They said it was natural causes; she'd just turned twenty-two. We found her in bed.'

'Was it serious?' Curtis asked.

'What do you mean?'

'Was it a serious relationship?'

'Oh yes, fairly serious yes. She was my first real girlfriend. We were going to get engaged,' Nathan told the young guard. His eyes glistened – as if he was about to cry.

'I'm sorry for bringing it up, mate,' Curtis apologised and turned the phone off.

'Funny thing is – that song – the one by Olive - *You're Not Alone* - that was our song. Every couple in my generation had a song. That was our one. '

Curtis said nothing in reply. He felt as if Nathan had more to get out of his system regarding the loss of the girl.

'She used to say she'd wait until the end of time for me, and that's what the singer says in that song. It's like word for word the way we were. We were both very clingy towards the other.'

'Love, isn't it?' said Curtis, with a soft smile.

'Yes, it was.'

There were no further incidents that night, and weeks passed without incident. Paddy returned to the job and moaned to the boss when the security firm kept on Curtis on a part-time basis. Paddy didn't like the young man for some reason. All Paddy talked about was money, gambling on the horses and online poker. Curtis was interested in philosophy and the metaphysical, and the books he read on the long watches of the night annoyed Paddy. Nathan never mentioned the 'phantom music' incidents to the mundane-minded Paddy, so he was very intrigued when Paddy returned from his rounds one night with a strange tale to tell. He didn't just come out with an account of his experience; instead he asked Nathan if people with the early signs of Alzheimer's Disease had hallucinations.

'I really couldn't tell you, mate,' Nathan confessed. 'I'm not a doctor. Maybe Curtis could tell you when he next comes in; that kid's pretty clever.'

'He's just a boring bookworm him; that's not brains, it's just book-reading – ' Paddy started to rant.

'Anyway,' Nathan interrupted, 'I take it you've seen something strange, and being a hypochondriac you think you're losing your marbles.'

'Yeah,' Paddy admitted, shaking his head. 'Around half two when you were here, listening to the radio, I was up at the north end of the warehouse, where it's pitch-black, and Nathan – God as my judge – I saw all these people dancing.'

'Dancing?' Nathan was stunned by his colleagues words.

'Yeah, dancing – not like ballroom stuff – like the ravers – you know, the clubbers – waving arms, jumping up and down, and what looked like lasers and flashing lights. And then it all just went!'

'What do you mean – "went"? You mean disappeared?'

'Yeah, like a light being switched off. On my kid's life, there must have been about a hundred people dancing there – and then they were gone.'

'What music was playing?' Nathan felt an eerie sensation course down his spine.

'Now, this is nuts as well – there was no sound – no music – juts all dancing and lights flashing, but no sound at all.'

'Have you been talking to Curtis?' Nathan asked, full of suspicion.

'Eh? What do you mean? What's he got to do with this?'

'So you haven't talked to him?'

'Why would I want to talk to him? What are you getting at?' Paddy was puzzled at the question.

'Me and him both heard music from the old clubs era – in here.'

'Why didn't you tell me?' Paddy was annoyed at not being told about the alleged incidents.

'I thought it might scare you, that's all, mate.'

'These things don't scare me; robbers with guns – yes – but ghosts – no. They can't hurt anyone – Our

Lord wouldn't let them.'

'This was a club – did you know that? Back in the 1990s,' said Nathan.

'No, I didn't know that. I heard it was a Waterworths fruit warehouse.'

'Well you heard wrong,' Nathan told him, and his eyes scanned the darkness behind Paddy. 'Do you remember the Buzz club and the Drome over the water and the State? You're not that young are you?'

'I remember the State, yeah – but I was into metal bands like Slipknot mate, not ecstasy and all that crap.'

'Well this was a club, and I used to come here. I took drugs, hardly really drank though. Just loved dancing till we let out around three.'

'What?' Paddy asked with a condescending smile, 'You used to be a raver?'

'Yeah, I know, we were all young once you know? I was a lot thinner then, good head of hair, very sharp, and there was a buzz in the air mate. Sex in those days was – well, anyway – you've experienced a timeslip in here tonight mate.'

'Do you think it's an omen?' Paddy asked, with dread creeping into his eyes.

'Nah! It's a scientific thing, mate – nothing supernatural about it. You know what it's like? Years ago, people reported stones falling out the sky and they were either disbelieved or the superstitious said it was a bad sign because angels were throwing stones down at us. But now we know that those stones were just meteorites. I think they'll understand timeslips like that in the same way one day.'

Nathan expected some feedback from Paddy when he made this analogy between timeslips and falling stones, but instead the guard's face became slightly flushed and he said: 'Ever tried to break wind and you do something else instead?'

'Oh my God, you're disgusting – ' Nathan stepped back from the lost cause.

'Turn that radio right up, I'm going the khazi,' he said, and hurried towards the toilet.

Nathan went home that morning at eight, and had only been in bed for a matter of minutes when he awoke to a slap across the face. He looked at his wife Denise sitting up next to him with her curlers in, and she had an expression of utter disgust on her face.

'I know that Marianne one liked it that way, but if you ever prod me up there again I'll cut it off!' Denise roared.

'Did you just slap me in the face?' Nathan growled from a bone-dry throat.

Denise told him he had been calling out the name of his "childhood sweetheart" in his sleep as he made thrusts into her *derrière*.

Nathan started to recall fragments of a dream in which he had sex with Marianne in the middle of some rave in that long-gone club with flashing lights and people dancing around them in a frenzy. He apologised to Denise and said he was overtired.

'Not content with our sex life eh? Going all perverted in your old age?' Denise rambled on. 'Thought the male menopause was all nonsense but they're right; once a man gets over fifty he thinks he's in his twenties again!'

'I was overtired!' yelled Nathan, feeling the side of his face where she'd whacked him. 'Hitting me when I'm asleep you stupid cow! I could have had a heart attack!'

She told him to turn over and face away from her in case he tried to have another go at her, and Nathan turned, dragging most of the blankets with him. Ten minutes later, Denise's hand slipped under his arm and rested on his chest, and in a meek voice she said: 'I'm sorry I hit you. You were saying her name; I got jealous.'

'She died seventeen years ago,' Nathan replied, and his left hand squeezed her hand at his chest. 'How could you be jealous of someone who's dead?'

'I know, but I've always had a jealous streak, I can't help it. Plus you hurt me.'

'I'm sorry,' said Nathan, and fell fast asleep.

He was back on duty at the warehouse at 8pm, and a strange thing happened the moment he entered the place. His company for tonight, Curtis, said, 'Here we are again. This is the rhythm of our lives.'

That throwaway line immediately struck a chord in the memory of Nathan: a song from long ago called *The Rhythm of the Night* by the Italian band Corona. Another song he associated with Marianne. The DJ was always playing that Eurodance hit at the club which had once existed here. Surely it had to be a coincidence?

That night, Curtis said he had heard more faint dance music at the north end of the warehouse, and that was why he was back off his round a lot earlier; he was absolutely petrified of anything supernatural. Then, at one in the morning, when the two guards were on their break, they both heard the sounds of someone approaching from out of that darkness beyond the fringes of the light which fell on their little base. The shuffling sounds and the faint pad of feet became so clear, Nathan and Curtis expected someone to appear, but the sounds stopped dead after about a minute. Curtis was due to go on his rounds in that haunted area of the warehouse at three, but Nathan said he'd go instead, as he knew how scared his young colleague was.

'I'll go with you if you want, mate,' Curtis proposed, 'it's not fair on you doing my work.'

'Nah, it's alright lad, stay here,' Nathan told him with a brave smile, and set off into the extensive darkness with only his torch. Nathan was trying to pretend he was unfazed by the strange goings-on in the warehouse, but he left his locker door open – so he was obviously distracted by something. Curtis was surprised to see the baseball bat resting in a corner of his colleague's locker. If the guards suspected non-supernatural trespassers in the warehouse, they could throw a few switches and turn on all of the neon lights in the place, and Curtis said he'd do this if Nathan asked him to during the rounds, but Nathan said he'd be okay. However, at 3.07am precisely, the little walkie-talkie on the table where Curtis was tackling a Sudoku puzzle suddenly bleeped and crackled, and the frantic-sounding voice of Nathan came from it: 'Curtis turn the lights on! Turn them on!'

Curtis jumped clean off the chair and almost fell against the wall where the row of black plastic switches was mounted on a board. He clicked them all – but no neon lights came on.

'Curtis, switch the lights on now!' Nathan sounded hysterical.

Curtis held the walkie-talkie to his mouth and said: 'I

switched them on but nothing's happened! Nathan? Nathan are you there?'

From the northern end of the warehouse came loud pulsing music, and flashing lights of blue and green. No reply came from the walkie-talkie, so Curtis went to Nathan's locker and grabbed the baseball bat. With the bat in his right hand and the torch in his left hand he set out for the northern end of the vast building – towards the sound of the dance music and the flashing lights – the music and the eerie lighting effects faded away. Curtis searched every aisle and even climbed ladders and walked a gantry which crossed the entire warehouse, but he failed to find any trace of Nathan. He was about to call the police when the entire factory lit up. Every neon light in the place came on, and then Curtis spotted Nathan staggering along an aisle close to the brick archway where the music always seemed to originate. He ran down to his friend and saw Nathan looked dazed.

Before Curtis could ask him where he had been, Nathan said: 'She came back – and they were all dancing with her – but they're all dead. Every one of them is dead.'

'I've been looking for you high and low, what happened?' Curtis asked, and he reached out and helped his beleaguered-looking friend along as he fired more questions. 'Who came back? Who were dead?'

All the way to the table at the other side of the warehouse, Nathan said, 'She came back,' over and over. When he finally reached the table, Curtis sat him down, and finding no coffee in the thermos flask, he opened a can of Diet Coke he'd brought in and gently placed it in Nathan's cupped hands. Nathan took a few sips and started to cry. He wiped the tears away. 'Marianne was there, and the place looked exactly as it had in the 1990s. I couldn't find my way back. I turned and looked around and saw only a crowd of people dancing. She threw her arms around me. Her face though, it looked so pale – there was something quite not right about her. Her eyes looked bloodshot. I recognised a few of the people dancing – and realised they were all people who had died. Dead people dancing. Marianne kept kissing my ear and whispering "Stay with us here" over and over.'

'I heard the music, just after you went on the round, and I saw the flashing lights,' said Curtis, and he looked over towards that northern end of the warehouse.

'They wouldn't let me come back,' Nathan wiped his eyes now with the backs of his hands and sniffled. 'They kept barring my way – all the dancers – and they were deadly serious. Some of their faces were hideous.'

'Maybe we should leave this place, mate,' Curtis suggested.

'I think maybe we should,' Nathan nodded. 'We can't leave now, but in the morning I'm handing my cards in. Denise will go mad, but I'm getting far away from here. The past - *my past* - will keep coming back otherwise.'

Seconds after Nathan said this, he and Curtis heard an explosion of deafening dance music which echoed throughout the warehouse. Nathan recalled the old song – it was *Klubbhopping* by the Klubbheads. As the security guards looked towards the source of the music, they saw coloured light filtering through the aisles of boxes – and a steady file of shadowy figures came from these aisles. They were headed towards Curtis and Nathan.

'That's them,' said Nathan, hardly able to gasp out his words in shock. 'What do they want?'

'I'm not staying to find out!' Curtis didn't even bother to get his things from the locker; he got up off the chair and he ran as fast as his legs could carry him to the exit door. Nathan followed closely and he heard voices shouting behind him. He was sure one of those voices belonged to Marianne, and he thought she had called his name as Curtis fumbled with the keys as he tried to unlock the door. With the shadowy phantoms just feet away, the two guards fled. Nathan went back to the warehouse in broad daylight that morning, yet he could detect the sinister, menacing atmosphere still hanging in the air there. He told his boss he was quitting because the place was haunted, and the boss said he was considering taking Nathan and Curtis to court for breach of contract and abandoning their posts. 'I really don't give a damn,' Nathan told him crisply, 'this place is haunted, and if I stayed here I'd end up joining them.'

'Are you on drugs?' Nathan's ex-employer asked as the guard walked away, out of the warehouse for good.

About a month after this, Nathan and his wife Tracy went to town, and after a pub crawl they went to A Passage to India – the popular Indian eatery on Bold Street. They had intended to go home after the meal, but began to reminisce about the days when they'd stay out all night, and so the couple went to a club. They only lasted about forty minutes at the modern dance club, finding they did not like the rap being played, nor the 'lame atmosphere' as Tracy called it.

And do the couple came out, and finding great difficulty in getting a taxi, the couple set off to the nearest thoroughfare, but during the walk, Nathan said he needed to have a pee. Tracy told him to tie a knot in it, but her husband insisted he was bursting, and he went down a narrow street that was practically devoid of any illumination from a lamp. 'That's right, leave me here,' Tracy grumbled as she watched Nathan's silhouette vanish round a corner in the eerie gloom of the street. 'I could be raped for all you care,' she added, and she tapped her feet on the pavement as the cold invaded her body.

Nathan unzipped and relieved himself against a wall – when he suddenly realised that he was urinating against the wall of that warehouse – the one he had worked in – and he felt a strange shudder upon this realisation. He swore under his breath because there was no end to his stream, and he had the spinechilling feeling of eyes upon him; he just knew someone was watching him, and the watchers were not living people. At last the stream ended, and he shook himself and zipped up – and he saw fingers of bone clasp his left wrist. He turned his head left a few inches – and there was Marianne, only her face was completely white, and her eyeballs were black, but glimmered. 'Nathan,' she said softly, and gripped his wrist. Nathan swore at the top of his voice and wrenched his wrist away from her skeletal hand. She let out a scream he will remember till the day he dies. He ran down the alleyway, and feeling a bit drunk he almost lost his balance. He nearly collided with Tracy, who had rushed down the alleyway because she had heard the scream and had wondered if something had happened to her husband.

'What happened?' Tracy asked, but Nathan grabbed her hand and he almost pulled her over as he yanked at his wife's hand. 'What's going on?' Tracy yelled, and fell onto one knee, hurting herself. She swore at her husband to stop but he kept looking back with a scared expression, as if he was expecting the Devil to come after him out that alleyway. When the couple got to the well-lit thoroughfare, Nathan looked into Tracy's eyes and said: 'She tried to grab me in that alley – Marianne. Her ghost – it tried to grab my arm. That's where that club was down there!'

From the ESP-like faculty that is borne of years of marriage, Tracy knew her husband was not lying, and his words scared her. 'We'll have to say prayers for her, Nathan, and tell a priest. It's like she won't give up on you.'

'Do you believe me, Trace? I swear I'm not making this up!' said Nathan, with tears in his eyes.

'I know you're not lying, love,' Tracy replied, and hugged him. Her face snuggled against his chest. 'She's not at peace, love, it's sad really.'

'Taxi!' Nathan yelled, and managed to attract the attention of a passing Hackney driver.

All the way back home the couple held hands, and were so shaken, they did not say a word of reply to the poor cabby who was trying to make conversation. Nathan and Tracy went to see a Catholic priest, and told him about Marianne, and they thought he'd say the ghostly incidents were all in Nathan's mind, but instead, the priest went down to the warehouse and had a word with Nathan's former employer. The Holy man obtained permission to bless every corner of the warehouse, and when he returned to the church, he telephoned Nathan and told him there were some 'lost souls' in the warehouse. They were mostly people who had died young, and the spirits had all gravitated to the place they had truly loved – the place where they had felt most alive when they walked the earth, and that was the site of the club, a place where they had literally danced in ecstatic states. 'I can't guarantee that the spirits will find their way to the place allotted to them in the hereafter,' the priest admitted, 'and I don't expect you to attend church from now on to keep them at bay. Perhaps you should try and forget about Marianne and move out of the city.'

Nathan moved up to Southport, and apart from the occasional innocuous dream about Marianne, the ghosts from his clubbing past seemed to have been laid to rest.

TRIX

Many of the ghost stories I look into remain a mystery; there is simply no rhyme or reason behind some of the unsolved hauntings, and the following sinister story is a case in point. It all started one foggy afternoon in February 1982. A 32-year-old woman named Rose Robinson left her home on Falkner Street with her two nieces – Cheryl, aged 10, and Amanda, 12 – and set off for town to do a bit of shopping. Rose had agreed to look after the nieces for the day as their mother recovered from an operation in the Women's Hospital on Catharine Street. The nieces really loved their Aunt Rose, finding her very young-minded and not at all stuffy and authoritarian as their other uncles and aunties. As Rose and the nieces walked down Hardman Street, Amanda stopped and picked up a very unusual pendant: it looked and felt as if it was made of sterling silver. Rose thinned her eyes as she gazed closely at the piece of jewellery and saw that it depicted a jester nailed to a cross. Rose thought the mock-crucifixion pendant was very blasphemous and told Amanda to leave it on the wall near the Unemployed Resource Centre, and the girl appeared to do this, but she slyly pocketed the crucified jester and walked on. Cheryl accused her sister of keeping the sacrilegious adornment and when Rose asked Amanda if this was true, the latter replied loudly that Cheryl was a liar. The nieces started arguing and Rose told them to be quiet or they'd be taken home and they finally piped down.

Rose called in to Rapid Hardware on Renshaw Street to buy a small can of gloss paint to decorate a bookshelf, and when she came out of the store, Amanda and Cheryl started to argue again. Rose halted and turned to tell them to behave – but she saw that the nieces were gone. With a mounting sense of panic, Rose went back into the hardware store, but the girls weren't there, nor could she see them anywhere on Renshaw Street. A guard at the store said he'd definitely seen the girls follow Rose out of the place onto the street. To make matters worse, the fog started to get thicker. Rose went to a nearby telephone box and called her grandfather, Len, who lived up in Halewood, and he and a neighbour named Joe immediately went out and flagged down a hackney cab which took them to Renshaw Street. Joe and Rose went to the police station to report the missing children as Len walked up and down Renshaw Street and the neighbouring streets. Len had only recently given up cigarettes, but was now so stressed, he nipped into a newsagents and bought a twenty pack of Embassy Regal. Len waved to a policeman and told him about the missing girls but the policeman said he had already been informed of the disappearance by radio from HQ and was actively looking for them. Within the hour, more police personnel and countless friends and relatives of Rose were out looking for the nieces, but they seemed to have vanished into thin air. Len was not a religious man, but he said a prayer, asking for help from God to find the children. He then had a strange hunch that the girls had not gone far, and he began to focus on one part of Renshaw Street – Heathfield Street. Over the many years I have spent looking into local supernatural phenomena, I have noticed how Heathfield Street often crops up in timeslips and other strange goings-on – almost as much as its neighbouring thoroughfare, Bold Street. Keith walked down this poorly-lit minor narrow street to Bold Street, hoping desperately to see Amanda and Cheryl. To Len's left was the loading bay entrance of Rapid Hardware, and to his right was a Charles Wilson's corner Bookshop. The fog was so opaque he could only see for a few feet, and a few people walking in the distance behind him were just faint shadows. Then Len heard a strange high-pitched voice behind him say: 'You'll never find them!'

Len turned, and got the shock of his life for two reasons; firstly the voice was from a man with a white painted face dressed as a jester in weird crimson attire and two-pointed fool's cap, and secondly, this oddball was holding a huge spear with an enormous lethal-looking tip. He grinned with a deranged look, and said: 'The girls are as good as dead!' His height must have been a little over six feet, Len estimated. Len immediately sensed that the jester was evil and of a paranormal nature, and as he looked at him, he felt the hairs on the back of his neck stand up. The eyeballs of the bizarrely dressed stranger were black, and his irises were just white rings, which added to the menace of his appearance.

Len suddenly said: 'Jesus, send this evil spirit back from whence it came.'

The jester stood there for a moment, and then a look

of utter hatred formed on its painted face and it shook the spear at Len in an aggressive way before silently running off into the fog. Len looked around to see if anyone else had been about to witness the outlandish entity, but the fog was so thick he could see no one. He heard children crying, and the sounds were coming from round the corner – on Renshaw Street. Amanda and Cheryl came out of the fog on Heathfield Street holding hands and trembling. Len ran to them and hugged the children with one embrace. 'Where have you two been? You've had everyone worried sick!'

The girls seemed unable to reply because they were sobbing so hard, but the older child, Amanda, said something about being kept in a fairground. Len took the children to a telephone box, called his home to let some family members know that the girls had been found, and then he managed to hail a taxi to take them home to their father. The mother of the children had not been told about the disappearance yet because she was recovering from her operation in hospital.

Once the girls were home and seated in front of the fire, they managed to describe just what had happened to them. They had come out of the Rapid Hardware store with Auntie Rose, arguing with one another, and when Rose had turned to tell them off, they had skilfully hid behind her back. This was a trick Amanda had often played. Then the girls had hidden behind a white van, giggling, but then, as they peeped out, someone grabbed the hair of both of them from behind – and the next thing the girls knew, they were in some fairground, but there was no one about and it was night. All of the rides and attractions were lit up with coloured bulbs, but there wasn't a soul about.

And then Amanda and Cheryl saw a strange little fat man, and one of his eyes looked huge. This man smiled, revealing large square teeth with big gaps between them, and he shouted something at the children which they couldn't understand.

The girls tried to escape from the fairground but there was a fence and railings around it, and through the fence, Amanda and Cheryl saw "weird, horrible people" who were laughing at them, and one of these people, an old woman, spat at them. The girls hid from the weird man with the oversized eye, and he almost grabbed Cheryl when she hid in a waltzer, but she kicked at him and ran off. This nightmare seemed to go on for hours, and then the children saw a dark fog come over everything, and the next thing they knew, they could see the orange lamp post lights of Renshaw Street.

'You didn't happen to see a jester dressed all in red, did you?' Len asked the girls, but they both shook their heads. He didn't tell them about the spear-carrying jester he'd met on Heathfield Street, because he knew that the account would only scare the girls even more. Len later saw the silver pendant of the jester on the cross which Amanda had found on Hardman Street, and he suspected the weird jewellery item had some bearing on the creepy abduction, so he threw it away. Len and the father of the girls went in search of the fairground, but it could not be found. That is not the end of the matter. Many years after this weird incident, I gave an account of it on a local radio show, and was afterwards contacted by about a dozen people who had heard of the jester with the spear. Three of them said they had seen him climb over a wall on Heathfield

Street and descend an old rusted ladder down to what is now a private car park for Network Rail. I doubted these reports at first, but upon examination of the wall, I found the ladder concerned, and it did indeed lead down to a part of Liverpool I never knew existed. Then I received a report from a man named Ian, a former heroin addict who used to shoot up down in this almost subterranean area in the 1980s. Early one summer morning around 1981, Ian was sitting on a small inflatable mattress in a corner of the sunken car park, partially hidden behind some wildly growing tall grass, when he saw a man dressed as a jester climbing the ladder lading to the wall on Heathfield Street. At the top of the ladder, the eerie-looking man in a red jester costume and hat, began to peep over the wall, as if he was watching someone. He was there for some time, just peering over the top of the blackened sandstone wall. But then Ian suffered a fit of coughing. Straight away, the white face of the jester turned, startled, and looked in his direction. I asked Ian if he carried a spear, as the jester had who Len had seen, and Ian said he did not, but he did quickly descend the ladder, and Ian, naturally assuming that a man dressed as a jester had to be unbalanced, made himself scarce in case the oddball had a knife. I also received calls from people who had not seen the jester themselves, but had heard about him hanging around that part of Heathfield Street, the back of Lewis's (Cropper Street) and that sunken car park belonging to the railway company. The general consensus from the reports was that the jester was nicknamed Trix, but whether this was his real moniker or just a nickname given to him, I cannot say. The whole case is quite bizarre, and all I'd say is that, if you are out after dark in the city centre, and are considering taking a short cut between Bold Street and Renshaw Street via that alleyway which passes through Heathfield Street, then please think again – just in case you bump into Trix – whatever he is...

RADIO MOOLAH

With it being April Fool's Day, taxi driver Charlie Rogers thought his mate, window cleaner Cyril Clarke, was pulling his leg about the "Phantom Tipster". Cyril stabbed his chubby index finger into the cabby's chest. 'Look, Charlie, I'm serious - there's moolah to be made from this; the penny only dropped before when I was cleaning Mrs Hale's bay windows. She asked me for a tip for the Grand National, and I thought *that's it*.'

'Go on,' Charlie sighed, then dragged on half of a Woodbine cigarette, 'what's the punchline?' He really did think Cyril was having him on, but his little friend got a bit irate.

'It's not a bleedin' joke, Charlie. Listen, dumb-bell, come with me to Maureen's Cafe and you can hear it for yourself!'

So, in a huff, Charlie accompanied Cyril to the little cafe near Duke Street and Cyril guided him to a quiet corner where an ancient radio rested on the napkins cupboard. 'That's it,' Cyril said out the corner of his mouth.

The waitress approached and Cyril asked for two coffees, and then he switched the radio on as his eyes darted about. The other six people in the cafe were all oblivious to the radio being switched on. Some were reading newspapers, some were mopping up the remnants of sunnyside-up egg with corners of toast, while others were staring in a brown study sort of way through the windows at Duke Street. After ten minutes of weather forecasts and constant yawning from Charlie, the radio announcer gave the sports news and results out – and Charlie heard him give out *tomorrow's* results – and the astonished cabby was particularly struck by the racing results. He yelled to the waitress to bring a pencil and paper, and he managed to jot down five of the names of the steeds that were mentioned. Those horses netted Charlie a pretty penny at the bookies.

Cyril asked the cafe owner Maureen if he could buy the old 'wireless' and she said, 'Oh no love, it belonged to my old mum that did – no, it's of what do you call it? It's of sentimental value, yeah and it's not for sale.'

'Pity about that, Maureen,' Cyril replied, 'would've given you a score for that like.'

'Twenty quid for a wireless?' Maureen came over and shot a quizzical look at the window cleaner. 'You could buy a brand new one for a fiver, Cyril.'

'Well, to tell the truth, ' Cyril began his fib, 'that wireless looks exactly like the one my old mum had, and er, that's why I wanted to buy it.'

'Sorry Cyril, it's not for sale,' was Maureen's last word on the matter.

Cyril wondered if he could break into the cafe and take the wireless; then he realised that Maureen would know he'd taken it because of the strange interest he'd taken in it. He became so overcome with greed and the lucrative opportunities the radio presented, he even thought about burning the cafe down so hopefully no one would even know he'd taken it away before the place was torched. Cyril felt a little disappointed with himself with these evil thoughts he was having, and he gave a little painful smile to Maureen, who was now behind the counter serving someone.

On the morning of Friday 2 April 1971, Cyril and Charlie were at that corner table listening to the radio with notepads and pens. The results of the Grand National were given out a day early by that mysterious announcer, and Charlie scribbled them down in his spiral-bound notebook, whispering the names of the horses as he quickly wrote them down: 'Specify – that's 28-1 as well! Black Secret – my brother-in-law's picked that one. Astbury...'

'Keep it to yourself, Charlie,' Cyril said through gritted teeth, 'you know what these earwigs are like in here; they can hear the grass grow.'

An old man came over and asked Cyril: 'Did that man on the radio just say the National's *been* run?' and Cyril froze for a moment, then produced a false laugh and told the old man: 'No, mate, he was talking about last year's National,' was Cyril's rapid reply.

'Oh,' said the oldster, 'I was gonna say, the National's tomorrow; I thought I was having a premonition then!'

'Premonition!' Cyril laughed and shook his head. 'You wanna get your ears syringed, mate!'

The elderly man left the cafe with a puzzled expression.

'The money we'll make from this,' whispered Charlie, 'trebles, accumulators, and Pools results.'

'Yeah, thanks to yours truly here,' quipped Cyril. 'You owe me one for this mate,' the window cleaner told Charlie, who had pound signs in his eyes.

'I got you this Cyril,' Charlie took out a bar of Cadbury's Fruit & Nut and slapped it on the table at Cyril's elbow. 'Just to prove I'm not continually on the take.'

'Good Lord, Charlie, your generosity knows no bounds – a bar of chocolate!' Cyril sneered – but grabbed the bar and unwrapped it anyway.

And then the window cleaner and the cabby heard a newsflash interrupt the sports results. The announcer said a policeman had been shot dead during a bank robbery in Liverpool's city centre. There was a pause in the newsflash, and then the announcer said: 'We've just heard that the policeman who was killed by the bank robbers was – ' And a name was given out – a name that Cyril and Charlie knew; it was the name of a policeman nicknamed "Jinxy" who often came into the same cafe's as them.

'We'll bring you more on this incident as it comes in,' said the announcer, 'and that is the end of this newsflash.'

'Jinxy gets shot?' said Charlie, and his mouth fell open. He seemed shocked.

'Tomorrow,' Cyril gave a nihilistic nod.

The two men were no fans of Jinxy but they couldn't let him die. 'He's got a lovely daughter named Janet,' Cyril recalled, 'and she's getting married in May too Jinxy told me.'

'We'll have to warn him,' Charlie reasoned through a fog of confusion.

'We can't, he'll wanna know how we know!' Cyril replied with a vigorous shake of his double chins. 'The plod will probably think we're involved with the robbers and the robbers will say we're snitches!'

'We can't just let him die, Cyril,' Charlie persisted, and sipped his lukewarm coffee.

'I know what to do,' said Cyril, with an animated

look in his eyes. 'I'll make a certain call.' Cyril made an anonymous call to the bank that day and warned them about the robbery. The police were informed of the warning and gathered near the bank in squad cars. When the robbers approached the bank they saw the police presence and abandoned the job – and Jinxy lived.

The weeks went by, and Charlie and Cyril made amounts of money they couldn't even spend. Charlie was good at hiding his newfound wealth, but it was a different matter for Cyril. Jinxy heard about Cyril throwing his money about in pubs, buying rounds for everyone, throwing parties galore and even racing around town in a flashy sportscar, and so he confronted him – and Charlie – at the cafe one morning.

'Where are you getting all the money from Cyril?' Jinxy asked, pulling a chair to the table where the two latest members of the nouveau riche were seated.

'What's it to you?' was Cyril's audacious reply. He was a bit tipsy from his champagne breakfast and had a false sense of superiority.

Jinxy's face leaned in close to Cyril's supercilious gob. 'Oh it's my business you see, when a window cleaner starts buying sports cars, booking holidays to the Mediterranean, and throws parties almost every night. Where did you get the money from?' Jinxy slammed his fist down on the table. All of the customers looked to the source of the shouting.

'I've been saving, constable,' was Cyril's reply, and he turned to Charlie for back up, asking: 'haven't I Charlie? Cashed my insurance policy in as well.'

'Do I look stupid?' Jinxy asked Cyril, who grinned at

the question, more out of nerves than sarcasm.

'Alright Jinxy, I'll tell you why I'm loaded, but you'll never believe me!' Cyril told him.

'Try me, Cyril, I'm all ears,' Jinxy advised him.

'See that radio, there?' Cyril pointed to the wireless set on the napkins cupboard.

'Yeah,' Jinxy half turned to eye it, 'what about it?'

Cyril told him how a man on that radio could somehow give out results to horse races, boxing and football matches, as well as reports of news that hadn't even happened yet.

'Are you on drugs, or has all the drink addled your brain?' A sceptical Jinxy asked. 'Now come on, big spender, where are you getting all your dosh from?'

'Look, I can prove it,' Cyril leaned over to the radio and switched it on. He turned up the volume control a little, and then he sat back on his chair and said to the policeman: 'Just pin your ears back and listen to this – you won't believe it.'

Jinxy gave a slight smile and shook his head, then turned to look at the radio.

The announcer on the wireless was saying: 'Arsenal became Football League Champions last night when they beat Tottenham Hotspur one nil at White Hart Lane...'

'They don't play till tonight, that's phoney – ' was Jinxy's reaction to the news from the future.

'Yeah, but Arsenal *will* win tonight, just you wait,' Cyril said with a smug grin, 'now listen to rest Jinxy – all the gee gees that are going to win – and you can walk out of here in a minute and place your life savings on them if you want – and you'll make a fortune!'

'It's got to be a trick, ' Jinxy decided, and got out of

his chair and examined the radio. 'All kidology! There must be a wire going to a room in here where someone's got a microphone. Someone's having us on!'

'No one's having us on, Jinxy' Cyril assured him, 'and we know because we've profited from this little wireless.'

Jinxy examined the mains flex that went to a plug; that was the only wire leading to the radio. He was baffled by the strange situation. 'But how can this thing be picking up news before it happens? It's impossible,' the policeman muttered.

Cyril coughed and addressed the confounded constable. 'Jinxy, with all due respect mate, you – and I for that matter – are not scientists, so we'll never know how that wireless does what it does, but let's cut to the chase; you keep your mouth shut about this money generator and you can benefit from it as well.'

Jinxy noticed Charlie writing down the horseracing results, and he eventually realised where Cyril had obtained his sudden wealth. He smiled, and a strange expression came upon his face as he was overcome with unmitigated greed. He unplugged the radio.

'Hey, I was listening to that!' Charlie looked up at the dead radio with his biro still poised above the notepad.

'You two have had enough from this thing,' Jinxy looked wide-eyed at the radio. 'Now it's time this underpaid bobby had a slice of the cake.'

'Eh?' Cyril was baffled by the policeman's words. 'What are you talking about?'

Jinxy lifted the wireless and wrapped its flex around it. 'I'm taking it, alright?' he said. He carried it away from the cupboard.

'Hey!' Maureen squealed and came over. 'Aye-aye! Where are *you* going with that? That's mine!'

'It's stolen property, love, I'm taking it in,' Jinxy told her, then said, 'open that door for me,' as he negotiated his way around tables and bemused customers.

'I'll report you!' Maureen promised, 'That was my mam's wireless! It's a heirloom.'

'Hey, put it back, Jinxy,' Cyril got up from his chair, and so did Charlie. The two men followed him to the door. Cyril wanted to clobber the copper for taking the goose that had been laying so many golden eggs.

'Its stolen property, shut up!' Jinxy said, and as he tried to open the cafe door with his right hand, the radio slipped from under his left arm, and smashed to pieces on the floor.

'Timber!' some customer shouted.

'You've destroyed it you stupid plod!' Cyril cried, looking at the radio's tuning knob rolling across the floor. He bent down and looked at the slivers of glass from the shattered thermionic valves and the candy-striped resistors and greasy brown capacitors on a broken circuit board protruding from a huge crack in the bakelite body of the wireless.

Jinxy had the wireless repaired, but the Phantom Tipster never spoke on that radio again.

JEREMY

I've changed a few names in this weird story for legal reasons. One hot drowsy afternoon in the summer of 1960, PC Roger Marker, a hard-boiled street-wise bachelor in his forties, was on his Lime Street beat, when he heard a male voice cry out: 'Hey, plod!'

He naturally thought some juvenile delinquent had shouted the remark, as the voice sounded young – possibly teenaged. Plod is a derogatory slang term for a police constable that is rarely used nowadays, but it was in common usage back in 1960. There are four giant stone lions on the stretch of Lime Street where Marker heard the offensive outcry and this impertinent voice seemed to come from the second lion from the rightmost one. Marker hurried to the other side of the statue but there was nobody there. He walked backwards about twelve feet, hoping to see the name-caller behind the other stone lions – but saw no one.

'Up here!' said the invisible speaker. It was coming from the head of the lion he'd been passing when he first heard the prankster. Marker knew it had to be ventriloquism – some joker was throwing his voice – and yet, as far as the copper could ascertain, no one was near the lions. He therefore wondered if some adolescent driver or passenger in a passing car on the busy thoroughfare had yelled at him out of plain mischief. No, on reflection, Marker decided the cheeky young man was hiding nearby.

'Show yourself!' Marker shouted, and he got the

shock of his life, because the head of the lion nearest to him was no longer looking straight ahead – it was tilted down to face him! How could that be? It was a solid statue, one of the four massive lions sculpted by one William Grinsell Nicholl in 1855 and moved to their present positions in 1864. They were not jointed – they could not move, and yet the head of this one was now eerily angled downwards to face Marker.

'Who are you?' the astounded policeman found himself asking this statue, no longer doubting the origin of the voice.

'Jeremy, and your name's Marker,' came the reply, and the policeman's discriminating ears now fixed the origin of the voice – it was indeed coming from the apparently animated leonine sculpture. Marker stood there, mute with shock. Then he managed, 'This is impossible.'

'And yet I speak,' said Jeremy, 'so listen to me. The criminal, Eddie Croucher is in the Legs of Man.'

Then the statue became silent.

'Eddie Croucher? How do *you* know where he is? Hello?' PC Marker asked the graven maned head, but he found the silence unnerving, and so he backed away, doubting his sanity. He crossed Lime Street, walking between a slow stream of vehicles, and out of curiosity, he paid a visit to the Legs of Man pub on the corner of Lime Street and London Road – and, lo and behold, there was the lanky distinctive figure of Eddie Croucher, wanted for a string of bank robberies, leaning on the bar. He was wearing an obvious false beard and a long overcoat which did not look right in this summer heat. He was very surprised when Marker slapped his hand on his shoulder and called out his name. He claimed he wasn't Croucher , and that he was a Polish sailor, and talked in a poor attempt at a Polish inflection mingled with a heavy nasal Liverpudlian accent.

'You can tell Judge Laski all that, mate,' Marker replied, and pulled Croucher's beard off. All the drinkers in the bar roared with laughter at the unmasking of the fugitive bank robber. Marker took him to the station and the CID men asked Marker how he'd collared the most wanted man in the city. 'I just got lucky, that's all,' the constable told them, not daring to tell the unearthly truth, and he added: 'Just a matter of keeping your eyes peeled.'

Over tea at 5pm that day, Marker *did* tell his mother about the voice of the mysterious personage calling itself Jeremy down on Lime Street – and she knew her son had never once lied to her in his life – but she said Jeremy *must* have been someone who had it in for Croucher, throwing his voice as he hid somewhere.

'I didn't see anyone hiding behind those statues Mam,' Marker insisted, enjoying a chop, 'I looked, and saw no one.'

'You'd be surprised how sound travels, Roger,' his mother assured him, pouring him a cup of tea. 'Sound bounces off things and echoes. It's been some other ne'er-do-well who's known Eddie Croucher was in that pub.'

Marker grimaced. 'I don't think that's the case Mam, to be honest. You'll say I'm silly but I had the feeling Jeremy was – ah nothing; it *is* silly.'

'You think it was a ghost – ' Mrs Marker sugared the tea, poured a little milk into the cup and stirred it. She had a slight grin on her face.

'I don't know,' Marker admitted, 'I don't know what to think.'

'If you hear Jeremy again down on Lime Street, Roger, you have a good look about and you'll see him, but I bet you *won't* hear from him again now because he's been in the right place at the right time, this fellah, and pulled one on you.'

'I hope I *don't* hear from him again, Mam,' Roger told her, 'I got a right shake on when I heard him.'

'You *are* silly sometimes Roger,' Mrs Marker chuckled. 'Your late father was like you, very superstitious. There's always a rational explanation for any so-called ghost.'

A week later, Marker was back on the Lime Street beat, and this time it was 6am. He purposely slowed down and lingered by *that* lion. A lone Morris Minor van slowed down as it approached, and then it halted, and the front passenger wound down the window and asked for directions to Stafford Street. Marker duly gave the man directions, and watched the van drive off towards the Commutation Row and London Road junction, and then he turned and looked at the lion. He walked on a few yards on this early beat, when he suddenly heard that familiar voice. This time it sounded brighter and upbeat. It said: 'Morning Marker. Here's another tip-off...'

As it spoke, the policeman rushed around the plinth of the statue and returned to his starting point. He saw no one.

'Now, now, Mr Marker,' said the voice, 'you'll never find me. Now listen; if you will go to a gardenia green door on Back Bittern Street, you will see a sign on it that says "John Scilly, Printer" and if you go inside right now you'll find Mr Scilly printing copies of cheque books and other counterfeit documents.'

'How do you know this?' Marker asked the disembodied voice. Then he noticed that the lion he was speaking to seemed to have a slight grin on its face.

'Just go now,' came the reply, 'that is all.'

Despite further questions from the policeman, the stone lion remained silent. Marker walked away, trying to recall where Back Bittern Street was. He had a little pocket street directory, but before he could consult it, he noticed a postman walking from Copperas Hill, and so, Marker asked him where Back Bittern Street was and was told: 'The back of the Irish Centre, it runs parallel to Mount Pleasant. You can go via Pomona Street.'

PC Marker found the green door with the printer's name on it, and he placed his ear to this door and clearly heard the rhythmic mechanical sound of the printing equipment at work, as well as a few voices. He knocked, but nobody answered, so he backed up and then kicked the door with sole of his boot. The green door flew inwards, revealing two men standing in front of a printing press with shocked expressions. One of them, later identified as John Scilly, told Marker: 'You can't just come in here like this, you haven't got a search warrant!'

'Ah, you left the door open, didn't you?' Marker casually replied and inspected the batches of fake car tax discs, doctor's notes, plus dozens of copies of bank books copied from originals that had been intercepted by a gang. The original books were delivered by hand to their rightful owners once they had been copied.

'You two are nicked,' Marker told the men.

Marker knew promotion wasn't far away now, and most of his colleagues at the station were amazed at his spate of busts, and some of his associates were downright envious, with one workfellow sarcastically predicting that Marker would soon be awarded the Queen's Police Medal. Marker's mother, however, seemed very unnerved when she heard about the latest inside information from Jeremy. Her son told her that he was now one hundred per cent certain that no human being was responsible for the tip-offs.

'Keep away from Lime Street then,' she told him, and the anxiety in her eyes was magnified by the spectacles she wore as she read the newspaper.

'How can I keep away from Lime Street if they put me on the beat down there, Mam?' Marker asked softly. 'That's part of my patch.'

'There's something weird about this,' she told him, and looked down at the paper.

'You said there were no such things as ghosts,' Marker reminded her, 'so why have you changed your tune?'

'I'm not saying a ghost is responsible, Roger, but perhaps its an evil spirit. I believe in the Bible and the Bible says there are evil spirits.'

'What's the difference between a ghost and an evil spirit? ' Marker asked. 'And Mam, how can it be evil if it's helping me to catch criminals?'

'Ghosts are just things people imagine, but spirits work with the other fellah,' Mrs Marker folded up the paper and leaned from her armchair to put it on the dining table.

'The "other fellah"?' Marker asked with a skew-whiff

grin.

'Old Harry, down below,' came the reply from his stern-faced mother.

'Oh you mean – '

'Don't say that name in this house,' Mrs Marker's face flushed. 'Talk about Him and he'll appear!'

'Mam, this is the Twentieth Century – '

'I know it is, but that fellah's very old and cunning, and the human race still don't know everything,' she told her sceptical son. 'Anyway, I'm watching the telly now. I don't want to hear any more of this and I don't want you going anywhere near Lime Street, even if that *thing* does help to get you promoted. It's not worth it.'

At 9pm, Marker told his mother he was just going to the pub for a few jars, but instead he hopped on a bus and paid a visit to the Lime Street lion, and it told him some alarming news. On this occasion Lime Street was virtually deserted because a long-winded downpour of Irish Sea rain was drenching the city. Standing under an umbrella, Marker listened to the latest tip-off. Jeremy told him: 'Mrs Lunt, the wife of your friend, PC Lunt, will be stabbed to death in her bed tomorrow at 10pm unless you prevent the murder.'

'What?' Marker recoiled, appalled at the prediction. 'You mean Brian Lunt's missus? Who's going to try and kill her?'

There was no reply. Marker listened to the patter of the heavy rain on the brolly's canopy for a while, then realised that Jeremy had nothing else to add. He then detected the rich scent of a man's cologne.

'Evening Mr Marker.' The voice from behind the policeman startled him. He turned to see it was Richie Landford, a silver-tongued confidence trickster and occasional thief. He stood there in his usual pin-striped suit holding an expensive James Smith & Sons umbrella aloft.

'How long have you been standing there?' Marker asked the con man with a suspicious side glance.

'Just a moment or so, constable,' Landford replied, and his knowing eyes were smiling but the rest of his face was not joining in – as if he had heard Marker addressing the statue.

'Yeah, well, keep going, go on, beat it,' said Marker, grumpily.

'Have you ever read the works of Kahlil Gibran, officer?' Landford queried as he moved forward at a snail's pace.

'Can't say I have,' Marker confessed with narrowed, annoyed eyes.

'He was a very insightful writer and poet,' Landford told Marker with a vague grin, 'and I recall him saying "If you reveal your secrets to the wind, you should not blame the wind for revealing them to the trees." Very deep isn't it?'

'Are you insinuating something, Landford?' Marker asked, but the smooth-spoken swindler had started to march away by the time the question was hurled and without turning, Landford simply replied: 'Bye.'

Marker knew Richie Landford had a mouth like the Cheddar Gorge, and if the con artist *had* seen him talking to a statue, it'd be all over Liverpool and beyond by tomorrow. The off-duty policeman took refuge from the rain in the Punch and Judy cafe and dwelt on the nature of Jeremy and also the murder he had forecast. On the following evening at 9pm, PC Marker decided he'd have to leave his beat as he walked past the Bullring tenements. As he was still wearing his uniform, he was very noticeable and by raising his truncheon in the air it was easy for him to hail a Hackney cab - which took him to Roby – to the semidetached home of Fiona Lunt, the wife of his best friend. On the way to the house, Marker wondered how he'd explain his foreknowledge of the murder; it was a tough one. What would he tell his colleagues when they asked him why he had abandoned his beat to travel to Roby to prevent a murder? *I could say I had a premonition of the attempted murder in a dream*, Marker thought, Or would they think I was of unsound mind if I started mentioning dreams and visions?. Then he explored another explanation: a member of the public had the premonition and talked him into going to the house to save Fiona. That version sounded a bit cuckoo as well. He'd have to just save Fiona and then think on his feet afterwards. Marker was sure of one thing though; this would definitely see him promoted. He'd be all over the newspapers tomorrow; a simple police constable who was single-handedly cleaning up local crime left right and centre.

The taxi dropped Marker off on tree-lined Roby Road, and he walked to the house where – according to the omniscient Jeremy – Fiona Lunt would be knifed to death in her bed unless he intervened. A bedroom lamp was showing dimly through scarlet curtains and netting in the upstairs window at the house. Marker's fists, clad in black leather gloves, creaked as they gripped the truncheon hard. He went to the door, took a deep breath, and thought about his friend Brian Lunt. He was on duty in Kirkby tonight, and if he knew what the evening had in store he'd be racing back home now. Marker brought the large brass knocker on the door down heavily three times. There was no answer. He looked around, wondering if the knifeman was perhaps watching him from the shadows. Perhaps he was already in the house. Marker knocked three times again. There was still no answer, so the constable took five or six steps backwards, and then he trotted forward and delivered a powerful kick to the door with the heel of his boot. The door flew inwards and bounced off the hallway wall and came back at him as he rushed in. His gloved hand switched on the hallway light and he ran up the stairs and barged into a bedroom that was in darkness. It was empty. Then he tried the next one, and although a bedside lamp was on in this room he switched on the main light and he looked at Fiona Lunt - and a senior detective Marker knew well. The couple were clinging on to one another beneath the covers of the king-sized bed.

'Marker!' snarled the policeman's superior, his eyes screwed up because of the bright ceiling light. 'What the devil do you think you're playing at?'

'I'm sorry sir!' Marker's bulging eyes looked upon the scene of adultery. He was lost for words for a moment. 'I – I was told to come here by a member of the public, sir,' Marker stammered, and fidgeted with the truncheon.

'Told to come here?' the detective turned his head sideways in a suspicious manner. 'Told by who?'

'A man who'd had a premonition sir,' Marker replied, and his face turned crimson.

'And who the bloody hell was this man?' bawled the detective, as Fiona hid the bottom half of her guilt-ridden face with the edge of the pink duvet.

Marker had to think fast. 'John, er, I don't know his second name you see sir, but he's a gypsy and he seems to be able to foresee crimes.'

'Did her husband put you up to this, eh? Is that the truth?' the detective asked.

'No sir, it was the John fellow I mentioned – '

'Bollocks Marker! You're a close friend of her husband aren't you?' The detective got out of the bed naked and put his underpants on.

'Yes, but he didn't send me sir, it was that John fellow!'

The detective lit two cigarettes and gave one to Fiona, and then he drew on the other one before he gave Marker a grave ultimatum. 'You breathe a word of this to anyone and I'll have your guts for garters – have you got that?'

'Yes sir, I'm sincerely sorry, but I really was acting on information – ' Marker was saying when his superior told him to get out. The policeman was accompanied to the door downstairs, where he halted and said he'd pay to get the busted lock repaired, but the detective shoved him out into the night. As Marker walked away, he looked at his watch. The time was five minutes to ten. He hid at the end of the street and thought of two scenarios as the moon went in and out of the clouds. Perhaps the detective was violent, and maybe he would have some altercation with Fiona Lunt and end up knifing her. The second possibility that formed in Marker's mind was that Brian, Fiona's husband, might return home earlier than usual and in a jealous rage, knife her. And so Marker waited until 10.15pm, but there were no screams from the house of the Lunts, so he got the train back to Liverpool and reported at the station to say that he had had to leave his beat to visit his mother, who had taken a bad turn. He was an unconvincing liar and the sergeant who listened to the explanation knew there was some other reason for the serious matter of beat desertion, but he let it go. Marker went back on the beat and visted that lion on Lime Street just before midnight, and after a few people had passed by, he asked Jeremy why the knifeman had not turned up. He heard a strange sniggering sound.

'Why are you laughing?' Marker wanted to know, and the cackling began to annoy him; the idea of something, albeit a sinister something, mocking him.

The suppressed laughter stopped. Roger Marker stood there in a sharp steel-cold out-of-season wind from the north which buffeted his back. 'You there?' he asked the blustery night air, tapping the truncheon on his gloved palm. What he saw next would haunt him for the rest of his life. In the periphery of his vision, to the right, something shadowy flitted across the paving stones, going away from the statue across St George's Plateau. Marker moved to the right in a gingerly fashion, suspecting that this thing was Jeremy, showing himself at last. He peeped around the base of the lion and saw a black, oily-looking figure of something that looked like a man with abnormally long arms – and a tail – and that tail was pointed at the end. The thing was running silently along on all fours, on feet and fists, and it slowed, stopped, and a hideous face presented itself over its right shoulder. It looked like a gargoyle's face to Marker, who felt his stomach somersault in fear. The thing's eyes were faint orange lights, like torch bulbs running from a dying battery. A long thin tongue slithered out of the mouth of irregularly-shaped teeth of pale brown, and then the thing turned away and ran off. It vanished from sight as it descended the steps of the plateau leading towards St John's Lane, and Marker thought he heard faint screams. Were these the screams of some woman who had seen the same abomination, or were they just the mundane screams of some female reveller after a night out? Marker didn't find out, because he could not bring himself to go after that grotesque tailed entity. He now knew his mother was right; it had been something evil, probably toying with a mortal. He turned and reversed his beat, crossing Lime Street and heading back up London Road. He wanted to tell his colleagues about the thing on St George's Plateau but knew he'd only end up before a psychiatrist. He told his mother what he had seen, and she told him that a certain neighbour had told her that someone had mentioned the rumour going round about her son talking to a statue on Lime Street. Marker knew immediately that Richie Landford had been the originator of the story – which was, of course, true. Mrs Marker told her local priest to bless her son, and Roger went along with it, because he felt as if he had been targeted by the evil being for some unknown reason. The priest visited Mrs Marker's home and assured the Roger he was not cursed, and that the thing had just been having a bit of warped fun at his expense. 'They've impelled people to murder,' the priest told Marker and his frightened mother. 'They have made people obsessed with strange notions, finally driving them insane, and of course, the victims of these demonic beings are never believed; they're locked away, and in some cases hanged because the victim has been driven to murder. Faith is the only protection against them, but in this day and age, it's in rather short supply.'

The priest then made the sign of the cross, and Mrs Marker and her troubled son did the same. The priest clasped his hands together and began to recite Psalm 130, commonly known as De Profundis, and as the holy man spoke the first lines of the penitential psalm, soot began to fall down the chimney and black clouds billowed out of the fireplace, where a fire had not been lit for almost eight months. Roger and his mother saw what looked like little black scorpions crawl out of the fireplace grate onto the hearth, but the priest paused the prayer and told mother and son to ignore the insects because they were not real. Then there came the sounds of hearty laughter from up the chimney, which caused Mrs Marker to shake with nerves, but the priest reached out and held her hand. The loud laughter sounded just like the guffaws Roger had heard emanating from the statue. The priest continued to reel off the prayer, and the entire house seemed to vibrate for a few seconds, but then the scorpions disappeared and the laughter ended. There was a crash outside the house and the for a moment, Roger and his mother thought a bomb had gone off. An old sycamore tree had inexplicably fallen, demolishing the low wall at the front of the house. The priest said that the tree had been pushed over by that evil being in a final spiteful act. Mrs Marker attended church every Sunday after this, and although her son did not, he found himself reading parables from the Bible on some nights as he lay in bed. He never heard from Jeremy again.

What was Jeremy? From the description given by PC Marker, and by the way it seemed to have supernatural knowledge of things happening at a distance in space and time, it's possible that he was a demon. What was the thing's agenda though? That's a difficult question to answer. He helped Marker at first, but then deliberately fed him false information to get him – and others – into trouble, and heaven knows what it could have used Roger Marker for; he seems to have been a mere pawn, conditioned to trust "Jeremy" at first – until the entity wanted him to carry out a certain action. Perhaps the entity was not even a demon at all, but some being from the myriad of worlds and dimensions of this universe with some devious plan. As scientists look further out into the universe, they find more and more earth-like planets, and more and more physicists are telling us that this cosmos is one of an infinite amount of universes that seem to exist alongside one another, and this opens up many frightening possibilities – one of which is that beings from some of these other planes of existence and planetary worlds have noticed our little Earth and can easily mess with our minds and even snatch us if they so desire. And there's nothing we can do to protect ourselves.

KNOWSLEY'S EVIL
GHOSTLY NUN

On New Year's Day 2017 at around 8.15am, a 24-year-old woman named Jessica left her home on Seth Powell Way, Huyton, bound for her auntie's home in Stockbridge Village. Jessica had been minding her aunt's dog, George, all night (because her aunt had gone to a New Year's Eve party in West Derby), but the dog had kept Jessica awake for most of the night, scratching at her bedroom door and whining because it was pining to go home. On top of all this, Jessica had a hacking cough, the remnant of a bad case of flu over Christmas, which had also interrupted what little sleep she'd enjoyed. Jessica therefore set out at 8.05 am with the dog on a chain leash, bound for her auntie's home. George seemed to sniff and urinate on every lamp post, and so, it was around 8.15am as Jessica took a shortcut across the circular grassy island of the roundabout at Waterpark Drive and Haswell Drive. Jessica was that occupied shouting at the misbehaving dog as it dragged its paws and prodded its nose into every inch of the ground, she didn't notice the eerie figure ahead at first, but then she glanced up and there it was – a nun kneeling at a large boulder feature on the island of the roundabout. When the dog George saw this motionless nun, it began to bark at it, and its hackles rose up. George was so afraid of the nun, he pulled Jessica to the left with the leash and she almost fell over. The kneeling figure did not react in any way, and Jessica ran across the island of the roundabout with George pulling her along. Jessica then got another shock, because she felt as if the nun was behind her, and so she turned and looked over her right shoulder – and there it was, moving along after her as if she was on wheels – and it had nothing inside of its veil and cap – just blackness. Jessica could not remember seeing the hands or shoes of this alarming apparition. Jessica let out a scream – which kicked off her cough - and then wheezing, she looked about. Not a soul was around and not a single car passed within the vicinity. She kept on running, and the dog howled as it raced ahead of her. The home of Jessica's aunt was still 800 yards away, and the young lady looked back again – and she was utterly relieved to see that the figure had vanished. When Jessica got to her aunt's home, she pounded on the door and windows, but there was no answer. Her aunt had stayed out after the party and was sleeping at her friend's house on Blackmoor Drive, West Derby. Fortunately, the neighbour of the absent aunt heard Jessica knocking next door and she let her drop George off at her house. Jessica mentioned the ghostly nun that had chased her and the neighbour said she had heard about the ghost about a week before from a relative who lived in Stockbridge Village. This relative had been travelling down Waterpark Drive in her car when she had seen a nun hurry across the road and go down Chalfont Way. Jessica was so scared of meeting the nun again, she had to go home to Seth Powell Way via a long-winded meandering route which took her as far away as the roundabout on Waterpark Drive as possible.

That ghostly nun has been seen in the area before. In September 2009 I received a letter from a man named

Jimmy who saw the nun days before, darting about one evening as he stood on the balcony of his flat in the hi-rise Mosscraig tower block in Stockbridge Village. The time was around 10.30 pm in late summer, and dusk was gathering. Jimmy was scanning the horizon with a pair of low-powered 8 x 30 binoculars as his girlfriend Gina made him a sandwich in the kitchen. A keen amateur ornithologist, Jimmy had been looking at a sparrowhawk through the binoculars but now as twilight gathered, he'd lost sight of the bird, and had noticed something very strange under a quarter of a mile away. It looked like a black point to the naked eye, moving about rapidly on the island of the roundabout to the left of Haswell Drive, so he picked up the binoculars and focused on the spot – and saw it was a figure in a long robe and hood, and it was moving at an incredible speed into the path of oncoming cars before dashing back to the middle of the roundabout's island. Jimmy called Gina onto the balcony, and she had a look through the field glasses and decided the rapidly-moving figure was a nun.

'Nah, it looks like a monk,' Jimmy told her, but Gina had much superior eyesight and she said she had seen the white wimple part of the nun's habit clearly – but she was a bit spooked at the way the nun was flitting about at high speed. The figure went missing at around 10.40 pm, and Gina, feeling there was something obviously supernatural about the unbelievably agile nun, asked her boyfriend to come in off the balcony, but Jimmy was fascinated by the possible ghost, and he kept scanning the area around the roundabout for the sinister figure.

'Jimmy, will you come in and stop looking for *her*,'

Gina begged him. 'Come and get your sarnie – it's got loads of salmon on it.'

'I will now, stop nagging, Gina.' Jimmy took the binoculars from his eyes and scanned the nightscape with the naked eye, looking for the nun.

'Me Nan always used to say you should leave the supernatural well alone,' Gina recalled, looking at Jimmy on the balcony. 'No good can come of it – it should be left well alone. I might as well talk to the wall.'

Just before 11pm, Jimmy backed away from the balcony through the door to the living room and almost stumbled onto Gina as she sat watching the TV.

'She's down there,' he whispered, with a look of horror on his face.

'What?' Gina got up and expected him to say he was joking, but Jimmy swore and said, 'Honest 'a God - she's down there!'

Gina went out onto the balcony and Jimmy tried to stop her by grabbing her arm but she pulled her arm away from his grasp and looked over the balcony rail. Jimmy was right; he had not been trying to pull her leg. A nun was standing still on the corner of Little Moss Hey, next to a wheelie bin – and she was looking up at Gina – but it had not been a face that was turned upwards to the balcony, just a black oval – as if there was no head in the head-dress. A feeling akin to an electric shock jolted through Gina's chest, and she found herself doing what Jimmy had done a minute ago – she backed away and stumbled into the living room, where her boyfriend was muting the telly.

'I told you, nosey hole!' Jimmy said through clenched

teeth, 'But you had to see for yourself!'

Gina had never seen him so scared, and she herself saw her bosom moving with irregular jolts because of palpitations. 'Close the door, Jimmy,' Gina told her boyfriend and then closed the door herself anyway before he could even react. Jimmy dimmed the lights, and then he went into the kitchen and took a look out the window of another room – and the nun was still there below. Gina felt goosebumps rise on her arms. She whispered: 'She knows we're looking at her. This is so creepy!'

'It's not a ghost, Gina,' said Jimmy, in a poor attempt to calm down his girlfriend, 'it's someone dressed up as – ' And before he could finish, the figure flew across the road – towards the 15-storey tower block.

Gina let out a scream. 'She's coming up here!'

Jimmy went to the front door, put on the bolt and the safety catch of the Yale lock, and then he backed away into the living room, where Gina had her hands to her face as she looked in terror at that front door. Jimmy said over and over that the nun was just someone messing about, but Gina told him to be quiet. 'You've attracted her! You and those binoculars!' Gina yelled and started to breathe heavily.

Then, they both thought they heard a noise outside the front door. It sounded like a click. Jimmy wanted to look through the wide-angle door viewer but Gina clutched his hand tightly and refused to let him go. The frightened couple stood there listening, but heard nothing more – but they did smell something that reminded them both of church incense, and it seemed to come down the hallway from the front door. Jimmy went back out onto the balcony – and as soon as he looked over the rail, he saw the nun, "bombing down the road" until she stopped at the bottom of a neighbouring towerblock called Whincraig. Gina saw her too, and she had a look at the unearthly figure through the binoculars and saw that the figure didn't seem to have any hands in the sleeves of the habit. Jimmy was supposed to drive his girlfriend to her home on Longview Drive at around midnight, but Gina decided to stay at his flat because she was so scared of encountering the creepy nun. The couple watched the nun remain stationary for a while, until someone came out of Whincraig to go to their car, and then the figure moved off at a phenomenal speed down Little Moss Hey, and flew around the curve in the road below the block of flats where Jimmy lived. It then vanished into the night. At around 1am, Jimmy opened the front door a few inches and peeped outside. On the little bristly mat outside his door was something which looked like six large black grapes on a stalk, but Gina thought they looked more like huge berries, as they were rounder than grapes. The couple never touched them, and established that the berries were giving off that strong smell of church incense. The door was closed, and on the following morning, Jimmy and Gina saw that the unidentified fruit was gone. The significance of the berries is unknown; did the nun leave them there? Thankfully, Jimmy and Gina have seen no more of that freakish, spooky nun. I brought a medium to the area around Stockbridge Village and she felt the nun was connected to a ghostly nun that had been occasionally seen in Kirkby for some reason. I do not believe this though. The latter apparition was thought to be the ghost of a nun who was tragically knocked down in the area around Kirkby's Valley Road some years ago, but the nun was a saint in life and even after her death, her ghost was harmless. The ghostly nun around Stockbridge Village and parts of Huyton seems to be sinister and hellbent on distracting motorists to crash. She may in fact be some demonic being masquerading as a nun. She is hard to explain, but I will keep delving into this ghost and will hopefully be able to identify her in a future book.

STRANGE LIVERPOOL CULTS

This island nation has always had occultists, dating from the mysterious megalith builders thousands of years ago, to the Druids (and there are a few in my family tree) and in this era obscure cults still persist. We have the Lily White Boys, a solar-based group of allegedly superhuman disciples found across northern England (which have been documented in many volumes of the *Haunted Liverpool* series), and we have even more terrifying sects that very little is known about, such as the sinister faction that sacrificed hundreds of sheep on the 69,000-acre Dartmoor estate owned by Prince Charles a few years back – always on the night of a full moon. In the late 1960s in Liverpool, a well-known journalist named Sid received a tip-off (via a telegram of all things) about a group of Devil worshippers carrying out rituals and holding orgies at sites between Ainsdale and Southport, and this group allegedly had some very influential people as members. Sid drove to one of the sites, but on the way, his tyres were punctured by a triangle of wood with spikes left on a lonely road just past Ainsdale. As Sid was examining the punctured tyres a motorbike approached – and as it drew nearer, Sid saw the rider had on a black hood with what looked like a weird black cone protruding from its front. The masked rider with the bizarre beak slowed as he passed the journalist and hurled a metal ball attached to a rope at Sid. The rope lassoed Sid as the ball swung around his neck, and the other end of that rope was tied to the metal bar of the luggage rack on the motorcycle. The bike tore off, dragging Sid along, and quick thinking saved his life. He fumbled for his Swiss Army knife, managed to pull out its penknife with his teeth, and cut the rope, but by then he was badly-injured by friction burns to his buttocks and legs. He ran off in agony with blood-soaked trousers, hid in a field, and peeping through the long grass he saw the hooded man looking for him on the bike. A police car approached and the maniac shot off at an incredible speed, as if the bike possessed a souped-up engine. Sid later received anonymous threatening phone calls in the dead of night at his home, and he eventually abandoned the scoop on the Devil cult.

At a certain Liverpool church in 1992, a priest gave a sermon about dabbling with Devil worship, and later received a bizarre call at midnight. A voice said: 'Phone three people and say "The Devil eats cheese on toast" or you'll have very bad luck.'

'Who is this?' The priest asked, and getting no reply he hung up. He was then besieged by many parishioners who told him they'd received scary calls – all at midnight – from a man asking them to call three people with that surreal message about the Devil and cheese on toast. Many of the parishioners claimed they had lost loved ones and suffered all sorts of misfortune after failing to carry out the weird request, and some confessed to the priest that they'd done as the caller said because they feared dire consequences if they didn't comply. British Telecom (BT) was eerily unable to trace the warped joker, and the disturbing case was even mentioned on *Granada Reports*. The menacing caller claimed to know shameful secrets of the person he was calling on some occasions, and threatened to reveal these skeletons in the cupboard unless his nonsensical order was obeyed. The telephonic terror eventually stopped calling and the whole strange affair died down. Was it all a joke that got out of hand – or was it perpetrated by some anti-Church cult?

At the time of the aforementioned mass anonymous calls, BT promised a crackdown on half a million obscene telephone calls to women across the UK. BT set up a network of fourteen bureaux with specially-trained staff to tackle the sex pests. Victims of habitual anonymous obscene callers were given a code to key into their phone's push-button dial as the call was in progress, and this code linked the offensive caller's telephone to a BT computer which then printed out the sex pest's telephone number. Many perverts were found to be calling victims from public telephone boxes, but there were also some callers who could not be traced, and these were the most creepy ones who had a lot in common, namely that the callers seemed to know the victim was alone and appeared to know the most intimate details about the victim's life. In many of these cases the anonymous caller was obviously observing the victim and could even tell them what they were wearing – even though the targeted person was often in a room where the curtains or blinds were drawn. Some investigators believed that some of the callers were simply driven by a sexual urge, but a sizeable group seem to have belonged to some cult, because the calls were not only made at the same time – 1.13am – the dialogue spoken was almost identical, and involved the caller instructing the victim to draw a specific symbol upon their left breast with a biro or marker. Refusal to do this would result in a terrible curse. A 26-year-old woman named Daphne in Mossley Hill received one of these calls at precisely thirteen minutes past one o'clock one morning in October 1992. At first Daphne heard nothing – just silence – when she answered the call which had awakened her in her bed. Her husband David was in Ireland on business, and she knew he wouldn't be calling at such an unearthly hour. A voice which seemed devoid of any accent or emotion then said: 'Hello Daphne, I'd like you to do something for me.'

'Who is this?' Daphne asked, switching on her bedside lamp. Hearing the mention of her name convinced her that the caller knew her.

'That's no concern of yours, Daphne,' said the man in a casual manner, 'but if you hang up your husband David will die a terrible death within a year and you'll have an awful curse put on you.'

'I'm going to report you to the police – ' Daphne said when the calm voice interrupted her.

'And your husband will most certainly die, and you'll have a curse placed upon you which will not lift for years. That's a very nice duvet, Daphne. Salmon pink isn't it?'

'What do you want?' Daphne asked, her hand shook as it held the telephone handset. She looked at the curtains, wondering if someone could see in, but they were drawn together and there wasn't even a slight gap between them.

'You have a biro on your bedside cabinet there Daphne – the one you do the crossword with,' said the menacing voice.

Daphne didn't answer. She wanted to just put hang up and call the police and her husband.

There was now a little annoyance detectable in the voice of the ominous caller: 'Pick that biro up now or you'll be cursed for the rest of your life and your husband will die in agony within twelve months.'

Daphne reached out and picked up the pen.

'Take the cap off,' said the disconcerting man.

Daphne angled her head, keeping the handset in place under her jaw so she could hold the cheap biro in one hand and pull its black cap off with the other. She then awaited further instructions.

'Good. Now, Daphne, draw a circle on your left breast, about an inch above the nipple. The circle should be as big as a ten pence piece.'

'No,' Daphne told the crank caller, 'what do you want me to do that for?'

'It is no concern of yours, Daphne, just do as I say, and make sure the circle is complete; if the ink doesn't take and it leaves gaps, you must fill it in.'

'Piss off!' Daphne had had enough, and she almost smashed the handset into the telephone's cradle. She felt like crying as she recalled the threats the bizarre caller had made about curses and her husband having a terrible death.

The telephone rang again. Daphne sat there on the edge of the bed, looking at it. She swore and shouted: 'Stop it!'

As soon as the phone stopped ringing she picked up

the handset, bit her lip to prevent herself from bursting into tears, then started to dial 999 – but the line was dead and she could not hear an electronic tone as she depressed each button on the telephone keypad.

She heard the man's voice; he was still on the line. 'Daphne, just do as I say and you'll be fine – '

She hung up, then went downstairs, made herself a coffee and sat in the kitchen, wondering about the caller. How had he known her name, and why had he wanted her to draw a circle on her breast? The voice had not sounded like anyone Daphne knew – so who was he? The questions ran back and forth through Daphne's mind. She picked up the telephone in the hall – and there was no purring tone – which meant the intimidating and obviously unbalanced caller was somehow blocking the line. At 6am, Daphne heard her neighbour Frank coming out of his house on the way to work, and so she went out and told him what had happened. Frank picked up Daphne's telephone handset in the hallway, but now the purring tone was audible again. He kindly advised Daphne to sit in his living room if she felt at all scared, and Daphne did this. At 7am, Frank's wife Rita got up and joined her neighbour downstairs. She advised Daphne to go to the police about the strange call, but Daphne said she'd feel silly talking about the man trying to get her to draw on her boob. Almost a month after this, Daphne visited her dentist one morning for a filling in a molar, and as she sat in the waiting room, the dentist's secretary took a call, then looked around. She told Daphne she was wanted. Daphne got up and was puzzled as to who would call her when she was at the dentist. Her husband was at work and no one else even knew she'd be in the dental surgery. She took the telephone handset and as her ear pressed against its receiver she went cold, because it was *him* again. His voice sounded a bit muffled this time, but he clearly told her: 'You should have done what I told you to do, Daphne, because now you are cursed. Things will go horribly wrong when he tries to put that filling in. Goodbye.'

Daphne panicked and tried to cancel the appointment, and the dentist came into the reception area at that moment and saw Daphne crying. He asked her what the matter was and took her into an office with a dental nurse. When he heard about the spiteful and deranged anonymous caller, he assured Daphne that the filling was straightforward and nothing would go wrong. The dental nurse then said a strange thing. She said that her sister – who lived near Sefton Park – had also had a call from a man all hours in the morning who had known her name and had also known her husband had recently separated from her. This caller had also tried to talk the nurse's sister into inscribing some symbol on her breast.

The dentist finally calmed Daphne down and with extra care he put in a filling and didn't even charge for the procedure. Daphne suffered no mishaps and never heard from the threatening caller again – and to date, nothing untoward has happened to her husband. Had something happened out of pure chance to Daphne or her husband she would have put it down to the supposed curse. I once mentioned this case on a radio programme and received a number of calls about a male who telephoned females (who ranged in age from

19 to 57) and told them they had to wear his 'mark' on their breast or they – and their loved ones – would suffer from all sorts of curses and extreme bad luck. Most of these terrifying calls came in the dead of night and were all around 1992-1997. As far as I know, the culprit – if there was just *one* - was never traced and caught. Some believe a cult was involved which required victims to wear a mysterious symbol – a circle and triangle around the left nipple – and the significance of this symbol is not known to me.

Moving a little further back in time, to the 1970s, there is another case of some sort of weird cult being active in the Croxteth area. On the Wednesday night of June 21, 1978, at a quarter to midnight a young couple, Peter and Carol, both aged 17, stood embracing under the full moon on Deysbrook Lane, West Derby, when they heard the tramping approach of two policemen on their beat. The amorous teens decided to go somewhere a little more secluded, and Peter led Carol on a long-winded 'shortcut' which involved climbing over railings and squeezing through a hedge until, at last, he led his sweetheart to the grounds of Croxteth Hall – the former ancestral home of the illustrious Molyneux family, and up until 1972, the Grade II listed hall –built in 1575 - had been the residence of the Earl and Countess of Sefton. Now, on this moonlit night, the hall was owned by the local authorities after the death of the last Earl. Carol thought there was something romantic – magical even - about this midsummer night; the moonlight, the fragrance of flowers hanging in the air, and the way Peter was holding her in his arms as he gazed into her eyes. 'How about it?' he suddenly asked.

'How about what?' Carol was puzzled for a moment by his words, then realised what he was referring to when she saw him coyly take out a condom in a little cellophane packet from his inside coat pocket. She recoiled from him and gritted her teeth. 'No!' she almost snarled, and told him she was not that type of girl. Peter persisted and Carol turned and marched off. He ran after her and she told him he had ruined a good night. 'I was only joking, you have no sense of humour, Carol!' Peter replied, but her little hand pushed against his chest and she turned and ran off, close to tears.

'Carol!' Peter sighed, and trotted after her. At this point, a solitary cloud drifting across the night sky, blotted out the full moon, and in the short spell of darkness, Peter lost sight of Carol. He looked about and sensed that she was hiding somewhere, behind a bush or a tree. He knew her so well; she had hid from him after the last little tiff in Woolworths and he'd finally found her in the photo booth.

'Carol, if you don't stop messing about I'll go home and leave you here!' Peter threatened, not wishing to raise his voice too much in case those coppers heard him. He wasn't sure if he was trespassing. The cloud above sailed on and the moonlight flooded the greenery and lent an eerie ghostly aspect to Croxteth Hall as it lay nestled among the trees of the ancient park. It had been a scorcher of a day, and now a thin ground mist began to move in and it went up to Peter's waist. He saw a faint flickering amber light in a clearing among the trees, and it turned out to be a small fire in a bucket with holes in, and sitting at this makeshift brazier were two vagrants. One was rather corpulent and the other was well below average height with thick-rimmed glasses, and he reminded Peter of the comedian Ronnie Corbett.

The tramps were eating crisps and swigging the dregs from wine bottles.

'Excuse me, have you seen a girl passing by here?' Peter asked, keeping his distance from the derelicts.

The drifters looked at one another, then turned to face Peter and shook their heads. 'No, sorry, we haven't,' said the spectacled little man in a well-spoken voice.

'What's she playing at?' Peter muttered, and walked on, but the stocky tramp said: 'You wanna be careful tonight – ' but the diminutive down-and-out shook his head as he glared at his colleague and whispered something, and the latter promptly shut up.

'Why? What do you mean?' Peter asked, but the tramps looked into the flames in the bucket and said nothing in reply. Peter walked on, and he felt so concerned for his girlfriend's safety, and yet he was also so angry at her for running off. He regretted that stupid proposition which had caused her to storm off in the first place. He came to the front of the Hall, and here he saw something both surreal and scary – a crowd of naked men, all of them in black pointed hoods – except for one who seemed to be wearing horns – and they were dancing and springing about and some of them were contorting their bodies – bending backwards as if they had rubber spines. What really unnerved Peter was the way some of the hooded danseurs seemed to defy gravity as they leaped high into the air while performing their strange choreography. Peter thought there was something evil

– Satanic even – about the black hooded dancers, especially the one who wore the horns. That one also wore a long black curly wig, reminiscent of the periwigs worn by the likes of King Charles II. Peter could make out other details in the strong moonlight; the van dyke and turned up moustache the horned man sported. What on earth was going on? He then noticed a long table covered in a white linen cloth about thirty yards to the left of the nude frolickers – and upon this table, a huge multi-tiered cake stood with other dishes lined up on either side of it, and about a dozen or more chairs tucked under the fall of the cloth.

A terrible thought struck Peter: what if those dancing deviants had kidnapped Carol – perhaps as part of some Satanic orgy? He went cold and refused to entertain this notion, but then, like some nightmare from which he could not awake, he saw two naked women approach on the moonlit green, and they flanked Carol! They each held her wrist, and were leading her towards the table. Peter looked about for something to attack these depraved degenerates with, and found a thick old fallen branch about four feet in length. He picked it up, and saw the horned dancer run towards Carol, but the girl suddenly screamed, broke free of the stark-naked women, and ran as fast as her legs could carry her. The horned man laughed hysterically and leaped onto one of the *au naturel* women instead, and they both fell backwards onto the table and landed on the tall tiered cake, squashing it. Peter ran in a curve through the mist, managing to avoid being seen by the undressed cultists, and he caught up with Carol as she tried to climb a wall. She screamed when she heard Peter call her, then hugged him and told him how those two unclothed women had chased her and brought her to those hooded men. The couple escaped, and never ventured near the grounds of the Hall again. I have received many reports of what seems to have been ritual Midsummer Revels across the outskirts of Liverpool, and what's even more sinister is that the horned figure in the curly wig seems to be the ghost of some historical personage of aristocratic stock, and the hooded men were most probably members of the ancient sun-worshipping cult of the Lily White Boys, who celebrate their Sun God being at the height of his powers at the Summer Solstice. Try not to stay out too late this Midsummer night, as these revels still go on today...

One chilly October evening in 1972 in the parlour of a certain popular pub in Liverpool city centre, a 20-year-old girl named Kate consulted a Tarot card reader named Marlena about her future. For 50p, Marlena scanned the cards in tense silence before telling Kate: 'You live on a hill.'

'Yes,' Kate nodded, 'Highgate Street,' she gasped (realising she did indeed live on the hill in the Edge Hill district), and Marlena muttered something then said, 'You're looking for "The One" – aren't you?'

Kate blushed and said she was and Marlene told her a strange thing. 'On the last day of this month, around midnight, "The One" shall meet you at the bottom of that hill, near to a pub.'

'That'll be the Oxford pub,' Kate reckoned, at the bottom of Grinfield Street, on Oxford Street. 'But I don't understand, Marlena; can't I meet him earlier?'

Marlena gathered in the cards and shook her head of

curly black hair. 'No, don't dictate to Lady Fate, and be there – alone – and The One will appear.'

The last night of the month – Halloween – arrived, and Kate foolishly walked alone up Oxford Street from the slope of Grinfield Street, and bumped into a homeward-bound man in his thirties with a broken nose. He seemed slightly drunk and he asked Kate if she was on the game. She glared at him and said she was not, and the man – named Eddie – said: 'You shouldn't be walking alone this time at night, love, people might think you're punting like.'

Kate wondered if Eddie was "The One" promised by Marlena. All of a sudden, on a nearby stretch of grassy wasteland where a whole street of terraced houses had once stood, a fire flared into being, startling the couple, and as the flames leapt high into the still night air. Three abnormally tall men in black gowns of some sort appeared around the bonfire.

'The size of them,' Eddie remarked, for the three men in black were about 7 feet tall. Then, suddenly, in the flames, a pale blue glowing figure with folded arms appeared – and it was about 12 feet in height – and it had twisted horns like those of a ram. Kate screamed at the materialisation, and the giant horned figure said 'Kate,' in an eerie deep voice. Kate fled up the hill of Grinfield Street, followed by Eddie, who was now totally sober. A police car came towards the running duo from the direction of Smithdown Lane and blocked their way. 'What's going on?' a policeman asked, and Eddie pointed to the fire on the wasteland and told them that the Devil had been conjured up by three "giant weirdos", but when the police reached the spot, the fire suddenly died – and there wasn't a soul to be seen anywhere near it on this Halloween night. Kate began to date Eddie, and they went to find Marlena to tell her what had happened, but that Tarot reader was never heard from again. Eddie believed that Marlena had tried to set Kate up with something evil that Halloween night. For many years, a fire would appear on that grassy 'oller'(slang name for the field) near the Oxford pub, and a ring of huge black cats would sit around the flames for a while before fading away. Student houses now occupy the field where the mysterious bonfire used to appear, but apparently, if the many reports I receive are anything to go by, the same tall robed men in black – possibly powerful occultists - now appear around a fire that flares up out of nowhere on the field behind the Oxford public house. This whole area is apparently steeped in supernatural goings-on, many of them documented in the early *Haunted Liverpool* books. A black Rolls Royce is said to pull up near this field and nearby Abercromby Square with a passenger that many claim to be the Devil. There are also unsettling rumours of paranormal abductions of young people by ruthless cultists in this part of Liverpool which I recall from my own childhood, when I lived off Myrtle Street, which runs close to the site of the fire where Satan was allegedly conjured up. This area of Edge Hill, which borders on Toxteth, is just one of many locales in the North West where paranormal incidents seem to be concentrated – there are many others, and a lot of them are centred on crossroads. These cruciform junctions, traditionally associated with the meeting places of witches, wizards and demons, will be covered in the next chapter.

MERSEYSIDE'S HAUNTED CROSSROADS

On the evening of Saturday 6 October 1960, the Jones family of Netherley went missing while returning home from their relatives' house in Cronton. The Morris Minor Traveller the Joneses had been making the return trip in was found abandoned at the remote crossroads formed by Alder Lane and Prescot Road about 2 miles north-east of Widnes. The next morning, a farmer found the family cowering in a wood a mile north of the crossroads in a very agitated state. The police interviewed Mr and Mrs Jones and found them to be terrified, quite disoriented and all of them seemed to be suffering from mild amnesia. The adults and their 6-year-old daughter and 9-year-old son could not recall why they had abandoned their car or who they were hiding from, but several days later, all four family members suddenly recalled the chilling incident which had taken place on that Saturday around midnight. Mr and Mrs Jones had sat in the front of the vehicle with Mr Jones at the wheel, and the children, Archie and Allison, had been sitting in the back of the car guessing the words the other one was thinking. The vehicle approached the lonely crossroads when Archie, guessing the word his sister was thinking, shouted "Abracadabra!" And immediately the car shuddered and stopped dead, the inertia throwing Mr and Mrs Jones (who were not wearing seatbelts) against the window. The car refused to restart as bright orange light blazed through the windows of the vehicle and the family were suddenly gripped by an intense panic. All four family members fled from the car and when they looked up at the source of the orange light they saw a giant luminous head with a frightening face hovering in mid air. The eyes were like balls of fire and the head measured about 20 feet in height from its pointed chin to its bald pate. The mouth was open wide and a loud groaning sound filled the air. This sound was so loud, Mrs Jones felt it vibrate through her body. The family ran into the dark fields from this sinister and shocking apparition and hid in a wood, where they saw the glowing head roam around the dark fields for a few minutes with beams like searchlights radiating from its eyes before it suddenly vanished, leaving a pall of smoke behind. Mr and Mrs Jones felt they'd die if they left the cover of the wood and so they stayed there for the rest of the night, huddling together with their children. Mr Jones never drove anywhere near the crossroads where the petrifying phantasm appeared ever again, and believed the apparition had been of the Devil.

The crossroads where the giant head appeared was once known as Arran's Cross, and legend has it that an old Celtic wizard named Arran was either buried there or had carried out arcane rituals at the spot in a time before the Roman invasion. Perhaps little Archie Jones had inadvertently conjured up Arran by yelling that ancient incantation "Abracadabra" as the car reached the crossroads. In the 1970s there were reports of a huge unidentified cat of the same ilk as the Surrey Puma near Arran's Cross, and many older folk in the area said this animal was some sort of pet of the ancient wizard, and some occultists maintain that the cat *was* Arran in one of his many forms. Even today I get occasional reports from people who tell me of a strange force that seems to affect their cars when they drive through Arran's Cross. I know of many other haunted crossroads on Merseyside and will tell you about a few of them in this chapter, but first, let me explain a little about the occult significance of crossroads. Until the 1820s, some executed criminals and suicides were not allowed to be laid to rest in a Christian churchyard so they were buried in unconsecrated ground – usually at crossroads, at night, and often with a stake through their heart and a stone smashed into their face. In 1824, a suicide was buried in this fashion at a crossroads in Grosvenor Place, just behind Buckingham Palace. The reasoning behind the burial of destroyers of life (be it their own or someone else's life) is hard to understand to the modern mind, but in times past the Church showed no sympathy to suicides, and classed people who destroyed themselves as belonging to a band of outcasts that included pagans, murderers, witches, wizards and even vampires. Why was this so? In 1 Corinthians 3:16 it's stated that God gave us our body as a temple, and that His spirit dwells inside of the temple-body, and so to destroy oneself would be to destroy the temple, where God lives, and this would incur the wrath of God upon the suicide. There are other references of this sort in the Bible, and the Church upheld them until the House of Lords agreed that suicide should no longer be a crime in March 1961 (and even then a few peers only gave their assent with strict reservations). On a practical level the Bill that stopped suicide being a criminal offence also meant that insurance companies would no longer have the law behind them when they refused to pay out on life policies when the policy holder committed suicide. And by the way, I personally know that people who commit suicide will *not* go to Hell or be cut off from God because of the act of self-termination. What has this got to do with crossroads? Well, primitive minds believed that the spirit of a person deemed to be evil might rise from its grave after death, so in addition to staking the deceased through the heart, the spirit of the dead person – if it did rise – would be unable to decide what way to go when it was presented with the four paths of the crossroads! That's the common explanation trotted out by some occultists, social historians and anthropologists in an effort to explain the supernatural reputation of crossroads, but the real reason a crossroads is regarded as a place of unearthliness seems to have been lost in ancient times. I don't believe crossroads have anything to do with Christianity, for they are revered and feared in many other religions too. The Ancient Greeks placed stones to commemorate Hermes at crossroads, and the Romans did a similar thing with their equivalent of Hermes – Mercury. The Hindu deity Bhairava was assigned to guard the crossroads in India, and in Africa, a host of spirits are associated with the crossroads and the Haitians have Papa Legba as an intermediary between humans and spirits at crossroads. The general consensus in ancient times is that the crossroads represent a type of portal – a place in-between our world and some other realm – a location where our mundane everyday reality and some other strange and frightening dimension overlaps. In many cultures, sinister beings are summoned at the crossroads and one particular entity seems to be commonly reported, and he is known as the Black Man – not black as in someone belonging to a particular racial group – but a figure who is so black he is almost pure silhouette – and he is regarded as a teacher, a bringer of dangerous knowledge and also of highly-prized skills that will make the pupil wealthy and famous – for some unspecified price. The legends are told again and again of musicians past and present who went to a certain crossroads and sold their soul so the Man in Black (usually equated with the Devil) would teach them how to play a guitar or a certain musical instrument in an incredible, inimitable way that would ensure world fame. Jimi Hendrix was said to have done this, and Delta blues musician Tommy Johnson (and not, as commonly reported, Robert Johnson, another blues musician) also received an incredible musical education from the Man in Black. Or so the legends state. Some giants from the world of sport are even alleged to have resorted to making a rendezvous with the Man in Black; people like Ayrton Senna, the late Brazilian racing champion, and even a well-known professional golfer.

Locally, one of the most oldest crossroads is the one an entire district of Liverpool is named after – Hunt's Cross. The origins of the name "Hunt" have been lost in the mists of time, and while some historians think a Mr Hunt might have owned the land the crossroad was centred on, other scholars of local history think the crossroads was a place where the fox hunts started from. It's equally likely that the name was derived from the stone cross which once stood at the crossroads in medieval times. The pedestal of this ancient cross was rediscovered in the 1960s and now stands at the end of Hillfoot Road on a traffic island. The crossroads Hunts Cross is named after still exist as a busy junction, and you will find it at the intersections of Speke Road, Hillfoot Avenue and Woodend Avenue, situated about 177 yards south of Hunt's Cross Railway Station. This crossroads has been the scene of some strange goings on over the centuries and has many legends attached to it, from the hoary old tale of the notorious highwayman Dick Turpin staying at an inn near the crossroads in the 1730s whilst on the way to York on his trusty steed Black Bess (said to have been stabled in a barn where the NatWest bank now stands on the corner of Hillfoot Road) – to the numerous accounts of supernatural goings on at the crossroads. Here are just a few of these inexplicable incidences which have taken place at the cruciate intersection of Hunt's Cross. In 1995, a 27-year-old woman named Liz Lewis moved into a house on Mackets Lane (located between Woolton and Hunt's Cross) with her partner Jon Mason. The house had been left to Liz by her aunt Jacqui, who had recently passed away, and although Liz's parents urged her to sell the house, Liz – who had been close to her aunt since she was a baby – decided to live in the semidetached dwelling. Then came the big surprise, in the inventory of other things Liz's Auntie Jacqui had left her, there was a quaint old car in the garage – a Renault Dauphine – a vintage four-door saloon, and it had been sprayed amaranth pink – and pink was Liz's favourite colour. Liz had learned to drive a few years back, but after obtaining her licence she found she never had enough money to buy a decent car. She'd bought a few wrecks which had let her down but having a very low-paid job (a waitress in a cafe) she found it hard to save for a new car. Jon said the pink French-made saloon was ancient. 'They stopped making these in the 1960s – sell it and get a decent one,' was his advice, but it was too late; Liz had fallen in love with "Pierre" – her name for the candy-floss coloured car. It had belonged to her beloved Aunt Jacqui (who had been something of an early New Ager), and Liz felt as if her late aunt was in the car when she sat in it for the first time. Jon's Uncle Martin was a whiz with cars and he managed to restore the pink Dauphine, and even wanted to buy it for a good price, but Liz said it wasn't for sale. That vintage pink car turned heads that summer as Liz and Jon took it on the road. The novelty of the pink car soon wore off and the couple settled into their new home on Mackets Lane. Then, one evening around 8pm in November of that year, Liz decided to pay a visit to her friend Lauren in Speke, and so, Liz drove down Mackets Lane, turned right onto Hillfoot Avenue, and headed towards the busy crossroads at the Speke Road and Woodend Avenue junction – and here, Liz got quite a start, because there was another pink car – and it looked to her as if it was the very same model as her own. She recalled thinking that "Pierre" had a brother and smiling – but then she saw that the woman behind the wheel of this car *was her double*. She had blonde hair scraped up into a bun, a greenish sleeveless top, and her face looked exactly like her. This girl in her pink

Renault Dauphine was heading east from Hillfoot Avenue – going in the direction Liz had just come from. An impatient motorist behind the distracted Liz beeped his horn repeatedly because the lights were on green and Liz stalled the car, then eventually restarted it just in time as the lights were changing, and curved left down Woodend Avenue. Liz told Lauren about the other pink car and how the girl in it looked like herself but Lauren said: 'I told you to keep your original colour; every girl's going blonde and they all look like clones of one another. That's all it's been, Liz, another blondehead with the same tacky taste in pink cars as you!'

But that night, just before midnight, in the middle of a heavy downpour, Liz came home through the crossroads where she had seen her double in the replica of her car – and as she turned right into Hillfoot Avenue, she saw that there were only two vehicles on the road to her right – what looked like a black Transit van – and that other pink saloon. This time, Liz slowed her car and saw that the woman in the other pink car was looking towards her – and this time, the headlamps of that carbon copy car flashed twice – as if to acknowledge Liz. This really creeped Liz out and she picked up speed and almost took the corner too fast as she swung the saloon into Mackets Lane. Jon didn't doubt his girlfriend's story of the eerie counterpart car and its lookalike driver. 'It could be a doppelganger,' Jon told Liz.

'A doppel-what?' Liz asked, thinking her boyfriend was joking, but she had known him long enough to quickly realise that he seemed a bit unnerved about the thing he was trying to explain. 'A doppelganger is an exact double of someone,' Jon informed her, 'not just someone who looks like you – a perfect copy of a person, and they're supposed to be seen by a person who's about to have a skirmish with death.'

'What?' Liz went cold inside.

Jon back-pedalled. 'Not always though; I mean sometimes a doppelganger is a warning your life is in danger.'

Liz went on the defensive. 'Who told you all this shit?'

'It's not shit, it was on the telly – ' Jon stammered, sorry he'd opened his mouth. 'Anyway, you've probably just seen someone who looked like you. And doppelgangers are of people, not cars – you can't have a doppelganger car as well – '

'Just shut up,' Liz told him. She looked scared. On the following day she asked her Nan about doppelgangers and her Nan, who was a font of knowledge concerning the supernatural, said Jon was talking about a "fetch" – a phantom double of a person – but Liz's Nan did not mention that a fetch was just the Celtic word for a doppelganger, and that a dark tradition stated that anyone seeing their fetch would be dead within a year. Liz's Nan told her granddaughter not to be concerned – that she had not seen her fetch because inanimate objects such as a car could not have a double as well. 'You've just seen some other girl who has a pink car, you soft thing,' Liz's grandmother said – but Liz knew what she had seen with her own eyes had not been some mere lookalike; she had somehow seen herself – but what did the sightings of her own double driving a replica of the pink car signify? Liz wondered about it.

A few weeks later, Liz was returning from Lauren's house in Speke in the pink saloon, and this time Jon was with her. The time was half-past midnight, and it was a Saturday morning. Jon was yawning as the car reached the crossroads at Hunt's Cross. Liz tapped Jon's right leg repeatedly and in an excited voice she said: 'Jon, look! Straight ahead! Look! That's it!'

About twenty-five yards ahead, waiting at the lights, was the pink Renault Dauphine, and Jon, who had excellent vision, noticed something that really shook him – the other pink car had the exact same registration plate as the one he was sitting in. He told Liz this disturbing fact, and once again, as she looked at the pink saloon with her dead ringer sitting at the wheel, she saw the headlights of that impossible car flash three times in rapid succession as if the duplicate driver was attracting her attention – she obviously *wanted* Liz to see her and the car. The lights changed to green, and so the two pink cars passed one another – one going north and the other heading south. Liz was that afraid, she could hardly turn her head right to look at the 'impostor' in the other car as she passed. She found herself breaking out in a cold sweat – but Jon had a good look, and he gasped: 'Oh my God!'

'That proves I'm not seeing things,' Liz said, with a tremor in her voice, and she watched the twin car move off into the night in the rear view mirror.

'She looked exactly like you, Liz,' John said, over and over as Liz turned the car right onto Hillfoot Avenue.

'She was smiling at us.' Jon recalled as the car headed for Mackets Lane.

The couple got home, and Liz mixed a vodka and tonic without saying anything, and Jon was that shaken, he made himself a joint. He hadn't smoked for three months but now, after that weird encounter with a flesh and blood copy of his girlfriend, he sought sedation in cannabis. Later that Saturday morning just after four o'clock, the couple lay in bed, holding hands, when they both heard the distinctive sound of a car pulling up outside. They both knew the characteristic sound of the pink saloon's engine, and Liz squeezed Jon's hand hard. Each knew what the other was thinking: was it *that* car?

Jon got up, went to the window, and gently pulled a curtain back a centimetre. Through the net curtain he saw the pink saloon parked at the kerb outside the house, and there in the driveway was the *original* pink Dauphine. Jon's heart palpitated. He turned and whispered to Liz, who was now sitting on the edge of the bed. 'She's here – the other one in that pink car.'

Liz couldn't even speak, she was far too scared, and she went over and stood by Jon and saw the replica of herself get out of the car, leaving its door ajar a little. Liz grasped Jon's hand and held on tight without taking her eyes off her living clone. Then Liz noticed that her double's neck was a lot longer, and so were the arms, which lent an eerie aspect to the imitator. The unearthly twin opened the gate to the drive and walked to the front door. Liz and Jon tensed up, waiting for a knock at the door, but there was none. Then the couple heard the faint sounds of what sounded like someone rummaging in the cutlery drawer in the kitchen downstairs. Then there was a silent pause for about a minute, and then Jon glanced out the window and saw his partner's facsimile walk back to its pink saloon. The thing even closed the gate behind it as it returned to the car, but just before it got into the duplicated Dauphine, the mimic looked up at the window, then got into the pink saloon and drove up Mackets Lane, heading north, towards the roundabout. Liz turned the light on in the bedroom once the doppelganger in its copy of the car had vanished into the night, and Jon went downstairs. He called Liz from the kitchen and she went down to see what the matter was. A jumbo steak knife had been removed from the cutlery drawer and obviously placed in the centre of the kitchen table. That table had been clear when the couple went to bed and neither of them had used the steak knife in the past fortnight. Liz and Jon both felt that the menacing mimic had placed the knife in the middle of the table as a clear threat; it was as if she was saying she could have knifed them. How she gained access to the house was never ascertained. Enough was enough; Jon suggested that he and Liz should live in his mother's house in Hooton for a while till they decided what to do. Liz took up the suggestion and within a few days the couple had moved. Liz later put the house on the market and she even sold the vintage pink Renault because she wondered if the vehicle had somehow attracted her supernatural spitting image in the first place. Today, the couple live in Southport. What Liz and Jon did not know at the time was that the doppelganger case had nothing whatsoever to do with any car or the house on Mackets Lane – the genesis of the whole strange affair lies with the Hunt's Cross crossroads. I have many doppelganger cases in my files which have occurred either at the crossroads or very near to them. For example, in 1957, an elderly "cocky watchman" (a type of security guard) from Speke named Harry was walking to a roadworks that he had to oversee all night, and this site was literally a stone's throw from Hunts Cross railway station. It was 8pm on a rainy wintry November night, and this nightly trip necessitated a route through the crossroads at the Woodend Avenue, Hillfoot Avenue junction. As the watchman passed Kingsthorne Road, which runs off Woodend Avenue, he thought he heard someone shouting his name. Harry knew no one in that avenue but naturally slowed his pace and looked about. There had been something oddly familiar about the male voice which had called his name. There was only a young woman in a swing coat and a headscarf hurrying along Kingsthorne Avenue through the slanting wind-driven rain. As Harry looked at her he heard that tantalizingly familiar voice shouting his name again, but it seemed to be coming from his left – in the direction of the crossroads, about 150 yards distant. Harry turned up the collar of his overcoat against the raw chill, tugged down the peak of his cap, and with his hands thrust deep into the coat pockets, he walked on, thinking some other Harry was being called too. He crossed Hillfoot Avenue, passing through the heart of the crossroads, and there, just to his right, about twenty yards away, he saw a man dressed just like him on this inclement evening – and then Harry realised that this man was his exact double. The face was exactly the same, and the stationary double wore a smile, despite the sharp wind and glacial rain. Harry reached the other side of the road, and as he proceeded up Speke Road, he heard a faint cry that was almost lost in the wind: 'Harry!'

It came from that stranger who looked like a twin brother. Then Harry realised why the voice sounded so familiar; it sounded like *his own* voice. He heard the weird alter ego call his name again, and this time he heard loud laughter afterwards. Harry didn't even look at him this time, because he was disconcerted by two things – that man was like a living copy of him, and why on earth would anybody be standing there on that corner in this weather, laughing like that? It was possible that the man who was the 'dead spit' of him was merely a drunk, impervious to the rain and biting wind – but the watchman's intuition told him otherwise and Harry walked on as fast as he could. Harry never saw that mirror image of himself again, but friends and relatives did, and whenever they talked to the double it would never reply – only smile – and almost every encounter with the uncanny ringer took place at the crossroads. There are many more of these doppelganger reports based around the ancient Hunt's Cross crossroads, but just why this phenomenon takes place there is hard to explain. My own feelings on the matter is that there is some ancient force still persisting at the crossroads – perhaps an entity that was worshipped by the pre-Roman peoples of long ago – and the two local tribes – the Setantii and the Cornovii – come to mind. Altars were often built at crossroads and animal and human sacrifice was carried out there in an effort to appease the gods and to conjure up spirits. When gallows were later erected at crossroads, this was merely the continuation of a tradition which saw the location as an execution ground. Even today, many occultists believe that the crossroads is an ideal place to carry out spells, as well as a place to meet the

Devil, preferably around midnight. I have found in my own experiences that the arcane practices of the past seem to stain the very places where they were carried out, especially rituals involving the violent slaughtering of humans and animals. I feel that something – an intelligent force somewhere between mischievous and malevolent – still lurks at those crossroads in Hunt's Cross. Perhaps you should be mindful of this when you are next passing through that intersection.

We next head ten miles north to another haunted crossroads of yore, situated where Tithebarn Lane crosses the junction of Giddygate Lane and Waddicar Lane, less than a mile to the north of Kirkby railway station, in the Melling area. The crossroads here are, unlike the ones at Hunt's Cross, very secluded, set in a lonely expanse of farmland. Many years ago when I had a slot on local radio talking about the paranormal, a Melling man named Greg visited me at the radio station to show me a strange dagger with a skull-like face in its handle which his father had unearthed at "Old Nick's Crossroads" during the height of a metal detector craze in the 1970s. The crossroads Greg was referring to is the one I mentioned at the beginning of this paragraph, and the dagger was passed to various experts who could not date it and none of them could even agree on the composition of the metal it was made from. Some thought it was an alloy containing gold and some believed it to be a bronze amalgam. I found the blade to be surprisingly sharp, considering Greg's claim that he had not sharpened it in the years he'd had it in his possession. According to Greg, his family had experienced a run of bad luck which started from the day his father brought the dagger home, and

Greg had been told by a medium to get rid of the archaic weapon – or better still – rebury it where it had been found. The medium said she had visions of a bald-headed bearded man with long green robes on when she handled the dagger, and felt that it had been used to kill sacrificial people a long time ago. Months after the meeting with Greg, he emailed me to say that he had – against the wishes of his wife (who thought the dagger might be worth something) – reburied the dagger close to the place where his father had unearthed it decades before – at Old Nick's Crossroads. Perhaps the dagger was some sort of athamé – a ceremonial blade, traditionally with a black handle – used by some Wiccans and members of various neopagan cults to channel psychic and telluric energies. It is also one of the main tools in white magic Kitchen Witchcraft. The bearded green-robed man the medium picked up from the dagger through psychometry could have been a Druid or an independent wizard of old, like Arran, mentioned at the beginning of this chapter; it might have even been Arran himself glimpsed by the medium. The dagger is just one mystery concerning Old Nick's Crossroads. Old Nick, incidentally, is an old-fashioned way of referring to the Devil without mentioning his traditional title, as to even mention the Devil by name was said to conjure him up, hence the old proverb: 'Talk of the Devil and he'll appear.'

The other mystery concerning the Melling crossroads are two ghosts that seem to belong to different eras, and no one knows their identities, although researchers have tried to find possible historical incidents behind them. One ghost is that of a woman who seems to date back to the 1930s. She has a white (or pale blue) top, a dress with a floral print just below her knees, sand-coloured stockings and shiny black chunky Oxford shoes. This female ghost also wears a small black straw boater-type hat and she also wears white gloves – *which sometimes turn red.* She has been seen standing at the crossroads since the late 1930s, and was even seen during the Second World War years. She's about five feet five inches in height, medium build, with dark hair and a fresh peaches and cream complexion. From all of the reports I have of the unknown phantom lady, it would appear that she belongs to a class of ghost in which the apparition seems very solid and lifelike, even casting a shadow. She rarely speaks, but when she does the lady seems to have a middle class accent with a trace of a Lancashire dialect. The most recent report of the Melling Lady is Summer 2015, when several passengers on the 236 bus, en route for Aintree Hospital, turned into the crossroads from Tithebarn Lane to Waddicar Lane one afternoon. Many of the passengers on that bus probably assumed the woman was just a real person, perhaps waiting for someone or perhaps just enjoying a walk around the rural lanes in that area, but a 77-year-old woman named Mary Johnson, who was on her way to a hospital appointment that afternoon, had seen the very same lady when she was only twelve, back in 1950. She had been spending the summer holidays at her aunt's cottage in Melling at the time, and when young Mary told her aunt about the lady at the crossroads, the girl was told never to go near that place again. Mary's aunt never told her at the time that the woman was a ghost, but a few years later when

Mary was about fifteen, her auntie said that the woman at the crossroads had committed suicide there in the 1930s. Mary was a bit shocked by this information and her aunt asked her if the woman wore gloves. 'I think so, yes,' Mary answered, 'white I think they were.'

'If they'd have been red you would have heard of a death,' said Mary's aunt, and she explained that the woman had cut her throat at the crossroads with a razor and had then grasped her throat, perhaps because she'd had a change of heart about suicide, but when she was found, the gloves were soaked with blood, and so was the top that she wore. Sometimes the ghost is seen with white gloves, which foretells good luck for those who see the ghost, but those who behold the carnate form when it has gloves red with blood are supposedly sure to lose a relative or friend before the week is through.

In the 1960s, there was a man – we shall call him only by his first name – Jack – who was a real hard-knock criminal from Netherton. Jack was in and out of prison for violent assaults and robberies and those who knew him said he had a literal Devil-may-care attitude to life; he simply did not give a damn about anything or anyone and was truly fearless – and a little insane, as evidenced by the time when he stripped naked after drinking six pints of cider and wrestled with a Morris Dancer performing at Ormskirk. One pleasant late-summer evening around 9.30pm on Saturday 11 September, 1965, Jack was sitting with two of his cronies in the Bootle Arms, a beautiful quaint old pub which stands less than half a mile from the haunted Melling Crossroads. Jack was listening to a young man, just out of his teens by the look of him, named Ray, who was complaining to a friend that he just couldn't get a girlfriend. 'Birds just don't want to know you unless you're loaded,' Ray grumbled. Jack went over to Ray, tapped him on the shoulder, and said: 'I've got a Judy for you, lad, come on,' and he nodded at the door.

Ray returned a bemused and indignant look at Jack – a big mistake.

'I said come on!' Jack roared, and grabbed Ray by the collar of his jacket. Jack's two strong-arm men laughed as their boss dragged poor Ray out of the pub. Jack threw the terrified youth into the back of his Jag. The two heavies got on either side of Ray and Jack took off for the crossroads just a few minutes away. When the Jaguar cruised to a halt, Jack scanned the roads, which were lit by a full moon on this warm evening. Jack's lackeys had no idea what their boss had in mind – but they soon found out. From the glove compartment, Jack produced a pair of handcuffs, and then he delved about in the recess in the dashboard, cussing to himself until his fingers located the key. 'You'll score tonight, lad,' Jack muttered, and then he got out the Jag and his men got out and one of them held Ray with his arm shoved up his back. The three of them took Ray to a telegraph pole and pushed him into it, and they handcuffed his wrists together on the other side of that pole. Jack then unzipped the young man's trousers, pulled them down, along with his underpants. As Ray begged to be released, Jack punched him in the back, and with a look of delight he told Ray: 'We're going now, lad, but there's a lady who'll be here soon. She's a ghost, and she haunts here. You might be able to cop off with her.'

Jack and the laughing cronies then walked away, but then Jack halted with his hand on the handle of the car, then walked back to the youth and warned: 'If you mention my name to anyone, like the coppers say, I'll bring you back here and I'll pin you to this pole with an axe. Alright?'

'I won't tell anyone,' Ray sounded choked as if he was going to cry.

Jack spat on the ground, then added: 'And if your mate in the alehouse says anything, I'll do him in as well, so tell him that when you see him.' Jack and his two brawny subordinates then went to Netherton. On the way there, Jack told his foot soldiers that there really was a ghost that haunted the crossroads where they'd left the hard up young man. He'd seen the ghost himself, he maintained, some years back when he was digging a hole in the area to bury the proceeds from a robbery. Jack was many things but he was not a liar, and his flunkies knew he was telling the truth.

On the following morning, a postman found Ray unconscious, slumped at the bottom of the telegraph pole. Jack had not known that the lad suffered from epilepsy, and when he regained consciousness, he said he had seen the woman in "antwacky" (Liverpudlian slang for outdated) clothes, and she had approached him and touched his face with a glove that felt wet. The woman's eyes turned black, and she made a gurgling noise as blood came from her mouth and neck – and remembering what Jack had said about the ghost haunting the road there, Ray had then suffered a pit from pure fear.

The police arrested Jack, and afterwards the criminal put in every window of Ray's home and even attempted to burn the cottage down before he was arrested and subsequently jailed for criminal damage.

The other ghost that allegedly haunts the crossroads is never seen, but is heard to strike the body of vehicles that pass through the crossroads, and for some unknown reason, this invisible entity only seems to be active in the months of April and May. In March 2012, I received an email from a man who drove his motorbike through the crossroads up in Melling and received three hard blows to his helmet and shoulder in quick succession. At first the motorcyclist thought a heavy tree branch had fallen on him, but quickly realised that there were no trees in that area – just fields and hedgerows – and there were no branches or anything else that would have caused the blows on the road. This happened in broad daylight, and most of the other attacks by the unseen entity have also taken place during diurnal hours.

Fifteen miles to the south-east of Old Nick's Crossroads lies a crossroads with another supernatural reputation, and this one is not named (as far as I know). It lies on what was Runcorn Heath and is formed from the coming together of Moughland Lane, Clifton Road, Heath Road, and Heath Road South. This crossroad is probably as ancient as the one in Hunt's Cross, and it is said to be haunted by some hybrid man-beast which some have taken to be a werewolf. The legend dates back well over a century, but in the August of 1975, a tremendous thunderstorm exploded in the skies over Runcorn Heath, and the sound was so deafening, it was as if two mountains had been smashed into one another in the thick low-lying clouds. As mile-long crooked lines of lightning struck Runcorn Heath, motorists waiting for the long-winded lights to change on Moughland Lane witnessed a terrifying yet astounding incident. A wolf-like creature with an unusually long body seemed to appear in the middle of the crossroads. The animal, which had no tail, reflexively dropped down with its ragged underbelly fur pressed to the road surface when the thunder rolled. The motorists nearer to the unidentified animal estimated that its length must have been about nine feet at least, and they watched in horrified fascination as the animal rose up from the floor, and hurried forward on its hind legs – something no wolf could do. This animal ran to a playing field adjacent to Clifton Road and Heath Road, where it seemed to vanish in one of the worst downpours in living memory. That day, Runcorn was flooded, and as far as I know, there were no further sightings of the wolf that walked on its hind legs. Some of the older folks who heard about the strange creature recalled an old story of an alleged werewolf that called itself something that sounded like "Wolfen" or "Wulvarn" (curiously, the latter is the name of a brook that flows through the rural Cheshire village of Barthomley, named in memory of the last wolf in England that was supposedly killed in a wood there in 1486). The Wulvarn of Runcorn Heath was a werewolf-like being that supposedly befriended a 13-year-old schoolboy named Stanley, who lived on Moughland Lane, about a hundred yards from the crossroads, in the late 1950s. Stanley was playing football with six friends on the fields adjacent to Heath Road South, about a hundred yards from the aforementioned crossroads one overcast Saturday afternoon in April 1955, when someone volleyed the ball into the distance. Stanley was the nearest to that end of the field so he had to go and get the ball, which had rolled into a dense border of hedgerows and shadows cast by the overhanging trees near the backyard walls of a street. As he looked for the old scuffed casey football, Stanley saw a greyish face with thick hair and a black nose upon it among the umbrageous greenery – and then with a start he noticed the orange-gold eyes of this strange animal peering at him through the branches and leaves. Before he had a chance to turn and run, a huge hand, clad in grey fur with long black pointed claws was thrust out from a bush, and Stanley saw that this massive hairy hand was holding the football. The hand was so large, it held that ball as Stanley would hold a cricket ball. The thing threw the ball at Stanley, and he turned and ran as fast as his legs could carry him to his friends. When he told them there was some creature hiding in the bushes at the end of the field, a couple of the boys went to investigate the strange claims in a very gingerly manner, but saw nothing out the ordinary there. However, a few days later, Stanley and a friend were walking past the same field around noon when they both saw a hairy grey figure about seven feet in height, peeping out from behind the trunk of a tree. This figure was watching the boys and as soon as they drew the attention of a passing policeman to the bizarre hairy hominid, it crouched down, hid behind a bush, and then seemed to vanish. The policeman thought Stanley and his friend were joking and sternly told them to move on. At least Stanley now knew he had not imagined the strange creature, for his friend had seen it too. He told his mother, and she was of the opinion that some practical joker in a fur coat was just trying to start a scare. It was early April, Stanley's mother reminded him, so the prankster was probably staging a late April Fool joke.

Then, on the morning of Good Friday, at around 3.30am, Stanley awoke in his bed at his home on tree-lined Moughland Lane. He heard a faint noise at the end of his bed, and he also detected a strange musty aroma that reminded him of the smell a dog gives off when it's drying itself by the fire after being out in the rain. Stanley dared to peep over the blankets under his nose to see an unfamiliar black silhouette of something framed by the curtains behind it, which were lit by a lamp out in the street. He went cold and numb in his stomach with shock, and then the solid black shadow moved and it said his name in a gravelly voice.

'Who's that?' Stanley drew his legs up under the blankets so he was almost in a foetal position in the bed.

The reply sounded like 'Wulvarn,' and the ominous being added, 'I gave you the ball back the other day. Don't be afraid of me.'

Stanley immediately recalled those orange-gold eyes peering at him through the leaves and branches, and that giant claw of a hand tossing the ball back, and yet he could detect some warmth in the voice of the man-beast 'crossbreed'. Stanley did feel afraid, but he somehow knew the thing wouldn't harm him. Stanley slowly lifted himself up into a sitting position and rubbed his eyes. As his eyes became adjusted to the dark he saw that the figure was crouching down. If it straightened up, its head – from which two pointed wolf-like ears protruded - would have reached the ceiling. Stanley reached for the bedside lamp but Wulvarn asked him not to switch the light on. For the next few minutes, Wulvarn spoke in a low hypnotic voice about the danger the human race was doing to Mother Nature. He said that the chemical plants being built around Stanley's home would do untold harm, and he also hinted that he was very old, saying he once lived on the Heath before people came there, and that, somehow, the activities of people were somehow having negative repercussions on his world. Wulvarn told Stanley that he had chosen him to tell everyone to respect nature, but there was a rap at the bedroom door and Stanley's father could be heard on the other side of it, asking: 'Is there someone in there with you, Stan?'

In an instant, Wulvarn had vanished. The door opened, and Stanley's father came in and turned on the light. He remarked on the strange smell, and opened the windows. He asked Stanley if he had heard the deep voice in his room, but the boy shook his head, annoyed at the interruption. Wulvarn visited Stanley on six more occasions, all outdoors, always during the hours of dusk, and gave him instructions on how humans could return to nature. Stanley became an early sort of 'eco warrior' – and even wrote a letter to the local newspaper about the coming disaster to the environment, its animals and plants, because of man's greed. The letter was not published, and when Stanley told his parents about Wulvarn, a priest started to visit the house because he believed that the entity filling Stanley's head with 'rubbish' was some demonic visitor. The priest blessed the spot in the bushes where Wulvarn had first passed the ball back to Stanley, and after that, the boy received no further visits a from the ecologically concerned "wolfman". The priest seemed smug and proud about warding off the demon, but Stanley then had a nervous breakdown which affected him for over a year. When he emerged from the psychological maelstrom, Stanley could hardly recall anything Wulvarn had told him, but felt a sense of great loss and sadness, as if he had lost a close friend. The whole Wulvarn case is hard to grasp, but I think it is somehow connected to the ancient crossroads on Runcorn Heath. In a later volume of *Haunted Liverpool* I'll tell you about some of the other supernatural incidents taking place at other crossroads in our neck of the woods – including some fascinating cases in Wirral.

AS YOUNG AS YOU THINK

The following strange seasonal mystery unfolded on the Saturday evening of 22 December 2007 at a terraced house on Rundle Road, Aigburth. A 77-year-old widower named Mick, father of four and a grandfather to seven, was sitting in his usual comfy winged chair, feeling a bit sleepy because he'd just had his turkey dinner. The time was 7.45pm and his two sons, two daughters, and their spouses were watching a *Top of the Pops* Christmas Special on the telly, while the seven grandchildren were chasing one another around the house and persecuting the old tabby Pete. The sons and daughters of Mick had arranged to have the usual Christmas dinner three days earlier than usual this year because each of them had plans to spend Christmas in the country, and they knew their dad would never go with them. A bottle of "heather ale" left by Mick's old Scottish army mate Duncan was opened and only Mick would drink it; the peaty aroma and sweet taste of the traditional Celtic beverage was disagreeable to some but Mick loved the after-tang of the drink. After a few glasses of the stuff, Mick pulled a cracker with his oldest daughter – and out fell a paper horn that uncurled when it was blown into, with a piece of paper which stated: 'You'll be visited by an old friend.'

'Old friend? They're all dead,' Mick laughed, 'Only Duncan's left now.' And he dozed off with the cat on his knee and they all took pictures of him snoring in his party hat with the paper horn in his mouth.

The seven grandchildren sneaked upstairs to a room where Mick kept a train-set and all sorts of junk, and here they were joined by a strange boy. He wore a grey pullover, black shorts, grey socks and black shoes, and he was aged about seven. The children asked him his name and he said, 'Mind your own business' and went down to the kitchen, where he cut himself a hunk of Christmas cake. The children followed the boy all over the house, where he mooched about in wardrobes and drawers. He suggested a game of hide and seek and when the kids again asked him who he was, the boy said: 'Michael.'

'Michael who?' asked 6-year-old Emily.

'Michael row the boat ashore!' was the yelled reply and he flicked his finger at her face, stinging her lip. Enraged Emily chased Michael all over the house and the adults saw him and thought he was a neighbour's child. Michael found a packet of balloons, and filled two with water and he threw one at the kids in the hallway and one hit Mick's oldest son, drenching him. Michael was chased but no one could find him. He was later seen in the back parlour by Emily, the girl he had flicked in the mouth and she slapped him hard in the face, and then she screamed – because Michael looked at her with a shocked expression – before vanishing into thin air.

At that moment Mick woke up – and felt his face. He had just had a vivid dream of a girl slapping him, and when he heard about the 'phantom' boy Michael, he realised his childhood self had paid a visit – just as that cracker had predicted.

Cases of spooky human replicas have been reported many times throughout history, and they are called various names such as "fetches" and doppelgangers – but in the case of the grandfather Mick, we have a *Junger Doppelgänger* - a young double – a supernatural apparition of a younger self. It has always been my belief that the younger person we once were is still contained within us like the concentric growth rings visible in the cross section of a tree trunk. The smaller rings obviously show the earlier, younger stages of the tree, and in our minds, the old thought patterns of the child and younger self (from many ages) may still be there. This would explain the second childhood phenomenon which is often seen in old people, and also sadly in some stages of Alzheimer's Disease. Some people are blessed in that they have managed to retain the childhood sense of wonder and innocence, even though their physical bodies have aged somewhat. The long-sought after Elixir of Eternal Youth is not far away now, and geneticists and experts in the field of ageing (gerontology) are not only beginning to understand why we age – they are also able to slow ageing to a certain extent. It won't be long till ageing is stopped and then reversed, but what effect this would have on the world's ever-growing population is not known. I believe that to a certain extent, thinking old makes one act, look and feel older. We are often told that we are as old as we feel, but many people are as old as they *think*. The mind, being the product of complex electrical patterns cannot physically age, no more than a jpeg image or an MP3 file on a computer can. Energy can't age, and the mind is energy generated from chemical reactions in the brain. We get wiser as time goes on and sometimes we suffer from memory loss and cognitive slow-down, but this is the physical brain letting the mind down. The mind does not age, but the brain changes over time and so we might be under the mistaken impression that our very soul is ageing, when it isn't. If the mind is energy that is not subject to change, then, how do we know how old we are? Well, we gather experience and expand our knowledge of life and the world, and as time goes on we are *told* to "act" our age. 'He's acting like a teenager,' people say, and I've heard people say: 'She's a cradle-snatcher, going out with a man half her age.' Another classic is: 'You ever heard of growing old *gracefully*?' which is another way of saying 'act your age' – but acting is another word for pretending. We are what we are; we cannot act any age because the mind is ageless, but still people will tell you to 'grow up'. Certain individuals have a very optimistic outlook about everything, whether they are young or old, but if an older person (say, over 70) is very positive and tends to accept change and empathise with younger people, his peers will say that person is "young at heart" – another clumsy attempt to define the age of the timeless mind. The general consensus among biologists is that ageing is just a build-up of errors at the genetic level in us mammals, and that as time goes by, cells malfunction, and debris from them accumulates until the cells become sluggish. We do have error-correcting mechanisms in our cells, but these also ultimately fail over the course of time, and so our bones become brittle, hair thins and falls out, skin sags, the immune system starts to falter and we eventually expire – but in recent years incredibly small robots have been built by scientists, and some of them are as big as the full stop at the end of this sentence.

These ultra-tiny robots are called nanobot, and there are plans to release them into the bloodstream of a human so they can repair cellular damage by destroying unwanted mutated cells, and cellular debris, as well as cancer cells. The nanobots also have arms with scissor-like blades and grippers on so they can even edit our DNA. These nanobots would make us immortal and would be injected into us every so many years when we are due for the human body's equivalent of an MOT test. If the nanobots spot anything life-threatening in our body they'd laser it or edit its strands of DNA so it works to our benefit. The nanorobot immortality treatment is not that far away, but some hypnotherapists believe that the mind can be taken back along its timeline to an earlier stage in life with beneficial effects to the body – why, some hypnotherapists even claim that ageing can be reversed in a limited way to the physical body as well as the mind, and this bold and controversial claim is the subject of the following story.

In the mid-1960s an eminent psychologist visited a certain care home (then known as an Old Folk's Home) in Liverpool as part of a study of the physical and mental wellbeing of the aged. The psychologist consulted a chairman of the social services sub-committee as well as the administrator of the home and suggested that good old-fashioned entertainment, perhaps by comedians and singers, should be staged at the home to cheer the old folk up because they were, 'generally a miserable lot.'

The staff at the home was called to a meeting days later and agreed that a regular variety type of show, put on perhaps once a fortnight, would be beneficial to the psychological well-being of the residents. The secretary at the home was instructed to book a cheap cabaret comedian named Hugh Neek, but somewhere along the line, wires were crossed and a hypnotherapist named Hugh Meek was booked instead. The first show was a matinee, starting with a ragtime band playing old classics such as *On the Sunny Side of the Street* and *Don't Get Around Much Anymore*. Then, at 3pm, Hugh Meek came on the little stage and set up his slide projector. He had a mass of curly hair and wore large black-framed glasses, a pea-green suit, and a red bow tie with black spots. He seemed nervous as he tested the microphone out, and then he clicked the box in his hand and the slide projector shone a picture of what looked like a tangle of coat hangers onto a white curtain behind Mr Meek. The bemused audience wondered what the punchline would be.

'Good afternoon ladies and gentlemen. This thing here, on the screen, is a virus. A virus does not age, nor does a perennial plant – they are virtually immortal – but we age because of processes in our cells, and yet the Bible states that Adam lived for 929 years, and Noah reached 950 – and do you know why?'

'They ate their crusts?' shouted a 77-year-old Dovecot man nicknamed Tornado. Everyone laughed – including Mr Meek, but eventually he continued to talk about ageing, and rambled on about molecules and the power of the mind.

'He's shite,' a retired bus driver named Paul remarked, and the lady next to him, a former teacher, tutted.

'Give him a chance, it'll be funny,' Tornado said, leaning forward on the hard seat of an old classroom chair.

'He doesn't look like Hugh Neek,' 79-year-old Patricia (former manageress at a hotel) whispered, 'he looks too young to be him, and he's got a full head of hair. Hugh Neek's bald as a billiard ball. There's something fishy going on here.'

'Go and tell Mrs Johnson she's booked the wrong person,' 75-year-old Jeanie, the girlfriend of Tornado told Paul.

'Who's Mrs Johnson when she's in?' Paul asked, turning in his chair.

'The secretary – the one who booked him!' Jeanie replied.

'Oh let's just see what his act's like, ' Paul told Jeanie, turning his back, 'he might pleasantly surprise us.'

The old folks waited for the jokes, the patter, some slapstick – but all they got was some sort of lecture on how the ageing process could be reversed. The claims of Hugh Meek began to intrigue some of the audience, whilst others grumbled, tutted and shook their heads.

Meek showed diagrams of the brain on the screen as he claimed: 'Ageing can not only be slowed with this technique, it can even be reversed, but it has to start in your mind, and although my theory is still not fully ironed out yet, I can give you an amazing example of what it promises. I need some volunteers to be hypnotised, and I guarantee you will feel the effects of the age-reversal within minutes. Anyone willing to be a guinea pig? I promise you it's harmless and perfectly safe. Anyone like to come forward as a volunteer? Yes, you sir, and you too madam, splendid! Please come onstage! Mind that step!'

Five men and two women came forward, while the

rest complained that this was not even funny. Someone went to complain to the staff, and when the administrator came into the hall, he saw Mr Meek snap his fingers as he said: 'Young again!' The seven hypnotised pensioners smiled and said they actually felt younger, and as the administrator asked Hugh Meek what on earth was going on, the mesmerised seven went to their rooms, put on their coats and went out into the wintry afternoon. The staff and a male nurse objected to the residents leaving the home but the pensioners seemed very energetic all of a sudden and fended off the grabbing hands of the nurse and staff members trying to bar their way.

The pensioners visited a local pub where a group of Mods were drinking, and Tornado, who still wore his hair in the style of the Teddy boys in a huge back-combed quiff, was mocked by a Mod who called him an "old rocker". Tornado, who had been a bantamweight boxer in his day, knocked the Mod clean out and took the keys to his Vespa scooter. Two other 'rejuvenated' pensioners threatened the other Mods and took the keys to their scooters. People in the pub thought it was some *Candid Camera* stunt when the seven pensioners sped off on the stolen Lambrettas and Vespas down snowy roads. Tornado's girlfriend, 75-year-old Jeanie, hugged him as she rode pillion passenger. She couldn't stop laughing as Tornado overtook a bus. She felt eighteen again, and felt like crying. 'We must be dreaming!' she shouted.

'No, that fellah's done something to us!' Tornado yelled back.

They all went to a café at the Pier Head and made plans for their second lives.

Jeanie sat next to Tornado, who was spooning away into a bowl of hot chicken soup. She examined the back of her hands and saw that those veins were no longer visible. They were smooth and as white as porcelain. She stood up, went to the counter, and looked at her face in the mirror. She *was* becoming younger. She looked at her neck in the reflection – it was rejuvenated – the one part of her ageing body Jeanie hated – the sagging skin of the neck – now all gone! She turned and saw that Tornado's little bald spot had vanished, and his grey hair looked slightly darker. He looked up at her and said, 'Gear this, isn't it?'

Jeanie nodded and tears fell from her eyes. People in the café stared at her.

'What are you crying for?' Tornado got up from the table and stooped down to look at her face. 'You look – beautiful Jeanie,' he said, captivated by her returning looks. 'I mean you were beautiful before, but now, you look like you did when I first saw you, girl.'

'You've started me off again,' Jeanie blinked and tears oozed from her eyes. She wiped them away and in a choked-up voice she said: 'Say it wears off though?' She felt her smooth firm neck.

'You'll still be beautiful – you'll always be beautiful, Jeanie, and I'll always love you,' Tornado told her, and her little body vanished as his arms enclosed her.

A tinny-sounding amplified voice startled everyone in the café. It was a policeman speaking through a megaphone, and he was addressing the 'escaped' residents of the home. The police had spotted the stolen scooters and the monotone voice on the loud hailer told the seven pensioners to come out of the café immediately.

'Why's the law being like this?' Tornado asked, and Paul got up from his table and suggested going out to talk to them. Tornado said he was staying where he was, and reminded the other 'runaways' that they had not broken the law.

'Oh yeah, we just borrowed those scooters mate, didn't we?' Paul said, and he left the café.

'Hello, this Hugh Meek,' said the hypnotist via the crackly megaphone, addressing the fugitive senior citizens who remained in the café. And three times in a careful, measured manner he said: 'I want you to listen to my voice.'

'Don't listen to him! I know what he's going to do!' Jeanie tried to warn the other truant golden-agers. 'He's going to cancel that hypnotic spell! Oh Jesus! Don't listen!'

'What?' Tornado heard Meek's distorted voice begin the hypnotic instruction to counteract the one that had given them all a second chance. 'Listen to me and only me...that's right. Listen to me and only me...'

'Put your fingers in your ears!' Jeanie told Tornado, and he did what she said, and he began to hum random notes to block out the hypnotic instruction. Jeanie did the same, but the four other pensioners in the café didn't do this; they listened out of curiosity, and then they began to cough and wheeze and moan about rheumatic pains that had strangely been absent since that 'stage act'.

The police came into the café with a concerned looking Hugh Meek, and Tornado and Jeanie pretended they were back to normal, and as the youth finally drained from their five friends, Jeanie and

Tornado remained young – and later eloped from the home to start a truly new life far, far away.

AURAS OF TRUTH

In the early 1960s, a 22-year-old woman named Penny De Lion left her home in Huyton after a very heated argument with her parents, and she moved into a flat in Bootle. The row with her parents had arisen over the steady stream of people coming round to the house to have their Tarot cards read. Penny's parents were very religious and superstitious, and thought that dabbling with the occult was a sure way of inviting the Devil into the family home. Penny was a natural psychic, and from an early age she'd had what everyone assumed to be an imaginary friend known as John the Clown – but he seems to have been a ghost who was responsible for a lot of poltergeist activity which seemed to follow the young Penny about. Penny began to see auras - strange faint glows of many colours - around all living things, from about the age of five, and her mother, thinking there was something wrong with the girl's eyes, took her to the doctor. He carried out a basic eye test and then sent Penny to an optician just to confirm what he suspected – that the child's vision was perfect. The optician told Penny's mother that some people saw glows around objects because their eyes were either fatigued (a condition known as eye burn) – or, the aura was just a symptom of some neurological condition, such as a migraine. Penny told the optician she only saw the colourful glows around things that were alive – or alive for a while – such as leaves. The optician smiled, patted the little girl on the head and assured her mother that Penny just had a vivid imagination and there was nothing to be concerned about.

But Penny continued to see auras, and as she got older she became an avid reader of anything to do with the supernatural. Through her reading, Penny discovered that many of the world's ancient religions stated that we have a spiritual body that's separate from our physical body, and that this spirit-body sometimes gives off a colourful glow in those who are of a certain spiritual nature. Penny read that some clairvoyants were able to see these auras around people, and that the colour and intensity of the glow was an indication of a person's character and the state of their health. Penny could even see a 'corona' of light around her cat, and also noted that butterflies had auras too. She soon realised that anything living – from something as small as a ladybird to an African Elephant possessed an aura.

At the age of fourteen she became obsessed with the Tarot, and now it had come to all this. Penny had been forced to leave home because of her 'dabbling in the Devil's Cards' as her father had phrased it.

Just after Penny moved into the Bootle flat, she she met a girl around her age named Judy, and they became good friends. One evening Penny and Judy decided to go to Liverpool for a night out. Judy said there were some good clubs they could go to and they decided to try the Blue Angel on Seel Street first. As the girls were walking up Berry Street, not far from the bombed-out church, St Luke's, they saw a large group of smartly dressed men, and one of them – a very stocky square-shouldered chap aged about thirty – had an amazing aura about him, the likes of which Penny had never seen before. There was a halo of flaming orange around the man's head, and a fluctuating amber glow bordered the rest of his body. The intensity and colour of the aura gave Penny a very strong impression of arrogance and violence – and it was so intense it overwhelmed her. The faint auras of everyone else in the street were like glow-worms in comparison. Penny had to turn and walk in the other direction, and Judy was annoyed at her friend's evasive action because she wanted to meet one of those smartly-dressed blokes; they looked as if they had a few bob. Penny later discovered that the man with the fierce aura was Reggie Kray – one half of the notorious Kray Twins, and the smartly-attired men standing in a tight circle around him were members of his gang. Reggie's visits to Liverpool are still cloaked in mystery. Some thought he wanted to move in on the Liverpool club scene to set up a protection racket, while others believed he was interested in a million pounds' worth of platinum kept in a safe at the Automatic Telephone & Electric Company offices on Edge Lane. The Krays visited the city on several occasions, and being former boxers, they apparently went to see fights at the Liverpool Stadium, and a persistent rumour has it that Reggie once had a swift half at the Swan pub on Wood Street during one of his shadowy visits to what was then the second city of the Empire.

Penny's ability to see auras strained her friendship with Judy. When the latter met Sid, the man of her dreams, Penny noticed he had a murky pink aura, which meant he was dishonest. Judy refused to believe this but later bumped into Sid in Lewis's with the wife he'd forgotten to tell Judy about! Not long after this on a day out in Chester, Penny noticed a man with an amazing golden aura, and she even told him he had a very spiritual radiance. The man – Robert - didn't laugh; he was a reverend, and he ended up marrying Penny. Robert made it clear that he was not keen on Penny reading tealeaves, Tarot cards and auras, as the Bible clearly forbade dabbling with the occult, but the clergyman also believed that in modern times, Penny was perfectly entitled to the freedom of pursuing whatever interests she had – as long as she didn't tell him about it, so the reverend turned a blind eye to the many visits of clients to the vicarage, where Penny had the attic set up like a fortune teller's parlour. One evening Penny and her husband had very important guests around for dinner – a senior church official who some believed to be destined as the future Archbishop of Canterbury. We'll call this man Raymond – not his real name – and his wife Geraldine. Raymond was a constant critic of Penny's husband, forever quoting scripture to him, and he said he had heard the rumours about Penny's secret room at the vicarage. As Penny served the vintage port – Raymond's favourite tipple - the middle-aged ecclesiastic addressed Robert with a steely gaze. 'I know I need not remind you that the good book is unequivocal about the practise of astrology, dealing with spirits, fortune-telling, casting spells and all that witchcraft mumbo-jumbo.'

'Yes, I *have* read that too, but we have to live and let live,' Robert replied with a forced smile, 'there are modern times we're living in and – '

'Live and let live?' Raymond's face was contorted with an expression of disbelief. 'What – let them worship Satan and carry out Black Masses too?'

'Well no, I'm not saying that, obviously but – but – '

Robert stammered, and he couldn't finish the sentence anyway because Raymond cut straight in.

'No buts about it Robert, we either uphold the word of God or we get out of the Church altogether!' Raymond's face turned red and he grabbed the tulip-shaped glass of port and emptied the lot down his throat with his eyes closed – and then he shook his head. 'I'm sorry if I over-reacted then, but I have very strong opinions about this whole witchcraft mania sweeping the country – it's doing untold harm. Ouija boards and séances should have been left in the Victorian era.'

Raymond dominated the conversations for the remainder of the evening, and frequently talked over his wife Geraldine, who seemed rather afraid of him. Penny and Robert were glad to see the back of Raymond at 10.30pm, and Robert took off his collar, and his shoes, and he sat in front of the glowing red vestiges of the log fire as Penny brought him a coffee.

'So, what do you make of righteous Raymond then?' the reverend asked his wife. He really did value her opinion on account of the way she seemed to be able to read people's auras.

'Well, he had the aura of someone with a very high sex drive,' Penny told her husband, who, from his chuckle, seemed to be under the impression that Penny was pulling his leg, as she sometimes did – but she seemed very serious about her assertion.

'No, I mean it, Robert,' she assured her husband, 'the blood red glow fringed with orange, and he even looked at my legs – and my bust. I felt very uncomfortable around him.'

'What?' Robert almost spat out the coffee and

seemed very shocked at the claim.

'Auras don't lie,' Penny told him, 'and even if a person lies to himself as well as others, the aura of truth shows through.'

'But Raymond's well known for his firebrand sermons warning against promiscuity and casual sex,' Robert retorted, and he clinked down the china cup on its saucer and slowly shook his head.

Penny sat in the opposite fireside armchair. 'He obviously doesn't practice what he preaches then. You asked me what I saw, Robert – and that is exactly what I saw – the aura of a randy reverend, and that aura was like something I'd see in a much younger person, like a horny teenager. It was very worrying.'

'I've never known you to be wrong about someone, and I do believe you have a gift of seeing these auras, but if what you say is true, Penny, and I believe you are telling the truth, then Raymond must be like a real-life Jekyll and Hyde.'

Three days after this, Raymond visited the vicarage while Robert was working at a local youth club. Penny admitted Raymond, who said he'd mislaid his trilby and wondered if he'd left it on the hatstand in the hallway of the vicarage. Penny said she'd seen no such hat, but had another look anyway, and as she was searching, she happened to turn, and she saw Raymond gazing at her bottom.

'No, it's not here, I'm afraid,' she told him, and he didn't even look away, but held his lecherous gaze.

'Would you ever have an affair behind your husband's back?' he suddenly asked, and the lids of his eyes were half closed as he said this, and his expression was the very epitome of indecency.

Penny glared at him. 'I think you'd better go – right now.'

With the ghost of a smile on his face, Raymond turned and walked to the door. 'I'll let myself out.' He left the vicarage and walked some distance to his car.

When Robert came home, he listened in horror to Penny's account of Raymond's salacious behaviour, and he headed for the door, vowing to have it out with the loathsome cleric, but Penny begged him not to go, and she ran in front of her irate husband and pressed her back against the door. 'We can't prove anything,' she told him. 'He might even say you've defamed him and heaven knows what might happen – you might even be defrocked.'

'But how dare he ask you to have an affair!' Robert shook with rage.

Penny finally calmed him down, and when Raymond rang him a week later, asking him if he'd like to have dinner at his vicarage, Robert gave a blunt reply: 'No thankyou. Bye.'

Raymond then tried to spread malicious rumours about Robert, saying that *he* was sex-crazed and that he preyed upon anything in a skirt. He also claimed that Penny was nothing short of a nymphomaniac who had even tried to seduce him when he had found himself alone with her during an innocent visit to the vicarage. Before the rumours could take hold, Raymond was found red-handed, having sex with a cleaner at his vicarage one morning by a visiting clergyman. Raymond had the cleaner stretched over his office desk and was indulging in a bizarre sex act when he was caught. He claimed, rather bizarrely, that he had been possessed by an evil spirit conjured up by the 'witch wife' of Robert as he tried to bless her "Satan's sanctum" in the attic of the vicarage. Raymond was not believed, and with his ecclesiastical career in tatters, he voluntarily left the Church.

STRANGE GOINGS-ON IN LYDIATE

On a wintry morning around half-past one in January 1998, a 20-year-old girl named Alyssa left the Paradox nightclub in a huff and walked in a drunken state down Ormskirk Road with the song *Don't Give Me Your Life* by Alex Party looping round the auditory cortices of her brain. She'd had a silly falling out with her friend Emily over a discussion regarding who had the fatter legs (Alyssa said that Emily did and that there was no shape to them), and so now Alyssa was heading south towards her home in Trevor Road, Orrell Park, just under a mile away. As Alyssa walked along in a rather unsteady manner, she happened to turn to see if anyone else was about on this freezing morning. There wasn't a soul to be seen. The young woman wore only a flimsy sangria-red mini dress and a pair of Schuh wedge platforms. Alyssa rummaged about in her little handbag and located her Ericsson mobile – a present from her dad from last Christmas - but the battery was dying and so she swore at the phone and threw it back in the bag. She had hoped to tell her mother she was on her way home, because, for some unknown reason, Alyssa felt as if something ominous – life-threatening even - was hanging in the air this morning, and she would have felt better talking to her mum. The young lady thought she heard a clicking sound behind her and she turned – and to her horror she saw a huge black dog about thirty yards away. She had a phobia of dogs (caused by being bitten on the chin by one when she was 6) and so decided to cross the road to get away from the hound but it followed her. Alyssa was so afraid of the massive dog attacking her, she felt her legs turn to jelly, and in a desperate attempt to take evasive action she tried to run down Park Lane – but then she heard the heavy panting and growling of the dog as it charged at her. She turned and screamed as the animal ran at her before it jumped into the air and flew at her face. Alyssa felt the heavy body of the dog slam into her and she and the aggressive canine went backwards into someone's garden hedge.

Then everything went black. Alyssa thought she felt hands on her body, lifting her at her armpits and under her knees, but the impression was too vague to recall fully. She awoke and saw an enormous chandelier of guttering candles hanging from the darkened arched ceiling of what seemed to be a church. Someone was playing an instrument that sounded like a harpsichord, and the person at its keyboard must have been demented because the echoing melody sounded haphazard and random. Alyssa recalled the huge black dog that had attacked her and nervously turned to her right. She saw that there were about twenty or more people sitting there in rows, dressed in a very bizarre manner. They wore what looked like old-fashioned 18th century costumes – tailcoats and waistcoats of satin with prominent cuffs - and all of these people not only wore off-white wigs too, but strange green masks that covered the top halves of their faces, giving them quite a sinister appearance. This assembly of outdated-looking men naturally scared Alyssa. She tried to get up from some polished stone slab she was stretched out on, but she felt dizzy and disoriented, as if she'd been drugged. A white linen sheet covered her from her feet to the top of her bosom. She looked to her left and saw another man wearing a mask and the same old-fashioned attire as the others – only he was much closer – and he was holding a long-bladed knife as he looked down at her.

Alyssa screamed, and this man shouted to her: 'Be quiet you wretch!' And his voice did not sound local at all; it had no definable accent and he was well-spoken. Behind him, Alyssa could see sandstone pillars and stained-glass windows but everything seemed to be swaying about as if she was on a ship in heavy seas. She hoped she was dreaming, and that this was all some mere nightmare. She closed her eyes tightly and she could still hear that maniacal harpsichord player, and now the men to her right were shouting: 'Let's have her blood Claude!' and 'Drain her!' Alyssa opened her eyes and, seeing she was still in this unearthly predicament, she realised it was definitely no dream.

The man to her left – who must have been Claude – placed a white glazed bowl next to Alyssa, and next to this bowl there was a human skull with a lit candle upon its carapace. In a broken voice, Claude chillingly told her: 'I am sorry pretty one, but you *have* to die now, and there will also be more.'

'Please don't kill me! Please!' Alyssa begged, and she heard shouts from the ghoulish masked spectators. 'Get on with it!' and 'Let's have her blood Claude!' cried the masked watchers. One of the men, who sounded quite elderly, cried out, 'Put it in at the left breast!'

Alyssa turned right, towards the bloodthirsty crowd, numb with fear, and she noticed the silhouette of a towering statue of an angel with its wings spread out – but it also had horns – and this weird sculpture stood behind the cruel masked men baying for her blood.

Alyssa saw Claude lean over her, the knife poised to do something ghastly, when she felt a droplet of something warm fall upon her face. It was a teardrop, and more dripped from the blue eyes behind the green mask. 'I can't do it – I can't do it,' he whispered, hesitating to plunge the knife into Alyssa.

'Don't tarry Claude!' shouted one of the pitiless audience members.

'Do it quickly! Do it now!' boomed the voice of another.

Alyssa was so sure she'd die, she closed her eyes and from the depths of her overwhelming despair she asked for Our Lady to save her. Alyssa was a lapsed Catholic but just 5 years ago she had attended church regularly, and her mother had always told her that when she had been seriously ill as a child, a nun had prayed to Our Lady and Alyssa had made a miraculous recovery. So, as Alyssa sobbed, she began to recite the Ave Maria – commonly called a Hail Mary, and as she did, the harpsichord player immediately ceased to produce his sinister music, and Claude suddenly backed away from Alyssa and she heard the ringing sound of something metal fall to the floor. Claude had thrown down his knife. 'I can't do it! I will not do it!' he shouted, and backed away, knocking over a wrought iron floor-standing candle holder. Alyssa rolled off the slab, along with the sheet draped over her, and she instinctively landed on her palms, but felt her knees hit the hard floor with some force. She crawled along and listened to raised voices and what sounded like a scuffle. She got to her feet, and found that she was now barefooted – her platforms were gone. Somehow, Alyssa got the strength to run down the aisle to the heavy church door, and she heard a scream behind her. She turned and saw about five or more of those masked men plunging daggers into Claude, who was on one knee with his arms outstretched towards the merciless attackers. The sheer horror of the multiple stabbing made Alyssa run a lot faster to the door. She slid a bolt to the left, then yanked at a large metal ring, and the door opened silently and smoothly. She ran out into the night. She thought she saw the silhouette of that big dog, but ran down the steps and kept running, expecting the weird cultists to come after her, but they never did. Alyssa found herself on a road in Lydiate, six miles north from the spot where she had blacked out. She was picked up by a hackney driver who saw the girl walking down Southport Road at 3am in a terrified state. Her handbag, shoes and mobile phone were never found. The girl's father seemed to think that the whole affair was the result of too many vodkas and perhaps a few ecstasy pills, but Alyssa never touched drugs and knows beyond a shadow of a doubt that the ordeal was not some alcohol-fuelled hallucination. Alyssa could not trace the church where she had apparently been a sacrificial victim in some gruesome ritual – but I found what might have *been* the church once. It is now a ruin, although it was once a chapel long ago, back in the

15th century – but disturbing rumours of Devil worship at this little house of God dogged it for years and during the Dissolution of the Monasteries around 1541 the chapel fell into disuse and gradually the place of worship was abandoned. Hooded figures in long dark robes, some of them carrying flaming torches are sometimes seen in the vicinity of the chapel ruins even today. The ruins are located on a lonely road in Lydiate, set back a hundred yards off the Southport Road, just a few minutes from the spot where Alyssa was found wandering by the taxi driver that morning in 1998. Just over a mile from the gothic ruins of the chapel, at Ridgeway Park, an intriguing incident took place one night which may tie in with the masked immolators who were set to kill Alyssa that wintry morning in the last century. On a blustery March night around 11.20pm in 2015, Jake and Hannah, both aged fifteen, were embracing one another beneath a full moon, talking in hushed tones and occasionally enjoying a self-conscious kiss as they stood in the narrow opening between houses on Ridgeway Drive which gives access to Ridgeway Park in Lydiate. Jake saw movement out the corner of his left eye, and he turned to see about a dozen figures assembling in the moonlit park, some eighty yards away. Hannah turned her head to look at the figures too, and the love-struck teens stood there, curious and rather bemused, because the figures seemed to be dressed in old-fashioned clothes and white wigs (which really stood out in the moonlight). One of Hannah's favourite films was the Sofia Coppola-directed movie *Marie Antoinette* - a very stylish reimagining of the life of the doomed French queen, and Hannah thought that the figures in the park were dressed exactly in the same style of the 18th century noblemen in the film. She wanted to go and take a closer look, but Jake held her back and said he felt there was something 'weird' about the oddly-dressed strangers. Hannah became annoyed at the way her boyfriend was restraining her and tried to free herself, but as she did, Jake said: 'What are they doing? Look!' The figures held hands, forming a circle, then began to carry out some sort of dance steps. The circle moved anticlockwise, and a flickering reddish flame rose up with a faint hissing sound in the grass in the centre of the circle of men. At first, Jake and Hannah assumed this flame was a firework, but the flame turned into a red globe of light, a bit bigger than a football, and it rose about six feet from the ground, its luminance throwing spokes of shadow behind the linking dancers. All of a sudden, Jake and Hannah simultaneously found themselves filled with fear and both of them were struck with an overpowering urge to flee from the park. This they did, running down the narrow strip of grass between the houses. What happened next still haunts them. The teens ran up Ridgeway Drive, and just before they reached the thoroughfare of Coronation Road, Hannah chanced to look back – and she saw the men in the white wigs and quaint clothes emerging from the alleyway she and her boyfriend had just fled from. She yelped and told Jake the men were following her, and Jake saw them too. The teens ran with their hearts in their mouths, in sheer panic, and instead of continuing down the road, they quickly decided they'd have a better chance escaping from their pursuers if they hid on Highgate Road. Hannah hid behind a garden hedge and Jake hid behind a parked car nearby, and the teens waited, dreading the arrival of the antiquated stalkers. A few minutes went by, and Hannah was just going to peep over the hedge, when she saw something that chilled her to her marrow. The full moon was casting a shadow of the hedge onto the ground next to Hannah, and she suddenly saw the distinctive shadow of a wigged head as it looked over that hedge. She also saw the shadow of the head's profile – including its long curved aquiline nose, and she froze. The figure moved on, and Hannah thought he had gone, but then his head suddenly shot out from the side of the hedge, about three feet from the ground – and she saw that it was the head of a man in white periwig, and he wore a mask upon his face, only this one was black (unlike the green ones seen by Alyssa 17 years before. Hannah let out a scream, and she turned and ran. She hopped over the low wall which divided the garden from the one next door, and trampled flowers under her trainers as she fled. She heard footfalls close behind her and screamed, but when she turned it was only Jake, running off with her. They turned right at the end of the road and ran down Oakhill Road, then were unsure whether to turn right or left. Hannah decided to run to the left, and Jake followed. They crossed the busy Northway A59 road and didn't stop running until they reached the house of Hannah's auntie on Deyes Lane. The significance of the circle-dance ritual in the park is unknown, but I have a feeling that the location may have had something to do with the dance – perhaps in the past, the land now partly occupied by Ridgeway Park had some supernatural reputation. Are the masked men in the démodé attire ghosts of Devil worshippers of long ago, or are they living, modern-day self-styled Satanists who dress in their antiquated costumes for reasons best known to themselves? It really is hard to say given the scarcity of information at the present time. In the meantime, however, if you happen to be out after dark in the Lydiate area when you see these strangely-dressed individuals, avoid them at all costs...

MRS BROOME

In the summer of 1971, Brian and Mavis Cundle, a couple in their fifties, moved out of a five-bedroom house in Aigburth. Brian had claimed to have seen the ghost of an old man at the house on three occasions, and while his wife Mavis agreed that the old Victorian detached dwelling did have something of an unsettling atmosphere after dark, she was sure that Brian had either imagined the ghostly man or had been fooled by some trick of light and shadow. Brian disagreed and said the old man looked solid, and what's more, he had seemed very angry, perhaps displeased at other people living in a house that had once been his. In the end, the couple agreed to sell the place, and they moved into a five-bedroom house on Thingwall Road in Wavertree. To supplement their combined incomes, the Cundles took in two lodgers after they had redecorated the house. The first lodger at the house was a 20-year-old art student named Judy, and Mavis found her a delightful and considerate person who even helped her with the shopping. The second person to take lodgings at the house was 55-year-old Ken Broome, a man who had sold his house in Walton after the death of his wife a year ago. Ken said he couldn't stay at the old house now that his wife had gone, and having no children, he had found the loneliness unbearable. He was a very gregarious man, and told Mavis he really appreciated having company. Mavis told Ken he should consider himself a member of the family, and she got on quite well with him. Ken had worked in insurance but had given up his job because of the depression from the bereavement, but he believed he'd find a job later in the year once he felt up to it. He had savings and the money he'd made from the sale of his house to live on for the time being, and the rent as a lodger was only five pounds a week.

Brian Cundle seemed infatuated by the young student Judy, and had to be constantly reminded by his wife Mavis that the girl was young enough to be his daughter. 'I don't look at her that way, Mavis,' Brian told her, 'I look at her in a paternal way – as a daughter I never had.'

This talk about the daughter he never had upset Mavis, because she had tried to have children for years without any success, and Brian had assured her it wasn't his problem – and Mavis had never seen a doctor about the problem, and now, at 56, it was too late to have a child.

At teatime, the Cundles and their lodgers ate at the same table, and at one such teatime, Judy remarked that when she had been coming home from uni on the bus, she had passed a quaint looking Italian bistro that had just opened in town, and she said that she would have to check it out sometime as she loved Italian food.

'Do you fancy going there tomorrow?' Ken Broome asked Judy in a confident manner as he sat next to her, eating Mavis's speciality – a beef curry.

Brian's jaw dropped at Ken's audacious invitation.

Judy smiled at Ken with a mouthful of food and nodded enthusiastically. 'Okay, you're on!' she answered.

'Been so long since I ate out, but your food will be hard to beat Mrs Cundle,' Ken told Mavis.

'Ooh,' Mrs Cundle cooed, 'I wish someone would take me out like that,' and she looked left at her husband and added: 'hint hint!'

Brian Cundle looked as if he was about to have a coronary, and did not react to his wife's quip. He was green with envy.

'You and Brian are more than welcome to come with us, if Judy doesn't mind,' Ken said to Mavis, then gazed back at Judy, who nodded at the suggestion.

'No, no,' Mavis shook her head, 'some other time maybe. You two enjoy yourselves. The break will do Judy the world of good; she's always studying, and it's about time you enjoyed yourself after what you've been through Mr Broome.'

Brian Cundle spent the rest of that evening telling his wife that Mr Broome was delusional if he thought he'd have a chance with a girl thirty years his junior. 'What gets into fellah's heads once they reach fifty, eh?' he asked Mavis, who was smirking as she watched the television. 'I admit that Judy is a beautiful woman, but I wouldn't dream of asking her out.'

'It's platonic, Brian,' Mavis told her perturbed husband, 'Mr Broome just wants a bit of company, that's all. The man lost his wife a year ago and hasn't been living since then.'

'You're so naïve, Mavis, you really are,' Brian told

her, standing with his back to the fireplace with his hands deep in his pockets. 'I've seen the way he looks at her – he's only got one thing on his mind – you can see it a mile away. She's just an innocent young girl and he's taking advantage of her.'

'Well, they're both grown-ups, let them do what they want to do,' Mavis told him, 'or maybe you wish you were taking Judy out.'

'Oh I'm going for a walk,' Brian said, and he went to the door, 'I can't have a sensible conversation with you.'

And he slammed the door behind himself and went out, intending to go for a walk around Wavertree, but bumped into his next door neighbour, a man named Ralph he hardly knew, for he and Mavis hadn't lived on Thingwall Road that long – just over a month. Ralph invited Brian into his home and explained that his wife was visiting her mother. Brian talked about the tiff he'd had with his wife Mavis and Ralph cheered him up with an offer of a drink. The two men had a little chat about sport, politics and the opposite sex, and then at 11pm, Brian went home.

Ken and Judy started going to the pub together, and then one night at eleven, after they'd been to see a film at the Abbey Cinema, Brian looked over the banister from the upper landing and saw them kissing in the hallway. He heard Ken Broome say, 'This is wrong, Judy, I could be your father.' And Judy had softly replied: 'I don't care, I want you in my bed.'

Ken had then gone into Judy's room with her. Brian stood on the stairs facing her door, and he heard giggling, then minutes later he heard the rhythmic sounds of those springs in Judy's bed, and her soft exaltations of pleasure.

The jealousy welled up in Brian, and he felt like kicking the door in. Mavis appeared at the top of the stairs and told him to come to bed. She knew what he was going through as he stood there in the darkened hallway.

'I'll be up now,' Brian said, 'just locking the front door.'

The next day at three in the afternoon, Brian boarded a Number 79 bus in town to take him home, and he went upstairs, sat down, and noticed that the back of the man's head two seats in front of him belonged to his lodger Ken Broome – and there was a woman sitting next to him. The woman was apparently nagging Ken. 'You're *my* husband. Stay away from this Judy one – she's a child, Ken. Thirty years of marriage and you start cradle-snatching,' she told Mr Broome. He took no notice and looked at his watch. 'You can't even answer me can you?' Mrs Broome asked.

Brian Cundle was elated. He'd found the adulterer out. Wait till Mavis – and Judy – heard about this. Mrs Broome was alive and well! So much for Ken's sob story about her death and all the lonely nights and the depression and having to give up his job – all lies.

Later, as the vehicle started to slow down at the approach of Wavertree High Street bus stop, Brian quickly got to his feet and descended to the bottom deck before Ken could get downstairs. He bowed his head and hid behind the queue of other passengers waiting to disembark. Brian Cundle then walked up the High Street but deliberately slowed down to let Ken catch up.

'Hello Mr Cundle,' Ken said to his landlord.

'Oh hello there,' Brian replied, 'I've just been to town to have a look at some carpets for the house. Have you just come off that bus as well?' Brian nodded at the back of the green Atlantean moving away into the heavy queue of traffic.

'Yes, I was upstairs,' he replied and they both walked on, talking about England's performance in the Third Test Match with India at The Oval.

Mavis Cundle said her husband had been mistaken, because Ken's wife had been dead a year. Brian fumed and said he'd swear on the Bible that he had seen a woman who could only have been his lodger's wife because she had even stated that she had been married for thirty years. 'It wasn't scotch mist, Mavis, it was Mrs Broome,' Brian told his wife, his flushed face inches from hers. 'I should have just gone up to him and asked him to introduce her,' Brian regretted.

'No wonder your older brother used to call you Pryin' Brian,' Mavis told him, pushing him away. 'You're always snooping into people's lives – you take after your mother, you do, she was always probing people's affairs.'

'You know what, Mavis? I'm starting to wonder if you've taken a shine to Mr Broome,' Brian said with a raised right eyebrow. 'You won't hear anyone say a bad word about him.'

Mavis threw her head back and projected a deep-sounding mock laugh at the ceiling. 'No one says anything bad about him, only you, and it's all because he's having a relationship with Judy. You're obsessed with the two of them.'

'I'm not obsessed, Mavis, I'm just concerned that Mr Broome is an adulterer and he is going to break that girl's heart!'

'Oh just let it go, Brian, please,' Mavis groaned. 'You should be more concerned with our life, never mind the lives of others.'

On the following day, when Ken was out, Brian rummaged through his room and found a picture of Mrs Broome – it was, beyond a shadow of a doubt, the very woman he'd seen on the bus with Ken. She had the same large head of curly dark hair and the same profile as the woman who had been nagging his lodger yesterday. When Brian showed the photograph of Mrs Broome to his wife, she shook her head and told him he was now 'beyond help'.

'That is proof, Mavis,' Brian flicked his finger against the photograph he was holding. 'He's been lying all along, but I'll bide my time and then I'll confront him in front of Judy when the time is right.'

Mavis buried her face in her palms. 'If you do, I'll leave you - I've had enough of all this, Brian. This has taken over your mind – it's an illness.'

On the following Saturday morning Ken came into the dining room with a bouquet of red carnations and said he was going to put them on the grave of his wife in Anfield Cemetery. Today was her birthday.

'Oh, they're beautiful,' Mavis remarked, and she smiled sympathetically at Ken. 'How old would she have been?'

In a broken voice, Ken muttered: 'Fifty-one Mavis.'

Brian sat at the dining table looking over the edge of the newspaper he was reading with a slight grin on his face.

Judy asked Ken if she could go to the cemetery with him but he grabbed her hand, squeezed it, then slowly shook his head. 'No, I'll go alone if you don't mind, love. Call me old fashioned but it doesn't seem right - going to the grave of my old love with my new love. I hope that hasn't offended you dear.'

'No, I understand Kenny,' Judy replied, and she lifted his hand and kissed it.

'Have a nice cup of tea before you go,' Mavis pulled a chair from the table, and Ken sat on it, and murmured: 'Thanks Mavis.'

'I've made some of those Eccles cakes you're fond of,' Mavis said with a big smile, and she patted Ken's shoulder. She brought the plate of cakes in and put them in front of her lodger. Judy sat next to him.

Convinced that Ken was going to see his living wife, Brian went next door to see his neighbour Ralph and asked him if it would be possible to borrow his car, as he had to go and visit a sick relative soon. 'The wife's taken the car to town but I have my old runaround if you want to take that, Brian,' Ralph told his new friend.

'Yes, of course,' Brian replied, 'I'll give you some petrol money for this, mate.'

'No you won't,' Ralph dismissed the offer, and beckoned him with a nod to come to the garage. 'Come on, it's an old Hillman Hunter.'

'Oh, I used to drive one of them,' Brian said gleefully, 'must get back on the road with a set of wheels soon.'

Brian got into his neighbour's car, drove about a hundred yards, then parked near the gates to an allotment. He saw Ken Broome come out of the house with the bouquet of red carnations and the lodger was in luck, because he managed to flag down a Hackney cab. Brian experienced a rush of excitement as the taxi passed him. He moved off in the Hunter slowly, so as not to attract attention, and then he kept his eyes on the Hackney cab. He almost lost it at the first set of lights, but caught up with it within the minute. Half an hour later the Hackney cab halted at the Walton Lane entrance to the cemetery, and Ken Broome got out and had a conversation with the taxi driver for about a minute. In this time, Brian drove 200 yards to reach the break in the central reservation so he could turn the car around and park on Bodmin Road, facing the cemetery gates. He hurried into Anfield Cemetery and could see his lodger walking slowly down the path, about eighty yards away. Brian kept his distance and followed Ken. At one point, Brian hid behind the thick trunks of the old trees in the cemetery and watched carefully as Ken halted at a black rectangular headstone, less than forty feet away. Ken crouched down and laid the bouquet of carnations in front of the headstone, then straightened up with his head bowed. What Brian then witnessed would haunt him for the rest of his life. A woman rose up out of the grass of that grave as if she was coming up in an invisible elevator. Even from forty feet away, Brian could see this was the same woman he had seen sitting next to Ken on the bus. She wore the same brown coat and her hair was a huge mass of dark curls. This was obviously the ghost of Ken Broome's wife, Brian realised with an icy shudder, and he heard her scream at her husband: 'Never mind flowers! Stop seeing that girl!'

Ken did not react, and it occurred to Brian that he could not see nor hear the ghost of his late wife.

Brian turned and he ran as fast as he could. When he reached his car on Bodmin Road, he recalled the ghost of the old man he had seen in the house in Aigburth – the ghost that Mavis had been unable to see, and with mounting horror, Brian concluded that he was psychic; that was why he had seen Mrs Broome sitting next to Ken on that bus, and it explained why his lodger had not reacted to the ghost – he hadn't been able to see her or hear her as she nagged him. The ghost must have followed her husband onto that bus, and if she could do that, she could pay him visits at the house on Thingwall Road as well, Brian reasoned. Sure enough, for the next couple of months – till Ken Broome left the house to live with Judy – the ghost of Mrs Broome stalked her living husband, and not only did Brian bump into the solid-looking apparition several times, he also heard her shouting at her oblivious husband on just as many occasions, and the visitations of the wife from beyond the grave almost resulted in Brian Cundle having a nervous breakdown. He rejoiced when Ken Broome and Judy finally left the house.

THE EVERTON WITCH

In the 1970s a young doctor named Stephen began his practice in North Liverpool, and the first time he went out on call was in late October 1974, to a family in Everton. The oldest son, 9-year-old Kevin was delirious, and the doctor soon established that he had a high temperature, swollen neck glands and a severe sore throat. 'Your son has the flu,' Stephen told the parents, and he noticed the crucifix on a chain around Kevin's neck and also saw the corner of what turned out to be an old copy of the Bible protruding from under his pillow.

'It's no fever that,' said the boy's grandmother, 'that's the work of that witch.'

There was a heavy pause, and then the skin between the doctor's eyebrows lifted up as if he was sympathising over something, but he smiled lopsidedly too, then turned his head a few degrees and the word he spoke was just audible. 'Witch?'

Kevin's mum Sheena stepped forward between Stephen and her mother and explained that her son had smashed the window of a woman who lived in a squat by the park, and that she had cursed him loudly. 'That woman's a witch as sure as we're all standing here, doctor,' Sheena asserted, and Stephen could see the fear in her sincere eyes. 'She's cursed other people round here and people have even died.' Sheena then gripped her mother's hand and squeezed it.

'Oh come on, it's 1974, not 1674,' the doctor laughed and assured them that Kevin's illness was due to a virus doing the rounds, not some curse, and he prescribed rest, plenty of water, and minimal food until Kevin regained his appetite.

Three days later, on the evening of Halloween, Stephen was called out again by the family in Everton. Kevin's younger brother Mark was now ill, and again it looked like a simple case of the flu. The boy's Nan said the witch by the park was to blame for Mark's illness, and after the doctor had left the house, he happened to see a large gang of men of all ages passing by, and some of them were ranting about the witch and how they should drive her out – and some of them had sticks. The doctor could not believe how superstitious the mob were and out of curiosity he got into his car, gave the gang a head start of a minute, and then he slowly followed them.

The rowdy scrum travelled about a quarter of a mile to a dilapidated-looking terraced house where the woman was squatting. Stephen realised he was witnessing a modern witch hunt. The men were chanting 'die witch!' and waving their sticks as they looked at an upstairs window at the house. The young doctor shook his head, disgusted at the pathetic ignorance and hysteria of the mob. A lady of about thirty with long reddish brown hair appeared at the upper window, and the men threw stones at her. The rabble then rushed up the three steps at the entrance of the derelict dwelling. The woman flitted away from the window, and then the doctor gasped, because the woman jumped out of another window at the side of the house on the same floor, and she seemed to *float* down into a yard, and during the inexplicably slow descent, the silhouette of the woman crossed the disk of the full moon which was then just rising. The figure landed somewhere behind a yard wall, and Stephen stood there, absolutely baffled as to how the woman had effected such a slow descent from that window. It had looked as if the woman had been suspended from some ultrafine wire. The mob rushed around to the back of the run-down house and chased the woman, and the doctor drove after them. Stephen beeped his horn as the crowd spilled into the road, and had to drive around them because they were so caught up in the witch-hunt, they were oblivious to his car and others on that road. Stephen eventually overtook the herd of excited and jeering locals and caught sight of the 'witch'. He wound down his window as he followed her, and heard her screams of laughter as she ran barefooted in long bounds down a cobbled road. The doctor wondered what he would say and do when he caught up with this incredibly agile lady. Something deep down in his logical, rational mind told him that she really had floated down from that window, and that only an Olympic athlete could jump along in amazing bounds the way she was doing now. Another part of Stephen's mind told him that the lighting conditions were abysmal round here, and dusk could simply be playing tricks – even on his scientifically-trained mind.

The woman ran to a church, and was seen to wrestle with the large brass handle on the door before she managed to get into the building. Stephen got out of his car and went to the church door, but now it was locked.

All of the lights went out inside the church and only the moon's light poured through the stained-glass windows. The priest came to investigate the manic laughter and saw the silhouette of a woman against the moonlit window – and she was hanging in the air about five feet off the ground. She was out of breath and she asked for sanctuary and when the priest refused, the church statues rocked about and some toppled over as candles were blown out by hissing blasts of air. The priest asked the lady if she was an agent of the Devil and she screamed "Oh f—k No!" before flying over to a doorway which led to a side exit from the church. The priest ventured outside via that exit and eventually saw the doctor. Stephen had caught a fleeting of glimpse of the woman before she leaped clean over a six-feet tall sandstone wall into the night. The doctor was invited into the priest's house, where the holy man told the medical man about the levitating witch and the statues that had sustained damage after being pushed over by invisible forces. The doctor in turn told the priest about the woman apparently jumping out of an upper floor window in slow-motion and her strange way of running by making leaps of about twelve feet into the air. Stephen did not want to be referred to the Medical Council to have his ability to practise questioned – and that would most probably happen if word got out about the things he had seen tonight – so he only told the priest what he had witnessed with regards to the unknown woman on the condition that it would be held in the strictest of confidence. The doctor did eventually tell me about the witch though when he retired, many years later. I mentioned his story on a radio programme I was on and several people who had lived in Everton in the 1970s recalled the incident, and some claimed that the woman was thought to have been what was then termed a hippie, who originated from Cheshire. One caller named Betty told me that the woman was definitely a witch, and that she had called at her home in August 1974 and had asked her mother for some flour and other ingredients. Betty's mother closed the door on the woman, who had on a long black dress, and the caller shouted something through the letterbox. At that moment, the large full-length mirror in Betty's room cracked in two upstairs and no one was in the bedroom at the time.

The "Everton witch" was seen no more in the area after that Halloween night and Kevin and his brother instantly recovered from the so-called flu. I have been unable to find out who the mysterious woman was, but I am sure that someone, somewhere out there, knows her story, and for all I know, maybe the lady herself is reading these very words; if that is the case I'd dearly love to hear from her.

A BIKE NAMED GEOFF

The following strange story began one hot drowsy afternoon in the summer of 2013. A couple in their thirties – Dominic and Eva – had decided to live together. They clubbed together and took a mortgage out on a semi on Huyton's Tarbock Road. Dominic's 76-year-old widowed grandfather Cyril, who lived in Speke, began to visit the couple almost every day, and although Eva got on really well with him, Dominic thought his grandad was wearing out his welcome and told his partner he intended to have words with Cyril soon. On the day Dominic was going to have it out with Cyril, Eva was clearing out the garage (which should have been cleared out by the previous owners of the house) when she found an old bicycle. Dominic wanted to throw it into the skip he'd just hired but Eva said she wanted to keep the old bike. She couldn't say why she wanted to keep it, but to her, the old bicycle just seemed to have a personality, and she also felt that there was something quite sad about the vintage machine. Dominic said she was barmy, wanting to keep the wreck of an old bike, and then Cyril turned up with parcels of fish and chips for the couple, and before his grandson could pull the old man up about his daily visits, Eva showed Cyril the superannuated cycle.

'What are you going to do with it?' Cyril asked, stroking the royal blue frame of the bike. He squinted at the faded lettering and logo on the down tube. 'Well stuff my old boots!' Cyril exclaimed with excitement in his eyes. 'A Geoff Clark bike. My old mate Banksy used to have one of these; I wanted a Geoff Clark so badly when I was fifteen. They came out in the early Fifties. This'll be worth a few bob – it's vintage.'

'Does it need much doing to it?' Eva asked Cyril.

'It needs dumping in the bleedin' skip,' Dominic butted in before his grandfather could answer.

'Seriously, is it salvageable Cyril?' Eva wanted to know.

Cyril examined the bicycle and muttered unintelligible things about callipers, chain stays, inners, binda straps and Benelux gears. Then in layman's terms Cyril told Eva: 'It's in a fair condition, but it could definitely be saved with a bit of tender loving care and a bit of oil.'

'Well, if you can restore it to its former glory Cyril, you can have it,' Eva stipulated with a broad smile.

'Are you serious?' Cyril asked, squeezing the rear flat tyre of the bike. Eva had never seen the old man smile so much; he looked elated at the offer. 'This would be a tonic to me, Eva. You sure you don't want it yourself?'

'No, I don't want it and Dominic obviously doesn't want it. It'd save you a few bob in bus fares if you got on the road with that,' Eva reasoned.

'I've got bus pass, Eva,' Cyril reminded her, 'but I'd love to get back into cycling.'

Overhearing all this, Dominic stopped his clearance of the junk in the garage, wiped the sweat from his brow with the back of his hand, and approached his grandfather and his fiancée. 'I did hear you right then, didn't I?' he asked Eva. 'About you suggesting that he could take this on the road?'

'Yeah, what about it?' Eva asked, sensing there'd be some objection to her simple notion.

'He can just about walk, never mind ride a bike,' Dominic indicated his grandfather with his thumb. Then he added: 'If you cast your mind back to last Easter, you may recall he suffered a mini stroke.'

'And that's all the more reason for him to get some exercise and keep in shape,' Eva retorted. 'You're ageist Dominic – just because Cyril's 76, you treat him as if he's past it.'

'Past it?' Dominic raised his eyebrows, smiled and nodded. 'That Imhotep out *The Mummy Returns* is in better shape than him.'

'You'll be old yourself one day, mate,' Cyril glared at his disrespectful grandson.

'I'm not having a go at you, Grandad,' Dominic rolled his eyes. 'But you're round here every bleedin' day, and whenever I go anywhere you latch on and follow me – you're like some probation officer supervising a young offender!' Dominic took a sharp intake of breath; he'd got what he had wanted to say for some time out of his system at last.

'Dominic!' Eva snapped at him, 'Take that back! Cyril will always be welcome here!'

'Well I'll stop coming round if that's how you feel,' Cyril bowed his head and looked at the pedals with unshed tears in his eyes.

'I – I don't mind you coming round now and then Grandad,' said Dominic, his voice sounding fainter as he went on. He looked ashamed of his outburst. 'You know we love you coming round and that, but everyday's too much – I don't mean too much for us, but too much for your health.'

'Cobblers!' Cyril told him straight. 'You don't want me around because you think I'm too old and in the way.'

'If it was the other way round and you were the younger one you would have well told me to stop bothering you - especially if you were with a bird.' Dominic asserted. 'And it isn't cobblers about me being concerned for your health. If you get on that bike it'll be like something out of *Holby City*. We've had three funerals in the family in the last two years – I don't want to see another one!'

'I can ride a bike better than you can, even at my age,' Cyril shook the old bicycle by the handlebars as he made this claim. 'You're all flab, mate. I'm like a whippet.'

Dominic paused for a second, and his eyes seemed to burn with anger. He pressed his front teeth against his bottom lip, then produced the most painful attempt at a laugh in his life. 'This proves what we've long suspected - he's got Alzheimer's,' he told Eva, who was cringing because she knew Dominic's recent weight gain was a touchy subject at the best of times. She felt for him but he was mean to his grandfather and she could see Dominic walking straight into this one.

'I haven't got anything wrong with me,' Cyril told him, screwing his eyes up and gritting his teeth. 'and I can run rings round you on a bike because I'm in better shape than you.'

Dominic shook his head and glanced down at his legs. 'I look as if I've put a bit of weight on because I've got a water retention problem – '

'Yeah, through lack of exercise. You're always eating

pizzas in front of the telly and drinking cans of lager like it's going out of fashion,' Cyril told him. 'Admit it.'

'Lager and pizzas?' Dominic returned a puzzled look, and turned his gaze to Eva: 'Can you remember when this took place?'

Eva nodded with a resigned expression. 'Yes, last Friday night. You were asking me and Cyril why McDonalds and the KFC don't do deliveries.'

'Anyway, I'll be off,' Cyril told Eva, 'I'll take this on the bus. Shouldn't be any bother.'

Eva seized the old man's arm. 'No, Cyril, you're not going. Come and have a coffee – come on.'

'There's your fish and chips there,' Cyril sheepishly told his grandson as he pointed to the parcel on the folding square table on the lawn. He then went inside the house with Eva.

'I don't want your fish and chips!' Dominick shouted to his grandfather's back, 'I'm too fat remember! You eat it!'

Without turning, Cyril gave him the V sign as he used his other hand to steer the old bike up the path.

Dominic hurried into the house and issued a challenge to his grandfather. 'Oi, Bradley Wiggins,' he said to Cyril, who was kneeling next to the old bicycle, examining its back tyre. 'I've got a challenge for you – we have a race from here to some destination – you can choose it, I don't care – and if I win, you have to stop coming round here every day, but if you win you can live with us if you want. How does that grab you?'

Eva was infuriated by the challenge. 'Dominic, are you listening to yourself? Just let this little disagreement die out, please!'

Cyril stood up and told his grandson: 'You're on!' He

offered him his hand to seal acceptance to the challenge.

Dominic gave a weak handshake but avoided eye contact.

'Dominic, you haven't even got a bike – ' Eva begun, but her fiancé interrupted her with a raised voice.

'I'll buy one, Eva! Yeah, that's right, a real top of the range one, carbon fibre and graphene – and I'll make you two eat your words!'

'Why are you involving me?' Eva asked, 'Have I knocked you?'

'Oh you had a go at me indirectly love,' Dominic told her, and his voice sounded uneven, broken, like he was going to start crying. 'You brought all that up about me being some couch potato who wants home deliveries from McDonalds and Colonel Sanders. You never back me up!'

'Don't be bringing Eva into this,' Cyril interposed, '*you* started all this, making out I'm a danger on the roads and can't ride a bike! Go and get your highfalutin bike and I'll still race rings round you, you big Jessie!'

'Big Jessie eh?' Dominic sounded really choked up now. 'That's nice, isn't it? Talking to your grandson like that...' he said, and his voice trailed off as he turned and went back outside. He picked the parcel of fish and chips up, threw them into the air a few feet, then performed a rugby punt kick.

'I can't believe you just did that,' came Eva's voice from behind him. 'Your grandfather bought you those fish and chips and he's only on a basic pension. You're insane, do you know that?'

'Oh I am at the moment, fuming mad, because

certain people have driven me that way!' Dominic yelled at her and went out of the baking sun into the garage to continue the clear out.

Cyril enlisted the help of a retired mechanic named Charlie Latimer to help him restore the Geoff Clark bicycle, and within a fortnight the bike was working perfectly with brand new brake blocks, a new chain, and new tyres. Charlie even sprayed the frame a shade of Zaffre blue, which was exceedingly close to the frame's original colour. Charlie had a test ride of the bike and found it to be in perfect order with no handling problems. Cyril was like an impatient boy that day, and after adjusting the seat to his liking, he took off from the kerb outside his Speke home, and when he returned about ten minutes later, he said something odd to the retired mechanic. 'Something quite strange happened when I was going round that curve on Alderfield Drive – you know by Almeda Road?'

Charlie Latimer nodded.

'Some dog started chasing me – a huge big thing – it should have been on a lead. Anyway, I thought it was going to take a chunk out my leg – but the bike started speeding up – on its own.'

'It's flat there though, Cyril,' Latimer recalled that stretch of road. 'How could it speed up?'

'I know Charlie, but the bike just speeded up as if it had an engine attached, and I was pedalling a bit faster than usual because the dog was gaining on me, but I must have been doing nearly forty.'

'No way, Cyril – a pro could do that type of speed but not you or I, mate. It must have just *felt* faster.'

'I'm telling you Charlie, this bike flew round that bend in the road and it was going that fast, I couldn't see because the air was striking my eyes and they were smarting and tears were streaming out of them.'

'Well what are you trying to say, Cyril? That the bike's haunted or something?' Charlie asked him and grinned.

Cyril shrugged. 'I don't know what was responsible for it, mate, but you've known me for nearly sixty years, and you know I don't tell fibs.'

'Cyril, you've probably had the wind behind you – the river's only about 500 yards away when you go down Alderfield Drive. It's been a blast of wind from the river that, and its pushed you round that corner.'

'It was calm Charlie but we'll never know what caused it, it's just one of those unexplained things that happen in life, unless it happens again.' Dominic presented his grandfather with a computer print-out of the route of the race. The starting point was the junction at Tarbock Road and St John's Road; they then had to travel about a mile down Tarbock Road and turn left onto Wilson Road. The route then went a mile up Wilson Road until they turned left onto St John's Road and on to the finishing line back at the Tarbock Road junction, where Eva would be waiting with a stop watch. Cyril insisted on Charlie Latimer being an independent judge with a second stopwatch. Dominic begrudgingly agreed to it. The race was to start on the following Sunday at 6am, so that there would hopefully be hardly any traffic on the roads. Eva tried to get the competitors to call off the race but grandson and grandfather were determined to go ahead with this race of two-and-a-half miles. On the Sunday morning at a quarter past five, Cyril arrived at his grandson's house in Charlie Latimer's Ford Transit van. Cyril took his restored bike – now nicknamed "Geoff" by him after the make of model, Geoff Clark – out the van and gave it a cursory inspection. Eva asked Cyril and Charlie to have some breakfast, and Cyril declined, saying he'd already eaten a special energy meal. Charlie went inside the house with Eva and had some scrambled eggs, black pudding, beans and bacon with her and Dominic. Cyril went into the van and put on a pair of banana-yellow baseball leggings, a high-vis skin-tight cycling jacket, a pair of brilliant white 'Nuke' trainers. He then went into the house carrying an expensive aerodynamic Kask Mojito cycling crash helmet – borrowed from Charlie Latimer – under his arm.

'Very impressive, Cyril,' said Eva, sitting between Dominic and Charlie. She thought Cyril cut a fine figure in the cycling wear, and she could see how thin he was now that he wasn't wearing his usual baggy attire.

'You look like an anorexic version of Tron,' said Dominic, and he beamed what was obviously a painful forced smile. He looked green with envy. No one even reacted to his feeble attempt at a joke.

'Are you wearing your bike gear, Dominic?' Charlie asked.

'Just the basic stuff, shorts and a tee shirt and trainers. The clobber's irrelevant; it's the stamina and skill at handling the bike that counts,' was his confident reply to Charlie. And he started to sing *Eye of the Tiger* as he dipped a soldier of fried bread into a sunny-side egg.

The race started at exactly 6am as Eva blew on an old referee whistle. Dominic shot off first and pedalled like mad down Tarbock Road, frequently glancing back over his shoulder to see where his grandfather was. Charlie and Eva laughed at the whole thing and sat on a bench near the traffic lights, each eyeing their own stopwatch. 'I told Cyril to watch it at his age after that mini stroke but he won't have it,' said Charlie, shaking his head. The two competitors were just two spots in the distance now.

'Yeah, that's what I'm worried about Charlie,' said a concerned Eva, 'and Dominic has a heart murmur you know? He's in denial as well. He hasn't even been dieting or anything for this event, just eating an extra Shredded Wheat of a morning. I'll be glad when it's all over.'

Charlie looked at his wristwatch. 'The average person takes about three to four minutes to cover a mile, travelling at say – about 18mph. If it all goes without incident they should be back here in about ten minutes.'

As Dominic passed Meadow Drive, he saw to his horror that he was being steadily overtaken by his grandfather, and not only that, he was beginning to find it hard to breathe. He saw Cyril look back over his right shoulder with that silly helmet on, and then the old man started to accelerate. 'He's got some engine fitted to that thing, the cheating bastard,' gasped Dominic. He watched with a burning heavy sensation in his legs as a man forty years his senior rocketed ahead of him down the tree-lined road until he could no longer be seen. Cyril, meanwhile, felt his stomach turn over as he realised that strange speeding up of the bicycle was happening again. The old man felt as if he was riding some silent motorbike and estimated he must have been doing at least 50 mph. The broken centre line stripes in the road were a continuous blurred line now and trees and bus stops were flashing past, and yet Cyril had stopped pedalling. He knew that if he exerted the slightest pressure with his index fingers on the front and back brake levers, he'd be thrown clean over the handlebars, and despite the safety helmet he was wearing, he'd either be killed or sustain life-changing injuries. The bicycle started to slow down, and Cyril realised that Wilson Road was coming up on the left now. This was the second leg of the race. Cyril wanted to get off the bike with a mind of its own, and yet he also wanted to win this race, and so he turned the bike into Wilson Road and began to pedal again, but within seconds "Geoff" was at it again – accelerating at speeds Cyril could never hope to attain – so who was pushing this bike along? The clue came when Cyril looked at his right hand gripping the handlebar: he was wearing an onyx ring on his third finger. Since his wife had died three years ago, Cyril had stopped wearing his wedding band, and had never been one for jewellery – so where had that onyx ring come from? He glanced back at his hand about twenty seconds after noticing the ring, only to find it had gone.

Eva's mobile rang and she saw it was Dominic calling. She answered it and heard her fiancé all out of breath as he told her: 'I'm coming back! I've turned around. Do you know what he's done?'

'No, what?' she asked, expecting Dominic to tell her that his grandfather had crashed.

'He and that mate of his – that Charlie Latimer – have fitted some engine to the bike. He must have took off at about fifty!' Dominic then wheezed, coughed and spat, then told Eva. 'Anyway, I'm coming back. I can't believe he's cheated. I should have checked his bike before we set off. I thought he was a sportsman - I'm too trusting.'

Eva told Charlie about Dominic's bizarre claim and the former mechanic returned a puzzled look. 'How could we fit an engine to a racing bike and keep it hidden?' he asked. 'You'd see the fuel tank and the engine. Sounds like a sore loser to me.'

A few minutes later, they saw the approach of Cyril as he came down St John's Road. As he reached the finishing line, Dominic came on the scene from his aborted attempt on Tarbock Road. He staggered to his grandfather's bike, seized the handlebar, then looked closed at every part of the frame. 'Where is it?' he asked. 'You've taken it off now!'

'Taken what off?' His grandfather dismounted from the bike and saw Dominic on his knees, looking under the saddle.

'I bet its hidden under the seat. No one can go that fast unassisted. I'm not stupid grandad!'

'What are you talking about?' Cyril asked, but he had an idea what Dominic was referring to.

Dominic looked at Charlie Latimer, narrowed his eyes and said: 'You must have stuck one of those engines on this thing!' he then turned to Eva and explained: 'They're only 48cc two-stroke numbers but they fit them onto bikes and the bike becomes a moped!'

'Well where the bloody hell is it then?' Charlie asked, quite annoyed. 'You're paranoid, mate. Your grandfather won fair and square because he's in better shape than you. That's all there is to it.'

A police car pulled up a few feet away, startling the four of them. A tall policeman got out the vehicle and approached Cyril. He said: 'I clocked you before doing over fifty down St John's Road. You flew over that zebra by the school. Have you got a licence for that thing?'

'See?' shrieked Dominic, with a huge grin on his face. To Eva he said: 'I told you he was using some engine!' He got back on his bike and pedalled along the pavement towards the policeman.

The policeman examined the Geoff Clark bike. 'Are you a professional cyclist?' he asked Cyril.

'No! He's a professional cheat, officer!' Dominic butted in.

'No, but I'm sorry I went that fast officer,' said Cyril, 'I was taking part in a race with my grandson there. I must have got carried away.'

'Are you on amphetamines or something?' the policeman asked with a crooked grin.

'The only drugs that I've taken are alcohol and caffeine officer,' Cyril told the intrigued officer.

'He's lying,' Dominic told the constable. 'He had some little engine attacked to the bike – he must have done – he's 76, I mean, it's obvious.'

The lanky policeman looked down at Dominic. 'Sir, no engine has been rigged up to this bicycle. I've had a look, and it's just a ten-gear bike propelled by legs and nothing else.'

'Thanks for clarifying that officer,' Charlie Latimer said, and he smirked at Dominic.

'I give you my word I'll never go that fast again on these roads.

'Thankyou sir,' said the policeman, and he looked at Dominic and said: 'Keep your bike off the pavement sir. A court can fine you five hundred quid for that.'

When they all got back to Dominic and Eva's house, Cyril self-consciously voiced his theory about the vintage bike and its inexplicable bursts of speed. He told them about the onyx ring he had seen on his hand as he raced along Wilson Road. 'I think the previous owner of this bike was some professional cycle racer, and perhaps he died. I think his ghost is somehow making his old bike go as fast as it used to. I know it sounds far-fetched but I can't explain the things I've experienced any other way.'

Eva said she believed Cyril's theory, for she had somehow sensed an 'aura of sadness' about the bicycle when she had found it in the garage. She made enquiries with the neighbours, and one neighbour, a woman of eighty, said she recalled a man in his thirties named David, who was always on a bicycle, and he had lived in the very house Eva and Dominic now lived in. This David, the old woman recalled, had been knocked down and killed whilst riding his bike somewhere on Queen's Drive in the 1960s, or possibly the early 1970s. She could not recall anything else about him – and she certainly didn't know if he wore an onyx ring – but Eva and Cyril believe his ghost was somehow responsible for propelling the old bicycle. Not wishing to risk his life by taking Geoff on the road, Cyril gave the bike back to Eva, and she put it back in the garage, and once again she felt an aura of sadness hanging over the renovated bicycle. Dominic later apologised to his grandfather and told him he was welcome to visit anytime he wanted.

NEVER OVER

In Liverpool, strips of grassy areas and rectangles of rubble where houses and buildings had once stood were called 'ollers. The etymological origins of the word 'oller are now lost in the mists of time, but might be derived from "hollow" – a small valley between mountains and also a stretch of land devoid of trees. Some etymologists have even mooted whether the name 'oller comes from the craters created by bombs dropped by the Luftwaffe on Liverpool in World War Two, reasoning that such craters would leave a hollow ground. I can't see this being the case, although some derelict houses in Liverpool in times past were referred to as "bombdies" – probably a slang version of bombed houses which had been left as shells during the same war. What follows in this chapter is a description of a weird incident which took place on an 'oller in Everton.

In 1966 in Everton there was a 70-year-old man named Alf, regarded by most people in his neighbourhood as an eccentric. They say he'd seen action in the Somme in World War One and had come back a changed man after seeing most of his friends die in the battle, and in those days there was no counselling. The horrors of the 'Great War' had turned his mind and Alf, like millions of other soldiers, was soon forgotten after the conflict ended. He volunteered to wallpaper a woman's room one day in August 1966, and after just half an hour had informed the lady that the job was finished, but when the woman went up to the room she saw that Alf had created a huge Union Jack cross by plastering the roll of wallpaper at various angles across the wall. Not long after this, a couple of local crooks – Terry and Joey - both aged 18 – tried to break into Alf's dilapidated house one Sunday afternoon when they thought he might be out, but Alf was in, and he scared the house robbers by yelling at the top of his voice and charging at them with a brush – as if he was wielding a Lee Enfield rifle fixed with a bayonet. Terry and Joey fled but began to play games with the old man. They'd knock on his door and shout 'Achtung!' through the letterbox and Joey even put a few windows in with ball bearings fired from a catapult. A neighbour of Alf named John chased the cowardly criminals and asked Alf if he was alright. Alf brought John into his parlour and showed him how he'd barricaded himself in and was ready for further attacks. John was so saddened at the way the old soldier seemed nervous. He rambled on about 'going over the top' and John told him that war of almost fifty years ago was long over.

'No, it never ended, not up here,' Alf tapped his forehead, and then he said he was putting on his old uniform – but it was all imaginary – he had no such uniform.

John vowed to himself that he would give Terry and

Joey a right beating for upsetting the old veteran. Later that evening, in thick fog, the taunting teens turned up in Alf's backyard and called him a deserter. Alf charged out of the kitchen into the yard – thrusting at the two yobs with a knife tied to the end of a brush pole – and the teens fled, screaming with laughter, but when they came out of the entry onto a strip of wasteland known locally as the 'oller, they found themselves in the middle of a battle. The 'oller was crawling with soldiers – and some sort of military tank with no turret. Machine-gun fire, whistling shells, screams and explosions filled the air, and the terrified teens fell into thick mud. There was not a blade of grass to be seen, just a quagmire of boggy ground that gave way under the feet of Terry and Joey. The teens could see silhouetted figures flickering into existence against flashes of light and flame from the explosions. The shadowy outlines of the backs of the terraced houses that formed one side of the 'oller were now ghosting away into the mist, and Terry and Joey grabbed one another as they tried to get out of the maw of the squelching mud. Joey trampled over his friend's back and shoulder as he panicked and tried desperately to find solid dry ground. Terry swore at him, and grabbed at his shoe, but Joey accidentally kicked him in the face as he thrust his foot backwards. The kick dislodged Terry's front teeth, knocking them inward. The resulting pain in Terry's mouth made him feel faint and weak.

From his bedroom window, Alf's neighbour John witnessed the eerie transformation of the misty wasteland behind the houses into some vast battlefield. Those were Germans and British soldiers down there!

He saw a Mark V tank lunge out the fog.

'I'm stuck!' Terry groaned, waist-high in the mud, and Joey couldn't yank him out. The teens felt bullets rip through them and found their lungs and throats filling with salty warm blood. In a state of shock, Joey stuck his fingers into the holes in his chest but the blood still found a way out. Terry lay there, his mouth open wide, trying to get in some air, but he began to throw up blood-soaked vomit – and then, suddenly – silence.

The teens found themselves on the grassy 'oller again – back in their own time, back – thank God - in 1966. They saw John running towards them. He asked if they were alright. Neither of the teens could answer because they were in shock. Joey almost ripped his shirt off and examined his chest, but could see no bullet holes.

Alf, the old war veteran, came walking over to the lads as they lay on the floor, and he had that brush pole with the knife tied to the end of it. The teens froze in terror.

'Leave me alone, please!' Alf said to the frightened and confused teenagers, and tears began to pour from his eyes. He gently grasped the knife blade on the pole, but not hard enough to cut himself. 'Stop bringing it back!'

'It's alright Alf, it's over – it's over,' said John, standing over Joey, who was trembling violently as if he was having a fit.

Alf turned around and walked back towards his home with his head bowed. 'No, it's never over,' he muttered, 'never over.'

After that horrific experience of some paranormal

re-enactment of a World War One battle on a wasteland in Everton, Terry and Joey never ventured anywhere near Alf or that old 'oller again.

HUYTON'S PHANTOM HOUSES

There are certain mysteries I've investigated over the years that have that extra eerie quality because they reoccur again and again, sometimes within days, most often over the years and decades, and an example of this is the strange case of the phantom houses of Bakers Green Road which has baffled me for many years. In the 1960s, two 13-year-old Huyton girls, Tina and Joyce, received their pocket money at the same time one November afternoon, and around 5pm they decided to go to a sweet shop. As they walked up Bakers Green Road, they noticed two houses they had not seen hours before, and both girls were absolutely sure of this; they had passed the spot that very morning. Someone's garden had existed there earlier on, and it was now occupied by two houses that shared a common wall – in other words, they were semi-detached. The site of this mystery was the corner of Bakers Green Road and Reeds Road, not far from Wellcroft Road. With the exception of a Hollywood film set, houses are not erected in hours, and Tina and Joyce were fascinated by the appearance of the dwellings, which both had lights shining through their curtains. The two houses also had thick hedges about five feet in height and ornamental gates set into these hedges. A young lady of about twenty years of age with long straight black hair and a friendly smiling face came to the gate of the semi on the left, and she called to the girls by their names – even though they had never set eyes on her before.

Tina went to walk to the woman but Joyce warned her not to, saying, 'Tina don't! Remember what our teachers said about talking to strangers!'

'Oh shut up, it's just some lady,' Tina replied, and walked on. Joyce reluctantly followed her friend to the gate.

'Could you two take a box of kittens to a house down the road?' the woman asked, smiling. She did not have a local accent and Joyce thought she sounded Welsh, as her Aunt Gwen, who lived in Wrexham talked just like her.

'Kittens?' Tina asked with a big smile. She loved cats.

'Yes,' the young woman answered, 'do you two know where Hillside Road is?

'I do!' Tina nodded, all wide-eyed and impatient to see the kittens.

'Tina, let's go to the shop – ' Joyce tried to pull her friend away by the arm of her school blazer, but Tina went to the gate of the house, which had the number 711 carved into it. The woman opened the gate, stepped aside, and then she beckoned Joyce to follow her friend – but Joyce stayed rooted to the spot and shook her head. Tina went to the doorway of the house and turned, realising her friend wasn't with her, before shouting out Joyce's name. Joyce still didn't move from the spot.

'Joyce! Come on!' Tina waved her arm in a circular exaggerated windmill motion, but Joyce suddenly ran off to the shops, intending to tell a shopkeeper. She could hear Tina crying out her name as she went into the sweet shop. She told the man serving in the sweetshop about the 'new houses' and with a dismissive look in his eyes he said 'Pull the other one it's got bells on! New houses!'

An older lad was in the shop and he heard what Joyce had said about the houses that had appeared on Bakers Green Road and he called her a liar. She bought a bag of sweets and told the lad, 'If I'm lying, I'll give you these sweets!'

'Yeah, alright,' said the boy, excitedly, and he looked at the shopkeeper and said, 'and you're a witness!'

The two youngsters then went back down the road – and the semi-detached houses were gone. There was just a garden there on the corner of Reeds Road. As Joyce stood there experiencing a rising sensation of nausea in her stomach, the lad snatched the bag of sweets out her hand and walked away, saying, 'Knew you were lying you stupid mare!'

Joyce burst into tears and ran home to Blue Bell Lane. Her mother hadn't returned from work yet, but the girl's father listened to Joyce's absurd account and eventually went with her to Bakers Green Road. When he reached the road, Joyce pointed out the lad that had whipped her sweets and her dad grabbed him by the collar and took the bag of sweets off him. Most of them were gone by now.

'She said I could have them if she was a liar, and she was!' the boy complained, and Joyce's father pushed him onto a grass verge. Then Tina's mother came up the road, and she asked Joyce if she had seen Tina because her tea was ready and she'd been calling her to no avail. Mobile phones were unheard of at this time and parents had a habit of almost yodelling the name of their children across the neighbourhood when they wanted them.

Joyce explained the weird situation to her friend's mother: 'There was this house over there where that garden is – no, sorry there were *two* houses – and this woman called me and Tina over and said she wanted us to take a box of kittens to erm, where did she say? Yes, Hillside Road, and your Tina went in the house but I didn't so I went to tell the man in the sweetshop – '

'Oh my God,' Tina's mum threw her hands to her face, 'she went in someone's house! Which house? Which house, Joyce?'

'It's gone now, that's what I mean,' Joyce struggled to explain what had happened. And then her eyes widened and she yelled: 'There she is! There's Tina!'

'Where?' said Joyce's father and Tina's mother simultaneously.

Tina was walking from the direction of Midway Road with her head bowed. They all ran to her and Joyce noticed she was walking in her bare feet. The returned girl was embraced by her mother, and then she was bombarded by questions from her mum and Joyce, and Joyce's father, and she seemed to be half asleep. 'Where are your shoes, Tina!' her mother asked, 'I've only just bought you them, where are they?'

Tina held her hands to her ears and started to let out terrible screams, creating such a disturbance, the police arrived at the scene. The officers of the law, the girl's mother, Joyce and her dad, and a huge crowd of people who had gathered around the hysterical girl listened to her strange account. She had gone into the house and the young woman who had invited her in to take the box of kittens had turned into an old woman with huge black eyes with no white to them. Tina ran to the door and tried to open it but it was jammed shut. The old woman kept telling the terrified girl she was now a slave and that she'd never see her parents again. The woman produced a small bottle with a little girl in it. She was just a few inches tall, and she was wearing a white dress with lace trimmings which looked very old fashioned. The frightening woman put this bottle over a candle flame and laughed as the miniature figure screamed. 'I'll put you in that bottle when I've finished with her!' the woman promised. Tina somehow escaped from the house by climbing over a fence in the back garden and had found herself on land overgrown with weeds near to where Coppice Crescent is now located. Tina had a nervous breakdown after this incident. Teenage hysteria was blamed but I have many accounts of phantom houses – sometimes semi-detached, sometimes a cottage – that have been seen all over Huyton, Dovecot and Prescot, and there are some occultists who believe these vanishing dwellings are traps, and may be responsible for the many cases in the North West of people who disappear without a trace each year.

SOMETHING IN DISGUISE

In the 1990s, a beautiful 18-year-old girl named Lorraine had a baby, and the father callously left Lorraine when the child – a girl named Carmen - was just a year old. Lorraine constantly asked her mother, aunt and grandmother to mind the baby at weekends and sometimes on Thursdays when she would go out with her friends on the town. Lorraine's mother Joanne said that her daughter should never have had the baby because she was too immature to be a responsible mother. Joanne was given weekend late shifts in her job, and had to take them because she needed the overtime pay, so Lorraine began to ask her Auntie Rea to mind the baby. Rea minded baby Carmen on four Saturday nights in a row, but became ill from what was subsequently diagnosed as fibromyalgia – and she told her niece she simply wasn't up to minding Carmen for the foreseeable future because she felt so ill and weak. Lorraine thought her aunt was just putting on the illness and they had a row. Lorraine therefore paid a visit to her Nan, Sian, who lived on Aysgarth Avenue in West Derby, and asked her if she could mind the baby this coming Thursday evening from 7.30pm till 11pm. The girl's Nan told

Lorraine: 'Of course I can love, but listen - you'd be better letting me keep Carmen overnight till the Sunday afternoon. I don't want you turning up drunk on a Saturday night in a minicab to take the baby back. You might drop her or something. Let me have her overnight.'

'Ah, thanks Nan,' said an elated Lorraine, 'you're always understanding and right there to lend a helping hand.'

'That's what Nans are for,' joked Sian.

Lorraine hugged her grandmother, went to put the kettle on and then she brought the packet of chocolate Hobnob biscuits out of the cupboard. She always did this when she visited and had a chat. While Lorraine was in the kitchen, she detected a peculiar scent of some sort – it reminded her of church incense because although the aroma was sweet, it also reeked of something burning too. She asked her Nan if she could smell it.

'Yes I can Lorraine,' said Sian, sniffing the air, 'it's been coming and going since last Wednesday. Don't know where it's coming from.'

'Maybe someone's having a barbecue around here and the smoke's drifting in here,' Lorraine speculated.

On Saturday, Lorraine called at her Nan's house with the baby and was surprised to find the front door open a few inches. 'You alright Nan?' she asked, as she ventured into the hallway and took Carmen out of her pram. That incense smell was back and seemed stronger.

'Yeah, come in Lorraine,' said her Nan, sitting in her usual winged high-back chair. Lorraine asked her why she'd left the door open. It was July, and Sian said she'd opened the door because of the stifling summer heat, but Lorraine warned her never to leave her front door open or unlocked with so many criminals knocking about. 'Well, you probably got rid of some of that awful smell by having the door open for a bit. It's back isn't it?'

'Is it?' Sian asked.

The teenager then kissed little Carmen on the cheek and pointed to Sian, saying: 'There's Nanna! Hello Nanna! Say hello Carmen – stop being antisocial.'

Sian looked at the little girl without even smiling, and then she said: 'Listen Lorraine, I've just been thinking about you girl - you know what you'd be better doing?'

'What, Nan?' Lorraine asked, ready to hand the child to grandmother.

'You'd be better giving that child away. Just leave her in someone's garden.' Sian said, eyeing Carmen.

'What!' Lorraine recoiled in shock.

Sian went on: 'There's a woman on Eaton Road been trying to have a baby for years; I can give you her address if you want. Leave the baby with her. Once she comes to the door, just walk away. Carmen will be alright.'

'Are you serious?' Lorraine asked, thinking Sian was winding her up.

'Yes, I'm very serious. Once a fellah gets wind of you having a baby he'll be off,' said Sian, 'so give the baby away.'

'Jesus Christ Nan!' exclaimed Lorraine, and she found herself stuck for words. All of a sudden, before her very eyes, her Nan turned into a strange hooded little old woman with a sinister grotesque face. She wore an ankle-length purple robe which matched the colour of the hood. Her head looked globular, and her tongue was hanging down out of a smiling mouth, but what really scared Lorraine were the eyes of this entity – they were pale blue and they held her in an icy stare. Lorraine isn't sure what the weird impostor said next, but it sounded like the c-word uttered in a low gruff voice. Lorraine ran out of the house with the baby, and didn't even stop to get the pram in the hallway. At the end of Aysgarth Avenue, Lorraine bumped into her Nan's neighbour – a woman named Mary – who told Lorraine that her Nan had been taken to hospital less than an hour ago after falling down stairs. Lorraine was unable to get her words out for a moment, and then she told Mary what had just happened. Mary naturally seemed sceptical at the account given by Lorraine, but she took the girl and her child into her home and got her husband and son to go into Sian's house. The two men found the place deserted, but they too said there had been a sickly sweet smell present in the place. Sian had suffered a broken collar bone and a fractured wrist in the fall, and she was soon discharged from hospital. Lorraine told her what had happened and it really frightened her Nan. She had never seen anything remotely supernatural in the house in all of the years she'd lived there, although she too recalled the baffling smell of incense which had recently started to invade the house. Thankfully, Sian never experienced anything paranormal at her home and Lorraine still went round to see her Nan till the day she passed away, but rarely took Carmen. Lorraine eventually faced up to her responsibilities and only went out about once a month. She later met a man named Luke and married him in 1997.

Just what the thing was impersonating Lorraine's Nan remains a mystery, but I have investigated similar incidents over the years where something inhuman has tried to pass itself off as one of us terrestrials. A case in point which stands out in my mind is the story told to me many years ago by a woman named Catharine Faye. In 1966, Catharine was a 17-year-old girl working as a waitress in a Kardomah café in the city centre of Liverpool. Cathy, as she was known by her workmates, was a beautiful girl, but she suffered from a common condition known as Amblyopia – a weakness in her left eye – and Cathy's mother constantly told the girl to have the "lazy eye" looked at by her doctor, but the girl just couldn't be bothered. You couldn't tell Cathy had a lazy eye – she didn't have a 'turn' in it or a squint – but she could hardly see clearly with the eye concerned, because it was more farsighted than the other eye. In the autumn of 1966, Cathy was asked out by a very tall and handsome customer named Robin Tremarco. He had shiny black hair cropped short in the classic short back and sides style, and a large pair of cornflower-blue eyes. Robin said he was a shipping clerk down at the docks and on the first day he met Cathy, he asked her out. She went to the cinema with him, and afterwards they went for a drink. Cathy's female work colleagues at the Kardomah were green with envy when she started seeing Robin Tremarco; he was everything most girls at the time wanted; he had great looks, a charismatic personality, and he also had a few bob. Just a few weeks after the first date, Robin talked about getting engaged to Cathy, but then something quite strange happened. Cathy arrived at her workplace an hour late one morning, and she was in a dreadful state. Her workmate Tina asked her what the matter was.

'Robin – he's – I don't know what he is,' she stammered and seemed to have difficulty composing a reply.

'Cathy, where on earth have you been it's nearly half-nine!' her boss, Trevor came out of the kitchen and confronted her. 'This won't do!'

'Leave off Trevor, something's happened to her,' Tina told him and then she curled her arm around Cathy's shoulder and led the distressed teen into the kitchen.

'He's not human, he's a thing,' Cathy told Tina, and tears welled in her eyes.

Tina looked at Trevor, who had a look on his face somewhere between puzzlement and mild amusement.

'Cathy, have you been taking something or smoking that happy backy?' Trevor insensitively asked.

'No!' Cathy yelled at him, making her boss jump. 'I haven't been taking anything. You'll never believe me – no one will.'

'Take her in here, Tina,' Trevor opened the door to his office. It was a small room situated next door to the kitchen. He slapped his hand on the light-switch and closed the door once the girls had entered. He told Cathy to sit down, then grabbed a tissue from a Kleenex box and handed it to her. He sat opposite his young employee and Tina stood behind her, bent over the girl with a sympathetic stroke of her hand on Cathy's golden hair.

Trevor smiled. 'Right, Cathy, tell me what happened to make you an hour late.'

After a few false starts that deteriorated into sobbing

fits, Cathy finally got her words out in a coherent manner, and the account she gave was very strange indeed. 'He has a flat on Campbell Street – ' Cathy began.

'Where's that?' Trevor asked.

'It's off Duke Street,' Tina told Trevor, then patted her friend on the shoulder. 'Go on, Cath.'

'I stayed with him last night,' said Cathy, and she seemed to be fighting her emotions to get the words out. 'And I decided to get up a bit earlier this morning, around half-past six, to get a bath, and I didn't realise he wasn't next to me in the bed. He was in the bathroom, and I walked in, and he usually locks the door when he's in there, but he must have forgotten. I went in and he was lying in the bath, under the water, with his feet up by the taps, but his skin was like dark grey, and his nose was like this long hairy funnel sticking out of the water.'

'What?' Trevor squeezed his eyes to thin slits and grimaced, showing his teeth. He almost smiled, then added: 'He had a nose like a funnel?'

'I know it sounds silly, but I swear before the Seven Sacraments that I'm telling the truth.' Cathy told him as she dabbed her eyes with the tissue.

'Go on,' Trevor said, and looked at Tina's face before listening to the rest of Cathy's bizarre tale.

'He made this high-pitched sound. It sounded like a flute or a recorder when you blow too hard. This noise came from his nose, and he sat up dead fast in the bath, and the water went everywhere, and the face was horrible. It looked like Robin but it was all grey, and the eyes were golden, and the long nose – the funnel thing, hung down. I ran out of the bathroom and into the bedroom, screaming, and I grabbed my clothes and I was going to get out the window but the flat's on the second floor. I heard running sounds, and then one of the other people in the flats came down and knocked on the door and asked if I was alright. I let him in and then ran out onto the landing and told him about the thing in the bathroom. He went in there, but came out and said no one was there.'

'Cathy, are you saying that Robin Tremarco is from another planet or something?' Tina asked, and then she looked at Trevor with a raised eyebrow and a facial expression which conveyed that she was worried about the sanity of her work colleague.

'I don't know, Tina, but I'm telling the truth, and you can go to the flat with me if you want and see for yourself. He's left all his stuff behind – his wallet and clothes and things. He's gone. I feel as if I'm dreaming, like I'm living in a nightmare.'

'So there was no sign of anyone in the bath when that person from the other flat went in?' Trevor queried, trying to get his head around this unearthly story.

Cathy nodded. 'Yeah, the bathroom was empty. The fellah from the other flat is Mr Burke – I don't know his first name. Why don't you come and see for yourself?'

'Look, just think of what you're saying Cathy, and calm down a minute,' said Trevor, looking down at the desk. He paused, then looked up at Cathy and asked: 'Could you have had a nightmare and – '

'It wasn't a bleedin' dream!' Cathy shouted.

Trevor raised his palm to his employee's loud protestation. 'Just hear me out a second, Cathy – listen

– maybe Robin whatshisname hasn't even been home yet, and you got up out of bed as you said you did, still half asleep, and you were sort of sleepwalking. My cousin does it – he stayed at a friend's house and got up starkers in the middle of the night and went downstairs – in his sleep - and started cooking things in the kitchen.'

Cathy shook her head as Trevor voiced his explanation. 'I know it wasn't a dream – I know I was wide awake – and I knew you wouldn't believe me. What am I going to do? Will they think I'm insane and lock me up?'

To Tina, Trevor said: 'Look, Tina, go with Cathy to this flat and see if this Robin fellah is there – '

'No!' cried Cathy, 'I'm not setting foot in there!'

'Oh come on, Cathy, Tina will be with you,' Trevor told her, but Cathy just shook her head and refused to carry out his suggestion.

'I'll go,' said Tina, 'have you got the keys Cathy?'

'No, I left them behind,' Cathy realised, 'I was in that much of a rush to get out.'

'Tina, just go and knock on the door and see if he's there then,' Trevor told her, 'and you can put Cathy's mind at rest then. She'll see it was all a dream.'

'No, don't go Tina,' Cathy implored her, rising from the chair, 'he might get you.'

Trevor got up from his chair and reached over the table to gently grab Cathy's forearm. 'Don't start Cathy or the men in the white coats *will* be coming to put you away!'

'I'll go now then,' Tina said, and patted Cathy's back before she headed to the door. Cathy went after her but Trevor called her back.

Tina was gone about twenty minutes. She returned to find Cathy sitting in the office with Trevor with a mug of tea and a biscuit in her hand.

'Was he there?' Trevor asked straight away.

Tina nodded. 'Yeah, he said he only got in around ten-past nine this morning. He was playing cards with friends all night.'

'He's lying,' Cathy told Tina, then turned to look at Trevor, who was now looking at her from under his bushy eyebrows.

'What did I tell you?' he asked the young waitress. 'You had a dream.'

Cathy sighed and lowered her head into her palms. She looked up again and told her employer. 'But I know I was awake, and how would I even dream something up like that?'

Trevor looked at Tina and asked her: 'Did you tell her boyfriend what Cathy told us?'

Tina shook her head. 'No, I just told him that Cathy was worried about his whereabouts and he asked where she was. He told me to tell her he was sorry for staying out playing poker and that he'll never do it again.'

'Look, Cathy,' said Trevor, avoiding eye contact with the teenager, 'maybe you should go and see your doctor – '

'I'm not mad,' Cathy interrupted, 'and I was not seeing things. If I told a doctor what I've told you he'd send me to Rainhill. That happened to a woman in our street; she said fairies were following her everywhere and they locked her up.'

'Let me finish,' said Trevor. 'No one's going to have you committed Cathy, but if your nerves are bad they can give you pills until you feel alright.'

'Well, I'm not going to any doctor,' Cathy replied, 'so you can either let me continue working here or you can sack me, I don't care.'

'I'm not sacking you,' Trevor told her in a nonchalant manner. 'I've had enough of this rigmarole, anyway, so I want the two of you back to work now, and I don't want to hear another word about this.'

The young ladies left Trevor's office and both were berated by Peggy, the older waitress who had been singlehandedly serving customers in the absence of Tina and Cathy. Cathy told Tina she was not going back to the flat she had shared with Robin and Tina said she could stay at her house in the Dingle, where she still lived with her parents – on the condition Cathy did not mention the 'far-fetched' story about Robin changing into some monster. Cathy was grateful for this offer and accepted it with both hands. At 7.30pm, Cathy and Tina ended their shift and left the café in the city centre. They headed for the bus stop around the corner on Paradise Street to catch the Number 20 to the Dingle. On the way, Cathy noticed a man of about thirty years of age following her and Tina and there was just something about him which gave Cathy the creeps. He was staring at her intently and he had on glasses and long blondish-brown hair in the hairstyle popularised by the Beatles. He wore a dark-blue suit, white shirt and a dark tie.

'What are you looking back at?' Tina asked her friend.

'That man's looking at me; see him?' Cathy replied, 'The one with the lightish-coloured hair and glasses on.'

'Oh come on, Cathy,' Tina urged her to hurry to the crowded bus stop. 'He's looking at you because you're looking at him.'

The bus arrived and the girl went upstairs and sat in two vacant rear seats where Tina lit a cigarette and kicked her shoes off. After nearly twelve hours on her feet, it was bliss to lay her stockinged toes on the cool floor. 'How come you don't smoke, Cath?' she asked her friend.

'Tina, there he is again,' Cathy whispered harshly.

The spectacled man she'd seen earlier came up the stairs, looked straight at Cathy, then went to a seat at the front of the bus.

'Will you shut up about people following you?' Tina sighed, exhaling a cloud of blue smoke. 'Your nerves are terrible. Here, have a drag on this and calm down.' She offered Cathy her ciggie.

'No thanks,' Cathy said with a troubled smile, then gazed at the back of the head of the man in the dark blue suit. When the girls got off at the Dingle, Cathy turned around and saw that the man in the glasses had also disembarked too. He walked behind the waitresses all the way to Tina's home on Allington Street. 'He probably just lives round here, Cath, stop being all suspicious,' Tina said, and she took her into her house and introduced Cathy to her mum and dad and 13-year-old brother Ozzy (short for Oswald). Tina told her parents that Cathy had broken up with her boyfriend and that she'd love to stay for just a few weeks and would be more than happy to pay for her keep. Tina's folks were perfectly okay with this and Cathy moved into Tina's room, sleeping "toptail" until she could get her own bed.

Then one Sunday afternoon, Cathy hammered on the door and Tina answered it because her parents were out visiting and she was the only one in the house.

Tina pushed past Tina and closed the door behind her. She was out of breath as if she had been running. She gasped: 'That man in the glasses – do you remember him? The one I said was following us? He got on the same bus that day and followed us to this street?'

Tina rolled her eyes. 'Yes I remember him, you never stopped talking about – '

'It's Robin! It's him!' Cathy had so much fear in her wide eyes as she told her friend this.

'You're starting all that again,' Tina told her, and she went into the kitchen where she had a radio on.

'Just listen to me please,' Cathy implored her. 'He was on Aigburth Road, and I saw him coming towards me as I went to the shop. So I turned and started to run, and I heard Robin's voice shout my name behind me. No one sounds like Robin – I know his voice, it's very distinctive. He started running after me and I just legged it back here. What if he's followed me?'

'Cathy, you're really starting to scare me now,' Tina told her. 'How could that man be Robin? Your fellah's got jet-black hair, and the fellah with the glasses is almost blonde, and he's not as tall as Robin Tremarco.'

'Why would I lie, Tina? Why on earth would I make this up?' Cathy said, and her voice was breaking as if she was about to cry.

There was a heavy ran-tan at the front door, and Cathy jumped at the sound. Tina left the room.

'Don't answer it! It'll be him!' Cathy begged, but

364

Tina went down the hallway and opened the door.

Her young brother Ozzy ran in and told his sister something very strange. Ozzy said that at the bottom of the road, in the alleyway which runs into the next street (Alwyn Street) he had been sitting on a backyard wall, looking for the family's cat Horace, when he had seen a man come down the alleyway and stand by a backyard door. This man had then looked up and down the alleyway, but had not noticed Ozzy, who laid flat on the backyard wall to watch the furtive-looking stranger. The man then crouched down, and then the next thing Ozzy knew, a black dog was standing in the same spot – and the man he had seen earlier had not passed by beneath him. Ozzy had followed the dog into Allington Street and had noticed that it walked in a peculiar fashion and not at all the way a dog normally walks.

'Ozzy, did the man in the alleyway have glasses on?' Cathy asked.

Ozzy's eyebrows shot up and vanished under his combed-down fringe. 'Yeah! He did, why? Who is he? Do you know him, Cathy?'

'Did he have a dark blue suit on as well by any chance?' Cathy asked.

'Yeah! He did!' said an excited Ozzy.

'Ozzy, you'd better not be just agreeing with what Cathy says as a stupid joke,' Tina warned her brother.

'I'm not,' replied Ozzy, annoyed at the accusation. 'Who is he? Is he a magician?'

Ozzy went back to the front door, opened it and went out. He stood on the pavement, and then he rushed back into the girls and said: 'He's coming up the street! The fellah I saw!'

Tina grabbed her young brother by the back of his collar and stopped him from going out again. Ozzy and the girls went into the front parlour and peeped out through the bay windows at the spectacled stranger. Tina and Cathy could see that it was indeed the very same man who had boarded the same bus as them from Paradise Street that evening. He stopped directly across the road, and looked at the bay window, as if he knew he was being watched. The three observers stepped away from the window and watched him as he then walked back down Allington Street the way he had come.

That night around 8pm, he returned to the street, and Ozzy ran up the stairs to his sister's room, where Tina and Cathy were reading magazines. 'That fellah's back!' Ozzy told the girls. They all went down the stairs and Tina's mother came out of the back parlour and shouted: 'Aye aye! What's all this noise? Your father's trying to watch the telly here!'

Tina didn't even acknowledge her mum; she went straight into the parlour with Ozzy leading the way. This time the atmosphere was very eerie. It was now dark outside, and by the feeble streetlights the girls and the young lad could see the stalker as a shadowy figure. He walked slowly up the street on the side opposite the house, and there was not another soul around at the time, perhaps with it being a Sunday evening. He stopped almost directly opposite, and again looked at the bay window where six eyes were watching, and this time he crossed the road, heading for Tina's house.

'Ozzy! Get away from the window!' Tina told her brother in a voice that was almost a whisper.

The man stopped outside on the pavement, less than

six feet away beyond the panes of the windows, then suddenly hurried away to the left. What happened next was very unnerving. About twenty seconds after the creepy man had vanished from sight, a black dog came walking from the left, and Tina and Cathy noticed it was walking in a very awkward manner. 'That's the dog I saw in the alleyway!' Ozzy said, his nose pressed against the window. 'See the way it walks? Didn't I tell you it walked funny?'

The dog stopped, sat on the pavement, and looked at the three people watching it from the darkened parlour. That dog seemed to *smile*. This really freaked out Tina and Cathy, and Ozzy remarked: 'Hey, it looks like it's grinning, doesn't it?'

The dog got up from the sitting position and walked back in the direction from whence it had come, and Ozzy pressed the right size of his face hard against the glass so he could see where it was going. He let out a yelp.

'What's wrong Ozzy?' Tina asked him.

Ozzy turned with his face half illuminated by the street lights. He looked shocked. 'The dog turned into a man,' he said in a trembling voice. 'It grew into a man – I'm telling me Dad!' The boy ran in a panic out of the parlour and into the next room where his father was watching the television. The girls held onto one another, afraid, as they left the parlour and lingered in the hallway for a moment, listening to Ozzy being shouted at by his father.

That night, and for several nights afterwards, Ozzy suffered terrible nightmares that had been darkly inspired by that weird metamorphosis he had witnessed outside his home – of a dog into a man.

Enough was enough as far as Tina was concerned, and she coldly told Cathy she could no longer stay in her home. Cathy burst into tears, and asked Tina if she could stay for just a week until she found some other place to stay, but Tina swore at her and told Cathy to go and stay with her own family. Tina's mother told her daughter off for talking to her friend in such an uncivil manner, and she told Cathy she was welcome to stay, but Cathy left the house sobbing.

Cathy did not return to her job at the Kardomah cafè, and Trevor became so concerned by the teenager's absence he visited Cathy's home – only to be told by her mother that the girl had been taken to a psychiatric hospital. A psychiatrist had told Cathy's mother and father that their daughter was suffering from acute paranoia as well as experiencing disturbing hallucinations, including those of a dog that changed into a former boyfriend and one of a bizarre being with an elephantine trunk. Another psychiatrist said that he had recorded similar types of hallucination without the paranoia in elderly blind patients and patients with cataracts and other visual disorders – so it was therefore possible that Cathy's lazy eye – Amblyopia – was having some bearing on the strange visions she was experiencing. Cathy's parents visited their child at the hospital, and Cathy told them that Robin Tremarco was visiting her in differing forms almost every night, including his real form – that of a grey scaly humanoid with a long snout which wormed about. The shapeshifting entity sometimes hurt Cathy and threatened to kill her if she told anyone about him. In the end, Cathy refused to talk about her surreal and terrifying persecutor and she was eventually discharged. She never set eyes on Robin Tremarco again, nor was she visited by him in human or animal form. I have so many reports of these shapeshifters (as I call them, for want of a better name), and I do not know where they come from or whether they have a common agenda. All I do know is that from the sheer number of reports (and that includes many in the Liverpool area) something very sinister is going on, and I wonder if any have ever passed me on the street in some acceptable form – perhaps as a man, woman, child, or some cat, bird or dog...

THE LIFE-SWAPPERS

I've changed a few names in this strange story for legal reasons. Michael Claridge, a 34-year-old out of work actor, woke, as usual, in another man's bed with another man's wife – Jenny - and he hated himself. He'd done this so many times in his life – committed adultery without an iota of concern for the repercussions it would entail. He simply couldn't help himself and had no self-control. His lecherous actions had broken up families and on one occasion the husband of the woman Claridge had bedded had put the barrel of a pistol to his head and pulled the trigger, but the gun had jammed and so the frustrated husband resorted to using his fists and feet to give the actor a beating. After the hiding, Claridge had vowed to himself that he would live like a Trappist monk in future, but he returned to his lechery after getting a bit tipsy at a Christmas party at a pub in Runcorn. That episode had ended when the landlord discovered Claridge having intercourse with his wife in the pub cellar. The pub owner never laid a finger on him, but he did put out a contract on Claridge and the actor never returned to Runcorn. Now, some thirty-something 'conquests' later, Michael Claridge had awakened in the bed of his neighbour Gordon, a builder by trade currently working on a house down in

Crewe. The womaniser was up to his eyeballs in debt, and down to his last cigarette, which he smoked as he lay beside Jenny. She was lying face down in the pillow, softly snoring as his eyes followed the curve of her back, bottom and legs. He wondered about his sexually-driven motives. Why did he do this? She had not even been keen on him. He had persecuted her to go to bed with him and she kept saying she loved Gordon, but he had persisted until she yielded to his warped wishes. It hurt him to recall the seedy mission to get her between the sheets, and so he turned his attention to his future – a very bleak place indeed. The cigarette was soon finished. He sneaked out of the bed, stole a pound note from sleeping Jenny's purse, took her cigarettes, got dressed, and went into the bathroom, where he used his absent friend Gordon's Wilkinson Sword razor and stick of shaving soap to improve his ghastly appearance. He left the house in Aigburth and headed to a local cafe, where he found himself surveying the curves of the waitress – a dead ringer for a young Diana Dors. From the cafe he rode a bus into the city centre, and paid a visit to his agent Freddie Micklemass. Freddie shook his head – no roles, just bit-work as an extra down in London, and Claridge didn't have the train fare to get to the capital. It was March 1966 and he hadn't worked for a year now. His sex addiction had become so bad he simply couldn't concentrate on work, and last Christmas he had even been turned down for a minor role in a panto. He had scrapped his empty account with Lloyd's Bank – an account he'd held since he was seventeen, because he had been unable to pay back a £500 pound loan. Two months ago he had closed his vacuous account with Martin's Bank because of another loan he couldn't repay. He pawned his mother's jewellery (including her engagement ring) without her knowledge and the pawn tickets for the rings and bracelets had long expired – so Claridge's father had warned him to never set foot in the family home again or he'd give him a pasting.

A fortnight ago, the down-and-out actor had been evicted from his lodgings at a house on Upper Parliament Street because his landlady Mrs Briggs had finally had enough. She was owed nearly two months' rent and despite constant promises to pay up, Claridge had instead changed the lock on his room door. Claridge sat on a bench behind St Luke's Church and stretched his brains to the limit as he tried to formulate some plan of action to get his life back on track. He was joined by another derelict of society, a failed poet named Nightingale, who told Claridge there was a secret place where he could stay on Oldham Street, at the back of Renshaw Street. This emergency abode was an old cocky watchman's hut which had been forgotten by whoever owned it. Two homeless men had tapped electricity from a lamp post and run the wires into the hut so it had light and power. As far as Nightingale knew, the place was currently uninhabited. The hut was in the yard of a derelict house and Nightingale gave Claridge detailed directions to find the place. However, when Claridge found the hut, there was a drunken Irishman asleep in it, and he looked as if he could take care of himself. Claridge knew that he could either try the Labour Exchange or even the Salvation Army, but for some deeply repressed reason, he was too proud to claim benefit or accept charity, and so he began to have suicidal thoughts. The soliloquy of Prince Hamlet echoed in his melancholic mind: 'To be or not to be, that is the question...'

He wanted to cry. He saw his father's face when he told him never to return home ever again after the pawning of his mother's jewellery – and the faces of those many friends he had done the dirty on by screwing their wives; friends who had helped him out and trusted him. 'I don't want to be me anymore,' he whispered through gritted teeth as sorrow throttled him. 'Time for me to give up this role and leave the stage for good I think.'

He saw poor Nightingale in the distance, looking at the daffodils in the gardens of St Luke's, lost in some poetic contemplation, and Claridge walked on through the sloping streets until he had reached the Landing Stage at the Pier Head.

Husbands were out to kill him, creditors wanted his blood, and now he had no place to live, so he decided he'd take a last look at the sun in the sky, and then he casually climbed over the rusty chains at the edge of the stage and jumped into the Mersey with his eyes shut tight. Unknown to Michael Claridge, another suicide jumped into the waters too, seconds after his leap, less than a hundred yards away – and this suicide was a well-dressed man in a bowler hat, an expensive camel-hair coat, razor-pleated trousers and highly-polished brogues. His name was James Orchard, a merchant banker, aged fifty. Two brave tramps jumped in the river, and each one respectively saved half of the duo from self-destruction. Claridge was dragged through the brown swirling waters to a set of stone steps – watermen's stairs - reaching out of the river's silt up the waterfront walls of the Pier Head, and Orchard, meanwhile, was likewise dragged out of the heroic vagrant's arms onto the landing stage by the arms of three people and a policeman. The two would-be suicides were breathing, but out cold. They were taken to the Northern Hospital and had some water drawn out of their lungs. Claridge regained consciousness first, and when the doctor asked him: 'What's your name sir?' to ascertain if the actor was brain damaged, Claridge said 'My name is Orchard – not sure of my first name though. I think it's James.'

James Orchard came to sometime later and when the doctor asked for his name, he replied: 'My name is Michael Claridge, and I'm an actor – well I used to act- when I could find work.'

The bemused doctors had already looked at Michael Claridge's soggy driving licence as well as his British Actors' Equity Association card, and they had also read James Orchard's soaked chequebook, so they knew what the real names of the men were – so why on earth was each man claiming to be the other one? The doctor had a word with a psychiatrist and the latter assumed the men knew one another as friends or work colleagues and were possibly confused about their identities because of the attempted suicide traumas. The psychiatrist recalled a case in which a male student, recovering from serious head injuries after a car crash, had given his name as Leo Tolstoy because he had been reading *War and Peace* just before the accident.

James Orchard somehow managed to escape from the hospital during the night and Michael Claridge remained under a psychiatrist for a while because he maintained *he* was the real Mr Orchard. Through some mysterious process, the actor Claridge realised his mind had been transferred into the body of James Orchard during the double suicide attempt, and he went 'home' to his palatial mansion in Formby and was doted on by his wife Jemima, who had been frantic with worry when he had not returned home yesterday. Claridge was living in an older body but it was a new start and he discovered that he was an incredibly rich business wizard – a merchant banker as well as the president of cutlery manufacturing business in Sheffield. The mind and soul of the real James Orchard on the other hand, now inhabited the body of the tumble-down thespian Michael Claridge, in a younger, slimmer body – and a body with powerful lustful urges and a pathological sex drive. Nevertheless, the former merchant banker was now a person who was unemployed and facing gross liabilities of three grand, and he could only vaguely recall who he had been. He felt he had been some clever man who worked with figures and money, and parts of his previous life were coming back. He had feared a mammoth fraud which he had perpetrated just before the jump into the river. He wanted to end it all because he believed he would be uncovered as a fraudster who had used other people's funds to make himself millions of pounds! He had no difficulty recalling that part of the ghostly life before this one. He tried to get his head around it all. He had been carrying the driving licence of a Michael Claridge in his wallet, yet he knew this was not his name. It was James Orchard, but who was he? He would have to see if he was listed in a telephone directory and perhaps go to the library to find out if he was anyone well-known. At the moment, Orchard was living on benefits and had to visit the Labour Exchange until he could find work. Meanwhile, Michael Claridge's soul was living in Orchard's body, and that body was now enjoying a luxurious lifestyle in a suburban mansion. Claridge was making love to Mrs Orchard each night and she was stunned at her husband's knowledge of the *Kama Sutra*; and she wondered why he hadn't shown her all those positions before. Of course, Claridge was also using the body of the older man Orchard to make love to secretaries, casual pick-ups in bars, and even the Avon lady who called to the mansion one evening. Claridge took holidays on the French Riviera while the real James Orchard existed in a bedsit with a communal toilet, a one-bar electric fire, and a cockroach problem. While Claridge enjoyed the finest wines and indulged in his favourite dish - charcoal-grilled Chateaubriand with pommes soufflés – Orchard was clawing baked beans out the can with a fork.

People who knew the real James Orchard heard the strange rumours about his sexual predatory behaviour and dismissed them as nonsense because Orchard was known as a cold fish who never even gave his wife a peck on the cheek in public. However, some thought Orchard's apparent neglect of his business and the number of holidays he was taking was very out of character for a man who was a workaholic and rarely went on vacations lasting more than a week. Some thought that he had perhaps suffered a nervous breakdown because he really did not seem to be himself of late – and of course, unknown to his workforce and business colleagues, he wasn't.

The real James Orchard, trapped in the body of Michael Claridge, opened a newspaper one day, and there on the business pages he saw a monochrome picture of a very familiar man; it was himself – James Orchard. He cut the article out and vowed that he would find the impostor who had stolen his life and confront him. Around this time, Orchard also started to recall his wife's face, and felt so sad at being apart from here while another man was sleeping with her each night.

The life-swappers lived their strange existences until one morning on Bold Street, when Orchard passed the man he had once been, and with a jolt in his stomach he recognised himself – and Claridge, seeing his wretched old self, flinched, hesitated in his step, but walked on.

'Hey!' Orchard cried out to the tall man in the bowler and tailored suit, 'I was you!' he cried.

Passers-by slowed and some halted at the strange exchange that was taking place near the Cripps department store.

'I beg your pardon?' asked Claridge - the fake James Orchard.

'You know very well what I am referring to, you – you damned impostor!' the real James Orchard bawled, and he grabbed Claridge by the arm.

'Unhand me you insane man!' Claridge shouted with the timbre of Orchard's rich voice.

'You swapped places with me, didn't you?' Orchard gazed into eyes that were once his, and saw the flicker of fear in them. 'You did it when we were in the river somehow!'

'Get off me you madman!' Claridge roared and he punched his old face, but Orchard was so angry he recovered from the smack and grabbed the poseur by his lapels. A crowd formed and they watched as the men from different classes wrestled and moved out into the road. A grass-green GPO van hit the two of them. There were screams and a few cruel laughs from the crowd as Claridge and Orchard went in different directions from the impact.

The two men awoke in the Royal Infirmary with sprains and minor fractures, and now there had evidently been some reversal of the mysterious process which had caused them to swap bodies in the double suicide attempt in the River Mersey, because they found themselves back in their respective bodies.

The doctor shone a pen light into the eyes of James Orchard and asked: 'What's your name?'

'My name is Michael – no – my name is James Orchard, sir.'

The same light was shone into the squinched eyes of Michael Claridge, and he too was asked: 'Can you tell me your name?' The doctor saw this patient was unable to speak for a moment, and then he replied: 'I can't feel my arse! Oh, what happened to me? My name's Michael Claridge. I've been on the telly.'

James Orchard was transferred to a private hospital and Michael Claridge remained at the Royal for almost a week until he was discharged, and when that day came, he had a visitor just as he was about to leave. It was Mr Orchard. The two men compared notes, and eventually realised that something very strange had taken place which they were at a loss to explain. Orchard believed some higher intelligence had wanted to show him how the other half lived, perhaps as some form of atonement for the dishonest and materialistic way he had been living his life. James Orchard became very sympathetic towards Michael Claridge, for he knew he was the victim of a sexual addiction and had hated himself for the life of lechery he was leading. Orchard loaned him £500 and gave him top calibre financial advice of the kind he usually only gave to paying clients. Claridge had limited success in his acting career, appearing in minor roles on stage and even in film as well as the small screen. James Orchard's fraud was never detected and he transferred all of the funds he had used in the crime back to the accounts of the people he had siphoned it from.

You'd be surprised how many accounts there are of people becoming another person, usually for just a short duration, and these incidents are always explained away as personality disorders, identity crises, dissociative disorders, fugue states and so on. Many years ago, a woman was about to be married at a church in Liverpool, and the bridegroom turned to her just before the marriage service commenced and asked her: 'Who am I marrying?'

The eyes of the bridegroom were a sky blue, and yet now they had changed to a dark brown colour, and the bride thought that the man she was looking at was some stranger. The priest coughed, hinting for the bridegroom to stop talking and to pay attention, and suddenly, the bridegroom pinched the top of his own nose, closed his eyes, and seemed unsteady on his feet. He turned to the bride, and his eyes were pale blue again. The marriage service went ahead, and the newly-married husband later told his wife that he had felt as if someone else had stepped into his space as they stood in the aisle that day, and then this separate identity had fled. Stress of the big day was blamed, but I wonder – was it a case of a 'life-swapper' attempting to take over the life of the bridegroom, but perhaps (and there's no pun intended) he got cold feet and returned from whence he came...

THE PURPLE GIRL MYSTERY

The entity known as the Purple Girl (and sometimes Purple Mary) was first reported to me around 2009 by a man named Jed, who used to be a fairground worker at New Brighton and North Wales in the 1960s and 1970s. In the summer of 1968, Jed was fixing a fairground generator near the "Big Slide" – a helter-skelter amusement ride in New Brighton when a man and woman in their thirties approached him with their three children and pointed out something quite odd – a child of about ten years of age, who had on rather old fashioned clothes – black stockings and a black knee-length skirt. This girl also wore a jacket and straw boater which were black too – but her hands and face and neck were purple. Jed smiled at first, thinking the girl was wearing makeup and was perhaps part of some attraction at the fairground, but when the child drew nearer, he saw that her eyeballs were dark, with no white or any colour in them at all. The couple told the fairground engineer that this weird looking girl had been following them round for the past half an hour, and at one point she had tried to grab one of their children. The purple-skinned girl turned about face in what seemed a mechanical manner, spinning on her heel, before marching silently off into the crowds of holidaymakers at the resort. Jed told the couple, who hailed from Liverpool, that he had no idea who she was, and he felt a bit spooked by the child. The Purple Girl was seen by Jed again later that day on New Brighton Pier, and he watched her as she seized passing children by their arms – and some of these kids were holding the hands of their mothers and fathers at the time, and when the parents pulled the kids from the strangely-coloured girl's clutches and shouted at her, the girl would pay no heed and simply turn 180 degrees and calmly walk away to vanish into the crowds. Jed mentioned the uncanny girl to another fairground worker named Alf, who told him that the girl in black with the purple skin was a ghost. Jed thought Alf was having him on at first but an old man who overheard Alf backed up his claim and said the child had been seen on both sides of the Mersey, and had been known as Purple Mary, but no one knew the story behind the ghost and why she was that colour. A vascular birthmark – known as Port Wine Stain – caused by abnormal development of blood vessels in the skin, can give the person who has such a birthmark a purplish patch on the dermis and outer skin, but this rarely covers the entire face, neck and both hands. The black eyes of the apparition are also hard to explain but are reminiscent of the eyes of the so-called Black-Eyed Children – alleged paranormal beings who have been reported in mostly tabloid newspapers in recent years.

The Purple Girl was allegedly seen in Liverpool on a number of occasions, and seems to have had a thing for parks – and children. One Spring afternoon in 1973, a woman named Nancy took her 6-year-old daughter Jane out for a walk in Newsham Park with the family dog, a young Jack Russell named Ace (because he had a black patch that looked like an Ace from a playing card). Nancy and little Jane and the dog walked along Judge's Drive in the park, and the sun started to break through the clouds. Ace started to make a whimpering noise and kept looking behind at something. Nancy slowed down and turned around and saw the figure of a young girl wearing a type of boater and a black dress and stockings approaching, but she could not see the face because the dark brown (possible black) boater obscured it as the girl walked along with her head bowed. Nancy did notice that the girl had on what looked like purplish-blue gloves, but when the girl passed the mother and daughter, Ace started to growl and snap at her, and so she turned to look at him – revealing a face that was a shade somewhere between a dark magenta and purple. What startled Nancy even more was that the eyeballs were black with golden irises in them. The unearthly-looking girl ran ahead of Nancy, then stopped, facing her in the middle of the path, with her arms stretched out sideways, barring the mother from passing. Ace the Jack Russell was barking hysterically by now, and Nancy, unnerved by the unnatural appearance of the girl, and suspecting there was something supernatural about her, turned around and walked out of the park. She felt little Jane being jerked backwards and when she looked down, Nancy saw that the purple-skinned girl had hold of her daughter's right wrist. Nancy screamed for the freakish girl to let go, and let go of Ace's leash so she could tackle the creepy child. Ace jumped up at the Purple Girl, and bit at the straw boater hat she wore, and the girl let go of Jane's wrist as she tried to slap the dog's head. Nancy picked up her daughter and ran screaming out of the park with the dog following. She glanced back a few times and saw the bizarre girl hurrying after her with an expression of utter hate on her face. By the time Nancy and her crying daughter had reached their home on Onslow Road, about four hundred yards from Newsham Park, there was no sign of the sinister girl, and Ace refused to be taken out on walks for days after the incident. Nancy herself kept away from the park for weeks and only ventured in there again in the summer when she went in the company of her husband. Almost ten years after this, on a sunny November morning in 1982, a 77-year-old Wavertree man named Johnny Lewis left his house on Alderson Road and went for his customary daily one-mile walk which took in Kensington and Edge Lane. He would then stroll through Wavertree Park (known locally as The Botanic) to get to a cafè on Picton Road. Mr Lewis was well-known and respected by the locals in the area, and he was always kind to children, often giving them money for sweets. On this morning, as he was walking through the park, he saw a gang of children near a small wooded area, and despite his age, Mr Lewis had excellent vision for seeing and discerning objects and people that were far-off, and he could see that the gang was made up of children he knew from the streets around his home. They were all good well-behaved children; not one of them was a vandal or a scally. All of a sudden, the gang in the distance scattered, and Mr Lewis heard shrieks and yelps. Four of the children were so afraid, they almost ran into the pensioner, and he wondered what they were running from. Mr Lewis's long-sightedness enabled him to see that there was a girl dressed in quaint, dated-looking clothes, walking towards him, about fifty yards away. But why on earth had the gang

384

of lads fled from here? Mr Lewis wondered, and then he saw the strange colour of her skin – a pale bluish purple in colour. She had on the black straw boater that had been noted by witnesses so many times before, and Mr Lewis thought it looked like the boaters young girls wore from Edwardian times right up to the 1950s (especially as part of the uniform in some girls' schools). Mr Lewis did not get close enough to report if the peculiar girl had black eyes. She walked in a curve around him and he bravely shouted to her: 'Hello there!' but she did not react or reply. She walked into a walled section of the park grounds called the Botanic Gardens, and Mr Lewis followed her but he found no one except a few frightened members of the gang that had ran away from the creepy child. These boys told Mr Lewis that the girl had been hanging around the park, watching a woman pushing a pram near the swings, and when the lads had approached her out of curiosity, she had loudly hissed at them like a snake and her mouth had opened to reveal pointed teeth like that of an animal. Mr Lewis passed through the park almost every day after the incident on his routine long walks, but never again set eyes on the Purple Girl. In August 1998, a gang of children playing in Walton Hall Park at 9pm one evening claimed that they had been chased by a girl of about twelve who had reddish-purple skin. She was wearing old-fashioned clothes, all in black, and had on 'a round black hat with a flat top' – which sounds like a good description of a boater. The girl chased the gang of children (ages ranging from about 10 to 13) out of the park and onto Moor Lane, where she seems to have vanished near to the back of a row of houses that front onto Queens Drive.

I have many vague and nebulous reports of what seems to be the Purple Girl being seen in the parks of Huyton, Kirkby, St Helens, Calderstones, as well as the parks and open green spaces of Wirral, including Birkenhead Park, Coronation Park and Arrowe Park. I always enjoy a good ghost story that has a solid back story, or even an alleged history, but in the case of the Purple Girl, I have to admit that I'm stumped – I have no idea whose ghost she is. It's unusual for a phantom to be seen over such a wide area, in places divided by a major river, and what does the colour of her purple skin signify I wonder? I have read of the skin of cholera victims turning purple after death, and have wondered if the Purple Girl is perhaps a ghost of some child who died of cholera, but my intuition tells me that is not a valid explanation at all. The black eyes seem to suggest something demonic, but why on earth would a demon constantly go in the guise of a girl from some bygone era? The whole case is a real puzzler, and I have a feeling we'll continue to hear of reports of the Purple Girl for some time to come.

MORE LIVERPOOL VAMPIRES

On many, many nights as Liverpool slept, I waited alone, in cemeteries, or encamped on windy hillsides, waiting for the vampires to show. Most of the time I waited in vain, but now and then I would catch glimpses of them; shadowy hyper-agile beings that are able to move at superhuman speeds, on foot and through the air, sometimes so fast that the eye can barely register them. Most 'educated' people in the West think the vampire is but a mythical bloodsucking creature, but 'vampire' is just one of the names we assign to the creatures which, in reality, are holes in our knowledge. We find the vampire in Eastern and Western culture, and in every era. They are contradictions – slick, romantic seducers and also repulsive zombie-like monsters. What the human race fails to understand is that there are many species of what we dullards call vampires (and the name is derived from the Hungarian *vampir* as well as the German *vampyr*). Not all vampires are derived from East European legends, and I even wrote a book called *Vampires of Great Britain* which chronicled vampire reports going way back into the history of the United Kingdom.

The Ancient Greeks knew of a dark convent of vampiric female bloodsuckers that were active at night. These alluring vampires roamed remote roads and country lanes at night, seducing male and female travellers and draining the blood of their victims. Further back in time, the Jews chronicled the terrifying exploits of Lilith, the first wife of Adam, who refused to lie beneath him during sexual intercourse and went flying about at night to suck the blood of animals, and later, men and newborn infants. Earlier, there was a vampire knocking about with a similar name to Adam's first missus – Lilitu, and she was an Assyrian vampiric-demoness with a huge mane of tangled hair and large fangs. The terrifying antics of Lilith/Lilitu were so feared by the Jews, they carried talismans and resorted to protective magic to ward off vampires well into medieval times. Likewise, Ancient China documented her vampires – the Kian-si, for example, a bloodthirsty demon who prowled the night looking for victims. The Native American Indians have stories about parasitic supernatural beings with trumpet-like mouths that can suck out the brains of victims through their ears as they sleep in the dead of night. These American Indian vampires can also draw off the life force energy, leaving a victim weak and near death. On the other side of the world we read ancient accounts of the Hindu vampire who seems to have a preference for women who are drunk or insane. We could easily fill many volumes documenting the vampires of the world's cultures, but this chapter is concerned with vampire reports I have unearthed which can join the ones detailed in the earlier *Haunted Liverpool* and *Haunted Cheshire* books.

In February 1963 it looked as if the New Ice Age long promised by the doomsayers for decades had finally arrived. The seas around Britain's coast actually froze solid, and it was possible to walk across the ice-crust of the Mersey. A thick blanket of frozen snow covered the UK and a rural Lancashire police station had been cut off by the unrelenting blizzards which swept the land. The telephone lines to the station were down and the electricity kept failing. A Liverpool-born police doctor named Richard Llewellyn was one of the seven men stranded at the station the night they brought in an unconscious couple found by a farmer in a snowdrift. The woman regained consciousness and claimed that the man with her was a vampire who had stalked her for miles. The unconscious man had bluish skin a very slow heartbeat, and crimson eyeballs – all symptoms of hypothermia to prolonged exposure to subzero conditions, some believed, but not Dr Llewellyn; his trained eye and the skill that comes from twenty-five years of being a doctor told him otherwise; he believed there was something decidedly odd about the man who had been brought in from the arctic cold. The unconscious stranger wore an expensively-made wig of straight long black hair and a tailor-made suit. He carried no identification on him or any documents or money.

The lady brought in with the man said her name was Harriet Brignall, that she was aged 20 and had been living in Ormskirk for the past six months with a relative. A shivering Miss Brignall begged the police to keep the 'vampire' locked up. 'He'll kill you all – he's very strong!' she claimed.

When the stranger opened his red eyes, he muttered what sounded like "Da-mi sange!' (possibly Romanian for 'Give me blood'). He then sat up, grabbed the doctor by each arm and pushed him across the room with great force as if he was a doll. The doctor slammed into the wall and was almost knocked out. Four policemen finally subdued the man, and believing he was mentally unbalanced, he was put in a straightjacket and kept in a locked cell.

The violent stranger stood up in his cell and in perfect English he shouted: 'Let me go before sunrise!'

'Shut up you!' a sergeant yelled at the prisoner, then turned to Miss Brignall and said: 'So you hadn't met this man before, miss?'

'Well, I had never seen him before in everyday life, but er,' the young lady faltered in her reply.

'You either know him or you don't know him, miss,' said the sergeant, sensing that the girl was hiding something.

'Well what I mean is, well – the dreams,' she said, and seemed embarrassed by her admission.

'Dreams?' Dr Llewellyn angled his head sideways and cast a screwed-up eye at Brignall.

Miss Brignall gave three staccato nods. 'I had dreams about him, and I know it will sound silly,' she said, 'but I used to have funny dreams about him, so when I saw him in real life I was quite scared.'

'But beyond your dreams you've never clapped eyes on this fellow before?' the sergeant asked the girl, pointing his thumb back at the caged mystery.

'No, never,' Harriet told him firmly, then she asked: 'Please, sir, can you keep him locked up till the sun comes up?'

'Don't worry miss,' said a young smiling policeman, 'he isn't going to turn into a bat and bite anyone.'

The sun was due up at 7.55am – and it was now midnight. Miss Brignall sipped hot broth as she filled in more gaps in her story. She explained that she'd eloped from her aunt's home in Ormskirk, and her boyfriend had not met her at the rendezvous point as arranged – but 'that abomination' instead. She had run away from him and he had pursued her, running at a phenomenal speed, but during the chase he was hit by a car and knocked out cold, and Harriet ran on blindly in the snow, hoping he'd been killed - but he followed her, shouting for her to come back because she had 'special blood'.

There was then a loud racket from the cells. The foreign man was somehow bending his limbs into impossible angles as he tried to get out of the straightjacket. His wig fell off as he struggled to be free. He was completely bald, and his mouth opened to reveal long pointed fangs. Harriet screamed and ran to the door of the station, but the young policeman intercepted her, saying: 'It's alright miss, don't go out there!'

As the sergeant took an old Army pistol out of the firearms cabinet and loaded it, Dr Llewellyn had the girl put in a tall cupboard in a corridor where the coats were hung, and then he hurried into the kitchen. The blue-skinned man slipped out of the jacket. He shook the cell door violently and it came off its hinges! The sergeant emptied the pistol into the fiend, hitting him in the chest at point blank range, yet he never flinched.

Only then did the police realise that they had something unearthly on their hands, and they stood there in shock, not knowing how to tackle this bald ghastly-looking being.

'She's in there!' the red-eyed monstrosity pointed to the cupboard, and smiled, showing his terrifying array of long razor teeth. 'I know this because I have her scent, but before I have her, I will kill all of you!'

Dr Llewellyn suddenly came running out the kitchen with a burning torch of paper and a cup of paraffin. He threw the paraffin at the man's face and thrust the burning paper forward. Before the thing could throw up its long-fingered hands to its head, the face was in flames, and it screamed.

'Come on you docile bastards!' the doctor ran to the rack in the corridor where a number of truncheons were hanging, and he seized five of them and threw it to the policemen. He didn't have to tell the men what to do – they ploughed into the strange figure, and forced it backwards towards the door of the station. The youngest policeman opened the door and watched in horrified awe as the half-blinded blue-skinned freak fell backwards into the snow, shrieking in agony. The station door was then bolted and two heavy filing cabinets were pushed in front of it to act as a barricade.

Until sunrise, the burned and disfigured face of the thing appeared at the station's windows, but was kept at bay by makeshift torches that the men would place near to the panes. The thing – whatever it was - seemed to be very afraid of fire and would draw back into the darkness when it saw the flames of the torches being thrust at it. Brignall ended up in a hysterical state and was eventually escorted to Ormskirk, where she took to sleeping in a priest's house for round the clock protection from that abomination. Dr Llewellyn advised the sergeant and his men to say nothing about the alleged vampire to their superiors, and the loss of six bullets from the inventory had to be explained away as a clerical error. The story did get out though, as some of the policemen told their wives and family and friends, but the whole story was eventually regarded as just some local urban myth. When Dr Llewellyn was questioned about the story he said there were no such things as vampires, just haemotolangiacs – people with a sexual fetish for drinking blood. From my own experience of delving into the supernatural, I know beyond a shadow of a doubt that vampiric beings exist, and a majority of them seem to be very old creatures, perhaps stretching back centuries. Modern scientific tests seem to prove what the occultists have been saying for hundreds of years – that young blood absorbed by a vampiric host can make him or her younger. Old mice have been injected with the blood and plasma of young mice, and the results showed that the 'vampire mice' not only gained vast amounts of energy, their memory and ability to learn was boosted. This was quite unexpected among biologists – that an old mouse could experience a burst of brain cell growth in its hippocampus – that part of the brain which, in us humans, deteriorates with age and leaves us with impaired memory and thought processes. In recent years there have been numerous experiments (viewed by many to be very unethical) carried out involving the donation and sale of teenaged blood to scientists who then inject the youthful blood into older people to rejuvenate them. This controversial new bio-science of putting young blood into the old has been tried out on humans at major universities across the world in an effort to combat ageing and neurodegeneration. It's a sad fact that as billions live longer today, they will not necessarily live with a better quality of life, as diseases such as

Alzheimer's and Parkinson's develop on a massive unprecedented scale in ageing brains – but it would seem that transfusions of young blood into the old might be some sort of unsuspected panacea. Of course, there are doubters, just as there were doubters in the 1660s when Robert Boyle first proposed blood transfusions as a way of prolonging life.

In 1971, a 19-year-old student nurse named Emma started work at a major hospital in Liverpool. Since the age of six, Emma, who hailed from Garston, had wanted to be a nurse, and now she had started her apprenticeship, and each day she would look at herself in the mirror as she wore her nurse's outfit and feel so proud for seeing her ambition through. She was put on what was then known as a geriatric ward, with some twenty-five beds, and one afternoon, the staff nurse Gladys informed Emma that one of the patients – a 78-year-old lady named Elsa – had just passed away. 'Your job now is to assist me in the dressing of Elsa's body, Emma,' Gladys told her calmly, 'and I know it's the first time you've seen a dead patient, but I have every faith in you and I'm sure you will not be distressed at all.'

'Of course Sister,' Emma told her superior, 'all experience for me to absorb.'

And off they went into the geriatric ward, Sister Gladys pulled the curtain around Elsa's bed and Emma saw that the old woman was laying there with a slight smile, her large eyes wide open, and her hands folded on her bosom. The staff nurse and student nurse set about washing the body in a most dignified manner, and then they dressed it, in preparation for the attendants to take it away. After the memorable task was completed, the staff nurse praised Emma for her calmness at undertaking the unpalatable task. Emma herself was surprised at how composed she'd been, washing and dressing the dead woman, and when she got home to her flat, which was less than a mile from the hospital, she told her boyfriend Jack about the grim job. He said he was proud of her and he had always supported her and encouraged her in her nursing aspirations.

The couple went to bed around midnight, and Jack fell fast asleep. Emma sat up reading Wilson Harlow's *Modern Surgery for Nurses* by the light of her bedside lamp. Around one that morning, Emma felt a little thirsty and decided to go and get a drink of water, so she placed a bookmark in the medical volume and slowly got out of the bed so as not to disturb Jack, who by now was snoring lightly. She closed the bedroom door almost silently behind her and in her bare feet she padded down the hallway to the kitchen, switching on the light just before she entered it. As the neon strip flickered in the ceiling, Emma stepped into the kitchen, which was unusually long for such a small flat, and straight away she saw a figure out the corner of her right eye. In that split second, the nurse knew the figure was a woman and that she had long white hair, and she turned right to face her, thinking that someone had broken in.

The naked woman sitting there at the breakfast table was, without a doubt, Elsa, the woman who had died on the geriatric ward yesterday. Unable to rationalise and take in what she was seeing, Emma turned and ran out of the kitchen and along the hallway to the bedroom without even looking back. She entered the room as quiet as possible, for even though she was terrified by what she had just witnessed, she was still mindful of her boyfriend Jack having his well-deserved sleep. She sat on the bed, then got in it, leaving the bedside lamp on, and looked at the door over the top of the blankets. Emma could feel her heart pounding. She expected the door to open or the handle on it to turn, but the door remained closed and that handle did not turn. Emma lay there, replaying what she had just seen over and over in her mind. She knew she had not been seeing things. She knew most psychiatrists would explain the apparition by stating that Emma had obviously been affected by the washing of her first dead patient and that her mind had repressed the trauma – until it had sprung forth in the guise of a ghost which only existed in her mind. She knew that what she had seen had been real. It had somehow been a solid-looking ghost of Elsa – but why was she haunting Elsa? The student nurse couldn't answer that question. She *did* live reasonably close to the hospital where Elsa had passed away but why pay a visit during the night? And why on earth would Elsa's ghost sit in a kitchen in the dark?

Jack suddenly startled the student nurse by turning to his left in the bed and throwing his right arm around her. 'You alright, love?' he muttered, without opening his eyes, then began snoring again.

'Yeah,' Emma whispered, 'go to sleep, hun.'

Jack's eyes opened slightly and he murmured: 'Turn that light off please.'

'Okay,' Emma reached out with her left hand and switched off the bedside lamp. Only the luminous green dial of the alarm clock was visible now in the engulfing pitch-black darkness.

She turned to face her sleeping boyfriend, closed her eyes, and tried to avoid thinking about that apparition of Elsa in the kitchen. Somehow, Emma fell asleep, but then she had a strange and erotic dream in which Jack was kneeling at the foot of her bed sucking her toes. Emma woke, and found the room was still in darkness. She was lying on her back and she could still feel a mouth sucking her left big toe. She felt the bed to her right, and her hand touched Jack's back – so if he was still there in the bed, *who* was slowly sucking her toe? Emma drew her legs up, and as her toe left that mouth she felt it move against something sharp – was that a tooth? She reached out with her left hand and switched on the light – and there, crouched or kneeling at the end of the bed, was the naked pale figure of Elsa – and her eyes were blood red. She rose up slowly, revealing her sagging small breasts and folds of skin which resembled smoothed contours of white putty. She had a smile on her face, and as a shocked Emma looked on, that face seemed to become slightly younger, and this slight metamorphosis of the face and the piercing red stare really unnerved Emma, who began to shake Jack awake as she tried to scream.

Jack awoke, and just before Elsa vanished into thin air, he saw her and swore. 'Who was that?' he asked, and sat up in the bed, gazing at the spot where the old lady had stood. 'Was someone in here then?' he asked Emma without even turning to face her.

'Thank God you saw her too, Jack,' Emma told him, and she pulled her left foot up and threw back the blankets. There was a small red spot on the underside of her big toe, and a corresponding spot of blood on the other side of her toe, just below the nail. Only then did Emma realise that the "ghost" of Elsa had been sucking out her blood through the toe, and she went cold inside. Emma did not see the ghost of Elsa again after that, but over the next twelve months, she would find strange bruises with two red spots in them all over her body. She found them on the soles of both her feet, on her breasts, under her arms, near her navel and Jack even spotted one of these strange wounds on the back of Emma's neck. The couple were so spooked by these suspected vampire bites they eventually found another flat to live in miles away in the suburbs. Emma tried to find out who Elsa had been from the staff nurse and was told that the old lady had died from heart failure and had been born in Poland in the 1890s. Elsa had been buried at a certain well-known cemetery but Emma and Jack wondered if she had somehow risen from her grave. That wouldn't be necessary for some types of vampire who exist only as a form of energy which takes on the shape of a humanoid when they float about at night, looking for victims to prey upon. I believe that Elsa was a vampire, and this would explain the way her face became slightly younger after she had imbibed the teenaged blood of Emma. Elsa is probably still prowling the night in search of victims who may never even suspect that their blood is being siphoned off. Have *you* checked your body for any unusual marks recently?

In May, 2010 another strange vampire-like being – and this was quite a bizarre one - was encountered by a 47-year-old woman named Lily at her home on Broadgreen's Milton Avenue. Lily was suffering from a bout of insomnia, and had been to her doctor to seek a remedy to her condition, which affects millions across the world. The doctor was reluctant to prescribe sleeping pills, and asked Lily if her sleeplessness was perhaps being caused by worries over something. Lily said she had landed herself in a lot of debt, and constantly worried about how she could pay it all off. Most nights she would get into bed with her husband and he'd be asleep minutes after his head touched the pillow, but Lily would lie there, worrying herself sick about the debt hanging over her. The doctor suggested that perhaps Lily should try and resolve her debt problem first before he'd try her on sleeping tablets. That night, Lily lay in bed at midnight, and her husband was snoring beside her. She heard her 27-year-old son playing on his X Box in his room, but by 1.20 am, the noise from the game console had died and then came the faint rhythmic sounds of snoring. Now Lily's son was asleep too. Feeling lonely, Lily got up at 1.45 am and went into the kitchen to make herself a cup of tea. She sat at the kitchen table, reading a *Martha Stewart Living* magazine, then decided to have a go at the Sudoku book she'd bought herself a few days ago. This book was in the lounge, which was only illuminated by the light filtering in from the kitchen. Lily went looking for the book (which was on a coffee table under a bundle of newspapers), and during the search she happened to glance at the blinds on the lounge window. They were normally closed at night but had been left open. Lily saw movement through the horizontal gaps in those blinds, so she went over to the window and peered out through the plastic white slats – and at first, Lily thought a balloon was floating over by the corner of Milton Avenue and Greystone Road. She lifted a slat in the blinds up to get a better view, and saw what appeared to be a child with a cloak on, floating close to the top of a telegraph pole. 'What the –' she heaved, and never finished the sentence. What in God's name *is* that? She wondered. It looked like a boy dressed in black with a flowing black cloak, and this gravity-defying person had a globular head with a white face and large black spots for eyes. As Lily watched the weird figure, a neighbour's cat came strolling down Milton Avenue from the Greystone Road junction, and that floating figure of a boy noticed the cat, and began to descend towards it in a slanting path which would take the figure down towards Lily's house. Lily froze, and her stomach somersaulted. She wanted to go and wake her husband or son and tell them about the weird little cloaked being, but she never had time. Within seconds the airborne minor was hovering over the hedge of her garden. Next door's cat was suddenly scarce, as if he had been frightened by the creepy cloaked boy and had gone into hiding. Lily was so afraid, she did not dare to move in case the thing saw her. She remained stock still as she peeped over the sofa, watching the levitating lad. She saw him clearly now, and he looked like the archetypal vampire as depicted in the old horror films, only he was very young, perhaps about ten or twelve. He had on a black velvet suit and dark boots, and his rippling black cloak looked as if it was made of shiny satin. The boy's almost round head had black hair that was so closely cropped or shaven, it looked as if it had been painted on, and came to a point in the centre of the forehead as a widow's peak.

The bizarre-looking boy floated backwards slightly, away from the hedge, and Lily rose a few more inches from her hiding place to get a better view. The 'junior Dracula' was now hovering over Lily's car. She decided she'd try and capture the amazing vampire boy with her iPhone and quickly realised the phone was in the kitchen. She moved a little along the sofa and her hand accidentally pressed on her car's key fob (which she'd left on the arm of the sofa). The car bleeped loudly and the doors unlocked, and the resulting brief flash of lights on the car and its clunking sound scared the figure, for he reflexively flew upwards, then shot across the rooftops of the facing house. Lily swore to herself and pressed the fob again to re-lock the vehicle. She waited at the window for an agonising long ten minutes, hoping to see the weird yet strangely cute cloaked boy, but he didn't return. Lily then went and made herself a fresh cup of tea and sat in the kitchen, thinking of what she had seen. She knew she had not dreamed the little vampire up, and she could not explain just what she had seen, but she decided she would not tell anyone about the boy, because she knew she would not believe a story like that herself if she had not witnessed it firsthand. She eventually emailed me and told me what she had seen, and I was at a loss to explain it. I'd had no similar reports of any vampiric children, but then in late December 2012, I received another email from Lily which was quite interesting. She said that on Boxing Day she had gone to visit an old friend named Julie, who lived on Pilch Lane, just a quarter of a mile from Lily's house on Milton Lane. Julie's husband and children were out visiting relatives in Huyton at the time, and Julie had remained at home because she had the flu. Lily doted on her sick friend and made her a hot toddy with rum to soothe her cold. The two friends talked of old times, of old boyfriends and funny incidents, and then somehow the course of the conversation turned to the supernatural, and Julie told her friend something which literally caused her heart to flutter. 'Well, I didn't believe in ghosts and all that stuff until six or seven weeks ago,' Julie said, and Lily asked: 'Why, what changed your mind?'

Julie sipped her toddy, then told her friend: 'It was the day after Bonfire Night, a Thursday, and it was around 11 o'clock at night. I had an argument with *him* [meaning her husband] because I wanted to do the washing, and he said it was too late to put the machine on, but it's dead quiet our new washing machine and our neighbour's an old woman who's deaf as a doorpost. Anyway, he stormed off to bed, and I'd had a bad bout of insomnia – '

'Oh, don't mention that to me, Julie,' Lily interrupted, 'I had that for six months.'

'Anyway,' Julie continued, 'I put the washing on, watched the telly with the sound right down, and on this night, there was a big full moon out; I've never seen it so big, and it was shining through the curtains and the nets right?'

Lily nodded, wishing her friend would get to the point.

'I saw this shadow in the moonlight go from one side of the window,' Julie told her, and she got up and pointed at the window concerned, saying: 'that window there. The shadow was like that of a kid, only about three feet tall I'd say, and Lily, on my fellah's life – may I never recover from this flu – he must have been floating outside the window.'

The feeling in the pit of Lily's stomach was like the sensation you'd feel if you were in a lift when the cable snapped, and her heart palpitated. Lily realised her friend was probably talking about the little vampire she'd seen four years before. She interrupted Julie by asking: 'Did he have a cloak on?'

Julie looked stunned, and she asked: 'How did you know?' And then she nodded.

'Julie, I saw the same thing four years ago. I was sitting up around two in the morning, and I saw him as clear as I'm seeing you now.'

'Shurrup!' Julie threw her hand to her mouth and seemed so shocked. 'That's what I was going to say, Lil; I went to the curtains, opened them, and I saw him fly from outside here right over there over Margaret Marys School. I could see his cloak flapping. I nearly crapped myself. I got him out of bed and he looked out the window but by then the thing had gone. He said it was an owl and then he said I was seeing things, but I know what I saw. Oh my God, you saw it too?'

The two friends compared notes about the little vampire and by one in the morning, when it was time for Lily to embark on the walk homewards, the two women stood on the doorstep of Julie's house on Pilch Lane and scanned the starry night skies – just in case that 'boy' was still about.

Every now and them I still get reports of a vampire in the Toxteth district, and they all seem to be referring to the legendary Manilu, also known as the Lodge Lane Vampire, a local bloodsucker I have written about in my previous books. He seems to date back to Victorian times, and seems to be quite an audacious creature. The following report of a vampire in Toxteth makes me think it's Manilu at work, and I know for a fact that there are people out there, some of them occultists, who know more about Manilu than I do and some may even be in league with him.

In September 1994, at the third-floor flat of a house with sharp gothic-looking gables on Toxteth's Bentley Road, Oonagh, a 19-year-old Irish economics student, noticed that a very eccentric man lived opposite her. She had seen his wiry shadow darting about on the blinds after dark, and on most mornings around 3am, this man would be seen sneaking out of the house. He was completely bald, well over six feet in height, and wore a long black knee-length coat and narrow trousers. Oonagh was seeing Neil, a musician with a grunge band named Grave of Dreams, and he stayed at her flat one night and he too saw the weird man come out of the house opposite.

'Baldy head!' Neil shouted, then ducked down, sniggering.

Oonagh was furious at him for doing this because the man in the street looked up to the windows of the flat before wandering off towards Lodge Lane.

'He could be a psychopath you childish idiot,' she chided Neil, and they had a row. Oonagh went to bed and Neil lay down on the sofa, sulking as he puffed on a roll-up with the sash window open. After the last drag on the ciggy, Neil flicked it out the window and tried to get some shut eye. After about five minutes, the musician opened his eyes and noticed that something outside the window was blocking off the lamplight from the street below and casting a shadow on the ceiling. That shadow then flitted away. A few minutes passed, and then a man's pale face glided into Neil's field of view as he lay on his back, gazing at the ceiling. In a state of sheer terror, Neil could see that the bald man in the street he had skitted at earlier was now floating over him, face down. The levitating entity then descended rapidly towards the musician. The gaunt and wrinkled face with bulging red eyes was suddenly inches from Neil's face, and the levitating figure said something unintelligible in a raspy voice. Neil rolled sideways off the sofa and fled into the hallway. Too afraid to leave the flats – Neil stayed put on the stairs for a while, then listened. The door to Oonagh's flat flew open, but it was not the baldy ghoulish figure coming after Neil, it was the young Irish woman. Oonagh asked Neil what all the shouting was about, and he told her. Oonagh reassured the musician that there was no one in her flat, and she'd closed the window. Neil searched the place anyway and even looked in the wardrobe. He hardly slept that morning, and on the following night, he and Oonagh sat in the dark at the flat, keeping watch on the house across the road. At around 3am, the couple both experienced dizziness at the same time and then they simultaneously blacked out, then both awoke at 7.30am. Both had puncture marks in the crease where their arms bent. Enough was enough; suspecting that the bald man opposite was some vampire, Oonagh moved in with her cousin in Oxton, and Neil stayed at his brother's flat in Heysmoor Heights, a tower block overlooking Sefton Park, but that thing even followed him there, and Neil and his brother saw a ghastly face peering through the window ten storey's up. Neil moved back in with his parents in West Derby, and thankfully the vampiric entity did not follow him there.

In the summer of 1972 there were some very strange rumours in circulation across Mossley Hill, Allerton, Aigburth and parts of Wavertree, carelessly spread by that early form of social media known as the grapevine, and these whispers were eerie ones, for they concerned stories of people waking in the morning – and sometimes in the wee small hours – with alarming puncture marks in their necks, upper back and sometimes their wrists. The general consensus was that a vampire was at large, and some people – usually friends of a friend of a 'victim' – maintained that a giant black bat with glowing red eyes had been seen flapping across the skies of south Liverpool. Around this time, there was a self-styled occultist and vampire hunter prowling the night streets of the city, and he was Stephen Ainsworth, a 25-year-old accountant and a dead-ringer for John Lennon with his wireframe NHS spectacles, long brown centre-parted hair, and his predilection for wearing white suits and tennis shoes. Coincidentally, Stephen lived (with his parents) in a mock-Tudor house on Menlove Avenue, just a stone's throw from Lennon's old home, "Mendips" at Number 251. When Stephen Ainsworth heard about the vampire rumours as he drank in the Rose of Mossley pub one evening, he smiled, and the few who knew him, including his girlfriend Audrey, could see that Stephen had found his cause at last. He was a fan of the Hammer horror films and thought of himself as Liverpool's answer to Van Helsing. While everyone else in the pub shuddered at the uncanny accounts of the alleged vampire doing the rounds in the locality, Stephen acted as if he'd had a win on the Pools. He told Audrey as they sat in a corner of the pub: 'I must set to work at once, and sharpen the stakes and bottle some holy water. I might even have to borrow my father's old army revolver.'

'No, Stephen,' panted Audrey, the small brandy catching her throat, 'you could get into trouble.'

With his left arm curled about his concerned girlfriend, Stephen gave a wry smile as he looked up at the ceiling. 'Ha! Trouble – I've had that all my life. I'm afraid trouble and danger are part and parcel of my job, my love, and you *were* told that when you hooked up with me.'

'You told me you were an accountant when I met you, you never mentioned vampires and Satanism and all that,' Audrey reminded him.

'Had I told you the truth about my double life, you would have dismissed me as some fantasist,' Stephen said, and he turned to Audrey, kissed her forehead, then looked at the moon's orange crescent, just visible through the pub window. 'These things – these vampires – remain at liberty because the human sheep are just too stupefied to take them in. We are just like the cattle in the field, unaware of the horrors of the abattoir, but I aim to change all that.'

'You're not going to start going on walkabouts of a night again are you?' Audrey asked, and unconsciously pulled a face which showed her vexation at his plans.

'I've never been an armchair type, Audrey,' Stephen told her sternly, unaware that he was crushing her towards him with his left arm. 'If there is a vampire at large – and you've heard several people tell their stories here tonight about men, women and even *children* being preyed upon, then it's my duty to protect the hoi polloi and destroy this abomination, regardless of the cost!'

'You're hurting me – ' Audrey winced.

'I'm sorry Audrey!' Stephen relaxed his arm-lock immediately. 'I don't know my own strength sometimes; it's just that I'm raring to go.'

That night at 11pm, Stephen escorted Audrey from the Rose of Mossley to her home on Archerfield Road. It was a pleasant walk on such a hot summer's night, and they covered the mile from the pub to Audrey's house, frequently stopping in the moonlight and kissing under the shadows of trees. They kissed at the gate of the house, and just before they separated, Stephen came out with a dramatic line that was typical of him, Audrey thought.

'Audrey – promise me one thing until we meet again,' he said, his hands wringing the top crossmember bar of the garden gate.

'Yes Stephen?' Audrey sighed, halting a quarter of the way down the path to her home.

'Well, I know it's a hot night, but please do not sleep with your bedroom window open,' Stephen said, and he looked up at the moon.

Audrey said nothing in reply, but shot him a baffled look.

'That *thing* is at large tonight, and you heard the stories – it gets in through open windows.'

'Oh, okay, I won't open the window – '

'You have to promise, Audrey!'

She turned and walked towards the house, 'Yes I promise, now get home Stephen – as soon as you can!'

'Oh, don't worry about me, love – night,' he said, and as soon as he saw Audrey let herself into the house he walked away. As Stephen went up Booker Avenue he bumped into a friend he'd gone to school with – Brian Bromsgrove, a giant of a young man, but quite docile. Brian's parents had separated and he was returning to his mother's house on Menlove Avenue after spending a few hours at his father's home. He accompanied Stephen on his homeward journey, and Brian, knowing his friend was obsessed with the occult, asked him if he had heard the rumours going round about the vampire. 'Yes, and I aim to track it to its lair and destroy it – even if I have to kill myself in the process,' Stephen assured him.

'So you really believe in them? Vampires?' Brian asked, with a slight smile.

Stephen threw his head back, inhaled the night air in a rather macho way, before replying: 'No, I *know* they exist, Brian, and from that inane grin on your face you obviously think this is all some joke?'

'No, I just wanted to know if you believed in them, that's all. My dad said it's all rubbish, all these stories of vampires. He said they never existed and Hollywood invented them. Why would anyone want blood, anyway?'

Stephen smirked and looked at the pavement as he walked along. 'Your dad says...'

'Yeah.'

'Your dad knows nothing, Brian. And you ask why anyone wants blood?'

Brian seemed hurt because Stephen had said his father knew nothing.

'Let me tell you a story, Brian boy. I know many stories about vampires and I don't want you wetting the bed tonight or having nightmares but here goes – '

'I don't wet the bed!' Brian protested.

'Anyway, listen: hundreds of years ago, there was a very cruel woman named Countess Bathory. This was in old Hungary. She discovered that if you drink and bathe in blood, you stay young. She chanced upon this discovery one day when a maid in her boudoir accidentally yanked at the her hair. The Countess slapped her so hard, the maid's nose started gushing with blood. It went all over the Countess's hand, and she thought the blood was very smooth and fresh, and seemed to make her skin softer. The Countess thought this was because the maid was a virgin. She summoned a few heavies and they slashed the maid's throat and drained her blood into a vat so the Countess could bathe in it. She was naked of course. For the next ten years, the cruel Countess took bloodbaths – made from thousands of gallons of virgin blood - to preserve her beauty, and her men would throw the bodies of the drained virgins over the castle walls so the wolves would eat the evidence. They kidnapped thousands of girls, all virgins, and took them to the castle to be squeezed like berries for their blood. They caught the Countess torturing the virgins in her castle in the end, and she had a tap with a pipe rammed up one girl's bottom. It was horrific. The soldiers raided the castle, beheaded and burned the Countess's men, and then they bricked her up in her bedroom but left a narrow slit so she could be fed through it. She died four years later, and her room was full of turds.'

'You're weird,' Brian told Stephen, and his face went into a spasm. He had obviously been affected by the gruesome story. 'It never happened. You made it up.'

'It's in the history books Brian, go and look it up in

the library. That's why vampires want blood,' Stephen told him, 'it is the elixir of youth to them.'

Brian cried out and threw his arm across his face as if something was going to attack him, and a shadow of something passed over the two young men.

'What was that?' Brian tried to follow the trajectory of the thing moving towards the west as it flitted through the sky.

'Aha! Well now!' Stephen remarked, looking up into the night air.

'It must have been an owl,' Brian wished, and his eyes bulged.

'That would have to be a prehistoric one, Brian,' remarked Stephen, and he realised that the thing was heading towards Audrey's home. 'I'd better warn my fiancée.' He went in search of a telephone box, and Brian followed out of curiosity. Stephen telephoned Audrey's house and her mother answered. Stephen asked for Audrey, and her mother said she was upstairs having a bath. 'Look, please tell her to keep her window closed tonight,' Stephen told his girlfriend's mother.

'Are you drunk or have you been taking drugs?' was the haughty reply, and then the telephone call ended as Audrey's mum slammed down the handset.

'I'll have to go and see Audrey at work tomorrow and tell her what we saw tonight,' he murmured as he came out of the telephone box.

'Does she still work in the library?' Brian asked.

Stephen nodded and then he and Brian walked onwards to Menlove Avenue, and Stephen slowed at one point and drew an imaginary line in the air with his index finger, saying: 'It came from that direction, which means... it came from the Calderstones Park area.'

'It was just a big owl,' Brian insisted, 'but it startled me because you were telling me about that woman having baths in people's blood.'

'Stay in your small world, Brian,' Stephen told him with air of superiority. 'Keep listening to your dad – see how far that gets you in life.'

On the following day during his lunch break at the accountancy firm on Allerton Road, Stephen dashed over to the library to see Audrey. The librarian was just starting her lunch break too.

'Audrey,' he said, as soon as he walked into the building, 'you won't believe what I saw last night on the way home from yours!'

'Stephen, why did you telephone our house last night?' a red-faced Audrey asked him. She looked incensed. 'You woke my grandfather up.'

'That's what I've come to tell you dear Audrey,' Stephen threw his hands out and tried to clasp hers, but she slapped them away. 'Audrey, I saw the vampire last night! And I have a witness who saw it too!'

'Shhh! Be quiet,' the senior librarian reprimanded Stephen, who responded by rolling his eyes.

'I'm sorry,' he whispered.

'Excuse me,' said a slim dark-haired man around Stephen's age. He had been sitting at a table reading a newspaper but now he was getting up.

'Yes?' Stephen replied, wondering if the man was going to lambast him too.

'Did you say you saw the vampire?' the man asked.

'Er, yes, I did, why?' Stephen replied.

'I'm going over to the cafè,' Audrey fumed, and

headed for the door.

'No please don't go yet,' Stephen stepped in her way but she walked around him and once again the top librarian scolded him about talking too loud.

'I think I know who the vampire is,' the man whispered to Stephen and introduced himself as Jim Smith. Stephen asked Jim if he would like to come to the cafè on Allerton Road to have a coffee and a sausage roll on him. Jim reluctantly agreed, and so, he ended up sitting at the table in the cafè with Stephen and a disinterested Audrey. Jim gave his information to the self-proclaimed vampire hunter.

'I'm unemployed at the moment,' said Jim, 'I have a bad bronchial chest condition, and it's hard for me to sleep. I live right by the park – Calderstones Park that is – and most nights when the telly ends, I listen to the radio till all hours in the morning, and I sit with the lights out, just looking out the window till I start feeling sleepy.'

'Is there a point to this?' Audrey asked, stirring her tea impatiently.

Jim looked down at the tablecloth despondently. 'Er, yes, er - '

'Audrey please! Do continue Jim,' Stephen assuaged him.

'Well, I noticed something really weird. I saw this thing – I thought it was some bird at first, flying up from a house. I have a pair of binoculars that I use for my bird-watching hobby. I had a look at this thing through them and I soon saw it was no bird – it was a black silhouette of a man. His arms were at his sides and his body was inclined at about thirty degrees. His hair was dark, and swept back. I do not know whether he had a suit on, but he seemed to be dressed all in black. He came out the attic of a house on Druid's Cross Road, and I even know the exact house he came from.'

'And would you be willing to supply me with the address of his house?' Stephen asked with an excited look.

Audrey gently kicked her boyfriend's feet under the table and looked at him with her eyelids half closed as if to say: 'You don't believe this rubbish do you?'

Stephen ignored her subtle communications and listened to the rest of Jim's account.

Jim continued. 'I see him almost every night. He goes to the attic, switches off the light, then opens the window. He seems to look about first, to see if anyone's around, and then the next thing I know, he's flying up into the air. He does this between midnight and about three in the morning. He isn't out long; I'd say about fifteen minutes, and then he's back again. What do you think? I'm not seeing things I swear.'

Stephen slowly nodded. 'I know you're not seeing things; you look pretty sane to me.'

Audrey almost spat her tea out as she chortled to herself. She thought Jim looked anything but sane; he looked barking mad in her eyes, even though she was used to the outlandish claims of her boyfriend concerning the mumbo-jumbo of the occult.

'If you give me the address, Jim, I'll watch the house from some vantage point, and then I'll attract his attention when he takes flight – and I shall destroy him.'

'How will you kill him though?' Jim wanted to know.

'Oh I have my methods,' Stephen told his informer,

'but now, the address.'

Jim produced a pen from his pocket, then picked up a paper napkin from the chequered tablecloth and wrote down the address of the vampire's house.

'Look, don't involve me, mate,' Jim told Stephen with a very worried look, 'I don't want this thing coming after me.'

Stephen tried to allay his fears with a soft smile as he pocketed the napkin with the address on. 'Oh, you needn't be concerned there Mr Smith, but I do advise you to keep your curtains drawn at night and to keep well away from your windows. Twitching curtains seems to attract these creatures of the night.'

Smith still seemed very scared and did not even touch the coffee or the sausage roll. He rose from the table and said: 'If you lay this vampire – or whatever it is you do when you kill it – will you let me know?'

'I certainly will, I'll call round to your place,' Stephen replied, 'where do you live?'

Jim shook his head and stipulated: 'I'd rather we met here, in case there are more than one of those things. I'll be back here every Thursday afternoon for the next few weeks if you want to meet me.'

And then he left the cafè.

'What do you think?' Stephen asked Audrey, and clasped her hand on the table.

She pulled her hand away, then smiled, then told him: 'Absolute hogwash. You seem to be a magnet to all these loonies.'

'So you think he's seeing things or just making it all up?' Stephen asked, and then he sincerely added a few flattering words. 'Audrey, I value your take on people - you're rarely wrong about folk.'

'Well, I admit he doesn't look like your common crackpot; he did seem to be afraid, and he didn't really add anything to what he said – which liars usually do – they embroider their lies; with Jim it was pretty straightforward.'

'Well look who's changed her tune,' Stephen raised his eyebrows and smiled.

'I know, but a wise person changes their mind, a fool never,' Audrey told him, and sipped her tea. 'Look, I think Jim saw *something*, but not some vampire; I think it's been some trick of the light; at that time in the morning, shadows take on all sorts of forms if you stare at them long enough.'

'I think Jim saw more than shadow and tricks of the light, love,' Stephen said, and slowly let go of her hand.

She grabbed his hand back. 'I knew you'd say that. Sometimes I think you're just like Don Quixote charging at far-off windmills, seeing them as all sorts of monsters of the night.'

That evening, Stephen packed his Gladstone bag with crucifixes of metal and wood, rosary beads, small bottles of holy water, bottles of powdered hawthorn, two wooden stakes, a mallet, and an old black leatherbound copy of the Bible. Laying beside the bag on his bed rested his father's Army pistol, loaded with three rounds. Stephen looked at the clock – it was almost twelve. He went down to the kitchen, made some coffee and laced it with whiskey, and poured it into a thermos flask. At midnight, Stephen left his home on Menlove Avenue wearing a black trilby and a long dark trench coat, and he discovered, to his joy, that a fog was invading the district. He visited the address supplied by Mr Smith and saw that the house on Druid's Cross Road was not a semi like most of the other dwellings, but an abode that stood alone, and Stephen thought this detached residence had quite an eerie atmosphere about it, especially now in the fog with a ghostly moon high in the sky. The neighbouring house was pebble-dashed, but the house of the alleged vampire had walls as dark as soot. The garden had no gate, just a wide gap in an ancient sandstone wall, and Stephen felt the handle of the pistol in his trench coat pocket as he walked down the gravel drive as slowly as possible. The front door of the house was white, and the black wrought iron knocker was shaped like the spade in a playing card, so that the entire door reminded him of the ace of spades. Stephen went to the Elizabethan-styled windows and peered in. Through a gap in the curtains he saw a familiar face which gave him a start – it was a framed photograph of the infamous occultist Aleister Crowley – which was a very strange photograph to be hanging in this suburban house.

'Shall I draw this fiend out or play the waiting game?' Stephen whispered to himself, and he thought he should wait. The house facing the dwelling of the Calderstones bloodsucker was rather dilapidated, given that it was in such an affluent area, and the garden was overgrown with wild-looking shrubs and the hedge had spilled over the wall. In that unkempt jungle of a garden, a huge irregular-looking tree was arching over the road, the gnarled and twisted branches of which could pose a hazard to any passing tall vehicles. But what a place to hide and keep watch, Stephen realised, and he looked about, and seeing that the fog, diffused with moonlight, was enshrouding a road as dead as the grave, he hid behind the garden wall of the facing house. He was about to take out the thermos of fortifying whiskey-infused coffee when he heard what sounded like a rustling sound above. He knew on such a still night of sodden fog hanging in the tranquil air, it could not be a zephyr rustling the leaves of the tree, and then he saw him.

The vampire was returning to its lair! He had imagined it hadn't even left the house yet, but it had obviously embarked on his nocturnal prowling earlier, and now it was gliding down, a pure black shadow wearing some sort of diaphanous veil – or was that something ectoplasmic trailing from the face? Stephen swiftly pulled out the pistol, rushed out into the road, and the vampire seemed to slow down as he took aim. It was hovering about twenty feet from the attic window. He fired once and perhaps with nerves, as the shot echoed throughout the neighbourhood, Stephen found himself crying out a prayer from his altar boy days: 'Lighten our darkness, we beseech Thee, O Lord!'

Bang! The second shot must have hit the vampire, because it clutched its chest, and he could see its pale hands feeling the point of entry. 'And by Thy great mercy defend us from all perils and dangers of the night!'

Bang! The third and last shot rang out, and now the pale hands flew to that veil – as if he'd hit the fiend in the head. The body of the vampire flipped and turned as if it was performing a manoeuvre on a diving board, and it fell somewhere behind the house.

Windows in the street lit up, and windows started opening. The police would be here soon! Home was only 400 yards away, but Stephen's legs felt like jelly. The door of the vampire's house opened and a man in a dark green satin night gown came out, and he had a gun trained on Stephen. In a voice that sounded slightly foreign – perhaps East European, the man asked: 'Who sent you? What is your game, eh?' The man then clutched at his chest and seemed to be in pain. His face became contorted.

Stephen slowly reached into the Gladstone bag, and took out the crucifix.

'I will shoot you! Put that down! I will shoot you!' shouted the man, and he raised the gun so it was aiming at Stephen's head.

'Then shoot me you bastard!' Stephen cried, thrusting the crucifix out further. He solemnly prayed out loud: 'In the name of the Father, the Son, and the Holy Ghost, deliver this abomination back unto the Gates of Hell!'

The man fell to his knees, fired the downwards-pointing gun once, and Stephen felt a piece of the blasted gravel sting his cheek. The man lay there, motionless. Stephen then simply walked away, and somehow, he avoided the law. A police car with its roof lights flashing passed him. Then an ambulance tore past him, and he went home and could not believe he had actually laid the vampire that had been causing so much fear in the south of the city. He hardly slept that night. He went to buy the newspapers the next day, and then he went to the library to tell Audrey all about it, but they could find no mention of the vampire slaying. That evening, Audrey telephoned him and told him the disturbing news. The man who had died had not been some vampire, but actually a vampire hunter. He was originally from Hungary, and had settled in London, but had moved to Liverpool after the authorities accused him of desecrating graves in the course of his occult activities in the local cemeteries. He was something of a laughing stock in the supernatural sphere because he claimed he had come to England to destroy a cunning vampire from his own village in Hungary. All of this had been on a radio bulletin which said the man – who had a history of heart trouble - had died from a cardiac arrest.

Stephen felt physically sick and an icy sensation shuddered down his back from the nape of his neck. And then it hit him: had that man – "Jim Smith" – been the real vampire? He told Audrey his theory and she told him to just drop the whole thing.

'No, Audrey, I can't – ' Stephen said, squeezing the handset.

'Yes you can – and you'll have to - unless you want to lose me!' Audrey told him.

'Audrey, listen, that thing I shot at – that must have been Smith! He was heading to the house to make it look as if he lived there! Those bullets probably went straight through him, it was all play acting. He was placing the blame on that poor man – what was his name?'

'I can't even pronounce it – it was something like Varga – but please promise me that you'll drop it, before you go too far. Imagine if you had shot that man last night!'

'Maybe that's what Smith wanted,' Stephen speculated, and his throat dried up at the thought.

That evening, Audrey had a shower, and then she went to bed, and with it being an unusually warm night, she decided to lie on the bed in just her underwear, with the chair leaning against the door so no one could enter. She put on a pair of headphones and listened to the radio with her eyes closed. She dozed off, and woke up on her front – a position she never slept in. Something icy was on top of her, and it was having sex with her. She tried to cry for help but her head was pushed hard into the pillow, and she thought she was going to suffocate. She saw Stephen's smiling face in her mind, and felt like crying, for she believed she was about to die and that would be the last thing to flash through her brain. Then she felt the thing withdraw from her, and then the weight lifted off her body. She slowly turned over on the bed, gasping for air – and saw that the room was empty. She looked at something pale to her right which seemed out of place. It was a man's face, reflected in the mirror of her wardrobe, but it did not make sense because there was nobody standing in front of that mirror – and then she saw that it was the face of that man she had laughed at – Jim Smith. The face was still sneering at her as it faded away. Audrey almost fell off the bed, for her bottom was a fire of intense pain, and she found it difficult to walk. She went to the toilet, and started to cry so hard she threw up in the wash basin. Her mother heard her crying and asked what the matter was, but Audrey could not bring herself to tell her why she was sobbing.

'Is this because of that Stephen?' her mum asked.

'No, no, just leave me alone!' Audrey cried, and had a long hot shower.

When Stephen was told about the rape, he became quiet, and then he cried. He said he would not rest until that vampire was destroyed, by fire, by stake or by gun – it didn't matter how – but he swore to Audrey that he would move Heaven and Earth till he exacted his revenge.

All the big talk came to nothing. Stephen walked up every road near to Calderstones Park, because Jim Smith – whoever he really was – had said he lived in that area – but that entity which had masqueraded as a man was never seen again by Stephen, and he imagined that the monster was mocking his attempts at revenge. The vampire was seen by Audrey, in recurring nightmares in which the sickening sexual assault was cruelly re-enacted – and sometimes when Audrey awoke in her bed with her heart pounding and the blankets and pillow moist with perspiration, she would sense that *he* was still there.

The rumours of the vampire attacks in the south of Liverpool continued, and Stephen, feeling a complete failure, almost turned to drink, but eventually Audrey steered his life back onto the rails and they married years later and moved to Wirral.

Every now and then I get a flurry of reports about people who have experienced something - some presence - pressing down on them as they lie in bed, often with their sleeping partner just inches away from them. The presence usually goes away after a while, but sometimes it stays and begins to molest the victim. When no molestation takes place, the occultist will recognise the incident as an "Old Hag" visitation – a demonic female succubus that is drawn to men, and sometimes women. But when molestation, penetration, the sensation of blood being drawn (and sometimes even semen) then the experienced occultist (and vampirologist) will suspect a vampire attack. But of course, who is going to report such a sinister violation, even in this so-called New Age era of enlightenment?

LETTERS TO THE LOST

It was New Year's Eve, 1998, and just coming up to 8pm when 50-year-old Tony Gullano walked into a wine bar on Allerton Road. He should have been in a good mood, with so many merry hours of drinking with friends ahead of him, but he recalled that it was upon this date, back in the year 1963, when his mum had passed away from a long illness. He'd just turned the tender age of fifteen when he had lost the best friend he ever had. Girlfriends had come and gone, and he'd gained some great companions over the years, but even now, there was no one who could take the place of Tony's mother, and he wondered why he was dwelling on this – why he was being such a spoilsport when there was such a buzz in the air with the approaching New Year celebrations.

Tony's friend Matt Parker saw that he looked down and asked him what the matter was. Tony wouldn't open up at first, but after a lager he told Matt about his mum passing away on New Year's Eve, long ago.

'I've lost people too, Tony,' said Matt with a rueful look in his eyes, 'but you've heard of that saying: "Laugh and the world laughs with you..." '

Tony nodded and smiled and finished that saying off: 'Cry and you cry alone. Yeah, yeah, I know, I'm wallowing.'

'It's allowed,' said Matt, 'I think we start to think of time around the New Year; Old Father Time and his hourglass and that thing – ' Matt swung an imaginary golf club, attempting to give Tony a clue about the thing he couldn't name.

'Scythe,' said Tony.

Matt nodded. 'That's it. Yeah, I think we look back over our shoulder this time of year and see where we've been.'

Over My Shoulder by Mike and the Mechanics came on the wine bar juke box, and Tony and Matt looked at one another, amused at the coincidence. Matt ordered a bottle of Sangiovese, and he and his friend talked further of people they'd lost as everyone else in the bar was in high spirits.

Matt reminisced about a summer that had long gone to its grave. 'I made a friend when I was six with a black lad from Newcastle named Danny,' and we both promised we'd stay friends forever. This was in the summer school holidays like. He was visiting his Nan in Liverpool. Those summer holidays seemed to last forever, but on the last day, Danny had to go home to Newcastle so we planned to both run away and live in a park so we could go on being mates. But his father caught him, and I remember him crying his eyes out, and I was upset. It was like we were soul mates. But I never saw him again. I suppose that's a loss in a way; we could have had a friendship lasting decades.'

Around 8.40pm, Matt went outside to see if he could spot a lady he liked who drank over in Yates's Wine Lodge. Instead, he noticed something odd — a green pillar box down by Woolworths. He told Tony about it and the two men went to look at the peculiar box. A man in a peaked cap and the same type of uniform as a postman approached, carrying a sack — but this uniform was dark green. He opened the pillar box and put the letters from the box's wireframe cylinder into a sack. Over his shoulder, Matt asked the man if Royal Mail had started some new service.

'No, this box is for sending letters to people who have passed on,' the 'postman' casually replied.

Matt and Tony were naturally taken aback by the reply.

'How is *that* possible?' Tony asked, 'I've heard of dead letters, like,' he joked.

'You write your letter, you put their address on the envelope, and I deliver it to them. Include your own address if you want a reply – and no stamp needed.'

'Is this a practical joke?' Matt asked, and he watched the green postman lock the pillar box and walk off with the sack of mail. He seemed to vanish near Woollies.

'He's just disappeared Tony,' Matt said, and he turned to look at Tony with a baffled and bemused expression. 'Honest mate, he's gone.'

'There's an alleyway to Auckland Road there, Matt, he hasn't vanished,' Tony assured Matt, but Matt went and had a look and saw that the alley in question was gated.

The two men then read the notice plate of the green pillar box; it said: 'Next collection at 1am'.

'It's got to be some practical joke this, Matt,' said Tony. The wine had reached his brain and he felt a little slow as reality was buffered by his alcohol-dulled senses. 'Must be a student arsing around.'

'Why do people always blame the students?' Matt replied in a narky manner. 'Tony, listen, that postman vanished by Woollies. There's something a bit strange going on here I'm telling you.'

'You've been watching too much of the *X Files*

mate,' said Tony, and he hiccupped. 'Someone's having a laugh and the joke's on us.'

'Don't you think it's funny how we were talking about people we've lost and then this happens?' Matt reasoned. He was annoyed because Tony couldn't see this tenuous but probable link in tonight's strange state of affairs.

Tony waved his hand dismissively at his friend. 'You're starting to wig me out now, Matt, just let it go. Let's go and sink a few pints and get stuck into the talent.'

'Tony, look, that's solid – look!' Matt tapped his knuckles on the tall green pillar box. 'Someone's gone to an awful lot of trouble mate if this is a joke.'

'Matt, it could be some telly company staging a practical joke,' said Tony, looking about, 'and they could have us on camera now.'

Matt shrugged and said, 'You're probably right. Let's go and get bladdered.'

But then as Matt decided Tony probably was right and there *was* a rational explanation for the green postman and pillar box, Tony's mind suddenly opened up to the possibility that perhaps the postman was some paranormal being, and as Matt went back into the bar and started singing along with the karaoke, Tony couldn't stop thinking about that service the man in the green uniform had mentioned: a means of sending letters to people who were long dead. Could such a thing be possible? Who on earth would dream up a cruel stunt like that?

Just before midnight, when everyone was gathering outside the bar to sing the mandatory *Auld Lang Syne*, Tony suddenly ran to his nearby home on Mayville

Road with tears in his eyes, and he ransacked drawers till he found an envelope and notepaper. With a short bookmaker's pen he wrote to his mum, telling her he was now a mini-market manager, had a son of 25, and had amicably divorced from his wife Lucy five years back. He told his mother how much he missed her, and how he loved her more than words could say and he urged her to write back. He wrote the address in block letters on the envelope – that address was of a house long demolished – and then he ran to that green pillar box through singing crowds as the fog horns ushered in 1999. A drunk was leaning against the strange pillar box, eating chips and gravy from a polystyrene tray. Tony pushed him aside and received a barrage of four-letter insults, but he didn't care. He believed that his letter would somehow be delivered to his beloved mother, and for once, he felt as if she was not dead but simply separated from him in space – as if 1963 was just a few miles away now.

He turned to the ruffled drunk and apologised, and then he took him into the bar and asked him what he wanted. 'Kronenbourg please,' the startled drunk told him, adding, 'you've got a golden heart, lad.'

Matt suddenly appeared at Tony's left elbow and said: 'I've been looking for you everywhere you drama queen – where did you get to?' He had a beautiful lady with him, and Tony realised it was the girl he'd had his eyes on for weeks.

'I'll tell you later, mate,' Tony said, and he asked Tony's girlfriend what she was having.

'Tell me now,' Matt insisted, then said, 'Oh by the way, this is Jessica Elizabeth – '

'Oh shurrup,' said Jessica Elizabeth, coyly shielding

her blushing face with her hand, 'it's just Jess!'

'Pleased to meet you Jess,' Tony said, and then as he went to get the drinks, Matt grabbed his arm and whispered: 'Did you put a letter in that green box?'

With a poker face, Tony nodded.

'I knew you would,' Matt told him.

On New Year's Day, a little envelope was posted through Tony's door. The handwriting was unmistakably his mum's. Tears welled as he read the letter in the hallway. She had written back immediately, telling Tony she was so proud of him, missed him every day, talked about him every day to other people who had passed over, and she said she looked forward to the day when she'd be with Tony again. 'Even as I was carrying you, before you were even born, I knew you'd be a boy, and I knew you'd be a good son, Tony,' she wrote, 'and when I first saw you walk, I said to your father that I dreaded the day you'd walk away to find your own life, and your own children.'

'Oh mum,' the tears fell from Tony's eyes onto the pale blue lined notepaper with a gentle patter.

The last line read: 'Well, I better sign off lad, look after yourself, and wrap up and keep warm, because I know it's cold over there now.'

Tony sat down and poured his heart out into another letter, but when he got to Allerton Road, the green pillar box was gone. He went to the road every day, hoping to see it, but Tony never set eyes on it again.

Please, just for once, don't question what I'm about to tell you. If you've lost someone and still love them – they know about it, believe me, they know.

SPRING-HEELED JACK VIGILANTE AND SANTA CLAUS

The top of my time-travel bucket list is 'pay a visit to Spring-Heeled Jack'. Today, Jack is dismissed by most historians and folklorists as some mere Victorian bogeyman wrapped up in embellished far-fetched claims, but doctors, soldiers, farmers, policemen and even solicitors backed up the eerie reports of a cloaked man in a strange helmet who could make tremendous leaps from pavement to rooftop and back, and I have hundreds of newspaper clippings of reports of the "Leaping Terror" dating from 1837 till the 1970s. Even the 69-year-old Duke of Wellington made it his mission to hunt the Jumping Devil down, all to no avail of course. The amazing long life of Springy cannot be explained – unless he was not human, or maybe he was but several people took up his gravity-defying boots at various times – and no, we cannot explain how a man can make a standing jump of over 25 feet when the record for such a jump (without a run-up) is about 5 feet 7. But then we know virtually nothing about gravity, and we are just as ignorant about the athletic potentialities of the human frame. If Olympic records continue to be broken, where will it end? Will we eventually see someone jump twenty feet into the air? Spring-Heeled Jack outran horse-mounted police and even trains, whereas Usain Bolt, the fastest human ever timed, just managed 28 mph – but this record *will* be surpassed. Fossilized foot prints found in Australia indicate that an ancient man ran faster than Bolt through mud, and physiologists now believe we may be able to run at around 50 mph one day. Many years ago an old man named Jack Walmsley came to see me at the studios of BBC Radio Merseyside to show me a curious entry from the diary of his grandfather, a policeman in the Liverpool of the 1880s. PC Walmsley claimed in the diary that he was on the beat near Mansfield Street, Everton one night in October 1887 when he was attacked by a violent drunk named Chandley with a poker. Seven of Chandley's associates joined in the ambush, but Walmsley somehow wrenched the poker from the drunk and fought some of the attacker's off. Several women who had tried to come to PC Walmsley's aid then started to scream, and the policeman turned to see an odd-looking man in black in a billowing cloak land in the road with a gentle thump. This sinister figure wore a helmet and his entire body was surrounded by a scarlet aura. The startled policeman also noticed that the stranger had pointed ears. He stood there, shrieking with laughter, then ran at a phenomenal speed at the gang of ruffians, knocking some of them down like skittles. The helmeted and cloaked man seized one gang-member and comically held him in his arms as he jumped clean over a wall, but as the super-fit superhero was high in the air, he let go of the roughneck in his arms and that man felt into a yard, breaking his arm.

The rest of the gang fled down an alleyway. One thug who was punched by the caped figure flew backwards through the air and hit a lamp post with such force he was knocked clean out. 'Spring-heeled Jack!' one woman screeched as she hid behind PC

Walmsley. And then, the unearthly helmeted vigilante made a mighty leap up onto a chimney stack, where he paused for a while, cackling as a silhouette against the moon. Walmsley had heard the rumours of this figure of mystery, but now he had seen him with his own eyes, and he longed to thank him for fighting off the gang, but Jack bounded off into the night.

It's odd how two mysterious Jacks went on to terrorize our country in Victorian times: Jack the Ripper carved out a grisly niche for himself in history of course, and Spring-Heel Jack left a mystery in his wake which has resisted all attempts to be solved. One Jack killed in eerie silence with a blade and the other one struck fear into the hearts of victims by screaming with laughter as he sprung from rooftop to pavement with his black flowing cape and demonic grinning face – a sinister cross between Batman and the Joker. Both Jacks evaded capture and vanished back into the darkness from which they came, leaving generations of armchair detectives to speculate upon their identities. Spring-Heel Jack was encountered by my great-grandmother Elizabeth Slemen in the 1880s when he visited her Sunday school in Everton, and scores of other people saw him across Liverpool on his many visits at that time. In 1884, Lancashire Police questioned an almost supernaturally agile Blackburn man named John Higgins, who called himself The Human Kangaroo because of his amazing leaping ability. Police questioned Higgins about his whereabouts during a recent Spring-Heel Jack scare across the North West, and examined his caped costume and special boots. Higgins could jump in and out of a basket of eggs without breaking one of them by "neutralizing" his weight, and could leap clean over a hansom cab. Higgins proved to have a perfect alibi however – he was being seen by a hundreds of theatregoers as he performed on stage at the Pavilion in Piccadilly on the night Spring-Heel Jack was at large, so he was not charged with being the Leaping Terror. The bounding bogeyman visited Liverpool as late as the 1930s (although some claim he was even here in the 1970s), and I have many statements from local people who met him during this time, and some of them have sadly passed away. A woman in her eighties named Anne told me how, one snowy moonlit morning at around 2am on 19th December 1926, when she was just 5 years of age, she was awakened by the excited voices of her older brothers as she slept in a draughty garret at her home on Havelock Street, Everton. Anne went to the window and saw a man in a scarlet suit and black cloak, sitting on the top of a chimney stack. He had pointed ears, a prominent beak of a nose, glowing eyes and a pair of calf-length boots. He smiled at Anne, and she recoiled in fear. The girl and her brothers then watched as three policemen with drawn truncheons came out of nearby attic windows and inched along slippery snow-covered ledges to confront the peculiar caped man. Crowds in the streets far below laughed, cheered and whistled, and all of a sudden, the strange figure opened his mouth and emitted a chilling type of yodelling sound. He then made an impossible leap to the rooftop across the street, some sixty feet distant. From there, Spring-Heel Jack jumped into a back alley, where, before he vanished into the darkness, he shouted something unintelligible which sounded to witnesses like the garbled words a parrot comes out with when it mimics the human voice. On the following night Jack was seen in Toxteth and then Warrington. A rumour went round Everton that night that Jack had thrown a sack stuffed with toys (stolen from a Dale Street shop) into the yard of a very poor family – acting as a Spring-Heel Santa!

It could be wishful thinking on my part, but I have a sneaking suspicion that Spring-Heel Jack will make a startling comeback in Liverpool one night…

TIMEWARPS AND SPACESLIPS

I'm sure most readers of my books know by now that Bold Street in the city centre is the place for timeslips, and I'm still not entirely certain as to why this is so, but I have taken into consideration that the grand Lyceum building, situated at the foot of the street, is made from sandstone, a sedimentary rock which contains a few micrograms of uranium and a great quantity of quartz. Quartz crystals vibrate when they are subjected to a small electric charge, and when you use a crystal of quartz in an electronic oscillator circuit, it vibrates – just like a tuning fork - at a very precise frequency, and that's why quartz is used in electronic timekeeping circuits, the type you find in alarm clocks, wristwatches, and even your mobile and computer. It's now known that gravitational waves, first detected in February 2016, affect the curvature of space-time, and any material moving or oscillating at relativistic speeds produces gravitational waves, and one material which definitely moves back and forth at relativistic speeds is quartz. Even a tiny quartz crystal, the type you will find in sizable quantities in the Lyceum's bricks, will vibrate back and forth 32,768 million times per second when you subject it to even a small charge of electricity. I believe that time machines will one day be manufactured that will have a component at their hearts which will be made of an arrangement of quartz crystals that have been doped – a term used in electronics for intentionally introducing impurities into a material to modify its electrical properties, and this quartz-based component will generate and manipulate gravitational waves, allowing us to gain access to the past and future.

Outside of the city centre, up in the suburbs, I have noticed other sites which seem to be rich in timeslips – and also 'spaceslips' – the latter being a strange poorly-documented effect where a person covers the distance A to B in an incredibly short duration, as if the space between A and B has somehow momentarily contracted. A case in point is the incredible journey of David Weller, a 39-year-old from Woolton who intended to cycle to a friend's house on Childwall Valley Road one evening in March 2010. David's father, a man who always claimed to know the quickest way to any destination, advised his son to go by a specific route to the house in Childwall by way of a little-known shortcut. David said he'd go the way he was familiar with, as it would be getting dark soon and his mountain bike was brand new. 'No,' his dad insisted, 'listen, get me a piece of paper and a pen and I'll show you the shortcut to Childwall; it'll save you going all the way round Gateacre Brow.'

He began his terrible sketch of the route. 'That there's where we are now, right? Obviously, that's the start point, now you go down here past the chippie...'

David kept looking at the clock. He respected his father and rarely criticised him but it was already 8pm and dusk was descending on Woolton. 'Dad, I'll be okay, honest, I'll go down Acrefield – '

'No, look, see that line there?' his father dug the tip of the ballpoint right through the paper. 'That's Sandfield Road – it goes through that part of Gateacre, and it's like a tiny alleyway that'll bring you out onto Gateacre Brow. The rest of the route is a piece of cake then, lad.'

And so David did as his father advised him. He went up Hunts Cross Avenue and he turned right into Glenville Close, and then he took some time finding the entrance to the 'secret alleyway' which would supposedly provide him with an amazing saving of journey time, even though there were staggered railings there where a sign plainly stated: 'Pedestrians only'. The time was now exactly 8.25pm, because David looked at his watch and shook his head. He'd told his friend he'd be there at 8.15pm at the latest. David slowly rode the mountain bike down the alleyway, when suddenly, he felt something slam into the back of the bike. For a moment, he thought a car had hit him. Everything was a blur. Now, this shortcut, Sandfield Road, runs straight for 90 yards before it takes a sharp 90-degree turn to the left where it runs 60 yards until it takes a 90 degree turn to the right, and after 25 yards, Sandfield Road takes a 90 degree turn again – to the left - and runs about a hundred yards to Gateacre Brow. In other words, the road is certainly not straight – it is crooked - and yet David Weller felt his bike move along in a straight line at a phenomenal speed, and the velocity seemed so high, the Woolton man had to hang on to the handlebars or be thrown backwards off the bike with the sheer inertia. As he bulleted along towards Gateacre Brow, David saw that he was in some cylindrical tunnel, and it was made up of pulsing light. He began to slow down, and suddenly he found himself within twenty feet of a police car that was blocking the end of Sandfield Road. David thought he'd hit that car, but the bike stopped dead, and yet he was not thrown over the handlebars by the momentum. The police officers in the car witnessed the high-speed approach of David Weller, and one of them got out the car and approached him. The policeman looked lost for words, and he asked David, 'Do you know you have just covered around a hundred meters in a second?'

David was still in shock and he said: 'You're not going to believe this, officer, but one second I was going down an alley on Glenville Close, and now – now I'm here.'

'That was unbelievable that!' the other police man in the car shouted from his side window.

David looked at his watch – it was 8.26pm – but that was impossible, as it had been 8.25pm as he rolled into the 'Pedestrian only' alleyway. The driver of the police car got out the vehicle and joined his colleague. He told him: 'I had a better view than you because I was looking towards him as he flew down here. This whole road lit up with a blue glow.'

The policemen eventually returned to their car and left, and David visited his friend in Childwall with an incredible story to tell. The almost instantaneous transference of David along Sandfield Road – a distance of almost 300 yards (900 feet) – might have been a case of teleportation – a method of transferring matter from one place to another without it traversing physical space in-between. Teleportation of humans –

even bacteria – is not possible at the moment, although scientists are working on it, but the experience David Weller had might not have been teleportation, but what I call a 'spaceslip' – this is when something bends the very fabric of space-time. If you picture a sheet of paper with the letter A at the top of the page and B at the bottom, you would draw a line down the length of the page to join the letters, but if the page was folded so A and B touched, that would be a good analogy for the spaceslip – a way to get from A to B without moving along that line; space is bent instead.

Strangely enough, I have had a few timeslips reported to me from people who have been walking down Sandfield Road or in its vicinity. One woman walking down that road lost forty minutes she could not account for, and a retired fireman named John once told me how he and friend were walking up Sandfield Road when they saw three men dressed in farmer's smocks, leading three huge shire horses past them, heading towards Gateacre Brow. After passing John and his friend, the clip-clop of the horses ceased abruptly. John and his friend turned around and saw that the dated-looking men and the horses had vanished. These three men and their horses have been seen by others too over the years, on Sandfield Road and Gateacre Brow.

One bitterly-cold morning in January 2001, a certain criminal from Speke named Mike was chased along Woolton Street by a detective who caught him trying to break into a shop red-handed. Mike, not knowing the area well, ran down a cul de sac on Woolton Street which still exists between a chemist and a bookmakers.

The detective smiled to himself because now Mike had nowhere to run – but he saw Mike vanish into thin air as he was half way down this dead end. Mike found himself running into an old fashioned blacksmith's shop. The blacksmith, a giant of a man, picked up a hammer and chased Mike out the place and the confused crook found himself in a Woolton of cobbled roads and horse-drawn carts, but still Mike had no idea he had entered a timeslip. He somehow ended up running back the way he had come, and found himself racing into the arms of the detective. Mike dodged the detective and ran past him, out the cul de sac, shouting: 'Dickhead!' but because he was running blindly, he was hit by a moped and knocked over. He sustained minor injuries, and later, in his cell, when he had time to think about his amazing escape down the cul-de-sac, he realised he had somehow gone back in time for a short while. I have checked the history of that part of Woolton Street where the cul-de-sac stands and have discovered that a blacksmith did exist where Mike found it, but it was in the 1850s.

We move now but a short distance from Woolton to the district of Speke, which has many timeslip hotspots.

There is an old English idiom we often use when someone suggests that something unlikely could happen: 'Yes, and pigs might fly!' In broad daylight on September 2, 1905 scores of people, many of them respected astronomers, spotted a strange dark object high above the clear skies of Llangollen, and when powerful telescopes were trained upon this early UFO, it looked just like a pig! It had a bulbous fuselage, a head with a stubby snout, wings, and what looked like four legs. It moved against the wind, unlike a balloon, and hovered two miles up before being lost to sight. A flying triangle was also seen not long after this, high over the Welsh village of Llanbedr, and telescopic examination of this object revealed that it looked like a bird with a large beak. Today, Llanbedr is earmarked to be one of the UK's first spaceports, where rocket planes will ferry tourists and satellites into orbit and even around the moon – so is it possible that the Edwardian "flying pig" and the big-beaked bird were timewarp previews of future spacecraft? When the mind sees something unfamiliar, it often resorts to zoomorphism, and will liken it to an animal (which is why we find so many creatures in the Zodiac constellations).

Many years ago a woman named Mrs Hammond told me how her father had seen a very strange "beast" flying through the skies over South Liverpool during his duties as an ARP warden in WW2. At the time, her dad was on duty near to Hale village on a sunny Sunday morning in Spring 1942 when he looked up and saw a gigantic white object - which, to his eyes, resembled a dolphin with overgrown flippers and tail - slanting down silently out of the blue sky – and it was headed for what was then known as Speke Airport. The warden shouted to a farm worker named Ainsley who came running over. Ainsley said he had seen the very same thing in the sky the week before, and the two men stood in awe, watching the leviathan of the sky glide silently to earth – but then suddenly – it literally vanished into thin air. The farm worker shouted excitedly to his employer but the ARP warden told him: 'Don't say I saw it as well or they'll cart me off with you! Got that?'

Ainsley nodded, realising that what the warden was saying was true – and who could blame the authorities for thinking they were barmy? A story about a flying dolphin was simply crazy.

The description of the vanishing gigantic plane makes me wonder if the warden and the farm worker were seeing today's "Beluga" Airbus – a gigantic plane that can actually carry planes because of its cavernous 150,000 cubic foot interior. The enormous cargo plane was nicknamed Beluga because it resembles a Beluga whale with his oddly-shaped head and massive body, and it is a regular visitor to our airport – but how two people in the 1940s saw a craft that did not go into production till 1994 can only be down to the timeslip phenomenon. Imagine if the hi-tech Beluga and its 21st century crew had landed at Speke in the middle of World War Two; the whole outcome of the most violent conflict in history might have turned out so differently. Another timeslip seems to have taken place up at Speke in 2005. In the spring of that year, two brothers, aged 10 and 12, were interrogated by their mother and father at their home on All Saints Road in Speke one afternoon when they were found in possession of a cache of assorted chocolate bars and packets of sweets. The oldest brother had been in trouble the year before after he had stolen an item from the New Mersey Retail Park, and so his father was furious. The older boy finally owned up to opening a van and running off with all the bars of chocolate. As the father was screaming and shouting at his sons, the mother noticed something quite strange – among the collection of stolen sweets there was a bar of plain chocolate called Terry's Oliver Twist. The mother showed this bar to her husband and asked if he'd heard of it – he hadn't, and he looked at the "Punch" bar, Fry's Chocolate Sandwich, one half-eaten Bolero bar, and various packets of fruit gums and Opal Fruits and he realised that these products looked vintage – and yet they were brand new.

'What shop did you get these from, eh?' the father enquired.

'It wasn't from the shopping centre,' said the oldest son, 'it was from a van – a red van.'

'I don't believe you, now stop lying!' the father roared. The parents of the boys found more of the outdated confections upstairs hidden under the beds of their children. The father visited the New Mersey Retail Park and could not find a store which sold vintage sweets, and a few years later out of curiosity, the wrappers of the chocolate bars were taken to a collector of 1950s ephemera named Bill, and he said the wrappers were not reproductions, but originals from around 1959-1963, and he bought them all for £25. Did the boys somehow manage to steal those chocolate bars from one of the many mobile shops that did business in new towns such as Kirkby and Speke long ago in the 1950s and 1960s?

A security guard named Tony recently told me of what seems to have been another Speke timeslip. One clear warm summer morning in August 2014, at around 1.20 a.m., Tony was on his break at the factory he was guarding, and went outside for a smoke. From where he stood, he had a fine view of John Lennon Airport, and he could see the runways of the complex clearly because a huge full moon was hanging high above Speke. At 1.30 a.m., Tony was joined by Des, another guard from the factory who had also decided to go outside for a smoke on his break. The two men chatted about such mundane matters as wages, football and cars, when suddenly their conversation was drowned out by a loud thrumming sound coming from above. The two guards gazed at the skies, trying to see what was causing this deep droning noise, which was getting louder by the minute, and then Des said: 'Look at that!' and he pointed to the glaring white disk of the moon. Planes were crossing it, and then more of them, and soon, as the eyes of the guards adjusted to the night sky, they could see what looked like a hundred or more planes flying over the south of Liverpool.

'They're not jets them, listen to that,' said Tony, 'they're propellers.'

'Listen!' Des put his index finger to his lips and turned to Tony.

The guards could hear the rumble of what sounded like – bombs exploding.

Then came the eerie whistle of what sounded just like a descending bomb. Both guards were too young to recall such a sound from World War Two when bombs screamed to earth from the planes of the Luftwaffe but they had heard that sound in countless war films. The sound of the falling bomb became so loud the guards were about to run for cover, but they heard a massive explosion somewhere close – and then – silence. The sky was empty, except for that full moon. A third guard came out the factory in an excited state and asked: 'What the f**ck was that?' He had heard the explosion and had thought a plane had crashed at the airport. Des and Tony told him about the ghost planes silhouetted against the moon and of the phantom bombing, but the third guard said they had seen birds migrating, and this really annoyed his two colleagues, for they knew that they had obviously seen some spectral replay of a night-time bombing raid on Liverpool by the Nazi air force of long ago. Every night after that, the guards went outside on their breaks, wondering if they'd see and hear those ghosts of the sky again. I have a feeling they will indeed see the warplanes from the past again. I have a feeling a timeslip is responsible for the incident, and such airborne apparitions from WWII have been seen from Runcorn right up to Southport over the years. In recent years, the *Liverpool Echo* even ran a series of articles about the number of mysterious explosions and strange droning sounds heard over the city after dozens of citizens contacted the newspaper to report the alarming nocturnal sounds.

From the skies of Liverpool, we next turn our attention to timeslips on the roads of this area.

On a gloomy February afternoon in 2015, 30-year-old Tomi Laker and her 33-year-old boyfriend Finn Jessup were travelling along the East Lancs (A580 road), about three miles west of St Helens. The couple, who hailed from the Sandhills area of Liverpool, were in Tomi's new Ford Focus on a trip to their friend's house in Leigh. As the car passed Catchdale Moss Lane, the satnav had a nervous breakdown as her voice came out with gibberish, and then music on the vehicle's radio turned to white noise. 'Oh this is fantastic,' Tomi sighed, ' and she started fiddling with the auto-tuning buttons on the fascia, but the white noise continued.

'God, what a change in the weather,' said Finn, because now the grey sky was completely gone and the sun was burning down from a baby-blue sky. As Finn remarked about the abrupt improvement in the weather, Tomi became concerned about the satnav failure and the hissing radio. 'I'm taking this car back if this is some fault,' she promised, 'I knew this was too good to be true.'

'You've probably just gone out of range of a radio station and my dad's satnav does that now and then; you just reset it Tom,' Finn assured his girlfriend. Finn then gazed in the rear view mirror with a puzzled expression and he noticed that the red Volkswagen Polo and every other vehicle that had been trailing behind it had vanished. The road was completely empty behind the Ford Focus, and, what's more, the road ahead was also clear, and looked quite odd. 'The road's changed, look!' Finn nodded at the windscreen. The central reservation had gone, and the road surface was darker now.

Tomi looked in her rear-view mirror and said, 'Oh Christ, what's this? What have I done?'

'What?' Finn asked her, then seeing she was referring to something behind the vehicle, he turned in his seat and looked out the rear window. Behind the couple, a police car was hurtling down the road flashing its headlights – and Tomi noticed a weird bell on the front of the car, just above its old-fashioned chrome fender, which was jangling. 'I haven't gone over seventy,' said Tomi, and she decelerated, then pulled over, and immediately, Finn saw that the police vehicle coming to a halt in the road ahead was a Wolseley 690, and being a vintage car enthusiast he knew those vehicles hadn't been in production since the late 1950s. When Finn saw the stocky bearded policeman get out the car, he thought it was someone like Dom Joly, dressed up as a policeman as he pulled some prank on a practical joke reality TV programme – but the cop was deadly serious. He had a good look at the Ford Focus and then asked Tomi: 'What in blue heaven's name are you driving, love?'

The other policeman left the quaint old Wolseley and came down the road to inspect Tomi's car. He had a slight Scottish accent and said something to his colleague then asked Tomi to get out of the vehicle. She asked why and he made a very sexist remark and shouted, 'Were you trying to break the sound barrier love? Talk about driving with undue care. Get out! Come on, move it.'

He asked the couple what their names were, and upon hearing Tomi's name he smiled and quipped: 'Get out of it - a Judy with a man's name?' And then he looked at Finn and asked, 'Bet she wears the trousers eh, lad? Is this your car or hers?'

'Hers,' Finn replied, and he still suspected that the policemen were sinister impostors, and wondered what their game was; would they try and rob him and his girlfriend?

The sexist Scottish cop asked to see Tomi's licence and when she showed him her licence card he said, 'No, your licence, love; that's not a licence now is it?' He then showed the card to his colleague and he seemed puzzled by it too and remarked to Tomi: 'Born in 1985? What are you playing at? Let's see your licence. Stop larking about.'

'That is her licence constable,' Finn said, 'have you

got any identity yourself like?'

'Shut up, gobshite, and stay there,' said the policeman, looking Finn up and down with an expression of disgust. 'You're a funny-looking c**t aren't you?' he added, then walked away to the car. He got into the Ford Focus and the bearded one seemed fascinated by the airbag feature, and Tomi heard him say: 'Bloody Supercar! Where did they get this?'

The other policeman said to his colleague: 'See the shirt she's wearing? She's got no bra on. Bet she's a goer.'

The bearded policemen then left the car and quizzed the couple on the grass verge. 'Now, I don't know where you got this from, but you're going to tell me when we get to the station. You two from the Pool are you?'

'Yes we are,' Tomi told him, and she felt so confused at what was unfolding here, and she had a horrible foreboding that these men would turn out to be criminals dressed up as policemen. 'I don't see what the problem is officer – ' Tomi was saying when the Scotsman in the car shouted to his colleague: 'Paddy! Look at this!'

Before he went over to his colleague in the Ford Focus, the policeman warned the couple. 'Don't even think of trying to scarper, because you're in the middle of nowhere – stay put.'

Tomi and Finn stood there, wondering what on earth was going on. They heard one of the cops in the Focus saying: 'What in God's name is that?' They also heard the Scottish policeman talking about the car's airbag feature and the bearded officer was heard to say: 'Bloody Supercar.'

Finn's stomach turned over when the penny dropped, and he realised that he and Tomi had somehow gone back in time. He shouted to the policemen: 'Excuse me! What year is this?'

The bearded policeman looked out the window with a bemused look and gave no reply. Tomi realised why her boyfriend had asked the question and turned to him with a knowing look. The bearded policeman started the Focus, revved the engine and then stalled it.

Finn whispered to Tomi: 'Let's get out of here!'

'And where are we going to go?' Tomi asked him, 'It's just farmland and miles of fields.'

Finn kept his eyes on the two coppers in the car as he told her his vague escape plan. 'Just follow me, love; hide over there by that hedge, and then we can make it to that building over there.'

'I don't know – ' Tomi was saying as her boyfriend bolted into the field to his left and hid behind a tall hedgerow. Tomi ran after him, lost her footing, and fell on top of him. They could still hear the policemen talking in the Focus. The couple ran further down the hedge, and then they both heard the bearded policeman yell: 'You won't get far! Come back!'

The couple slowly walked along the hedgerow, keeping out of sight, but they could see a man in the field, about two hundred yards off, walking their way. They assumed he was a farmer. The couple heard the policemen shouting for them to come out of hiding, but then the sun dimmed in the sky and it started to rain. The couple emerged from the hedge and found that all of the road signs and the motorway's surface had apparently returned to modern times now. They reluctantly walked back along the hard shoulder and found the Ford Focus where they had left it. There was no one in that vehicle, and Tomi found her iPhone on the driver's seat, and the screen was active; it showed the keypad – as if someone had been trying to unlock it. At this point, Finn got the shock of his life, because he felt a hand grab his wrist, and he heard the Scottish constable say: 'He's here Paddy!'

Tomi also felt the car rock slightly, and something brushed past her – as if an invisible passenger was getting up off the driver's seat. She heard the word: 'What?' and then the sound of very faint voices somewhere. The grip on Finn's wrist was released, and then the faint voices stopped. Tomi said she was going home, but Finn said that they should continue on to Leigh and visit their friend. 'No, we're going home,' Tomi announced, 'I feel really sick.'

And so the couple returned to Liverpool, shaken by the timeslip experience – just one of many I've heard about on the East Lancs over the years. I interviewed the couple and asked them to think back, to the events shortly before the timeslip; had anything out of the ordinary happened? Had they seen anything which seemed a little out of date? Finn then recalled something that might have had some bearing on the development of the timeslip episode: about ten minutes before the timeslip, a Ford Zodiac Mark III had overtaken Tomi's car, and she had asked her vintage car mad boyfriend what model it was. The four-door saloon had been white and was possibly carrying two people. This car, produced from 1962-66, could have been a vintage model with a new engine, but it's equally possible that it was a real car from the late 1950s early 1960s, so the timeslip might have been coming into action a little earlier than the couple realised. Tomi never found her driver's licence, and one wonders if it is in an attic somewhere, a puzzling conversation piece of the son or daughter of one of those policemen from the past.

One of the strangest timeslips on our local roads was reported to me a few years ago by a retired traffic policeman, and this incident took place on the M62 in 1998. It is not as dramatic as the last one, but fascinating nevertheless. On a stretch of the M62 motorway that runs past Sutton Manor Woodland (close to the place where "The Dream", a public sculpture is now sited), a Vauxhall Corsa was crawling along at just 30 mph in the middle lane, in the direction of the Clock Face area. George, a policeman on a motorcycle, came alongside the Corsa, which had been beeped at by other annoyed motorists, and he saw that two young women, who both looked no older than 22, were in the vehicle. The driver was wearing large rollers and was looking in the pull-down vanity mirror as she put her mascara on! The other girl in the front passenger seat was waving her arms about and seemed to be singing, probably to a song on the car's radio. The police officer could not believe his eyes; these girls were apparently oblivious to being an obstruction and the driver was either somehow unaware of the tailback she was causing or she simply didn't care. George tried everything to catch the attention of the driver, but she was looking straight ahead. Matching his motorbike's speed with the crawling Corsa, George had a good look into the vehicle, and saw that the driver and the girl seemed to be moving in slow motion. The passenger moving her arms about was doing it as if she was in a film that had been slowed down, and the driver was also moving the mascara brush up and down at her eyelid in the same slow dreamlike motion. The pink furry dice hanging from the rear view mirror were also swinging in slow motion – and this meant that the girls were not merely pretending to be moving in slowmo – which baffled George. George drove alongside that Corsa with its slowed-down occupants for three miles, until suddenly, as the car reached the junction at Burtonwood, the driver and passenger moved in a speeded-up fashion, and then returned to normal. George cut in front of the Corsa and flagged them onto the hard shoulder. The girls (who were actually both aged 19) were from Netherley, and were headed for Winwick, where a cousin of the driver was having a party. They both claimed that they had felt very strange after they had passed the Rainhill Stoops junction, and likened the experience to being extremely drunk. George told them that they had been travelling along for over three miles at 30 mph and seemed to be moving in slow motion, and this revelation frightened the girls, especially when George told them that even the furry dice hanging from the rear view mirror had been swinging in slow motion. The driver of the Corsa then realised that her watch had lost about a quarter of an hour. The passenger did not have a watch, so no comparison could be made, and the clock in the car still marked the correct time. It is not known if the girls experienced any further slow-motion effects in that car. Perhaps this incident was an example of a highly localised type of timeslip.

From the M62, let me now escort you back to

Liverpool, and to Walton Road, where a number of intriguing timeslips have all revealed a structure from long ago. The first timeslip took place in a thick fog at the end of March 2002. Thousands of drivers across the land were trying to get away for Easter but the good old British weather put the boot in as usual. Fog crept slowly over the country, bringing fatal motorway pile-ups, and disrupting the UK's road network from Berkshire to Birkenhead and from Lanarkshire to Liverpool. By the Friday morning of March 29 of that year, a hackney cab driver named Jimmy was ready to call it a day. The visibility had dropped to mere feet and the headlights only made the situation worse – plus, in his own words, 'there were arseholes still driving with no fog lights and still speeding round Liverpool.'

Jimmy was going down Walton Road from the Spellow Lane end, when he saw a blue glow ahead. It was not a flashing blue light, the type you'd see from a police or ambulance vehicle, but a steady soft blue light, and it was very diffused, almost as if the fog itself was luminous. He was doing about twenty by now, and slowed down further. The light was a few feet after an old pub he used to drink in many years ago – The Springfield. Jimmy gingerly cruised to a halt at the pub. To his left was Springfield Square, a cul-de-sac which led to an MOT garage, and that glow seemed to be in this dead end street. Jimmy was startled by a gaggle of kids, most of them no taller than four feet. They were silhouetted by the blue light, and they all rushed at the hackney cab. Thinking this gang was out a bit early, Jimmy wound down the window and was going to ask them what that light was when he saw that the children were all dressed like extras out of a Victorian film. They were all barefooted, and wore ragged clothes; some had on caps, but the poor souls looked very thin and emaciated, and they came running up to Jimmy, and seemed in awe of the taxi.

'Where are you lot from?' Jimmy found himself asking. The fog seemed to clear a little at this point, and the taxi driver then saw something which will stay in his mind till the day he dies. He glanced up the dead end street of Springfield Square, and there, silhouetted against the blue glow, was a towering windmill, and its sails were not moving. In all the years Jimmy had lived in Walton, he had never seen this windmill, and instead of believing his own eyes, he swore and said: 'Where did that come from?' A little boy said something to Jimmy, but he was so spellbound by that windmill, he did not hear him properly. And then, in a flash, Jimmy realised that he had somehow entered a timeslip. Most people I talk to who have experienced slippages in time seem to be either terrified, or highly intrigued. In Jimmy's case, he was suddenly overcome with an incredible sadness, and he found himself almost in tears as he looked at the children in ragged clothes. 'Hang on lads,' he said, and the cabby picked up what he called his Sin Box – an old biscuit tin full of an assortment of sweets he carried with him on his job. He opened the tin, took out tubes of Polo mints, Mars bars, chewing gum and loose Cadbury's Roses, and he threw them into the eager hands of the children. The kids looked very surprised and some of them got down on their knees and grabbed the sweets, which would have been manna from heaven to them, and then Jimmy looked in the glove compartment for more sweets for the children, and found a box of Tic Tacs mints, but when he looked back out the window – those kids had vanished. Jimmy found himself dabbing his eyes with a hanky, and he got out the vehicle and looked about, and saw that the windmill was not there now, and that blue glow was fading, and the amber light of the sodium streetlamps was replacing it. A police car came down Walton Road and a policeman leaned out and asked the taxi driver why he had stopped and left his driver door open. Jimmy said he'd just dropped off a fare and got back in the cab. He told his father about the strange, and very moving, experience, and his father told Jimmy that there had indeed been a windmill at the top of what was once Springfield Place (now called Springfield Square) behind the pub many years ago. It had been there till the 1920s. 'So how did I see it this morning then, Dad?' Jimmy asked. His father just replied: 'Time's gone back, lad; I've heard of that, like.'

Jimmy was just as baffled at the way he felt so much sympathy towards those little street urchins he'd given the sweets to, and hoped the little treats he'd given them would at least have relieved the hard suffering of their daily lives, back in God knows when. In October 2015, a 24-year-old driver named Jake was travelling up Walton Road from the Everton Valley end caught a glimpse of the very same windmill at the back of the Springfield pub, and this was at around half-past three in the afternoon, so other people probably saw it too. On this occasion, Jake was moving along the road in a queue of slow-moving traffic when he saw the windmill, which was actually turning, but not being a Waltonian, he thought the windmill had always been there. When he went to pick up his girlfriend Sophie at her home off County Road, he mentioned the windmill to the girl's father, who was talking about the environment and solar power. Sophie's dad said there was no windmill in Walton. 'On Walton Road there is,' Jake begged to differ.

'Not in Walton Road or anywhere in Walton mate,' Sophie's father insisted, and Sophie said Jake wasn't a liar, and her father stated that he had not said that he was, and it ended up with Sophie's dad promising Jake he'd give him a thousand quid if there was a windmill on Walton Road. Of course, Jake drove Sophie to the spot where he had seen the turning windmill, and it was not there. Only later when Sophie's dad mentioned the story Jake had told in his local pub did someone confirm that there had been a windmill exactly where Jake had seen it about ninety years before. I still get reports from people who have seen this phantom windmill, and it is not the only windmill from the past which occasionally reappears either, for I have had a few reports from readers about a windmill which has been seen in Newsham Park over the years. I once mentioned one of these appearances of the mystery windmill on the Billy Butler Show on BBC Radio Merseyside, and a man in his seventies named Ray telephoned me on air, and said that in the 1980s, he was walking through Newsham Park one sunny morning when he noticed a windmill which was standing between the main boating lake and the smaller one. A group of people had gathered near the windmill, and one person even took a photograph of it. The windmill had not been there the day before, and some of the people present said that it must be a huge prop being used by a film company perhaps. In the afternoon, that windmill had gone. A local historian assured me and Billy Butler that no windmill had ever stood in Newsham Park, but on the following day, two people unrelated to one another came to the reception of the radio station with photographs of a windmill in Newsham Park circa 1952. I got a copy of the photographs and sent them to Ray, who had seen the windmill in 1980, and he confirmed it was the very same one he had seen. It would be intriguing to see the photograph that was taken of this timeslipped windmill in 1980. Someone out there might just have it in their album. No one seems to know when the park windmill was demolished.

I have not yet finished with timeslips, and in the next chapter you will read of a very sentimental one...

LOVE ACROSS TIME

I have had to change a few names and minor details, but beyond these legal requirements this strange story is allegedly true – yet so hard to explain. On a sunny Saturday morning in the April of 1978, a 45-year-old English literature tutor at Liverpool University named John Carrington was ensconced in his favourite chair at his Rodney Street flat, reading Edward de Bono's *Wordpower* - an illustrated dictionary of hip words - when he suddenly heard a woman's soft voice close to his right ear say, 'Doctor Rogers will be with you shortly Mr Dickson.'

Carrington naturally jolted at the manifestation of this voice. He had never been one to believe in ghosts, and was more worried that he might be suffering from the onset of some mental illness. After a tense moment of listening out for further suspected hallucinatory voices, but hearing only the rumbling stream of weekend traffic outside of his ground-floor flat, he turned his attention back to the paperback again. As he re-read the entry for 'homeostasis' he heard a woman yawn.

'Who is this?' he found himself asking the empty room.

The unseen woman's voice let out a startled 'Oh!' followed by: 'What was that?'

A listener to radio often forms a mental picture of how a DJ looks, just from his voice, and this was the case with Carrington. From the ghostly voice he had heard, he pictured a certain beautiful woman of about 25 perhaps, and where the face of this woman originated in his mind was a mystery, for it was the face of a woman he had never seen before in everyday life. He had not see the face in any magazine or any film, so Carrington surmised it was just a product of his subconscious. As he wondered about the genesis of the attractive face, he heard the silken feminine voice ask: 'Are you a ghost?'

'No, I'm alive and kicking,' was John's reply, followed by his half-hearted effort of a laugh as he added: ' so maybe you're the ghost.' He then heard her yelp again with shock. She asked if it was someone messing about, and John said it wasn't, and he asked her if *she* was a figment of his imagination.

'No, I'm real,' she assured him, and in an annoyed voice she firmly said: 'Stop trying to frighten me and show yourself.'

The tutor put down the paperback, paced around the room, finger and thumb to his chin, with a faint undecided smile on his face. April Fool's day had long gone, so what on earth was going on? 'Where are you?' John Carrington asked, and he waited in the corner, trying to home in on the direction of the charismatic voice.

'I'm here of course,' she told him, and he could actually make out that she was smiling by the changed timbre of her voice, which comes from smiling and speaking at the same time.

John gave a nervous simulated laugh and said: 'No, I

mean the address!'

'Here,' the invisible lady told him, in a tone which conveyed that she was plainly stating the obvious, and then she made it even more clear: '63 Rodney Street. This is so silly, whoever you are.'

'Ah, well that's also my address – that's where I am now,' John replied, and he tried to fathom out just what was going on. He looked around. Had someone – one of his students perhaps - placed hidden speakers in the room through which they were talking via some intercom? John thought of Brian Phelps, a student who had pulled off some well thought-out practical jokes over the last few years – but surely this would be beyond him?

'How can it be your address if I work here?' the out-of-sight woman queried.

'It's quite odd this,' said John, 'but I'm not pulling your leg – I do live at Number 63, in a ground floor flat. Perhaps if you – '

'Dr Rogers will see you shortly Mrs Chetwynde,' the woman said, interrupting John, and then she whispered to him. 'I can't talk now, a patient has just arrived.'

'Oh sorry,' John said, and then he smiled, thought of the absurdity of the situation, and turned towards the window, arms folded, shaking his head with a smile on his face. Is this insanity? He thought; am I actually hearing things? If I am, then the voice in my head is answering back as well; not really good is it? He knew schizophrenia rarely developed in people his age, and as far as he knew, no one had laced his coffee with lysergic acid at the cafè on Bold Street earlier this morning – so was this a genuine psychic occurrence?

'You still there?' he asked.

No reply came.

John considered his options. Should I go to the doctor? Or perhaps I should just have a word with Frederick (a clinical psychiatrist at the university). He thought of the numerous morbid reasons a person might hear voices in their head; lesions on the brain stem, acute sleep deprivation – but he'd had a good seven hours of kip, he recalled. What about...

'Hello? Are you still there?' asked the baffling woman who wasn't physically present.

'Yes!' John quickly answered. He moved about the large room, and gauged that the voice was louder near the wall separating the lounge from his bedroom. 'May I be so bold as to ask you what your name is? My name's John, incidentally. John Carrington.'

'Hello John, my name's Emily,' came the reply, followed by 'Are you going to tell me how you are doing this?'

John stood close to the partition wall and with great sincerity he answered: 'I'm simply talking, there's no trick, and I give you my word Emily, I am not pulling your leg.'

At this point, John detected a scent – a woman's scent – and he suddenly recalled how he had caught that scent a week ago, and had assumed it had drifted in from the street. Now he realised that it had been the scent of Emily. He asked her: 'What perfume is that you're wearing?'

There was a pause, a diffident chuckle, and then Emily told him: 'Bandit.'

'Bandit?' John tilted his head sideways, puzzled at the reply.

'Yes, it's a perfume by Robert Piguet,' she informed him, then asked: 'Can you really smell it?'

'Oh yes, I can,' John reached out with his right hand towards the wall, just in case he could somehow touch this beguiling woman of mystery, but his searching hand merely passed through the air. The couple then conversed for some time, and John gathered this: that Emily was just 22 years of age, and she was a doctor's receptionist in 1946, and the reception room was in the very room he was now living in – in the very same space, but in a bygone decade. When he explained that they seemed to be conversing across thirty-two years of time, Emily seemed a bit afraid, and she asked him what life was like in the future.

'Oh, I suppose it's just like life there in 1946,' said John, feeling very philosophical all of a sudden. 'The times change, the technology gets a little better, but the same people and their problems and emotions come around again, like a big non-ending cycle.'

'Is there a Mrs Carrington?' she enquired, with a little less volume to her voice.

'No,' John almost sang the word, 'there was, but we divorced five years ago. How about you?'

'I'm engaged,' she told him, then it sounded to John as if she was going to say more, but Emily curtailed it with a sniffle.

'Lucky fellah,' quipped John, and he moved about with his nose in the air, trying to get a fix on the place where the perfume was strongest.

'He's a soldier,' she said, 'his name's David. He's coming home soon.'

'I see,' John's heart went into free fall, 'sounds serious.'

'If David knew his fiancée was talking to a strange man he'd be ever so mad.'

'Ha! Well, you'd have to tell David I'm no romantic threat; I'm just fascinated by the way we can talk like this – two people in two different eras.'

'How is it possible?' Emily wondered out loud, and then she laconically stated: 'Someone's coming in. Bye for now.'

There was a rapping at the window, followed by a ring of the doorbell, and John shook his head and rushed out of the room. He hurried through the communal hall and opened the stained glass vestibule door. He knew it would be his friend Mike "Mince" Pye, before he even opened the front door, and John was thinking up excuses already, because he had no intention of going out with Mince tonight. All that mattered now was Emily.

'I can only stay for half an hour John, and then I'm off to that new barber on Leece Street,' Mince said, walking past his colleague into the vestibule area.

'Ah, yes, Mince, I should have rang you, but er, well you see, I can't go out tonight – '

'Why ever not? Have you joined a monastery?'

'I've just been prescribed a course of antibiotics – chest infection you see – '

'Your chest sounds fine to me old chap.'

'Oh no, the lungs are like a pair of lace curtains, and I've had an X-ray and that, and the doctor said I can't drink alcohol and take antibiotics – could be fatal – he said.'

'Oh, well, that's you snookered for tonight, Johnno,' Mince told him, and he pushed past his friend anyway and walked down the hallway towards the kitchen. 'I'll make some coffee and then after a little chat you can take to your sick bed.'

'Well, I was just going out – for some aspirins,' John said to the back of his pushy friend, but Mince went straight into the kitchen whistling loudly.

John grunted and slapped his hand against his forehead. Why did people always visit him when they were not wanted?

Minutes later, Mince – a biologist at the university - came into the lounge with two cups of coffee and a biscuit barrel wedged under his arm, and he told an uninterested John about his plans for a new job. 'Right, here's the gist of it: I'm thinking of applying for the post of a lectureship in agricultural biochemistry at Aberdeen University. I've got the required honours degree,' and he began to count the degrees on the fingers of his hand: 'in biochemistry, in agricultural chemistry...'

John nodded, and looked past him to the point where Emily was sitting at her desk in the reception of the doctor's surgery in 1946.

Mince stopped abruptly, and followed John's line of sight to see what was distracting him. 'What are you looking at?' he asked.

John snapped out of his apparent brown study. 'Oh, nothing sorry, was just thinking of you living up in Aberdeen.'

'Well, I have to think of the money side of things you see old boy. The salary on offer up in bonny Aberdeen is between four thousand and seven thousand per annum...'

John nodded, but his eyes kept swivelling to look at that spot, and he wondered if Emily would hear his loud visitor.

'John? You're drifting off again – are you ill?' Mince dipped a gingerbread biscuit in the coffee and consumed half of it. He seemed genuinely concerned.

'Mince, I am so sorry, but yes, I feel as if the room's spinning,' John told him, 'and I feel bad about it because I really am trying to listen to your plans, and I will miss you if you leave for Aberdeen.'

'Oh, I probably won't get the post anyway,' Mince ate the other half of the biscuit and crunched as he continued. 'It's very competitive, and you'd be surprised how many applicants they get. Well, Johnno, I'll get out your hair, and you can go to bed or do whatever you have to convalesce.'

'You're very considerate, Mince,' John got up, and as he headed for the door of the lounge ahead of his friend, Mince sniffed the air. The biologist smiled. 'What a seductive scent! Have you had a woman in here Carrington?'

'Yes, but unfortunately it was a cousin,' John lied, and opened the door.

'Oh, that never stopped the Royals Johnno – they're always marrying their cousins.'

As soon as Mince had left, John rushed back into his flat, closed the door behind him, and then went back to the partition wall and asked: 'Are you there Emily?'

There was no reply.

Just after noon, as John sat slumped in the leather two-seater sofa with his arms folded, he heard Emily say: 'John, I've done my half-day's work. I'm off home. Perhaps we'll talk again?'

John shot up off that sofa and went to the wall and asked, 'I forgot to ask you, where you live?'

'Well, I'm not sure whether I should tell you, because I live with my parents, and I think if they heard you, they'd have the house blessed. They're very old-fashioned and superstitious. Anyway, cheerio for now John.'

John heard no more of Emily throughout the rest of the weekend, and he telephoned in sick on Monday morning and told the university receptionist he was feeling very under the weather. At 8.50am that morning, John heard Emily again. She greeted him with: 'Good morning John – hope you can hear me.'

'Yes, I can Emily, good morning,' John replied and he noticed that her perfume seemed much stronger.

'What time is it there, John?' she asked.

He pulled back his sleeve and looked at his watch. 'Er, it's ten minutes to eight.'

'Of a morning I assume,' she said.

'Yes, a Monday morning,' John told her, relishing her perfume and not fully realising yet that its effects were aphrodisiacal. 'Monday morning of April 24, 1978.'

'It's Monday here too, and it's the 8th of April, 1946,' Emily told him Oh, by the way, did I tell you my surname was Wishart?'

'Emily Wishart. Nice name. Is that one surname or is it one of those hyphenated double-barrelled names? Is it Wish-Hart?'

'No hyphen, just one surname,' she said.

John had a vague suggestion forming in his mind, and he voiced it. 'Emily, perhaps we should not tell anyone that we can do this thing we are doing, because it might cause problems.'

'Why?'

'Well, because – I mean, I'm not a physicist or anything – but perhaps I could change history if I start telling you about events, which, to me, are just history, but to you – well, they're future events. If you get what I mean?'

'I'm not sure I understand that, but I'm telling no one about you anyway,' she said, and gave a little laugh which only served to make John even more enamoured of her.

'I've told no one this end, either,' said John, and he leaned on the partition wall with one hand, and the other hand was at his face. He pinched his chin between his finger and thumb, wondering what to say. He was like a schoolboy confronted with his first crush.

'John, what do you look like? I'm just curious. I picture you clean-shaven, looking like Ronald Coleman. Bet you have a beard though.'

'Well, no I'm clean-shaven. I'm a little over six feet, I have hazel eyes, and curly dark brown – almost black hair – going a little grey at the sides. I weigh about 200 pounds. Er, not much more to add, really. What are your measurements?'

'John!' Emily exclaimed, and gave a hearty laugh.

'I'm sorry, I phrased that wrong, er, I mean, how tall are you, hair colour etc – '

'I know, it's alright. I'm five-foot five, sort of dark brown hair, blue eyes. I have a piggy nose – '

'A what?' John laughed.

'Yes, people say it goes up a bit, but on some photographs it looks straight. I have big feet – size six.'

'That's not big,' John assured her, 'my wife was as tall as you and she had size 8 shoes.'

'Oh wait! There's someone coming in. Talk later!' she said.

As the weeks went by, John fell deeper in love with Emily Wishart, and his colleagues and the students at the university began to notice the change in him, and the number of sick days he was taking off. His friend Mince asked him if everything was alright, and John wanted to tell him his secret but thought it would backfire if the authorities got wind of the strange communication channel to 1946. He loved Emily too much, and the idea of the intelligence service moving into his flat to quiz his love and probe the time anomaly was simply not allowed.

And then, one September afternoon, Emily told John something in a broken voice which shattered his heart.

'John, David wants to marry me soon. He's having a word with the reverend this evening.'

'But Emily, I – I love you,' John told her, and he felt dizzy and confused, and then a burning sorrow chafed his heart. 'I love you, you can't marry him. Please don't marry him, Emily please.'

'I have to,' she said, and he could tell by the way her voice had changed that she was crying. He felt so close to her of late, he almost knew what she was thinking, and vice versa. If ever there were two soulmates in this world, it was these two, but they just lived apart in time – the most cruel type of separation.

'But I love you Emily, I love you!' John leaned against the wall, his face almost pressed against it, and her perfume engulfed him, and he slammed his fist into the wall with anger.

'We can still talk,' she said, and he heard her sniffle,

and her voice became muffled slightly as she spoke into a handkerchief. 'I'll still work here John. But I have to marry David, we both made promises, and he loves me too.'

'Damn him! Damn David!' John pounded the wall, and he began to sob. He had not cried like this since his mother passed away when he was just twenty. This was even worse somehow.

He had to accept it in the end, and a month later, he learned that the wedding service was to take place at St Agnes' Church on Ullet Road, not far from Sefton Park. She let slip the date and time, and John marked it on a calendar he'd drawn up of September 1946. He got there that Wednesday morning, at 10.30am, and although the church was empty accept for the cleaner with her mop bucket, John Carrington knew that back in 1946, the families and friends and relatives of the bride and groom would be at the church. He sat near the front, close to the altar, and he looked as if he was praying because he had his eyes closed, but he could hear Emily's voice clearly! He could not hear the words of the reverend conducting the service, but he knew what he would be saying now: 'Will you, Emily Wishart, take David to be your husband?'

All John heard was his love from so long ago saying: 'I will'. She was making her vows, and she was marrying a man who should have been John.

John ran to the altar and he got on his knees and prayed out loud for God to bring Emily to 1978. He made such a racket, the police arrived, and they escorted him out onto Ullet Road. He walked all the way back to Rodney Street, to his empty flat, and he felt empty inside. His heart felt hollow, and he thought he was dead. No feelings existed in him now, just a tremendous sense of loss.

He made allowances for the honeymoon she and David would have, but he never heard Emily again. He waited in his lounge every day, every night, and even slept in the chair in the lounge, just to ensure that he'd be there if she called to him, but she never did. Did David decide to take her away somewhere, or did he discover her secret and prevent her from returning to her work as a doctor's receptionist? John scoured censuses and hired genealogists and family tree experts and eventually, he discovered that Emily Wishart was buried at a certain cemetery in Liverpool. She had died just four years ago – 1974 – at the age of fifty. John found the grave, and saw that only Emily was buried in it. He lay on that grave for a long time, face down in the leaves, crying, and calling her name.

They say that love will go through stone walls, and perhaps it will also go through time. If you have not already found your soulmate, he or she may be out there now in the world, and a chance encounter with that person may change your life forever – but your soulmate might have been born too late, or too early, and still, love might find a way for you to know this, and it would be pure torment, for you might never meet because of time's impediment.

Printed in Great Britain
by Amazon